Creation out of
Nothing

Creation out of Nothing

A BIBLICAL,
PHILOSOPHICAL,
AND SCIENTIFIC
EXPLORATION

PAUL COPAN AND WILLIAM LANE CRAIG

APOLLOS

Baker Academic
Grand Rapids, Michigan

© 2004 by Paul Copan and William Lane Craig

Published by Baker Academic
a division of Baker Publishing Group
P.O. Box 6287
Grand Rapids, MI 49516-6287
www.bakeracademic.com

and Apollos
(an imprint of Inter-Varsity Press)
38 De Montfort Street
Leicester LE1 7GP England
email: ivp@uccf.org.uk
website: www.ivpbooks.com

Printed in the United States of America

Library of Congress Cataloging-in-Publication Data

Copan, Paul.
    Creation out of nothing : a biblical, philosophical, and scientific exploration / Paul Copan and William Lane Craig.
        p.   cm.
    Includes bibliographical references and index.
    ISBN 0-8010-2733-0 (pbk.)
    1. Creation—History of doctrines. 2. Cosmology. 3. Religion and science.
I. Craig, William Lane. II. Title.
BT695.C66   2004
231.7′65—dc22   2004004473

British Library Cataloguing in Publication Data
A catalogue record for this book is available from the British Library.
Apollos ISBN 1-84474-038-2

Contents

Abbreviations

AB	Anchor Bible [commentary]
ABD	*Anchor Bible Dictionary.* Edited by D. N. Freedman. 6 vols. New York, 1992
ANE	ancient Near Eastern/East
ANTC	Abingdon New Testament Commentaries
BECNT	Baker Exegetical Commentary on the New Testament
ET	English translation
ICC	International Critical Commentary
IDB	*The Interpreter's Dictionary of the Bible.* Edited by G. A. Buttrick. 4 vols. Nashville, 1962
IVPNTC	InterVarsity Press New Testament Commentary
LXX	Septuagint, OT in Greek, from third century BC
MT	Masoretic Text of the Hebrew Scriptures, the OT
NAC	New American Commentary
NCB	New Century Bible [commentary]
NIBC	New International Biblical Commentary
NICNT	New International Commentary on the New Testament
NICOT	New International Commentary on the Old Testament
NIDNTT	*New International Dictionary of New Testament Theology.* Edited by C. Brown. 4 vols. Grand Rapids, 1975–1985
NIDOTTE	*New International Dictionary of Old Testament Theology and Exegesis.* Edited by W. A. VanGemeren. 5 vols. Grand Rapids, 1997
NIGTC	New International Greek Testament Commentary
NT	New Testament

OT   Old Testament
PNTC   Pillar New Testament Commentary
TDNT   *Theological Dictionary of the New Testament.* Edited
            by G. Kittel and G. Friedrich. Translated by G. W.
            Bromiley. 10 vols. Grand Rapids, 1964–1976
TDOT   *Theological Dictionary of the Old Testament.* Edited by
            G. J. Botterweck, H. Ringgren, and Heinz-Josef Fabry.
            Translated by J. T. Willis, G. W. Bromiley, and D. E.
            Green. 13+ vols. Grand Rapids, 1974–
TLOT   *Theological Lexicon of the Old Testament.* Edited
            by E. Jenni, with assistance from C. Westermann.
            Translated by M. E. Biddle. 3 vols. Peabody, Mass.,
            1997
TNTC   Tyndale New Testament Commentary
TOTC   Tyndale Old Testament Commentary
WBC   Word Biblical Commentary

Introduction

I believe in God the Father Almighty, maker of heaven and earth." What does this terse creedal statement involve? In modern theological history, the idea of God as Creator has apparently not been thought significantly to involve—if it involves at all—creation *out of nothing*. In the early 1970s, George S. Hendry of Princeton Theological Seminary wrote of the "current eclipse" of the doctrine of creation:

> The doctrine of creation has received scant attention in recent theology. Little has been written on it, outside of systems which cover the whole field. Few theologians have made it a subject of monographic study.[1]

Indeed, until very recently, the doctrine of creation out of nothing had fallen on hard times. But today thanks to the work of noted theologians such as Claus Westermann,[2] Wolfhart Pannenberg,[3] Colin Gunton,[4] Robert Jenson,[5] and others, the doctrine of creation out of nothing is receiving the fresh attention and defense it deserves. The doctrine is not

1. George S. Hendry, "Eclipse of Creation," *Theology Today* (Apr. 1971–Jan. 1972): 406.
2. Claus Westermann, *Genesis 1–11: A Commentary*, trans. John J. Scullion (London: SPCK, 1984).
3. Wolfhart Pannenberg, *Toward a Theology of Nature: Essays on Science and Faith*, ed. Ted Peters (Louisville: Westminster John Knox, 1993).
4. Colin E. Gunton, *The Triune Creator: A Historical and Systematic Study* (Grand Rapids: Eerdmans, 1998); and idem, "Relation and Relativity: The Trinity and the Created World," in *Trinitarian Theology Today: Essays on Divine Being and Act*, ed. Christoph Schwöbel (Edinburgh: T & T Clark, 1995), 92–112.
5. Robert W. Jenson, *Systematic Theology: The Works of God*, vol. 2 (New York: Oxford University Press, 2000).

merely supportable biblically and theologically, but also scientifically and philosophically.[6]

Nonetheless, many thinkers still labor under the influence of Friedrich Schleiermacher, the fountainhead of much of modern theology. He contributed to the eclipse of the doctrine of creation by collapsing the ideas of *creation* and *conservation*.[7] The doctrine of creation was de-temporalized by referring to creation as the "sustaining relation of God to the world, not to his origination of its existence."[8] Schleiermacher emphasized religious experience or "absolute dependence"—thus eliminating any scientific or philosophical implications of religious truth.[9]

Schleiermacher's detemporalization of creation was not without significant precedent. For example, Thomas Aquinas emphatically stressed the universe's contingency or dependence upon God. As with the doctrine of the Trinity, Aquinas believed that reasons for believing that the universe began were available through special revelation alone. While Aquinas rightly emphasized the contingency of God's creation and its dependence on God for its very being, Aquinas basically disregarded the doctrine of a temporal creation out of nothing (not to mention the place of the Word of God—Christ—and the Spirit of God in creation). Colin Gunton goes so far as to say, "Although Aquinas affirms the doctrine of creation out of nothing, he makes little of it."[10]

In 1946, Karl Barth set forth the doctrine of creation in a Trinitarian context, showing how creation encompassed past, present, and future and how creation could not be separated from redemption.[11] In the wake of Barth (and later, Claus Westermann), a fresh generation of theolo-

6. For example, on the rationality of *ex nihilo* creation, see Thomas V. Morris, "Creation *ex Nihilo:* Some Considerations," in his *Anselmian Explorations* (Notre Dame, Ind.: University of Notre Dame Press, 1987), 151–60.

7. Friedrich E. D. Schleiermacher, *The Christian Faith*, 2 vols., trans. Richard R. Niebuhr (German original, 1821–22; New York: Harper & Row, 1963), 1:148–52.

8. Hendry, "Eclipse of Creation," 412.

9. Similarly, Langdon Gilkey sees creation as "a long, slow process of change," and the "symbol of creation" remains (reflecting Schleiermacher) "as an expression of the absolute dependence of all beings on the divine power and intention; but an absolute first moment becomes not only dubious but irrelevant" (Langdon Gilkey, *Nature, Reality, and the Sacred: The Nexus of Science and Religion* [Minneapolis: Fortress, 1993], 21). In an earlier work, Gilkey wrote that the scientist is "confined by his method" and that "God's creative activity is no part of any valid astronomical, biological, or geological textbook, although to the mind of the Christian it is the implication and inference of every study of natural processes" (*Maker of Heaven and Earth* [Garden City, N.J.: Doubleday, 1959], 152).

10. Colin E. Gunton, "Creation," in *The Cambridge Companion to Christian Doctrine*, ed. Colin E. Gunton (Cambridge: Cambridge University Press, 1997), 150–51.

11. Cf. Karl Barth, *Church Dogmatics*, trans. Geoffrey Bromiley (Edinburgh: T & T Clark, 1958), 3/1:231–32.

gians emerged who have begun to restore this doctrine and develop new lines of thinking.[12]

Still, today it is not unusual to find a comment such as the following in a Bible dictionary or encyclopedia: "Creation is not so much dealing with absolute beginning [i.e., creation out of nothing] . . . as with the world order as perceived by human beings."[13] Or one may read dismissive remarks regarding creation *ex nihilo* by those outside the field of biblical studies. For example, philosopher Wes Morriston, referring to Genesis 1:1–2, states, "When God began to create the heavens and the earth, the earth was a formless void (NRSV footnote)." Then he presses forward by declaring that there is "little scriptural support" for the traditional doctrine of creation out of nothing. The reason for asserting this doctrine is, we are told, due to "obvious theological motives" of postbiblical theologians.[14]

One German theologian, Gerhard May, in what has become a standard work on the doctrine of creation *ex nihilo* in early Christian thought, claims that this doctrine is biblically ambiguous and was a late second-century formulation by Christian theologians responding to Middle Platonic and Gnostic ideas.[15] He suggests that the doctrine of creation out of nothing is "not demanded by the text of the Bible."[16]

Unfortunately, May proffers little substantiation for this claim, and many who cite him simply take it on his authority that creation out of nothing is "not demanded by the text of the Bible." While his book is primarily, as the subtitle suggests, about the development of this doctrine in early Christian thought, his comment is regrettable and misleading. In one relatively recent doctoral dissertation, which, disappointingly, provides comparatively little—and rather selective—examination of biblical texts, James Noel Hubler (following May's work at many points) declares that creation *ex nihilo* not only "appeared suddenly in the latter half of the second century CE" but also "lacked precedent": This doctrine was "an innovation in the interpretive traditions of revelation and cannot

12. Brevard S. Childs, *Biblical Theology of the Old and New Testaments* (Minneapolis: Fortress, 1992), 405.

13. J. R. Porter, "Creation," in *The Oxford Companion to the Bible*, ed. Bruce M. Metzger and Michael D. Coogan (New York: Oxford University Press, 1993), 140.

14. Wes Morriston, "Creation *ex Nihilo* and the Big Bang," *Philo* 5, no. 1 (2002), online at www.philoonline.org/library/morriston_5_1.htm.

15. Gerhard May, *Creatio ex Nihilo: The Doctrine of "Creation out of Nothing" in Early Christian Thought*, trans. A. S. Worrall (Edinburgh: University of Edinburgh Press, 1994). One reviewer of May's German edition, *Schöpfung aus dem Nichts* (1978), calls it "a lucid and informative book" (G. C. Stead's review in *Journal of Theological Studies* 30 [1979]: 547). Another reviewer of the English translation calls it a "marvellous achievement" (J. C. M. van Winden's review in *Vigiliae Christianae* 49 [1995]: 307).

16. May, *Creatio ex Nihilo*, 24.

12

be explained merely as a continuation of tradition."[17] This, we shall see, is not simply overstated; it is plainly false.

Even the evangelical theologian Alister McGrath follows May's bold but inaccurate assertion.[18] McGrath says that patristic theologians would not have given creation out of nothing much thought had it not been thrust upon them by Gnostic and Platonic ideas. To some extent this is true, but the church fathers—even apart from the theological disputations they were involved in—held to the same assumptions that the biblical authors did: God *alone* is from everlasting to everlasting, which necessarily precludes the eternal metaphysical dualism of God and matter/chaos. As patristic scholar Eric Osborn argues, May's arguments fail to distinguish between *concepts* and *words:* While the *words* "creation out of nothing" may not be articulated in Scripture or by the early church fathers, the *concept* of creation out of nothing undergirds their assertions.[19] Yet with May, McGrath views the biblical evidence as ambiguous.[20]

Furthermore, we are also living in a time when certain influential theologians and philosophers involved in the flourishing dialogue between science and theology either tend toward *panentheism* or deny the theological significance of the origin of the universe as confirmed by contemporary cosmology. In either case, creation that involves a temporal origination is neglected in favor of other emphases such as "immanence" or "ontological dependence." For example, philosopher of science and theologian Ian Barbour pronounces, *"Creation 'out of nothing' is not a biblical concept."*[21] (In this, he goes even beyond May's assertion that the doctrine is biblically ambiguous.) Barbour rejects the idea of creation out of nothing in

17. James Noel Hubler, "Creatio ex Nihilo: Matter, Creation, and the Body in Classical and Christian Philosophy through Aquinas" (Ph.D. diss., University of Pennsylvania, 1995), 102. When commenting on Genesis 1, Hubler, for example, calls on commentator E. A. Speiser for wholesale support of his "construct" reading of Genesis. He shows the same lopsidedness in his handling of NT texts such as Romans 4:17; Colossians 1:16; Hebrews 11:3; 2 Peter 3:5; and others.

18. Alister McGrath, *A Scientific Theology: Nature*, vol. 1 (Grand Rapids: Eerdmans, 2001), 160.

19. Eric Osborn, *Irenaeus of Lyons* (Cambridge: Cambridge University Press, 2001), 65–68. Thanks to Carl Mosser for bringing this work to our attention.

20. McGrath, *Scientific Theology*, 159–66. We could say the same about Frances Young, who points to Gerhard May's work as offering the substantiation for rejecting creation out of nothing as being a "Jewish idea." Rather, the doctrine of creation out of nothing was "daring" and reflects the fact that "Christian intellectuals were not captured by Greek philosophy. For *creatio ex nihilo* was affirmed in the face of Greek assumptions" (Frances Young, "'Creatio Ex Nihilo': A Context for the Emergence of the Christian Doctrine of Creation," *Scottish Journal of Theology* 44 [1991]: 141, 139).

21. Ian Barbour, *Issues in Science and Religion* (New York: Harper & Row, 1971), 384. Philosopher of science Ernan McMullin states that the doctrine of creation out of nothing, "an act of absolute bringing to be," took "firm shape only in the first centuries of the

favor of the idea of the ontological dependence of the universe on God: "*Creatio ex nihilo* as an initial act of absolute origination" must be given up in favor of this idea of absolute dependence in which "God's priority in status can be maintained apart from priority in time."[22]

Arthur Peacocke is another theologian and philosopher of science who strongly emphasizes God's immanence and downplays the importance of the universe's absolute origination. God is present in the world that God is "continuously creating."[23] Of course, Peacocke is correct in pointing out divine immanence in creation (cf. Acts 17:28 NIV/NRSV: "In him we live and move and have our being"). However, on the basis of this text and others (e.g., Deut. 30:11–14), he affirms *panentheism*—that the world is *"within God."* That is, there is a "general sense of the intimacy of the presence of God" in creation.[24] God is, in Peacocke's view, *continuously* active in the *open-ended emergent* processes of nature.[25]

Peacocke asserts that, whether we may or may not be able to infer or assign a beginning point to the universe (such as with the big bang), "the central characteristic core" of creation would remain unaffected— that God is the Sustainer and Preserver of the created order.[26] Though not necessarily denying creation out of nothing, Peacocke denies its relevance.[27] He comes close to Barbour's (panentheistic) position but does not quite go so far as to reject creation *ex nihilo*. Peacocke takes panentheism to be the belief that "the Being of God includes and penetrates the whole universe, so that every part of it exists in Him but (as against pantheism) that His Being is more than, and is not exhausted by, the universe."[28] However, his belief in *ex nihilo* creation is incompatible

Christian era, in part at least in response to the prevalent dualisms of the day that represented matter as evil, or at least, as resistant to God's action." McMullin is at least willing to concede that hints of *creatio ex nihilo* can be found in Scripture (pointing to 2 Macc. 7:28 and Rom. 1:20) ("Natural Science and Belief in a Creator," in *Physics, Philosophy, and Theology*, ed. Robert Russell, William Stoeger, and George Coyne [Vatican City: Vatican Observatory, 1988], 56).

22. Barbour, *Issues in Science and Religion*, 458.

23. Arthur Peacocke, *God and Science: A Quest for Christian Credibility* (London: SCM Press, 1996), 13.

24. Arthur Peacocke, *Creation and the World of Science*, 1978 Bampton Lectures (Oxford: Clarendon, 1979), 352.

25. Ibid., 353.

26. Ibid., 79.

27. See Ted Peters, "On Creating the Cosmos," in *Physics, Philosophy, and Theology*, ed. R. Russell et al., 286–88.

28. See Arthur Peacocke, *Theology for a Scientific Age: Being and Becoming—Natural and Divine* (Oxford: Blackwell, 1990), 169, 208–9 n. Peacocke is not a full panentheist: he does not accept the idea that God utilized preexisting materials as a potter does to make a vessel. Any model of creation implying that "matter" was already preexistent prior to creation (and thus does not affirm the "essential" doctrine of creation *ex nihilo*) is "defective."

with true panentheism, which historically and inherently affirms the eternality and necessity of the physical world.

Thus, Barbour and Peacocke emphasize creation as nature's dependence on God but deemphasize its temporal origination—and assume God's creation from preexistent chaos. Barbour concludes: "We still need to defend theism against alternate philosophies, but we can do so without reference to an absolute beginning."[29]

One important point: Even if the biblical evidence for creation from nothing *were* ambiguous or unclear, the idea of *creatio ex materia* should not be simply assumed as the default position (whether by panentheists/process theologians or Mormon theologians).[30] Even if creation out of nothing were neither implicit nor explicit in the biblical text, creation from chaotic matter should not be taken for granted.

What Is Creation out of Nothing?

Theologian Thomas F. Torrance describes the doctrine of creation *ex nihilo* as follows:

> The creation of the universe out of nothing does not mean the creation of the universe out of something that is nothing, but out of nothing at all. It is not created out of anything—it came into being through the absolute fiat of God's Word in such a way that whereas previously there was nothing, the whole universe came into being.[31]

29. Ian Barbour, "Religious Responses to the Big Bang," in *Cosmic Beginnings and Human Ends: Where Science and Religion Meet*, ed. Clifford N. Matthews and Roy Abraham Varghese (Chicago: Open Court, 1995), 396. As we note below, various feminist theologians, while laudably pursuing models of God's loving relationship to the world, too closely tie God to the world—a variation of process theology. They follow in the wake of Alfred North Whitehead—the household name among process theologians—who rejected the doctrine of creation out of nothing because it presents God as playing too absolute a role: "He is not *before* all creation but *with* all creation" (Alfred North Whitehead, *Process and Reality* [New York: Free Press, 1978], 343).

30. Unfortunately, Mormon scholars create the false impression that solid biblical scholarship does not support creation *ex nihilo*, that there is no relevant extrabiblical evidence for *ex nihilo* creation, and that philosophical and scientific arguments can be adduced for creation *ex materia*. For a response, see our essay "Craftsman or Creator?" in *The New Mormon Challenge*, ed. Francis J. Beckwith, Paul Owen, and Carl Mosser (Grand Rapids: Zondervan, 2002); also, Paul Copan, "Creation *ex Nihilo* or *ex Materia*? A Critique of the Mormon Doctrine of Creation," forthcoming in the *Southern Baptist Journal of Theology*. The present volume is a significant expansion on the themes of these essays.

31. Thomas F. Torrance, *The Christian Doctrine of God: One Being, Three Persons* (Edinburgh: T & T Clark, 1996), 207 n. Technically, however, this is incorrect. Torrance needs to say that "it was not the case that there was anything previously." To say "previously there

Torrance explains that the creation is not an *emanation* from God—something that is in God, part of God, or created out of God.[32] Usually, emanationism implies that there is no reality other than the divine and that what derives from it is either illusory or a degradation. The idea of emanation was often prominent in the Platonist (and Gnostic) tradition, blurring the distinction between Creator and creature.[33] Instead, Torrance holds that the creation of the universe is "the unique positive act in which God freely brings into being *another reality utterly different from his own transcendent reality.*"[34]

Torrance adds that this created reality is still contingent on God's free activity, "existing and continuously existing under the affirming and sustaining power of his sovereign will as the Lord God Almighty." So the only meaningful distinction between beings is "Creator" and "creation." There is nothing in between.[35]

Thus, the idea held by ancient Greek and contemporary Mormon thinkers alike that there can be independent, eternally preexistent matter coexisting with God—a metaphysical dualism—affirms a form of *idolatry*, compromising both the ontological distinction between Creator and creature and the nature of divine sovereignty.[36] That is, such a dualism attributes an eternal, independent ontological status to something other than God, and it entails that something external to God limits or constrains his creative activity. Basil of Caesarea pointedly affirms in his *Hexaemeron*, "If matter were uncreated, then it would from the very first be of a rank equal to that of God and would deserve the same veneration."[37]

So when we describe what creation out of nothing means, we affirm that without God's initiating creation, only God exists. Upon creation, we have a universe because God willed it into finite, temporal being. Thus, creation out of nothing affirms that the universe is contingent on God, not just in having its (continued) existence in being (ontological dependence) but also in having its temporal origination from nothing preexistent, but simply by the will and word of God (*ex nihilo*).

As Ted Peters states, "One concrete form" of the ontological dependence of all things on God is expressed in the "cosmological assertion"

---

was nothing" implies that there was a moment of time prior to creation at which nothing existed; whereas, to say "it was not the case that there was anything previously" is to deny even the existence of the prior moment as well as anything else before creation.

32. Ibid.

33. Jenson, *Systematic Theology,* 5–6.

34. Torrance, *Christian Doctrine of God,* 207 (emphasis added).

35. Colin Gunton, *The Christian Faith: An Introduction to Christian Doctrine* (Oxford: Blackwell, 2002), 11.

36. See note 30, above.

37. Basil of Caesarea, *Hexaemeron* 2.4.

that "although God is 'eternal,' the created universe began at a point of temporal initiation, i.e., the world has not always existed."[38] Hence, even though the universe has a being and integrity of its own, its contingency indicates that the orderly universe is neither self-sufficient nor self-explanatory nor self-subsisting.[39] Indeed, through the idea of temporal beginning we best reach the idea of dependence.[40] Creation out of nothing expresses, among other things, the unhindered freedom, sovereignty, and graciousness of God. John Polkinghorne writes that the free act of God to create something distinct from himself is vividly expressed in the phrase creation *ex nihilo*: "Nothing else existed (such as the brute matter and the forms of the classical Greek scheme of things) either to prompt or to constrain the divine creative act. The divine will alone is the source of created being."[41]

Robert W. Jenson fleshes out the meaning and ramifications of creation *ex nihilo* in the following theses:

1. There *is* indeed other reality than God, and it is really other.
2. That there is other reality than God depends entirely on his will.
3. All the above holds precisely in the present tense. The world at any moment would not be did God not will it.
4. The reality other than God has an absolute beginning.[42]

---

38. Ted Peters, "On Creating the Cosmos," 274. Maurice Wiles has rightly observed that a meaningful doctrine of creation implies creation out of nothing. After all, only this doctrine answers the question Why should there be a world at all? "Creation is creation out of nothing or it is [not truly creation]. An indispensable element in any contemporary defense of theistic belief is the sense of mystery as to how it comes about that there is anything at all" (M. F. Wiles, *God's Action in the World* [London: SCM Press, 1986], 16).

39. Torrance, *Christian Doctrine of God*, 217.

40. Peters, "On Creating the Cosmos," 274.

41. John Polkinghorne, *Science and Christian Belief: Theological Reflections from a Bottom-Up Thinker* (London: SPCK, 1994), 73–74. Unfortunately, however, Polkinghorne does not place sufficient weight on the doctrine of creation *ex nihilo*: "There never was a theological stake in preferring Big Bang cosmology to steady state cosmology" (*Serious Talk: Science and Religion in Dialogue* [London: SCM Press, 1995], 64). But if this is so, why did so many contemporary scientists resist big bang cosmology? Because it too closely resembles Gen. 1! Fred Hoyle and Steven Weinberg may serve as examples.

42. From Jenson's "Aspects of a Doctrine of Creation," in *The Doctrine of Creation*, ed. Colin Gunton (Edinburgh: T & T Clark, 1997), 18–23. Jenson mentions two others, however, that strike us as problematic (and are not entailed by *creatio ex nihilo*): "Reality other than God has not only a beginning but a termination; . . . reality other than God is 'flesh' [i.e., transient, passing away]. . . . In Genesis creating is a purposive act." These statements seem to undermine the doctrine of immortality through resurrection. His final thesis is also problematic: "If all this last is true, then the initial posit that God is our end cannot simply mean that we have God as our boundary. . . . God is our end in that we will be taken into the triune life." Thus he inadvertently suggests a kind of universalism.

In these terse statements, Jenson presents the fundamental ontology of the biblical worldview.

Creatio ex Nihilo and Contemporary Cosmology

It has become apparent to many that the big bang has theistic implications. In the wake of the emergence of big bang cosmology as the prevailing scientific model, Robert Jastrow of NASA's Goddard Institute has observed the remarkable concurrence between Scripture and science:

> Now we see how the astronomical evidence leads to a biblical view of the origin of the world. The details differ, but the essential elements in the astronomical and biblical accounts of Genesis are the same: the chain of events leading to man commenced suddenly and sharply at a definite moment in time, in a flash of light and energy.[43]

He goes on to admit:

> For the scientist who has lived by his faith in the power of reason, the story ends like a bad dream. He has scaled the mountains of ignorance; he is about to conquer the highest peak; as he pulls himself over the final rock, he is greeted by a band of theologians who have been sitting there for centuries.[44]

Not all acknowledge the connection between the big bang and theism. In the "creation" entry in the *Oxford Companion to Philosophy*, Kwasi Wiredu declares, "In recent times some fallacious interpretations of the big bang theory have sought to boost *ex nihilo* creation."[45] In his book *Creation*, Hans Schwarz cautions against identifying the beginning of creation with the big bang: "We should not too quickly identify the temporal beginning of the universe in a creation out of nothingness with the cosmic big bang. Such identifications are subject to the winds of developing science."[46] William P. Brown suggests that we cannot refer to

43. Robert Jastrow, *God and the Astronomers* (New York: W. W. Norton, 1978), 14.
44. Ibid., 15.
45. Wiredu says that there is "a contrasting conception of a much longer ancestry" (creation out of chaos), and that "it is not clear how ex nihilo creation coheres with the principle *ex nihilo nihil fit* [out of nothing nothing comes] embraced by most classical Christian philosophers." This is a nonissue, however. Since the classical Christian tradition is creation out of nothing, the assumption is that *naturalistically* speaking, being cannot emerge from nonbeing. If God exists, this is not a problem. Available online at www.xrefer.com/entry/551716.
46. Hans Schwarz, *Creation* (Grand Rapids: Eerdmans, 2002), 174.

the big bang as the means by which God brought about the universe.[47] Langdon Gilkey states the same, creating a spurious dichotomy between "a cosmological fact about the universe" and "a theological affirmation about God"; thus Gilkey concludes that the universe's beginning "cannot be part of religious truth."[48]

Despite John Polkinghorne's earlier approving comments of creation out of nothing, he claims that "creation is concerned with ontological origin, not temporal beginning," and that the idea of creation *ex nihilo* "asserts the total dependence of the universe upon the sustaining will of its Creator."[49] Thus, he appears not to place sufficient weight on the doctrine of creation *ex nihilo* as it relates to the big bang. Elsewhere, he writes, "There never was a theological stake in preferring Big Bang cosmology to steady state cosmology."[50]

We disagree with such assessments. Not only do the Scriptures strongly imply creation *ex nihilo*, but the empirical evidence of an absolute beginning of the universe does seem to have momentous theological ramifications. While Schwarz is certainly correct to warn about rashly embracing whatever is all the rage in current science, we should not deny that God has still given us two "books"—the book of Scripture *and* the book of nature—which are not, in principle, in conflict since the God of truth is the Source of both.

Thus, even if big bang cosmology does not *fully* capture all that creation involves theologically, we should not diminish the theological significance of the big bang either. Given the biblical and theological grounds for the doctrine of *creatio ex nihilo*, we should *expect* to observe something like a big bang universe rather than a steady state universe or an eternally oscillating universe. Given the evidence, the big bang does plausibly represent the creation event. Actually, astrophysicists John Barrow and Joseph Silk (who are hardly theists) do see something remarkably biblical in contemporary cosmology: "Our new picture is more akin to the traditional metaphysical picture of creation out of nothing, for it predicts a definite beginning to events in time, indeed, a definite beginning to time itself."[51]

Moreover, the obvious theistic implications of the big bang *have* made many physicists and cosmologists uncomfortable. Fred Hoyle's

47. William P. Brown, "Creation," in *Eerdmans Dictionary of the Bible*, ed. David Noel Freedman (Grand Rapids: Eerdmans, 2000), 293.

48. Gilkey, *Maker of Heaven and Earth*, 314.

49. John Polkinghorne, "Science and Religion," *Expository Times* 101 (1989–90): 317.

50. Polkinghorne, *Serious Talk*, 64.

51. John D. Barrow and Joseph Silk, *The Left Hand of Creation*, 2d ed. (New York: Oxford University Press, 1993), 38.

philosophical preference for the steady state theory—despite the evidence for the universe's beginning—became legendary. Hoyle inveighed against the theistic implications of what he disdainfully called the "Big Bang."[52] Other cosmologists and physicists have likewise resisted what remarkably appears to resemble Genesis 1:1. Nobel Prize winner Steven Weinberg once remarked that the "steady state theory is philosophically the most attractive theory because it *least* resembles the account given in Genesis."[53]

Such thinkers have sought to avoid the implications of standard big bang cosmology by crafting alternative cosmogonic theories not involving a cosmic beginning. In his *God and the New Physics*, Paul Davies has suggested that the universe could have arisen out of a quantum vacuum: "The processes [of quantum fluctuations] . . . represent . . . the conversion of preexisting energy into material form."[54] Similarly, John Gribbin maintains that the universe could have emerged out of the quantum vacuum, which "produces virtual photons out of nothing at all."[55] Finally, astrophysicist Edward Tryon has alleged that "our Universe did indeed appear from nowhere about 10^{10} [years] ago."[56] *Why* did our universe come into existence? Tryon's "modest proposal" is that "our Universe is simply one of those things which happen from time to time."[57] The spontaneous and quirky quantum world, it is claimed, affords all kinds of naturalistic alternatives to divine creation. As we shall see, some scientists will resort to the most outlandish speculations rather than entertain the simpler metaphysical idea of a personal Creator.

Biblical scholar Bernhard Anderson correctly observes that the biblical view of creation is not an effort at primitive science.[58] For that reason, we reject as anachronistic eisegesis any suggestion that Genesis 1 teaches big bang cosmology. Nevertheless, we believe that contemporary science can and does confirm and reinforce the general biblical teaching of creation out of nothing.

52. See, for example, Hoyle's rejection of miracles as "contradictions" and his caricatures of theism/religion in *The Origin of the Universe and the Origin of Religion* (Wakefield, R.I.: Moyer Bell, 1993).

53. Cited in John D. Barrow, *The World within the World* (Oxford: Clarendon Press, 1988), 226.

54. Paul Davies, *God and the New Physics* (New York: Simon & Schuster, 1983), 31.

55. John Gribbin, *In the Beginning: After COBE and before the Big Bang* (Boston: Little, Brown/Bulfinch, 1993), 247.

56. Edward P. Tryon, "Is the Universe a Vacuum Fluctuation?" *Nature* 246 (14 Dec. 1973): 396.

57. Ibid., 397.

58. Bernhard W. Anderson, *From Creation to New Creation: Old Testament Perspectives* (Philadelphia: Fortress, 1994), 1.

Trinity, Resurrection, and Creation

Looking past the OT to the illumination offered by NT revelation, we come to see more clearly what creation means and what is its ultimate goal in salvation history. Creation does not only have a starting point, but it also has a *telos*, when all things reach their fulfillment as a result of the death and resurrection of Christ. From beginning to end, the persons of the holy Trinity have worked to bring about the climax of creation in the new heavens and the new earth, in which God dwells with his people forever. We cannot truly understand what creation means until we see where creation is heading and how Father, Son, and Spirit have worked to bring about this goal. And it is precisely by means of this Trinitarian approach, rooted in the new resurrection order brought about through Christ, that many creation-related theological concerns can be addressed.

German theologian Jürgen Moltmann, despite his fine exegetical arguments for creation out of nothing,[59] continues to pay lip service to panentheism in the conclusion of his book *God in Creation*, where he discusses various "symbols of the world." On the one hand, he rejects "the modern mechanistic world picture; for it is a view of the world that is one-sidedly patriarchal."[60] As a result of Newton's influence, this mechanistic picture makes God utterly transcendent and removed from the world. On the other hand, the concept of the World Mother or Mother Earth is more *pantheistic* (transcendence is swallowed up by the immanent). Veering off the *ex nihilo* trajectory of his good exegetical work, Moltmann opts for a *panentheistic* view of the universe as "feast," "dance," "music," and "play."[61] He seeks to bring together the transcendence-immanence interplay through this model. In light of the reality of our natural environment and who we are as human beings, a more "ecological worldview" is required.[62] Moltmann argues that if there is to be a world or realm outside of God, "the infinite God must have made room beforehand for a finitude in himself."[63] After all, Moltmann argues, if there were a realm outside God, God would not be omnipresent.

Such reasoning is both unconvincing and, ultimately, unbiblical. Admittedly, some Christians have so emphasized the transcendence of God that their view of the world is more akin to *deism*, according to which God winds up the universe, lets it run, and remains aloof from it. To be

---

59. See Jürgen Moltmann, *God in Creation: A New Theology of Creation and the Spirit of God*, trans. Margaret Kohl (San Francisco: Harper & Row, 1985), 86–93.
60. Ibid., 320.
61. Ibid., 318.
62. Ibid., 320.
63. Ibid., 86.

biblical, divine transcendence must be counterbalanced by the equally important aspect of divine immanence. Both reason and Scripture remind us that there can be a world external to God without excluding either divine omnipotence or interrelationship.[64] We can affirm divine transcendence without eclipsing divine immanence.

Indeed, the concerns raised by panentheists, many of which arise from a unitarian understanding of God's absolute transcendence and sovereignty at the expense of his immanence, are more adequately addressed by Trinitarian theology. In such a theological framework, the interpenetration or mutual indwelling *(perichorēsis* or *circumincessio)* of the divine persons furnishes a *relational* context for understanding Creator and creation, transcendence and immanence, God *over* and God *in.*[65] When we lay aside the "unitarian" or strictly "hierarchical" model of God, much of the discussion of God's relationship to the world can move forward because God is viewed as God-in-relation. God is necessarily relational even sans the universe.

The same Trinitarian response is appropriate for responding to concerns raised in feminist theology. Sallie McFague opposes a "monarchical" view of God, in which a powerful, disembodied God is distinct from the world and rules over it. Such an idea encourages harmful or oppressive attitudes and actions:

> The monarchical model is dangerous in our times: it encourages a sense of distance from the world; it attends only to the human dimension of the world; and it supports attitudes of either domination of the world or passivity towards it. . . . The monarchical model encourages attitudes of militarism, dualism, and escapism; it condones control through violence and oppression; it has nothing to say about the nonhuman world. The model of the world as God's body encourages holistic attitudes of responsibility for and care for the vulnerable and oppressed; it is nonhierarchical and acts through persuasion and attraction; it has a great deal to say about the body and nature.[66]

Hence, McFague seeks to establish a more relational, nurturant, loving God.[67]

64. Gunton, *The Triune Creator*, 141.

65. This is an example of how a Trinitarian—rather than unitarian—understanding of God is vital and concerns God and the public square. See Lesslie Newbigin, "The Trinity as Public Truth," in *The Trinity in a Pluralistic Age: Theological Essays on Culture and Religion*, ed. Kevin J. Vanhoozer (Grand Rapids: Eerdmans, 1997), 1–8.

66. Sallie McFague, *Models of God: Theology for an Ecological Nuclear Age* (Philadelphia: Fortress, 1987), 78.

67. Sallie McFague, *Metaphorical Theology: Models of God in Religious Language* (Philadelphia: Fortress, 1982). David A. S. Fergusson points out that feminist and process theo-

Grace Jantzen takes a similar view, arguing for a God whose body is the world:

> In the whole of our experience, eyes are necessary for sight (materially, if not logically), ears for hearing, a body for touching. Although we are not compelled by strictly logical considerations to say that this must be the case universally, we have no grounds within our experience for thinking it is not. It is therefore by no means obvious that we could look forward to disembodied survival as a time when sight will no longer be impeded by our eyes, hearing limited by our ears, or thought by the structure of our brain. Our experience points unequivocally in the opposite direction.[68]

Of course, such models of God and God's relation to the world necessarily exclude the doctrine of creation out of nothing. If God is responsible for the origination of the universe, it is difficult to avoid the conclusion that a disembodied Being has brought into existence physical time, space, matter, and energy and thus is not subject to physical constraints. And if the universe came into existence a finite time ago (with the big bang), did God not exist without a "body" (the world)? From cosmological/astrophysical considerations alone, these feminist models would seem to be untenable.

The Christian doctrine of the Trinity actually answers the objections to theism raised by Jantzen and McFague—without succumbing to the problems found in their theology (e.g., the elimination/diminution of the strong Creator-creature distinction so pronounced in Scripture). To portray God in a *monarchical* manner is, as we have seen, to portray God as being strictly *unitarian*. However, Christian theology views God as *God-in-relation*. The distinct persons of Father, Son, and Spirit—each possessing the divine nature—exist in a necessary and unbreakable relationship of love with one another. Jesus spoke of being "in the Father" and of the Father's being "in me" (cf. John 10:30, 38; 17:21). In the Christian understanding, the members of the Trinity experience a mutual, inseparable indwelling of one another. Theologian Cornelius Plantinga declares: "In the divine life there is no isolation, no insulation, no secretiveness, no fear of being transparent to another. Hence, there may be penetrating, inside knowledge

---

logians have expressed concerns about how the God-world relation is often characterized: a God who is apart from and transcendent to creation. This, they claim, reinforces an idea of divine sovereignty that runs counter to the need for "mutuality, love, connectedness, and wholeness" (*The Cosmos and the Creator: An Introduction to the Theology of Creation* [London: SPCK, 1998], 2–3).

68. Grace Jantzen, *God's World, God's Body* (Philadelphia: Westminster, 1984), 76.

of the other as other, but [also] as co-other, loved other, fellow."[69] As Christoph Schwöbel explains, God does not simply create as the result of "an arbitrary act of the divine will." Rather, from a loving God-in-relation, creation can be seen as a free "expression of the love of God, who remains faithful to what he has created in love."[70] The triune God *loves* in freedom, and the creation of a Trinitarian God is one of freedom and love.

God is a relational God—not only necessarily within himself but also freely and contingently with respect to creation. Rather than simply *ruling* the creation, God also *relates* to it intimately—without oppressing or militating, without crushing human freedom.[71]

Dietrich Bonhoeffer writes in his *Creation and Fall* that God's creating the heaven and earth "means that the Creator, in freedom, creates the creature. Their connexion is not conditioned by anything except freedom, which means that it is unconditioned."[72] Hence, there is literally *nothing* between Creator and creature. This "void" is not some "thing, not even a negative thing"; rather, it is "absolutely nothing."[73] Bonhoeffer goes on to connect the God who creates out of nothing to the God who raises the dead Jesus Christ of Good Friday as the resurrected *Kyrios* (Lord) of Easter Sunday: "That is creation out of nothing, creation from the beginning."[74] Just as through Torah God creates Israel, through his Word—his Logos—God creates the universe (Ps. 33:6, 9; John 1:1–3). Creation is *in* and *through* Christ. Thus, in a symbolic sense, Easter Sunday can be viewed as the *eighth* day of creation—the beginning of creation's reorientation toward its rightful goal through God's raising Jesus from the dead, so that creation is now being set in its proper direction.[75]

In this regard, Irenaeus proffered an illuminating metaphor: God the Father has "two hands" in mediating creation—namely, the Son and the Spirit. "For with Him were always present the Word and Wisdom, the Son and the Spirit, by whom and in whom, freely and

69. Cornelius Plantinga Jr., "The Perfect Family," *Christianity Today* 28 (4 Mar. 1988): 27.

70. Christoph Schwöbel, "God, Creation, and the Christian Community," in *The Doctrine of Creation* (ed. Gunton), 157.

71. Colin E. Gunton observes, "God remains in close relations of interaction with the creation, but in such a way that he makes it free to be itself. God's transcendence as the maker of all things is not of such a kind that he is unable also to be immanent in it" ("Creation," 142).

72. Dietrich Bonhoeffer, *Creation and Fall: A Theological Interpretation of Genesis 1–3* (London: SCM Press, 1959), 14.

73. Ibid., 15.

74. Ibid., 16.

75. Gunton, *Christian Faith*, 7.

spontaneously, He made all things."[76] Indeed, we have hints of Trinitarian involvement in creation in the OT Scriptures. They tell us that the Spirit hovered over the waters (Gen. 1:2), that the heavens were made by the *word* of the Lord and their host by the *breath* (*rûah*, the word for *spirit*) of his mouth (Ps. 33:6), that Wisdom was a craftsman at God's side when he created (Prov. 8:27, 30), and that God's Spirit gives life to all creatures (Ps. 104:30–31).

In the divine undertaking to bring creation toward its true end, the Word—Immanuel, God incarnate—comes into a sin-laden world by taking on human nature and living among his creatures (John 1:14). Through his death, hostile demonic powers are defanged. This is attested to by Christ's resurrection, which came through the working of the Spirit (Rom. 8:11; 1 Peter 3:18). Speaking in general terms, Colin Gunton summarizes the nature of the mediation of the Son and the Spirit this way: "The incarnation of the eternal creating Word in the human being, Jesus of Nazareth, betokens God's freedom *within* the material world, while the Spirit's sovereign action is the mark of God's freedom toward or *over against* it—from outside, so to speak."[77]

Furthermore, there is an integral connection between creation, incarnation, and resurrection, which should not be ignored. Richard Bauckham and Trevor Hart observe:

> Resurrection is a fresh creative act of God, giving back life to the creature[s] who would otherwise revert to the nothingness from which the first act of creation brought them. . . . Resurrection hope is radical faith in the God who remains faithful to His material and mortal creation, valuing it too much to let it perish. Christian resurrection hope is radical faith in the God who became incarnate in material and mortal human nature, setting the seal of his own presence on its eternal value for him. Christian resurrection hope is radical faith in the God who raised Jesus from death, thereby pledging himself to raise also those who believe in Jesus.[78]

Both in the doctrine of the Trinity and in the death and resurrection of Jesus Christ, we have available to us rich resources that enable us to view the doctrine of creation with greater fullness and clarity. Although an *ex nihilo* understanding is not all there is to this doctrine, it is a very crucial aspect, with many significant ramifications.

---

76. Irenaeus, *Against Heresies* 4.20.1.
77. Gunton, *Christian Faith*, 10.
78. Richard Bauckham and Trevor Hart, *Hope against Hope: Christian Eschatology at the Turn of the Millennium* (Grand Rapids: Eerdmans, 1999), 124.

The Theological Importance of Creation out of Nothing

While God's creative activity is not limited to bringing about the universe's existence from nothing a finite time ago (as differentiated from, say, the coming "new creation" in the eschaton), the doctrine of creation from nothing is not only biblically grounded but theologically illuminating. This is apparent in at least three ways:

First, creation *ex nihilo* reinforces the idea of God's *aseity* or necessary existence. Philosophers and theologians have spoken of God as "the being than which nothing greater can be conceived"; as the sole necessary, self-existent, self-explanatory Being; as the Being who exists in all possible worlds; as the Being who cannot *not* exist. When the ante-Nicene Fathers write about creation, they often speak of God as "uncreated [*agennētos*]" and "unbegotten [*agenētos*]" and all else as "created" and "begotten." God's bringing everything other than himself into being reveals that all else is contingent in its being. The existence of the universe and, indeed, anything outside the universe apart from God is a creature and grounded in God's creative act.

Second, creation *ex nihilo* underlines the doctrine of divine *freedom*. God acted freely by bringing about the created order without relying upon preexisting materials *(creatio ex materia)*. Neither was the creation some emanation from God. He speaks by his word, calling all things into existence.[79] God freely chose to create (rather than not) something distinct from himself. God could have chosen to remain alone, in the self-sufficiency of the intra-Trinitarian love relationships. But he freely elected to create finite persons in his image and to invite them into the blessedness of a love relationship with himself.

Third, creation *ex nihilo* exhibits God's *omnipotence*. Certain medieval theologians maintained that God must have infinite power, since there is an infinite qualitative distance between being and nothingness. On the other hand, God's omnipotence would be compromised if there were an eternal dualism of God and eternally preexistent *Urstoff*. If God desired to create, but could only create with preexisting matter, then this would place a limitation on God. The existence of an eternally existent, primordial stuff would be a matter of pure *luck*—a fortuitous coincidence![80] That is, God's ability to create would depend on whether

---

79. As Hans Schwarz succinctly puts it, "For God, creation was neither a necessity nor an accident" (*Creation*, 173).

80. The church historian Eusebius challenged those who claimed that matter was eternally preexistent to tell him "whether it does not follow from their argument that God by lucky chance found the substance unoriginate, without which, had it not been supplied to him by its unoriginate character, he could have produced no work at all, but would have continued to be no Creator" (*Preparation of the Gospel* [*Praeparatio Evangelica*] 7.20).

he had material available. It is difficult to imagine any more stunning display of God's almighty power than the world's springing into being out of nothing, at his mere command.

The Plan of the Book

While we could write much about the theology of creation,[81] our focus in this book will be on the specific dimension of creation *ex nihilo*. In defending the doctrine of creation out of nothing, we do not delve into many of its theological implications and ramifications. Others have ably done so. We see our contribution as gathering together various strands of data in one volume to offer a wide-ranging cumulative case for creation *ex nihilo*. We do so by examining biblical and extrabiblical writings, philosophical arguments, and scientific discoveries that point us in the direction of creation *ex nihilo*. We are restricting ourselves to the assessment of the available evidence for and against *ex nihilo* creation in hopes that this material will stimulate further research and discussion on this important topic.

In the first three chapters of this book, we shall see that the doctrine of creation *ex nihilo* has good support when we closely examine the OT (chap. 1), the NT (chap. 2), and the relevant extrabiblical writings (chap. 3).[82] We shall show that many of the exegetical claims that tend to undermine or diminish creation *ex nihilo* in a number of texts are often weak and implausible. We are familiar with the oft-repeated argument that the doctrine of *creatio ex nihilo* is not found in the Bible but is a theological innovation of late-second-century Christian theologians. But we contend, in the words of Mark William Worthing, that "the idea of creation out of nothing . . . is a doctrine that can lay legitimate claim to being biblical in its seminal form, if not indeed in its full expression."[83] That is, a *strong cumulative case* can be made for creation *ex nihilo* as a thoroughly biblical doctrine, and not simply a theological innovation. Some scholars may seek to undermine certain single strands of evidence here and there (e.g., contending that the Hebrew verb "create" does not necessarily express something from nothing). But just as in a court of law,

81. For helpful discussions of the biblical doctrine of creation, see Bernhard W. Anderson, *Creation versus Chaos* (Philadelphia: Fortress, 1987); idem, *From Creation to New Creation: Old Testament Perspectives* (Minneapolis: Fortress, 1994).

82. The first part of this book is a significant expansion on an earlier article: Paul Copan, "Is *Creatio ex nihilo* a Post-Biblical Invention? A Response to Gerhard May's Proposal," *Trinity Journal* 17 (spring 1996): 77–93.

83. Mark William Worthing, *God, Creation, and Contemporary Physics* (Minneapolis: Augsburg, 1996), 76.

while one strand of evidence may be insufficient to convict a criminal, the full range of evidence may be quite convincing.

This book offers reasons for claiming that creation out of nothing is a *biblical* concept. The biblical data are not ambiguous, as some contend; indeed, creation *ex nihilo* is the most reasonable inference to make in light of biblical texts. Even if the doctrine of creation out of nothing is not explicitly stated, it is an obvious inference from the fact that God created everything distinct from himself. "Implicit" should not be watered down to mean "ambiguous." (Or, again, we can distinguish between the *concept* of creation out of nothing in Scripture even if the *words* "creation out of nothing" are not specifically used.) That ancient Jewish and Christian exegetes and theologians believed in creation *ex nihilo* should therefore not come as a surprise. And even if, as many of them believed, God did create out of primordial matter, these Jewish and Christian thinkers held that this matter itself was *first* created by God and then at a later stage shaped by him into an orderly cosmos. They uniformly held that God alone is unbegotten and uncreated; everything else is begotten and creaturely.

The biblical doctrine of *creatio ex nihilo* needs to be carefully distinguished from God's conservation of the world in being. Chapter 4 provides a careful analysis of these two notions and argues that creation is properly distinguished from conservation principally in that only the former lacks a patient entity to receive God's action.

The doctrine that God created everything other than himself and therefore alone exists *a se* is significantly challenged by Platonism. Chapter 5 explores ways of meeting this challenge in a biblical and philosophically coherent way. This chapter is programmatic in character, and its conclusions are tentative.

The church fathers departed from Greek philosophical tradition in rejecting the eternity of matter in favor of the Hebrew idea of *creatio ex nihilo*, and engaged in philosophical disputes with Greek philosophers concerning the finitude of the past. For centuries this tradition continued in Christian, Jewish, and Islamic thought. Chapter 6 once more takes up this ancient tradition. The claim of the past's finitude is philosophically superior to the claim of the infinity of the past, and chapter 6 defends, in conversation with contemporary philosophy and mathematics, two independent arguments for the conclusion that past, physical events are not infinite but had a beginning.

In a revolution of almost Copernican proportions, contemporary astrophysical cosmology has abandoned the view of the universe as a static object in favor of the view that the universe is an evolving entity and so has a large-scale history. Remarkably, the evidence strongly suggests that that history is not infinite in the past, but is finite. According to the controlling paradigm of contemporary cosmology, the universe—indeed, space and time themselves—came into being out of nothing roughly thirteen billion years ago. Chapter 7 presents evidence from astrophysical cosmology for the finitude of the past and explores attempts to avert this absolute beginning through nonstandard cosmogonic models. It reveals why most cosmologists today think that no model not involving the finitude of the past is as plausible as models consistent with the prediction of an absolute beginning by standard big bang cosmology.

Therefore, there are good philosophical and scientific grounds for affirming the temporal origination of the universe ex nihilo. To complete the case for creatio ex nihilo, chapter 8 examines naturalistic attempts to stave off the inference to a transcendent, personal Creator of the cosmos. These attempts are desperate and reveal that the best explanation of the origin of the universe is that God created the universe out of nothing.

I

The Old Testament Witness to *Creatio ex Nihilo*

Gerhard May admits that the idea of creation out of nothing "corresponds factually with the OT proclamation about creation,"[1] even though the doctrine is *not demanded* by the text.[2] Upon closer examination, however, a solid case can be made for *creatio ex nihilo* in the OT—that it is indeed demanded by the text, even if "out of nothing" is implicit rather than directly stated. That is, there simply is no other plausible and consistent way to read the biblical text. That declared, the OT case for creation *ex nihilo* is a *cumulative* one, not relying upon one piece of evidence alone but upon a number of mutually reinforcing elements. When we combine them, the case for creation out of nothing is quite strong.

As we establish in this chapter, the case for creation out of nothing combines the following elements:

1. The contrast between the biblical creation account and other ancient Near Eastern epics.

1. Gerhard May, *Creatio ex Nihilo: The Doctrine of "Creation out of Nothing" in Early Christian Thought,* trans. A. S. Worrall (Edinburgh: University of Edinburgh Press, 1994), xi.
2. Ibid., 24.

2. The various literary/contextual reasons to take Genesis 1:1 as an absolute sentence ("In the beginning God created . . .") rather than as a construct ("When God created . . .").

3. Significant features of the verb *bārā᾽* (create), when used in the context of the initial creation (e.g., Gen. 1:1), point to creation out of nothing:

   a. God is always the subject of the verb *bārā᾽* (the relevant uses are in the Qal and Niphal stems).

   b. No material is mentioned in connection with God's creative action.

   c. God's creating by his *word* reflects an effortlessness and freedom not communicated by a doctrine of creation out of eternally preexistent matter.

   d. *Bārā᾽* captures the breadth of God's creation from start to finish—unlike words such as *make* or *form*.

4. The *totalism* of the OT creation passages (e.g., "the heavens and the earth," representing the *totality* of creation) strongly implies that nothing is left out of this comprehensive description; God and his creation constitute the sum total of reality.

5. The Creator-creature contrast in the OT (and carried over into the NT) takes for granted God's intrinsically enduring nature as opposed to creation's inherent finitude and transitoriness.

Whatever one says about the use of literary sources and traditions in Genesis, many scholars agree that the final form of Genesis 1 gives precedence to God's initial activity in creating the heavens and earth. They recognize that creation marks the beginning of time and earthly history, the very originating point of everything apart from God.[3] So we shall examine these key features and other arguments that strongly support the doctrine of creation out of nothing as clearly implied by the OT.

Genesis 1: Just Another Ancient Near Eastern Cosmogony?

The first tablet of the ancient Babylonian "creation epic" *Enuma Elish* begins this way:

> When heaven above [*enuma elish*] was not yet named
> Nor earth below pronounced by name,
> Apsu, the first one, their begetter

3. Brevard S. Childs, *Biblical Theology of the Old and New Testaments* (Minneapolis: Fortress, 1992), 385.

And maker Tiamat, who bore them all,
Had mixed their waters together,
But had not formed pastures, nor discovered reed-beds;
When yet no gods were manifest,
Nor names pronounced, nor destinies decreed,
Then gods were born within them.
Lahmu (and) Lahamu emerged, their names pronounced.
As soon as they matured, were fully formed,
Anshar (and) Kishar were born, surpassing them.
They passed the day at length, they added to the years.
Anu their first-born son rivalled his forefathers:
Anshar made his sun Anu like himself,
And Anu begot Nudimmud in his likeness.
He, Nudimmud, was superior to his forefathers:
Profound of understanding, he was wise, was very strong at arms.
Mightier by far than Anshar his father's begetter,
He had no rival among the gods his peers.
. . . .
And Ea and Damkina his lover dwelt in splendour.
In the chamber of destinies, the hall of designs,
Bel, cleverest of the clever, sage of the gods, was begotten.
And inside Apsu, Marduk was created;
Inside pure Apsu, Marduk was born.
Ea his father created him,
Damkina his mother bore him.
. . . .
The gods, unable to rest, had to suffer.
They plotted evil in their hearts.
. . . .
They crowded round and rallied beside Tiamat.
They were fierce, scheming restlessly night and day.
They were working up to war, growling and raging.
They convened a council and created conflict.[4]

The word *cosmogony* has to do with the origin or birth of the universe, and Genesis 1 indeed offers us a cosmogony. Most of us have heard scholars in the history of religions compare Genesis 1 with ancient Near East (ANE) cosmogonies, lumping them together as "basically saying the same thing." In their book *In the Beginning*, Robert Coote and David Ord, after citing the *Enuma Elish*, casually dismiss the uniqueness of the Genesis account: "Genesis 1 is a typical creation account, so it opens the

---

4. This translation is by Stephanie Dalley, in *Myth from Mesopotamia*, World Classics (Oxford: Oxford University Press, 1991). Available online at www.usd.edu/~dpryce/honors/enuma.htm.

same way."[5] Such frequently repeated remarks obscure the remarkable differences between Genesis and other cosmogonies.

Before looking at particular OT texts related to creation, we should at least examine other ANE cosmogonies to make a more informed judgment about how they compare with Genesis 1, since such a juxtaposition has a bearing on understanding biblical creation. When we recognize the remarkable differences between them, the similarities actually pale in comparison to the differences.

Genesis is quite unlike the Mesopotamian cosmogonies, for instance, which are intertwined with *theogonies*—accounts of the origins of the gods. In them, we are not told so much about how the universe came about—the origin of the worlds is really accidental or secondary in ANE accounts—but how the *gods* emerged. And in addition to the fact that these Mesopotamian cosmogonies are really concerned with the ancestors of the gods and how they got themselves organized, they do not even identify these gods as creators. So when it comes to the elements of the universe (the waters/deep, darkness), a deity either *controls* one or *is* one.[6]

As Umberto Cassuto puts it, the ANE creation epics tell about the *origin of the gods* who came before the birth of the world and human beings. They speak of "the antagonism between this god and that god, of frictions that arose from these clashes of will, and of mighty wars that were waged by the gods."[7] Also, these epics "connected the genesis of the world with the genesis of the gods and with the hostilities and wars between them; and they identified different parts of the universe with given deities or with certain parts of their bodies."[8]

Gerhard Hasel says that the author of Genesis 1 writes with an *awareness* of rival cosmogonies, but deliberately *rejects* them.[9] In rival cosmogonies, humankind is merely an afterthought, whereas in Genesis 1 man and woman are the crown and apogee of God's creation. Unlike the "exclusive monotheism" of OT creation, Raymond Van Leeuwen writes, ANE texts are characterized by polytheism in which gods are identified with "powers, parts, or aspects of cosmos and culture."[10] Even

5. Robert Coote and David Ord, *In the Beginning: Creation and the Priestly History* (Minneapolis: Fortress, 1991), 50.

6. John H. Walton, *Ancient Israelite Literature in Its Cultural Context* (Grand Rapids: Zondervan, 1989), 25–26.

7. U. Cassuto, *A Commentary on the Book of Genesis*, vol. 1, trans. Israel Abrahams (Jerusalem: Magnes Press, 1972), 7.

8. Ibid., 7.

9. Gerhard F. Hasel, "The Polemic Nature of the Genesis Cosmology," *Evangelical Quarterly* 46 (1974): 81–102.

10. Raymond C. Van Leeuwen, *"br," in NIDOTTE*, 1:728.

where imagery or action is similar in the OT and ANE accounts, the polytheism of ANE texts (e.g., primeval conflict, the world as having an ambiguous good-evil dimension) gives them a character completely different from the OT accounts (e.g., creation without conflict, the creation is entirely "good").[11]

Further, Yahweh simply speaks, thereby creating; in other ANE cosmogonies, deities struggle to divide the waters. Also, in Genesis 1, the astral bodies are not *gods* (as in ANE accounts) but are *creations.*[12] As Rolf Rendtorff points out, even the darkness in Genesis 1 is "an element of creation"—as well as the "waters."[13] (See also Isa. 45:7, where Yahweh creates not only light but darkness.) Gerhard von Rad makes the powerful point that Israel's worldview, as reflected in Genesis, drew a sharp demarcating line between God and the world. The material world is purged of any quality of the divine or the demonic.[14]

Old Testament scholar Mark S. Smith has compared and contrasted the Ugaritic cosmogony with that of Genesis 1. In Genesis, we read of something marvelously different than in the former, with its gods and hostile powers (darkness, the waters/the deep): "These cosmic monsters are no longer primordial forces opposed to the Israelite God at the beginning of creation. Instead, *they are creatures like other creatures* rendered in this story."[15] Genesis 1 depicts a "divine mastery" over these forces, which are "depersonalized" and "domesticated."[16] The language of ancient myths and powers serves as a literary backdrop to the Genesis imagery. Nevertheless, "the mythic assertions themselves are avoided, since a jealous God can brook no competitive primal powers."[17]

Contrary to the assertion by Laurence Turner that "chaos rules" in Genesis 1:2,[18] the waters and darkness have no force or power at all. (As just noted, God creates the darkness as well as the waters; darkness,

---

11. Ibid., 729.

12. On this, see Hasel, "Polemic Nature," 81–102.

13. Rolf Rendtorff, "Creation and Redemption in the Torah," in *The Blackwell Companion to the Hebrew Bible,* ed. Leo G. Purdue (Malden, Mass.: Blackwell, 2001), 314.

14. Gerhard von Rad, "Some Aspects of the Old Testament World-View," in *Creation in the Old Testament,* ed. Bernard W. Anderson (Philadelphia: Fortress, 1984), 3.

15. Mark S. Smith, *The Origins of Biblical Monotheism: Israel's Polytheistic Background and the Ugaritic Texts* (New York: Oxford University Press, 2001), 38. See also Mark S. Smith, *The Early History of God: Yahweh and the Other Deities in Ancient Israel,* 2d ed. (Grand Rapids: Eerdmans, 2002).

16. Smith, *Origins of Biblical Monotheism,* 38.

17. Robert W. Jenson, *Systematic Theology: The Works of God,* vol. 2 (New York: Oxford University Press, 2000), 11.

18. Laurence A. Turner, *Genesis* (Sheffield: Sheffield Academic Press, 2000), 21. Jon D. Levenson speaks of the "survival of chaos after the victory of God" in the first part of his *Creation and the Persistence of Evil* (San Francisco: HarperSanFrancisco, 1989).

like the waters, is a creation and not eternally preexistent: thus the OT presentation runs contrary to other ANE epics.)[19] There simply is no "dialectical tension" between chaos and cosmos.[20] Gerhard von Rad declares about Genesis 1:

> It is amazing to see how sharply little Israel demarcated herself from an apparently overpowering environment of cosmological and theogonic myths. Here the subject is not a primeval mystery of procreation from which the divinity arose, nor of a "creative" struggle of mythically personified powers from which the cosmos arose, but rather the one who is neither warrior nor procreator, who alone is worthy of the predicate, Creator.[21]

A further contrast to some ANE cosmogonies has to do with ontology or being: the created world does not somehow *emanate* from Yahweh. It is not an "overflow of the essence of deity, but rather an object."[22] It is clearly distinct from him. By his word, he calls it into existence, making it his own possession.[23]

In contrast to ANE myths, there are no rivals to the Creator in Genesis 1—let alone preexistent matter. This, according to Luis Stadelmann, is a "fundamental" difference between the two. There is no cosmic dualism or struggle at all.[24] On the other hand, the Babylonian creation story elaborately "features a succession of rival deities" rather than a simple monotheistic account.[25] As James Barr observes, the theomachies

---

19. The divine spirit and cosmic matter are coexistent and coeternal in these extrabiblical epics; thus, light emanates from the gods in the Babylonian epic. In Genesis, however, God creates matter and exists independently of it: God creates light in Genesis (E. A. Speiser, *Genesis*, AB 1 [Garden City, N.J.: Doubleday, 1964], 10).

20. Contrary to Karl Lönig and Erich Zenger, *To Begin with, God Created . . .* (Collegeville, Minn.: Liturgical Press, 2000), 18; and W. Sibley Towner, *Genesis* (Louisville: Westminster John Knox, 2001), 18: "[Various biblical passages cited] retain a remnant of the mythological tradition of cosmic warfare and divine victory."

21. Gerhard von Rad, *Genesis: A Commentary*, trans. John H. Marks (Philadelphia: Westminster, 1961), 47.

22. Ibid., 49.

23. Ralph L. Smith, *Old Testament Theology: Its History, Method, and Message* (Nashville: Broadman & Holman, 1993), 179.

24. Luis I. J. Stadelmann writes: "The idea of some primordial monster, coexistent with Yahweh from the beginning, was undoubtedly felt to be incompatible with the monotheistic outlook. When the biblical writers use mythological imagery to depict Yahweh's struggle with the monsters of primeval chaos, they are careful not to suggest a cosmic dualism but regard the primeval chaos as devoid of any power or resistance as soon as the creator-god overcomes it" (*The Hebrew Conception of the World: A Philological and Literary Study* [Rome: Pontifical Biblical Institute, 1970], 178).

25. Speiser, *Genesis*, 11; see also Kenneth Kitchen, *Ancient Orient and the Old Testament* (Downers Grove, Ill.: InterVarsity, 1966), 89.

(divine warrings) and polytheism of the ANE are in sharp contrast to Genesis 1, which is "magnificently monotheistic."[26]

According to John Sailhamer, the creation account in Genesis 1–2, in contradistinction to the ANE accounts, presents a threefold theological emphasis:

1. The identity of the Creator, who is also the God of Israel—and not part of a pantheon of gods
2. The origin of the world (Gen. 1:1)
3. The tying of the work of God in the past to the work of God in the future (e.g., the creation account parallels the building of the tabernacle later in the Pentateuch)[27]

John Walton says that the similarities between Mesopotamian cosmogonies and the Bible are superficial rather than substantial: "It is difficult to discuss comparisons between Israelite and Mesopotamian literature concerning creation because the disparity is so marked."[28] Walton sees three key differences:

1. Theogony versus cosmogony
2. Polytheism versus monotheism
3. Organization versus creative act

Contrary to popular belief, the Genesis account is not "just another myth" of the ANE. Genesis defines the God of Israel as being the one Creator—as opposed to the many gods in the ancient orient, who were limited in power, knowledge, and morality.[29] In a dramatic and revolutionary presentation, God is seen as creating the sun, moon, and stars, which were often thought to be gods in their own right.[30] While some similarities exist between Genesis and some other ancient creation epics

26. James Barr, *The Concept of Biblical Theology: An Old Testament Perspective* (Minneapolis: Fortress, 1999), 472.

27. John Sailhamer, "Genesis," in the *Expositor's Bible Commentary*, vol. 2, ed. Frank Gaebelein (Grand Rapids: Zondervan, 1990), 19–20. Victor Hamilton and James C. Moyer reduce these key differences to two: (1) to portray God as "sovereign, without challenge, and transcendent over creation"; and (2) "to present a pattern of relationship" with Israel's God as Creator, who eventually makes a covenant with Abraham and then establishes Israel as a nation after the exodus (*The Old Testament: Text and Context* [Peabody, Mass.: Hendrickson, 1997], 43).

28. Walton, *Ancient Israelite Literature*, 26. Walton notes that the god Marduk appears to create a constellation but actually destroys it to demonstrate his power to other deities. So there is no permanent cosmos at all.

29. Gordon J. Wenham, "Genesis," in *The New Bible Commentary*, ed. Gordon Wenham et al. (Downers Grove, Ill.: InterVarsity, 1994), 57.

30. Claus Westermann, *Creation*, trans. John J. Scullion (Philadelphia: Fortress, 1974),

(e.g., mention of dry land, heavenly lights, humankind; the gods' resting), the differences are far more striking and noteworthy.

Not only is there a difference in *content* between Genesis 1 and other ANE cosmogonies; there is also a striking dissimilarity in *style*. Archaeologist Kenneth Kitchen has pointed out the contrast between the simple creation account in Genesis and the more elaborate ANE creation epics. As a general rule of thumb with such writings, *the simpler the earlier:* "Simple accounts or traditions may give rise (by accretion or embellishment) to elaborate legends, but not vice versa."[31]

Furthermore, as Claus Westermann has urged, we ought not to feel threatened when we hear of other creation accounts from the ANE.[32] A closer examination of these accounts reveals that the Jewish-Christian doctrine of creation is hardly threatened in its uniqueness *and* that significant differences (frequently understated) readily emerge when we carefully compare other ANE accounts with Genesis.[33] Unlike the typical monistic cosmogonic myths of the ANE, only the Bible speaks of a God free and distinct from the world. Henri Blocher comments: "There is a danger in the obvious passing unnoticed: the beginning of Genesis proclaims first of all *creation*. The one God has created everything. At the time it was formulated, the proposition was anything but commonplace."[34]

Genesis 1:1: Construct or Absolute?

A not-uncommon view of Genesis 1 is that it was influenced by the Babylonian epic, *Enuma Elish*, and other ANE epics. Indeed, such a perspective has affected how Genesis 1:1 itself was to be understood in some recent translations. Allegedly, because "beginning" does not have an article "the" preceding it in Hebrew, it is not absolute but temporal.[35] Thus the New English Bible (NEB, 1970) translates Genesis 1:1–2, "In the beginning of creation, when God made heaven and earth, the earth was

44: "The utter creatureliness of the heavenly bodies has never before been expressed in such revolutionary terms, as far as we know."

31. Kitchen, *Ancient Orient and the Old Testament*, 89 (and note).

32. Claus Westermann, *Genesis 1–11*, trans. John J. Scullion (Minneapolis: Augsburg, 1984), 20.

33. For a brief summary of some of the issues related to alleged biblical borrowing from ANE myths, see Walter C. Kaiser Jr., *The Old Testament Documents: Are They Reliable and Relevant?* (Downers Grove, Ill.: InterVarsity, 2001), 53–66.

34. Henri Blocher, *In the Beginning: The Opening Chapters of Genesis*, trans. David G. Preston (Downers Grove, Ill.: InterVarsity, 1984), 60.

35. So Towner, *Genesis*, 15.

without form and void." The New American Bible (NAB, 1970) translates it, "In the beginning, when God created the heavens and the earth, the earth was a formless wasteland." The New Jewish Version (NJV, 1962) puts the alleged circumstantial clause this way: "When God began to create the heaven and the earth—the earth being unformed and void." In their (ironically titled) book *In the Beginning,* Coote and Ord declare that the traditional translation of Genesis 1:1, as in NIV ("In the beginning God created the heavens and the earth"), is "incorrect." They add, "Historians are generally aware of this, but translations continue to render the Hebrew in this way because it is so traditional."[36] The authors proceed as though there is no grammatical basis for the standard and historical translation.

These temporal translations of the text just cited imply that there is no absolute beginning to creation; in fact, so it has been argued, primordial (or chaotic) matter existed eternally and was organized by God. If Genesis 1:1 is a dependent clause, then the first thing God creates is light, not heaven and earth (i.e., the universe). One commentator on Genesis 1:2 thus says, "Creation of matter in the Torah is not out of nothing (*creatio ex nihilo*), as many have claimed."[37]

To the contrary, contemporary scholarship has, with increasing force, taken issue with such a construct reading. Furthermore, many prominent scholars have argued that there exists no substantive or significant dependence of Genesis 1 on Mesopotamian or Egyptian sources (although we readily acknowledge the biblical author's *awareness* of ANE cosmogonies); hence, distinctions should be more carefully drawn, and lumping them all together should be avoided.[38]

We identify four views on interpreting the first verse of Genesis:[39]

36. Coote and Ord, *In the Beginning,* 50.

37. Richard Elliott Friedman, *Commentary on the Torah* (San Francisco: HarperSanFrancisco, 2001), 6.

38. Much of this discussion is from Gordon Wenham, *Genesis 1–15,* WBC 1 (Waco: Word, 1987), 11.

39. This breakdown is from ibid. For a similar layout of positions, see Victor P. Hamilton, *The Book of Genesis: Chapters 1–17* (Grand Rapids: Eerdmans, 1990), 103–4. Biblical scholar James Barr trims the options to three by conflating views 1 and 2 (the construct/temporal renderings). Thus, Genesis 1:1 either (1) describes an *initial act* of creation (prior to the creation of light in 1:3); (2) is a *temporal expression* ("in the beginning of God's creating heaven and earth") and "thus attached to the description of the chaotic state in v. 2"; or (3) is a *summary* of the total work of creation, "placed at the beginning and followed by the detailed account that goes back over the same process of creation in seven days." See James Barr, "Was Everything That God Created Really Good? A Question in the First Verse of the Bible," in *God in the Fray,* ed. Tod Linafelt and Timothy K. Beal (Minneapolis: Fortress, 1998), 55.

Four Views on Genesis 1:1	How Genesis 1:1 Is Interpreted
View 1: Verse 1 is a temporal clause, subordinate to the main clause in verse 2.	In the beginning when God created . . . , the earth was without form.
View 2: Verse 1 is a temporal clause, subordinate to the main clause in verse 3 (verse 2 is a parenthetical comment).	In the beginning when God created . . . (now the earth was formless), God said. . . .
View 3: Verse 1 is a main clause and serves as a title to the chapter as a whole, summarizing all the events described in verses 2–31.	In the beginning God created the heavens and the earth—[and here is how it happened]. . . .
View 4: Verse 1 is a main clause describing the first act of creation. Verses 2 and 3 describe subsequent phases in God's creative activity.	In the beginning God created the heavens and the earth. [After he did so,] the earth was uninhabitable and desolate.

What is the practical significance of rendering Genesis 1:1 in a temporal sense (views 1–2) as opposed to an absolute sense (views 3–4)? Kenneth Mathews writes that a relative or temporal beginning ("in [a] beginning") to creation suggests "permitting the possibility of preexisting matter" (although not necessarily so). An absolute reading ("in *the* beginning") presents us with a definite or absolute beginning of the universe.[40] So, does creation have an absolute beginning or not? Did God shape eternally preexisting matter, or did God create everything out of nothing? According to Victor Hamilton, the standard alternatives are either *monotheism* (God as the ultimate, eternally existent Being) or an *eternal dualism* (God and chaotic matter are coeternal).[41] In the beginning, was there one existing entity, or were there two—God and preexisting, chaotic matter?[42] The differences are dramatic and significant.

After surveying the relevant scholarship, Gordon Wenham asserts that "the majority of recent writers reject [the construct] interpretation."[43] Indeed, the absolute view is superior to the construct. Let us look at some of the arguments and reasons:

40. Kenneth A. Mathews, *Genesis 1–11:26*, NAC 1A (Nashville: Broadman & Holman, 1996), 137.
41. Some scholars, however, simply see the origin of primal matter in Genesis 1 as an unresolved issue.
42. Hamilton, *Genesis 1–17*, 105.
43. Wenham, *Genesis 1–15*, 12. See also Gerhard F. Hasel, "Recent Translations of Genesis 1:1," *The Bible Translator* 22 (1971): 154–68; and Hershel Shanks, "How the Bible Begins," *Judaism* 21 (1972): 51–58. Compare John W. Rogerson, R. W. L. Moberly, and William Johnstone, *Genesis and Exodus* (Sheffield: Sheffield Academic Press, 2001), 74–76, who argue, weakly, that even the traditional reading ("in the beginning") itself implies creation out of preexisting matter.

First, the lack of an article (lit., "in beginning") *hardly entails a construct state rather than an absolute state* ("in *the* beginning"). Scholars such as G. Wenham,[44] N. H. Ridderbos,[45] James Barr,[46] John Sailhamer,[47] and others have shown that temporal phrases often lack an article (Isa. 40:21; 41:4, 26; 46:10; cf. Gen. 3:22; 6:3, 4; Mic. 4:14 [5:1 ET]; Hab. 1:12).[48] We can forcefully say that it just has *not* been shown that *bĕrēʾšîth* ("in [the] beginning") *cannot* have an absolute sense. Take, for instance Isaiah 46:9–10, where we read: "I am God, . . . declaring the end from the beginning [*mērēʾšîth*]" (lit., "from beginning"). Here, Walter Eichrodt urges, God's utterance seems obviously to be an absolute sense—God's "absolute disposition over beginning and end"—and with a historical sense in mind.[49] Besides Isaiah 46:10, with *mērēʾšîth* used in an "absolute state,"[50] Proverbs 8:23 also seems to have absolute force: "I was appointed . . . from the beginning [*mērōʾš*], before the world began." Indeed, in Job 8:7; 42:12; Ecclesiastes 7:8; and Isaiah 46:10, we see this word "beginning" used in opposition to the "end."

44. Wenham, *Genesis 1–15*, 12.

45. N. H. Ridderbos, "Genesis i 1 und 2," in *Studies on the Book of Genesis*, by B. Gemser et al., Oudtestamentische Studiën 12 (Leiden: Brill, 1958), 216–19.

46. James Barr notes this as well, pointing to Isaiah 41:4, 26; 48:16; Proverbs 8:23; Ecclesiastes 3:11 ("Was Everything That God Created Really Good?" 58).

47. John Sailhamer, "Genesis," 21–23, offers a number of grammatical and literary reasons why *rēʾšît* was chosen. For example, he notes the literary importance of an absolute beginning in Genesis 1:1 in contrast to the eschatological term *ʾaḥărît* ("end times") used at strategic places—in "poetic seams"—in the Pentateuch (Gen. 49:1 NIV, "days *to come*"; Deut. 31:27 NIV, "*after* I die!"). See also idem, *The Pentateuch as Narrative: A Biblical-Theological Commentary* (Grand Rapids: Zondervan, 1992), 35–37.

48. N. H. Ridderbos argues that Genesis 1:1 cannot be translated as a temporal clause ("Genesis i 1 und 2," 216–19); cf. Francis Brown, S. R. Driver, and Charles A. Briggs, *The New Brown-Driver-Briggs-Gesenius Hebrew and English Lexicon* (Peabody, Mass.: Hendrickson, 1979), 912; and William R. Lane, "The Initiation of Creation," *Vetus Testamentum* 13 (1963): 63–73, who nevertheless declares, "There is only one view of creation which is acceptable to us; that is creatio ex nihilo. Anything else is not creation" (65).

49. Walter Eichrodt, "In the Beginning," in *Creation in the Old Testament*, ed. Bernhard W. Anderson (Philadelphia: Fortress, 1984), 68; Hamilton, *Genesis 1–17*, 106, argues further that if Isaiah 46:10 happened to be the only text using the alleged construct usage *rēʾšît* in an absolute sense, then this one example is "sufficient" to show that this structure—*rēʾšît*—"may be used to express temporal meaning by use of the absolute state construction." Moreover, *bĕrēʾšîth* ([early] in/at the beginning) occurs in Jeremiah 26:1; 27:1; 28:1; 49:34 ("at the beginning of the reign of *X*")—each time followed by the occurrence of another noun, but in Genesis 1:1, the noun is followed by a finite (perfect) verb, and this construction is unique. However, this construction is quite common in Semitic languages, and a parallel is found in Hosea 1:2 (E. Kautzsch, *Gesenius' Hebrew Grammar*, trans. G. W. Collins [Oxford: Clarendon, 1898], 443, §130d). See also Ridderbos, "Genesis i 1 und 2," 228. For further comments, see Edward J. Young, *Studies in Genesis One* (Philadelphia: Presbyterian & Reformed, 1964), 6.

50. Young, *Studies in Genesis 1*, 4.

James Barr, arguing that there is *no* grammatical evidence that "be-ginning" is construct in Genesis 1:1,[51] calls such a reading "intrinsically unlikely."[52] The construct argument depends only on the absence of the article, and it simply will not work. According to Bernhard Anderson, on the basis of both *stylistic* and *contextual* considerations, Genesis 1:1 is indeed an independent sentence,[53] referring to an "absolute beginning," *"the origination of all things."*[54] Rolf Rendtorff agrees: Genesis 1:1 refers to a beginning in an absolute sense.[55]

Second, the literary structure of Genesis 1 militates against a construct rendering of Genesis 1:1. According to E. A. Speiser, the P (Priestly) ac-count of creation ends at 2:4a and the J (Jahwistic) account begins at 2:4b. Speiser, who tends to be overquoted in support of the construct view, believes that Genesis 1:1–3 parallels Genesis 2:4b–7. In both, he sees a temporal beginning, a parenthesis, followed by the main clause (thus allegedly paralleling the Babylonian *Enuma Elish* epic):[56]

Genesis 1:1–3	Genesis 2:4b–7
Temporal clause: When God set about to create the heaven and the earth	At the time when the LORD God made earth and heaven
Parenthesis: the world being then a form-less waste . . .	no shrub of the field being yet in the earth . . .
Main clause: God said, "Let there be light."	God Yahweh formed man from clods in the soil.

From a structural-linguistic vantage point, there are several problems with such a reading. Victor Hamilton points out that if Genesis 1:1 is a temporal dependent clause,

> then the additional facts are that verse 2 is a parenthetical comment, set off by the hyphens from what precedes and follows; and the main clause appears in verse 3, "And God said. . . ." The result is an unusually long, rambling sentence, in itself not unheard of, but quite out of place in this chapter, laced as it is with a string of staccato sentences.[57]

51. Barr, "Was Everything That God Created Really Good?" 57.

52. Ibid., 58.

53. Bernhard W. Anderson, *From Creation to New Creation* (Minneapolis: Fortress, 1994), 30.

54. Bernhard W. Anderson, *Creation versus Chaos* (Philadelphia: Fortress, 1987), 185.

55. Rendtorff, "Creation and Redemption in the Torah," 313.

56. Speiser, *Genesis*, 8–13, 18–20.

57. Victor P. Hamilton, *Handbook on the Pentateuch* (Grand Rapids: Baker, 1982), 31.

Hershel Shanks points out that the inferior literary quality of the construct furnishes a powerful argument in favor of the more majestic absolute translation. The attempt by some recent translations to make Genesis 1:1–3 into one long sentence is "a model of awkwardness" and "a clutter of thoughts crying to be sorted out," which is instinctively off-putting.[58] For the alleged sake of grammar and "scholarly" considerations, the construct interpretation in certain recent translations (NAB, NEB, NJV) sacrifices literary beauty. The main concerns behind the construct rendering are, in fact, resolved by an absolute one.[59] Edward P. Arbez and John P. Weisengoff see the construct reading as "clumsy,"[60] and Keil and Delitzsch go so far as to call it "intolerable."[61] Why then adopt a translation, Shanks asks, "that has been aptly characterized as a *verzweifelt geschmacklose* [desperately tasteless] construction, one which destroys a sublime opening to the world's greatest book"?[62]

Wenham, Hamilton, and Mathews offer extensive arguments against Speiser's alleged parallel, and they suggest that a new section in Genesis begins with 2:4a ("This is the account of the heavens and the earth. . . ."), not 2:4b.[63] This is borne out by the following six factors:

Factor 1: Genesis 1:1–2:3 forms a chiastic pattern, indicating a complete unit. Genesis 2:1–3 echoes 1:1 by introducing the same phrases but in reverse order: "[He] created," "God," "heavens and earth" reappear as "heavens and earth" (2:1), "God" (2:2), "created" (2:3).[64]

Factor 2: "This is the account/These are the generations . . ." (2:4a) is a standard marker in Genesis (2:4; 5:1; 6:9; 10:1; 11:10; 11:27; 25:12, 19; 36:1, 9; 37:2),[65] pointing not to what *precedes* but to what *follows*. It is designed to "move the narration forward."[66] It always announces a new section of narrative; this is its "usual function."[67] In the case of 2:4, the chiastic inversion from "heavens and the earth" (2:4a) to "earth and the heavens" (2:4b) focuses our attention on the elaboration of the general description of Genesis 1:1–2:3—the setting for, and the actual creation of, man and woman in Genesis 2:5–25.

58. Shanks, "How the Bible Begins," 51.

59. See ibid., 51–58.

60. Edward P. Arbez and John P. Weisengoff, "Exegetical Notes on Genesis 1:1–2," *Catholic Biblical Quarterly* 10 (1948): 141.

61. C. F. Keil and F. Delitzsch, *The Pentateuch*, vol. 1 of *Commentary on the Old Testament*, trans. James Martin (1866; repr., Grand Rapids: Eerdmans, 1986), 46.

62. Shanks, "How the Bible Begins," 58.

63. Wenham, *Genesis 1–15*, 5–10, 44–59; Hamilton, *Genesis 1–17*, 107–8; and Mathews, *Genesis 1–11:26*, 137–44, 188–93.

64. Wenham, *Genesis 1–15*, 5.

65. See also Numbers 3:1.

66. Mathews, *Genesis 1–11:26*, 190.

67. Wenham, *Genesis 1–15*, 55, 49.

Factor 3: Genesis 2:1 ("Thus the heavens and the earth were completed in all their vast array") *already* serves as a fitting summary of 1:2–31.[68] It, therefore, makes better sense to see Genesis 2:4a as introducing a new section rather than repeating what 2:1 has sweepingly stated.

Factor 4: It is quite a stretch to draw parallels between *Enuma Elish* 1–9 and Genesis 1:1–3. In fact, any similarity that exists is between *Enuma Elish* 1–9 and Genesis 2:4b–7.[69] Genesis 1:1 stands as unique, which even critical scholars such as Hermann Gunkel have admitted: "The cosmogonies of other people contain no word which would come close to the first word of the Bible."[70]

Factor 5: The various ANE accounts that begin with *enuma* (or *inuma*) could be translated "on the day that" or "when" (i.e., as temporal clauses), corresponding to the Hebrew *běyôm* (on the day)—which is exactly what we find in Genesis 2:4b, but *not* in Genesis 1:1. Indeed, "in the beginning" has no parallel in the ANE.[71]

Factor 6: Genesis 1:1 being followed by the *wāw* (and) reveals that Genesis 1:1 is not simply just a heading or title (which would read more like 2:4a or 5:1: "This is the account/these are the generations of Adam's line"). If Genesis 1:1 were a title, then 1:2 would not immediately begin with the conjunction *and (wāw)*.[72] The function of the *wāw* (and) in 1:2 is to connect the various *subsequent* acts of creation with 1:1, as "the *primary* foundation on which they rest."[73] Computer analysis of the Hebrew OT in which the construction of the (a) *wāw* plus (b) a nonpredicate plus (c) a predicate preceding the main verb (as in Gen. 1:2) reveals that the preceding clause ("In the beginning . . .") furnishes us with background information to understand 1:2–31. This means that Genesis 1:1, rather than being appositional or summing up what takes place in 1:2–31, is actually coordinated with the following section. That is, Genesis 1:1 serves as the historical context or setting for what follows in 1:2 and beyond.[74]

In light of these six factors, we affirm that both Genesis 1:1 and Genesis 2:4 are independent, rather than temporal, sentences. Such a view makes the best sense grammatically, literarily, and aesthetically.

---

68. John Sailhamer, *The Pentateuch as Narrative: A Biblical-Theological Commentary* (Grand Rapids: Zondervan, 1992), 82 n.

69. Hamilton, *Genesis 1–17*, 107.

70. Hermann Gunkel, *Genesis*, 7th ed. (Göttingen: Vandenhoek & Ruprecht, 1966), 101; see also Hasel, "Recent Translations of Genesis 1:1," 163.

71. Hasel, "Recent Translations of Genesis 1:1," 162.

72. John Sailhamer, *Genesis Unbound: A Provocative New Look at the Creation Account* (Sisters, Ore.: Multnomah, 1996), 102–3.

73. Keil and Delitzsch, *Commentary on the Old Testament*, 1:46 (emphasis added).

74. John Sailhamer has carried out just such an analysis. See *Genesis Unbound*, 102–3, 253 n.

Third, the phrase "the heavens and the earth" is a merism that refers to the totality. According to Hershel Shanks, many of the alleged problems (for the absolute reading) brought up by Speiser and others who take the construct reading are resolved when we see that "the heavens and the earth" is a merism (or merismus). This is a rhetorical device that refers to the extreme parts or to the first and last of something to represent the whole. (One example is the expression "from Dan to Beersheba" [Judg. 20:1; 1 Sam. 3:20; 2 Sam. 3:10; 17:11; 24:2; et al.]—the northern and southern boundaries of Israel, representing the *entirety* of the nation.)[75] In Genesis 1:1, the author is not telling us about the order of creation; instead, he is telling us that "God made the universe."[76]

Shanks further states that if "heaven and earth" speaks of totality—thereby eliminating a primordial preexistence—then *even if we take Genesis 1:1 as construct, creation out of nothing would still be implied:* "Perhaps more important, whether *creatio ex nihilo* is implied in verse 1," Shanks writes, "depends, not so much on how we begin the verse, but on how we understand 'heaven[s] and earth.'"[77] If "heaven[s] and earth" describes only organization and ordering, then some primordial existence is not precluded. But if "heaven[s] and earth" refers to everything—"the works"—that would exclude primordial matter.

As Wenham points out, Genesis 1:1 could thus be reworded: "In the beginning God created everything."[78] *Totality* rather than *organization* is the chief thrust of this merism. Westermann asserts, "[The 'beginning' in the title in Gen. 1:1] means not the beginning of something, but simply The Beginning. *Everything* began with God."[79] Of course, "universe" goes beyond what was the ancient—and more limited—understanding of the cosmos. Therefore, "totality" best expresses what "the heavens and the earth" attempts to capture.[80]

Fourth, further support for this absolute reading (and view 4 in particular) *stems from the fact that this particular absolute view is the oldest one.* Bruce Waltke lists "all ancient versions" as understanding Genesis 1:1 as an "independent clause."[81] Hamilton points out that "all the

75. Or, for example, "from Geba to Beersheba" (2 Kings 23:8), the northernmost and southernmost points (respectively) of the southern kingdom of Judah.

76. Shanks, "How the Bible Begins," 55.

77. Ibid., 57.

78. Wenham, *Genesis 1–15*, 15.

79. Claus Westermann, *Genesis: A Practical Commentary*, trans. David E. Green (Grand Rapids: Eerdmans, 1987), 7.

80. John E. Hartley, *Genesis*, NIBC 1 (Peabody, Mass.: Hendrickson, 2000), 42.

81. Bruce K. Waltke, "The Initial Chaos Theory and the Precreation Chaos Theory," *Bibliotheca Sacra* 132 (July 1975): 223.

ancient versions translate the word as an absolute and the whole as an independent clause."[82] Note the following evidence:

- This absolute understanding of Genesis 1:1 and its status as an independent clause is borne out by the LXX's rendering as well (*En archē epoiēsen ho theos ton ouranon kai tēn gēn. Hē de gē . . .* = "In the beginning God created the heaven and the earth. And the earth . . ."). According to Bernhard Anderson, the testimony of the LXX, which treats Genesis 1:1 as an independent sentence in Greek, reinforces the thrust of an absolute beginning of the cosmos in that passage.[83]
- John 1:1 (*En archē ēn ho logos . . .* = "In the beginning was the Word") itself relies on the LXX's translation of Genesis 1:1.
- Rather than understanding Genesis 1:1 as a construct, the first-century Jewish historian Josephus in his *Jewish Antiquities* follows the absolute rendering of the LXX in the outset of his work: "In the beginning God created the heaven and the earth [*En archē ektisen ho theos ton ouranon kai tēn gēn*]."[84]
- All ancient versions such as Aquila, Theodotion, Symmachus, and Targum Onkelos render Genesis 1:1 as an independent clause.
- Theophilus of Antioch (ca. 180) draws on the absolute reading of the LXX in Genesis 1:1 in *To Autolycus* (2.4): "In the beginning God created heaven [*En archē epoiesen ho theos ouranon*]."
- Pseudo-Justin (AD 220–300) cites the LXX's absolute rendering of Genesis 1:1: "For Moses wrote thus: 'In the beginning God created the heaven and the earth [*En archē epoiēsen ho theos ouranon kai tēn gēn*],' then the sun, and the moon, and the stars."[85]
- Jerome's Vulgate begins with the absolute rendering as well, treating it as an independent clause (*In principio creavit Deus caelum et terram*).[86]
- Saadia Gaon's tenth-century translation into Arabic takes Genesis 1:1 as an independent sentence.
- The various versions and the Masoretic pointing imply that "this was the standard view from the third-century BC (LXX) through to the tenth century AD (MT)."[87]

82. Hamilton, *Genesis 1–17*, 107; see also Mathews, *Genesis 1–11:26*, 138.
83. Anderson, *Creation versus Chaos*, 185.
84. Josephus, *Jewish Antiquities* 1.1.
85. Pseudo-Justin, *Hortatory Address to the Greeks* [*Cohortatio ad Graecos*] 28.
86. Hamilton, *Genesis 1–17*, 107; and Waltke, "Initial Chaos Theory," 223.
87. Wenham, *Genesis 1–15*, 13. See also Hamilton, *Genesis 1–17*, 107.

Therefore, all else being equal, preference should be given to antiquity.[88] Presumably, those closest in time to the composition of Genesis 1 would be the better informed about its meaning. Bruce Waltke reports the *unanimity* in "both the Jewish and Christian tradition" that the first word in the Bible is in an "absolute state," and that the first verse is "an independent clause."[89]

Fifth, the absolute construction of Genesis 1:1 is further supported by the structure of verse 2: The subject ("the earth/land") precedes the predicate ("was") rather than vice versa, and the predicate "was" is not omitted.[90] Rather, the phrase in verse 2 "And the earth [*wĕhāʾāreṣ*]" begins a new subject, which would not be the case if 1:1 were to be understood as construct. Cassuto declares forcefully that this particular syntax proffers a "decisive objection" and "proves"[91] that verse 2 begins a new subject:

> It follows, therefore, that the first verse is an independent sentence that constitutes a formal introduction to the entire section, and expresses at the outset, with majestic brevity, the main thought of the section: that in the beginning, that is, at the commencement of time . . . God created the heavens and the earth.[92]

Sixth, as recognized above, Genesis 1:1 stands out as unique when compared to the other ancient cosmogonies. Brevard Childs observes that to read Genesis 1:1 "as a temporal clause does not take seriously enough" the kind of contrast being made against the struggles so typical in other ANE cosmogonies.[93] Whatever one may say about verses 2–3 as reflecting mythological images of the ANE, verse 1 stands out as utterly unborrowed and distinct from ANE cosmogonies. As von Rad suggests, "One must not deprive the declaration in verse 1 of the character of a theological principle."[94] That is, God, in the freedom of his will, created "absolutely everything," establishing "a beginning of its subsequent existence."[95] Precisely because Genesis 1:1 precedes mention of "chaos"

---

88. Hamilton, *Handbook on the Pentateuch*, 41.

89. See Waltke, "Initial Chaos Theory," 217–28, esp. 225.

90. Cf. Jer. 26:1; 27:1; 28:1; Hos. 1:2; 1 Sam. 3:2–4 (note Cassuto's comments, *Commentary on Genesis*, 1:19–20).

91. Ibid., 1:19–20.

92. Ibid., 20.

93. Brevard S. Childs, *Myth and Reality in the Old Testament* (Naperville, Ill.: Allenson, 1960), 41.

94. Von Rad, *Genesis*, 46.

95. Ibid., 46.

in verse 2, "we cannot say that it is uncreated, that is, that it was found by God as pre-existent."[96]

Although some scholars are wont to do so, to conclude that the "chaos" is eternally preexistent is a huge non sequitur. There is very good reason—especially given the Bible's aversion to metaphysical dualism (since God alone is eternal or everlasting)—to embrace the idea that the "chaos" was itself brought into existence by God. Kenneth Mathews writes: "It is an unnecessary leap to conclude that the elements in verse 2 are autonomous, coeternal with God, and upon which he was in some way dependent for creation."[97] Brevard Childs remarks that some primordial dualism in Genesis 1:2 is simply out of the question.[98]

We have presented six reasons why Genesis 1:1 should be taken as absolute, which would negate the idea of an eternally preexistent chaos from which God organized the world. Indeed, in Claus Westermann's commentary on Genesis 1–11, he declares that Genesis 1:1 is a "principal sentence" that serves as an expression of praise to God.[99] This sentence dramatically sets apart the Genesis account from its ANE counterparts. Genesis begins like no other. And Westermann states that "had the question been put to [the biblical writer], he must certainly have decided in favor of *creatio ex nihilo.*"[100]

Theologian Robert W. Jenson comments on how decisively Westermann's analysis of Genesis 1 has undermined the construct rendering, rooted in radical biblical critical approaches to Scripture (which, among other things, failed to appreciate significant differences between ANE cosmogonies and the Bible):

> The Bible begins with a straightforward statement of doctrine: "In the beginning God created the heavens and the earth." Westermann established this as the right translation. . . . Resistance to Westermann's insight, and translations that make the first line a dependent clause, derive from residual prejudices of an earlier mode of critical exegesis.[101]

96. Gerhard von Rad, *Old Testament Introduction*, vol. 1, trans. D. M. G. Stalker (New York: Harper & Row, 1962), 144.

97. Mathews, *Genesis 1–11:26*, 141.

98. Childs, *Biblical Theology of the Old and New Testaments*, 386, adds that there is still the threat of creation's collapsing into nonbeing.

99. Westermann, *Genesis 1–11*, 97.

100. Ibid., 108–9.

101. Robert W. Jenson, "Aspects of the Doctrine of Creation," in *The Doctrine of Creation*, ed. Colin E. Gunton (Edinburgh: T & T Clark, 1997), 17. In order to make clearer demarcations between the *construct* rendering (views 1 and 2) and the *absolute* (views 3 and 4), we left out this segment of Jenson's quotation: "Westermann established this as the right translation, by showing that Genesis 1.1 is the caption of what follows" (which is view 3). As it turns out, view 4 is the more plausible rendering, as we explain below.

Elsewhere, Jenson states it even more strongly. Rather than taking Genesis 1:1 as a dependent clause, he claims this absolute rendering has surely been demonstrated for good. The dependent clause derives from "residual prejudices of a now-antique form of critical exegesis" that sought to find the "real" meaning of texts in earlier stages of the tradition prior to and outside the canonical text's structure. As a result, the interpretation of the canonical text was often forced onto the Procrustean bed of this critical exegesis to make it fit.[102]

Raymond Van Leeuwen sees Genesis 1:1 as communicating both an absolute beginning to the universe as well as God's absolute sovereignty by first bringing it into existence and then ordering it by his will.[103] According to James Barr, Genesis 1:1, while not actually asserting creation out of nothing, furnishes a "pointer" in that direction.[104] Von Rad declares that Genesis 1:1 stands as an overarching theological affirmation of creation out of nothing, coming before verse 2's reference to "chaos."[105]

We are convinced that Genesis 1:1–2 should not be translated, "In the beginning, when God created the heavens and the earth, the earth was a formless wasteland . . ." (NAB) or in some similar fashion.[106] Even Bernhard Anderson, who sees Genesis 1:2 as referring to creation out of chaos (although he affirms that later biblical writers affirm creation out of nothing, and so there is nothing to preclude a two-step process beginning with creation out of nothing), concedes that "stylistic studies" favor Genesis 1:1 as being an "absolute declarative sentence."[107]

Commentators Keil and Delitzsch declare that the phrase translated "in the beginning" *(bĕrē'šîth)* is used "absolutely," and a translation such as "In the beginning, when . . ." simply *cannot* be a reasonable treatment of the text.[108] In their estimation, the context indicates "the very first beginning."[109] Thus, the eternity of the world or the existence of

---

102. Jenson, *Systematic Theology*, 2:3 n.

103. Van Leeuwen, *"br'*," 732.

104. Barr, "Was Everything That God Created Really Good?" 65.

105. Von Rad, *Genesis*, 49.

106. Cf. E. A. Speiser, *Genesis*, 3, who takes Genesis 1:1 as a construct rather than an absolute: "When God set about to create heaven and earth . . ."; Luis Stadelmann follows Speiser here (*Hebrew Conception of the World*, 11). However, if what we have just argued is true, this would mean that Ian G. Barbour's assertion that Genesis argues for "the creation of *order from chaos*" rather than from nothing, is misguided (*Religion in an Age of Science* [San Francisco: Harper & Row, 1990], 130).

107. Bernhard W. Anderson, *Contours of Old Testament Theology* (Minneapolis: Fortress, 1999), 88–89. Mathews's analysis concludes that "v. 1 is best taken as an absolute statement of God's creation" (*Genesis 1–11:26*, 139).

108. Keil and Delitzsch, *Commentary on the Old Testament*, 1:46.

109. Ibid., 46. The same conclusion is drawn by Hamilton, *Genesis 1–17*, 106.

any "primeval material" is ruled out by language such as the absolute phrase "in the beginning" or the totalistic merism "the heaven[s] and the earth," which was, again, the very best the Hebrews could do to express entirety.[110]

Cuthbert A. Simpson concludes that the author of Genesis 1:1 is endeavoring to present the idea of a creation *ex nihilo* insofar as he could conceive of it.[111] The author is careful to counter any suggestion that the chaos did not derive its existence from God by prefacing his account with Genesis 1:1—God's creation of everything. (According to Simpson, God created in a two-step manner—first bringing matter into existence and then shaping it into order.)[112] Julius Wellhausen himself deemed the construct reading of Genesis 1:1 as "desperate."[113] Gerhard Hasel's survey of the literature concludes by noting the *unanimous* support of the independent/main-clause reading of Genesis 1:1 in light of the "combined efforts of lexical, grammatical, syntactical, comparative, and stylistic considerations."[114]

Moreover, it is quite telling that the Revised English Bible (REB), the successor of the NEB and involving some of the same scholars who worked on the NEB twenty years earlier, makes a *dramatic reversal* back to the traditional, absolute rendering of Genesis 1:1–2, rather than favoring the construct rendering. They now reject the reading they had earlier favored.[115]

NEB: In the beginning of creation, when God made heaven and earth, the earth was without form and void.

REB: In the beginning God created the heavens and the earth. The earth was a vast waste.

In light of contemporary biblical scholarship, this about-face should come as no surprise. Gordon Wenham writes: "Most modern commentators agree that verse 1 is an independent main clause to be translated, 'In

110. Ibid., 106. Cf. Werner Foerster, who says that this merism "embraces the cosmos" (*"ktizō," TDNT*, 3:1012).
111. Cuthbert A. Simpson, "Genesis," in *The Interpreter's Bible*, vol. 1, ed. G. A. Buttrick (Nashville: Abingdon, 1952), 467.
112. Ibid., 468.
113. Cited in Hasel, "Recent Translations of Genesis 1:1," 163.
114. Ibid., 167.
115. The NASB (1960) preserves the absolute reading of the ASV (1901). The New Jerusalem Bible (NJB, 1985) preserves the earlier Jerusalem Bible's absolute reading (1966), noting at Gen. 1:1 that the absolute reading is a "more coherent rendering of the text." However, the NRSV (1990) does use the construct reading—in contrast to the more accurate absolute RSV translation (1946).

the beginning God created. . . .'"[116] That is, views 1 and 2 (the temporal reading of Gen. 1:1) are generally rejected in favor of an absolute reading (either 3 or 4). And no wonder: It is the more majestic and elegant reading. It is the oldest and best-attested reading. There is no other way to express an absolute state (whereas there are alternative Hebrew temporal expressions, such as *běyôm* [on the day]).[117] And, finally, there are no good or overriding structural/linguistic reasons to overturn such a judgment.

The Verb *Bārā'*

Does the verb *bārā'*, used for "create" in Genesis 1:1 and elsewhere in the OT, imply creation out of nothing? It is well known that *bārā'* (create) is used elsewhere, as for God's creation of the people of Israel (e.g., Isa. 43:15) or his creation of a clean heart (Ps. 51:12 [10 ET]). Even after God's *initial* creation is complete (Gen. 2:1), God creates indirectly by continuing to create all creatures and to bring about his glorious purposes in history: "When you send your Spirit, they are created" (Ps. 104:30 NIV).

In their use of *bārā'*, the biblical writers are not *always* implying an *ex nihilo* creation at the beginning of the universe. We freely admit that the verb *bārā'* does not *always* speak of an *ex nihilo* creation, but can be used more widely than this.

That said, however, creation *ex nihilo* is implied in the relevant contexts surrounding *bārā'* and pertaining to the initial creation in particular (as in Gen. 1:1, 21, 27; 2:3). Furthermore, we can still pick up strong signals from OT writers regarding the uniqueness of the word *bārā'* (despite the LXX's obscuring it).[118] So we must look more closely at this word. While we must be careful not to load it with more freight than it was meant to carry,[119] we must not overlook its significance either.

To seek the meaning of a word, some take the precarious tack of appealing to its etymology and suggest that the verb *bārā'* may have originally meant "cut, divide, or separate."[120] This, however, is far from

---

116. Wenham, *Genesis 1–15*, 12.

117. Waltke puts it decisively: "Moses could not have used any other construction to denote the first word as in the absolute state, but he could have opted for a different construction to indicate clearly the construct state" ("Initial Chaos Theory," 224).

118. In the LXX, the more general verb *poiein* (to make) is often used instead of *ktizein* (to create). The verb *ktizein* occurs sixty-six times in the LXX, and thirty-nine of them are without a Hebrew equivalent. See Hans-Helmut Esser, "Creation," in *NIDNTT*, 378.

119. Westermann cautions that we not read creation *ex nihilo* into *bārā'* all by itself (*Genesis 1–11*, 100).

120. Karl-Heinz Bernhardt, "*bārā'*," in *TDOT*, 2:245, states, "The Heb. root *br'* probably has the original meaning 'to separate, divide.'" Cf. van Leeuwen, "*br'*," 731.

clear, as scholars such as G. Wenham and W. H. Schmidt observe.[121] Despite this, some scholars conclude that, based on the etymology of "cut" or "divide," there hence is some connotation of shaping as an artisan shapes from preexisting materials.[122] Stanley L. Jaki, for example, claims that *bārāʾ* is a verb that "exegetes love to raise to a quasi-divine pedestal."[123]

Modern linguists and exegetes have repeatedly shown that using etymology to establish word meaning is misguided. For example, the English word *nice* has been derived from the Latin *nescius*, which means "ignorant."[124] But we do not therefore imply that a "nice" person is an ignoramus! In most cases, the synchronic[125] usage of a word *rarely* means what it originally meant (i.e., etymologically). As biblical scholar Moisés Silva emphatically states, "Modern studies compel us to reject this attitude [i.e., appealing to etymology as giving us the 'basic' or 'real' meaning of a word] and distrust a word's history."[126] Similarly, James Barr asserts, "The main point is that the etymology of a word is not a statement about its meaning but about its history."[127]

Does *bārāʾ* by itself entail creation out of nothing? While admitting that the intertestamental book of 2 Maccabees (7:28) speaks of creation out of nothing,[128] Assyriologist Shalom M. Paul points out that *bārāʾ* by itself "does not imply" creation *ex nihilo*.[129] As we shall see, this state-

---

121. Wenham, *Genesis 1–15*, 14. W. H. Schmidt says that "the basic meaning 'to cut' (and similar meanings) does not echo anywhere in the usage of [*bārāʾ*]" in the Qal and Niphal (*"brʾ*, to create," *TLOT*, 1:253–54).

122. Despite this warning, Jaki himself appears to succumb to the "etymological fallacy" discussed below (Stanley L. Jaki, *Genesis 1 through the Ages* [Royal Oak, Mich.: Real View Books, 1998], 5–6).

123. Ibid., 7.

124. Anthony C. Thiselton, "Semantics and New Testament Interpretation," in *New Testament Interpretation: Essays on Principles and Methods*, ed. I. Howard Marshall (Grand Rapids: Eerdmans, 1977), 80.

125. *Synchronic* refers to the way a word was used *at the time of writing* (as distinguished from the *diachronic*, how a word was used over periods of time, for which the study of a word's etymology is quite useful). The etymological study is useful as a last-resort method—when the occurrence of a particular word is extremely rare and there is little else to go on.

126. Moisés Silva, *Biblical Words and Their Meaning: An Introduction to Lexical Semantics* (Grand Rapids: Zondervan, 1983), 51. See also D. A. Carson, *Exegetical Fallacies* (Grand Rapids: Baker, 1984), 26–32. Peter Cotterell and Max Turner state that the etymological fallacy is "a sufficiently dead horse in educated theological circles" (*Linguistics and Biblical Interpretation* [Downers Grove, Ill.: InterVarsity, 1989], 114).

127. James Barr, *The Semantics of Biblical Language* (Oxford: Oxford University Press, 1961), 109.

128. On this passage, see chapter 3, "The Extrabiblical Witness," below.

129. Shalom M. Paul, "Creation and Cosmogony in the Bible," *Encyclopedia Judaica* (Jerusalem: Encyclopedia Judaica, 1972), 5:1059, 1062. Paul does acknowledge 2 Macc. 7:28

ment is misleading; *bārā'* does have important theological significance that bears upon the question of creation out of nothing.

The relevant use of the term *create (bārā')* occurs thirty-eight times in the Qal stem or verb form and ten in the Niphal stem in the Hebrew Scriptures.[130] We are *not* here considering the Piel stem, which (as we noted, some scholars count as a distinct verb and doubt its *connection to bārā'* in the Qal or Niphal stems)[131] can mean "to cut, split" (Josh. 17:15).

The first point about the verb bārā' *is the utter absence of preexisting material in connection with it.* Though *bārā'* is used of God's creating human beings (Gen. 1:27), a new generation of people (Ps. 102:19 [18 ET]), certain historical events of judgment or redemption (Exod. 34:10; Num. 16:30; Isa. 48:7), and a pure heart (Ps. 51:12 [10 ET]),[132] there is no mention of preexisting material. On Genesis 1:1, Wenham observes that "the text never states what God creates out of."[133] It seems that the biblical authors intended to reserve this verb for uniquely divine activities, unhampered by preexisting materials.[134]

On Psalm 51:12 (10 ET), Ridderbos says that a new heart is a *completely new* creation.[135] In Werner Schmidt's view, this verb expresses that God "did not have need of already existing material. . . . Creation is deprived of any similarity to human action."[136] According to George Knight, "God has given man the power to refashion stuff that is already there; but man cannot *bārā'*; only God can create."[137] Stadelmann states:

> By analyzing God's efficient causality as well as his active control manifested in the world-order as a whole and in each of its aspects and details,

---

as referring to *creatio ex nihilo* and that Gen. 1 is radically different from ANE mythologies. Even the waters—indeed all things—are God's creation according to his will.

130. The verb *bārā'* occurs eleven times in Genesis and is always translated *poieō* (make) in the LXX.

131. Wenham notes that any "etymological connection" with the Piel of *bārā'* is doubtful (*Genesis 1–15*, 12); Schmidt, "*br'*, to create," 253–54.

132. John E. Stek, "What Says the Scripture?" in *Portraits of Creation: Biblical and Scientific Perspectives on the World's Formation*, ed. Howard J. Van Till (Grand Rapids: Eerdmans, 1990), 207–8.

133. Ibid.

134. Robert A. Oden Jr., "Cosmogony, Cosmology," in *ABD*, 1:1166: "The priestly writers are careful to reserve the term *bārā'* . . . for God's action alone."

135. Ridderbos, "Genesis i 1 und 2," 222: "*eine völlig neue Schöpfung.*"

136. Werner H. Schmidt, *The Faith of the Old Testament: A History*, trans. John Sturdy (Philadelphia: Westminster, 1983), 173. Schmidt notes that while the word *bārā'* by itself does not mean creation *ex nihilo*, God's creating by his word goes beyond representing a craftsman at his work.

137. George A. F. Knight, *Deutero-Isaiah: A Theological Commentary on Isaiah 40–55* (Nashville: Abingdon, 1965), 45.

we find that [bārā'] expresses, together with its basic meaning of creating,
the idea either of novelty or of an extraordinary result. Moreover, since
[bārā'] is the term par excellence for God's creative activity, it is only natural
that it also implies the idea of his effortless production by means of his
powerful word, without any help of outside intervention.[138]

As Brevard Childs states, the product is always mentioned—but never
any material. This, in addition to the "simultaneous emphasis on the
uniqueness of God's action," could not be brought into a "smooth harmony with the fact of a pre-existent chaos. World reality is a result of
creation, not a reshaping of existing matter."[139] Therefore, according to
Childs, *creatio ex nihilo* is implicit in the text.

One may ask: Why is *bārā'* used for the creation not only of the heavens
and the earth (Gen. 1:1) and of human beings (1:27), but also of great sea
creatures (1:21)? Is this theologically significant? The answer takes us back
to the ANE context, in which sea monsters figured as primeval forces that
hindered a well-ordered cosmos. Genesis 1 implies that this is a *false* theological view. The not-insignificant verb *bārā'* emphasizes that God created
the sea creatures; they are *not* hostile forces to be reckoned with.[140]

Furthermore, the verb "create" refers not only to God's originating creation (after which he rested), but can also rightly speak of God's creative
activity throughout history. For example, Ecclesiastes 12:1 expresses that
God is the "Creator" of each human being; Psalm 104:30 NIV similarly
states that the sovereign God continues to create all creatures and bring
about his glorious purposes in history: "When you send your Spirit, they
are created." Isaiah 48:6–7 NIV also speaks of things "created now, and
not long ago." We agree with Kidner that the precise sense of *bārā'* varies
with its context, which may emphasize "the initial moment of bringing
into existence" (e.g., Isa. 48:3, 7: "suddenly," "now") or "the patient work
of bringing something to perfection" (e.g., Gen. 2:1–4).[141]

Werner H. Schmidt observes that while the word *bārā'* by itself does
not mean creation *ex nihilo*, God's creating by his word goes beyond
representing a craftsman at his work. "He spoke . . . and it was so" expresses the truth that God "calls material objects into existence through
being uttered"—which marks out the Creator from the creature.[142]

So *create* can refer to divine activity even *after the initial creation* (e.g.,
God's creating a new heart). Thus, *bārā'* can apply to more than initial

138. Stadelmann, *Hebrew Conception of the World*, 5.
139. Childs, *Myth and Reality*, 40.
140. This point was made by David Wilkinson, *The Message of Creation* (Downers Grove,
Ill.: InterVarsity, 2002), 21.
141. Derek Kidner, *Genesis*, TOTC 1 (Downers Grove, Ill.: InterVarsity, 1967), 44.
142. Schmidt, *Faith of the Old Testament*, 173.

creation out of nothing, but we must not forget that *bārā'* is never linguistically connected to any preexisting matter. While *bārā'* does not by itself mean "creation out of nothing," in the relevant contexts (such as Gen. 1) it appears to mean that—especially when considered in conjunction with other linguistic and contextual factors. *Bārā'* does not speak solely of the temporal *ex nihilo* origination of God's creative work, but it does include this concept.

Second, in view of the fact that God is always the subject of bārā', *this verb appears to be without analogy and refers uniquely to divine activity.* Gordon Wenham says, "It should be noted that God, the God of Israel, is always the subject" of *bārā'*.[143] But some will shrug this off by pointing out that *bārā'* is used in conjunction with other words not necessarily associated with divine activity, such as *'āśāh* (make) and *yāṣar* (form); these appear to be interchangeable with *bārā'*. For example, God is said to *make* and *create* human beings in his image (Gen. 1:26–27). We read in Genesis about "all that [God] had *made*" (1:31) and about "all his work which God *created*" (2:3). In Isaiah, we see that God both *created* and *formed* Israel (43:1). In verse 43:7, God speaks of

> everyone who is called by my name,
> whom I created [*bārā'*] for my glory,
> whom I formed [*yāṣar*] and made [*'āśāh*].

Isaiah 45:18 states that God *created (bārā')* the heavens, *fashioned/formed (yāṣar)* the earth and *made ('āśāh)* it.

Does the fact that the verb *create* is used in parallelism with other verbs not necessarily restricted to divine activity diminish its theological significance? Can *bārā'* simply be reduced to another way of expressing "make" or "fashion"?

Here we must guard against linguistic reductionism. While such verbs may express *facets* or *aspects* involved in God's creative work (e.g., God "made" man in his image), the verb "create" goes beyond what they express and communicates something further. According to Walter Brueggemann, "While it may be used synonymously with 'make' or 'form,' the verb 'create' is in fact without analogy. It refers to the special action by God and to the special relation which binds these two parties together."[144] Karl-Heinz Bernhardt asserts that *bārā'* is used

---

143. Wenham, *Genesis 1–15*, 12.
144. Walter Brueggemann, *Genesis* (Atlanta: John Knox, 1982), 17. Schmidt echoes this view about *bārā'*: "To the extent that the OT reserves the verb exclusively for God, this type of creation has no analogy and is, therefore, beyond conceptualization" ("*br'*, to create," 254).

to express clearly the incomparability of God's creative work. It refers to the "nonpareil work of the Creator God."[145]

Thus we have a rejection of materialism (some "stuff" as autonomous and independent) and transcendentalism (a kind of dualism of God and matter).[146] Gerhard von Rad has observed that Genesis 1:1 utilizes a verb "retained exclusively to designate the divine creative activity."[147] The author could have used a Hebrew verb to designate "artistic creation," but he does not do so. The verb he chose, *bārāʾ*, is "without analogy" in the human realm.[148] When God creates the heavens and the earth (Gen. 1:1), a new heavens and a new earth (Isa. 65:17), or a new heart (Ps. 51:12 [10 ET]), these are things *only God can make.*[149] One Jewish commentator claims that while humans "form" and "make," only God is seen as "creating"—that is, producing something out of nothing.[150]

So when we look at Genesis 1:1 and 1:27 (where *create* is used three times) and 2:3–4, we recognize that the author has *theological* reasons in showing a preference for *bārāʾ* over the more manual deed of *ʿāśāh.* According to Westermann, this is evident by the fact that God is always the acting subject with *bārāʾ.*[151] Werner Schmidt agrees: "*bārāʾ* (Gen. 1:1; et al.) is a special word for God's creative act," used in order to "avoid any analogy between this act and human activity."[152] It is a verb that remains reserved for God alone.[153] Moreover, Schmidt adds, God's creation needs no raw material.[154] The inference von Rad makes from the lack of any mention of preexistent material is that the idea of creation *ex nihilo* is connected with it.[155]

Brevard Childs claims that *bārāʾ* is a "technical verb" to describe God's creative act.[156] And Henri Blocher aptly comments:

> The Old Testament uses [*bārāʾ*] most sparingly, and in that form, exclusively of the God of Israel. Never is any material mentioned. The creative

---

145. Bernhardt, *"bārāʾ,"* in *TDOT*, 2:246–47. He adds that in a redactional process, "P introduced *bārāʾ* into particularly important passages and thus implicitly prevented a misunderstanding of *ʿasah* in the earlier narrative" (246).

146. Ibid., 246.

147. Von Rad, *Genesis*, 47.

148. Ibid. See also Gerhard von Rad, *Old Testament Theology*, vol. 1, trans. D. M. G. Stalker (New York: Harper & Row, 1962), 142.

149. Towner, *Genesis*, 16.

150. J. H. Hertz, ed., *The Pentateuch and the Haftorahs* (London: Soncino, 1996), 2.

151. Westermann, *Genesis 1–11*, 86.

152. Schmidt, *Old Testament Introduction*, 109.

153. Ibid., 353.

154. Ibid., 352–53.

155. Von Rad, *Old Testament Theology*, 1:142.

156. Childs, *Biblical Theology of the Old and New Testaments*, 111.

act appears supremely effortless and its result sometimes miraculous (Ex. 34:10), frequently new (Pss. 51:10 [ET]; 104:30; Is. 48:7; 65:17; Je. 31:22). For God, it is a matter of "doing"—for that ordinary verb is used as a parallel for *bārā²*, and Genesis 2:3 speaks of "all his work which he had done in creation"—but "done" in a unique sense, reserved for God, from which arises complete newness.[157]

So even though *bārā²* is used in conjunction with other terms, this does not mean that they are fully equivalent and that *bārā²* has nothing significant to contribute beyond the verbs *make (²āśāh)* or *form (yāṣar)*. Indeed, *creating* may involve *making* and *forming,* but *making* and *forming* fall short of *creating.* Hartley points out that *create* refers to the creation of something *new* by God: only God creates. Arbez and Weisengoff state, " 'To create' is thus a suitable rendering [of *bārā²*], more so than 'to make,' 'to fashion,' or 'to shape,' or the like."[158] Other verbs such as *form* and *make* allow for "a variety of processes to come into play between God's speaking and the object's coming into existence."[159]

The uniqueness of *bārā²* is further reinforced by another fact. The earlier Greek version of the OT, the LXX, often uses the more general verb *poiein* (to make) instead of *ktizein* (to create). Nevertheless, later Greek versions—Theodotion, Aquila, and Symmachus—consistently use *ktizein* (to create) to translate *bārā²*.[160]

Thus, it appears that *bārā²* uniquely captures *the entirety and breadth of God's creation*—something these other supporting verbs fail to do. As Derek Kidner puts it, "The whole process is creation."[161] The *whole* range of God's creative activity is covered. But "until God spoke, nothing existed."[162] The point is that God undergirds all reality.

Third, the uniqueness of bārā² *is evidenced by its association with God's powerful word.* God's not needing preexisting matter for his action in creating is further reinforced by God's creating by his powerful word.[163]

---

157. Blocher, *In the Beginning,* 61. Kidner states that the verb *bārā²* in 1:1, 21, and 27 marks three great beginnings, but "it does not define a particular way of creating, since in 2:3–4 it is parallel with *²āśāh* (make) and covers the whole range of God's work" (*Genesis,* 44). But again, even though *²āśāh* here encompasses the sweep of God's work of creation, it still does not have the unique significance *bārā²* does in its specific connection with God.

158. Arbez and Weisengoff, "Exegetical Notes on Genesis 1:1–2," 144.

159. Hartley, *Genesis,* 45.

160. The Greek version of Theodotion is first century AD; Aquila, second century; and Symmachus, third century.

161. Kidner, *Genesis,* 45.

162. Ibid., 43.

163. God's creation by divine fiat is also reflected in 2 Esdras 6:38 (NEB): "O Lord, at the beginning of creation you spoke the word. On the first day you said, 'Let heaven and earth be made!', and your word carried out its work."

Wenham observes that while *bārā'* is not a term exclusively reserved for creation out of nothing, it preserves the same idea (citing W. H. Schmidt on "God's effortless, totally free and unbounded creating, his sovereignty. It is never mentioned what God created out of").[164] The verb *bārā'* in Genesis 1 speaks of the "absolute effortlessness of the divine creative action," of the God who creates merely by his will and word.[165]

Wenham adds: "That God did create the world out of nothing is certainly implied by other OT passages that speak of his creating everything by his word and his existence before the world" (cf. Ps. 148:5; Prov. 8:22–27). Moreover, there is no hint in the OT that there are powers or entities independent of God. God is sovereign over all, and all other entities do his bidding.[166]

Bruce Waltke adds the same: The genre of Genesis "represents the world as coming into being through God's proclamation so that the world depends on his will, purpose, and presence."[167] Again: "Since everything exists by the word of God, we must not think of creation independently of God."[168] Incidentally, in Waltke's view, the narrator of Genesis does not explicitly say where the darkness and waters come from,[169] but this in no way undermines the theological conviction expressed by biblical writers that God created everything from nothing. Any eternal dualism is implicitly rejected.[170]

In the context of Genesis 1, the verb *bārā'* does point us in the direction of creation out of nothing. As von Rad declares, "It is correct to say that the verb *bārā'*, 'create,' contains the idea both of complete effortlessness and *creatio ex nihilo*, since it is never connected with any statement of the material. The hidden pathos of this statement is that God is the Lord of the world."[171]

Because God is always the *subject* of *bārā'*, interpreters regularly recognize that the word *create* inescapably refers to *divine* activity.[172] The verb carries "considerable force" in Hebrew.[173] On Isaiah 42:5–6, Walter Brueggemann comments that the verb *bārā'* is "the most majestic of

164. Wenham, *Genesis 1–15*, 12.
165. Von Rad, *Old Testament Theology*, 1:142.
166. Wenham, *Genesis 1–15*, 16.
167. Bruce K. Waltke, *Genesis: A Commentary* (Grand Rapids: Zondervan, 2001), 78.
168. Ibid., 69.
169. So also John J. Scullion, *Genesis* (Collegeville, Minn.: Liturgical Press, 1992), 15.
170. Waltke makes clear this point: "One should not infer an eternal dualism from this silence" (*Genesis*, 68).
171. Von Rad, *Genesis*, 47.
172. Brown et al., *The New Brown-Driver-Briggs-Gesenius Hebrew and English Lexicon*, 135.
173. Blocher, *In the Beginning*, 61.

terms for God's action as Creator"—a verb used "with no other subject except Yahweh."[174] E. J. Young notes that with the verb *bārāʾ*, the "idea of novelty or extraordinariness of result seems frequently to be implied."[175] Thomas McComiskey concurs that *novelty* or the *initiation* of an object is implied by *bārāʾ*.[176] Schmidt makes this same point,[177] and so does N. H. Ridderbos: "When it is said that God 'creates' something, then that means that this 'something' was previously not there."[178]

Even though other parallel verbs are used to support God's action (such as *form* [*yāṣar*] or *make* [*ʿāśāh*]), the power of God's word to create is repeatedly highlighted throughout the Scriptures. To OT writers, it would have appeared *blasphemous* to suggest that human beings create *(bārāʾ)*.[179] Robert Jenson states that creating (*bārāʾ*) is something that only *God* does.[180] Genesis 1 rhythmically describes a God who simply *says*, "Let there be . . ."—and "there was . . ." God creates the world by his word alone. "By the *word* of the LORD were the heavens made" (Ps. 33:6 NIV). "He *spoke*, and it came to be; he *commanded*, and it stood firm" (Ps. 33:9 NRSV).

Thus, creation is not an "effect" of God; rather, it is "a work created in freedom in the Word."[181] Bruce Waltke says that *bārāʾ* "distinguishes itself by being used exclusively of God," revealing his vast power and might, imagination and wisdom, immortality and transcendence.[182] German theologian Jürgen Moltmann captures this well:

> To say that God "created" the world indicates God's self-distinction from that world, and emphasizes that God desired it. . . . It is the specific outcome of his decision of will. Since they are the result of God's creative activity, heaven and earth are . . . contingent.[183]

174. Walter Brueggemann, *Theology of the Old Testament: Testimony, Dispute, Advocacy* (Minneapolis: Fortress, 1997), 146.

175. Young, *Studies in Genesis 1*, 6.

176. Thomas E. McComiskey, "*bārāʾ*," in *Theological Wordbook of the Old Testament*, 2 vols., ed. R. Laird Harris, Gleason L. Archer, and Bruce K. Waltke (Chicago: Moody, 1980), 1:127. McComiskey mentions that *yāṣar* primarily emphasizes the *shaping* of an object.

177. Schmidt, "*brʾ*, to create," 255: the objects of the verb "create" are "special, extraordinary, new."

178. Ridderbos, "Genesis i 1 und 2," 221: "*wenn gesagt wird, dass Gott etwas 'schafft,' dan bedeutet das, dass dieses 'etwas' vorher nicht da war.*"

179. Smith, *Old Testament Theology*, 180.

180. Jenson, *Systematic Theology*, 5.

181. Dietrich Bonhoeffer, *Creation and Fall: A Theological Interpretation of Genesis 1–3* (London: SCM Press, 1959), 21.

182. Waltke, *Genesis*, 59.

183. Jürgen Moltmann, *God in Creation: A New Theology of Creation and the Spirit of God*, trans. Margaret Kohl (San Francisco: Harper & Row, 1985), 72–73. For commentary

Moltmann comments on *bārāʾ*, which is used "exclusively as a term for the divine bringing forth."[184] He points out that since *bārāʾ* does not take an accusative (i.e., some object) of a material out of which something has been made, this reveals that "the divine creativity has no conditions or premises.[185] Creation is something absolutely new. It is neither potentially inherent or present in anything else."[186] As Werner Foerster has written, creation in Genesis 1 "arises out of nothing by the Word of God."[187]

While *bārāʾ* does not automatically connote creation out of nothing in the context of Genesis 1, its being "without analogy" is part of a cumulative case pointing in the direction of *creatio ex nihilo*.[188] The idea of *creatio ex nihilo* is implied in Genesis 1:1 since no "beginning" for God is mentioned.[189] Thus, *bārāʾ* is a word best suited to express the concept of creation out of nothing. In fact, no other Hebrew term would do.

Fourth, the verb bārāʾ *in Genesis 1:1 is connected with the totality of God's creation* ("the heavens and the earth"), *which points us to creation out of nothing.* Walter Eichrodt expresses the implicit assumption that the OT makes regarding absolute creation: "The idea of the absolute beginning of the created world thus proves to be a logical expression of the total outlook of the priestly narrator."[190] For example, Isaiah 40:21—which refers back to Genesis 1:1 but utilizes the parallel ex-

---

on the inconsistency between Moltmann's exegesis of Genesis 1 and his panentheism (i.e., the confusion between creation out of nothing [*ex nihilo*] and continual creation [*continua*], rendering any distinction meaningless), see Allan J. Torrance, "*Creatio ex Nihilo* and the Spatio-Temporal Dimensions with Special Reference to Jürgen Moltmann and D. C. Williams," in *The Doctrine of Creation: Essays in Dogmatics, History, and Philosophy*, ed. Colin E. Gunton (Edinburgh: T & T Clark, 1997), 83–103; cf. Philip Clayton's discussion of Moltmann's panentheism (e.g., "absolute space" is seen as the presence of God in the whole material world and all it contains), in *God and Contemporary Science*, ed. Philip Clayton (Grand Rapids: Eerdmans, 1997). See also Wolfhart Pannenberg, *Systematic Theology*, vol. 2, trans. Geoffrey W. Bromiley (Grand Rapids: Eerdmans, 1994), 14–15.

    184. Moltmann, *God in Creation*, 73.

    185. Westermann makes these same points: Yahweh is always the subject of *bārāʾ*, and *bārāʾ* is never used with a preposition or an accusative of the material out of which God creates (*Genesis 1–11*, 98). Ridderbos notes this as well: "[The] subject [of *bārāʾ*] is always God. It is never connected with the accusative of matter = *[Das] Subjekt ist immer Gott. Es wird niemals verbunden mit dem Akkusativ des Stoffes*" ("Genesis i 1 und 2," 220).

    186. Ridderbos, "Genesis i 1 und 2," 220.

    187. Foerster, "*ktizō*," 1010.

    188. Brueggemann says that while Genesis 1:2 speaks of a kind of chaos, 1:1 (which he takes to be a later theological reflection on creation) "suggests God began with nothing" (*Genesis*, 29). According to Brueggemann, no attempt is made to resolve the apparent tension. He also notes that by the time of the NT, "it was affirmed that God created out of nothing (cf. Rom. 4:17; Heb. 11:3)" (*Genesis*, 29).

    189. Sailhamer, *Genesis Unbound*, 247–49.

    190. Eichrodt, "In the Beginning," 72.

pression "from the foundation[s] of the earth"—is "a clear reference to an absolute beginning" and not an "arbitrary judgment," according to Eichrodt.[191] He considers the doctrine *creatio ex nihilo* as being "incontestable"[192]—especially in light of the author's strict monotheism as well as his radical distinction between his own view and that of other ancient cosmogonies, in which the gods emerged out of preexisting matter. Eichrodt argues that "the ultimate aim of the [creation] narrative is the same as that of our formula of creation ex nihilo."[193]

Although this formula (creation *ex nihilo*) does not occur in the OT, the object of God's creative activity is "heaven and earth and all that is in them"; so God's creation cannot be restricted to "the stars and things on earth" but must include "the entire cosmos."[194] The fact that "heavens and earth" is a merism signifying "the totality of cosmic phenomena" points us toward an absolute beginning of the universe—including matter.[195] In fact, there is "no single word in the Hebrew language" to express totality; thus, this phrase is used.[196] As we noted with Westermann, Genesis 1:1 refers to "the Beginning. Everything began with God."[197]

So it is clear that while *bārā²* by itself is insufficient to establish the idea of creation out of nothing, when seen in conjunction with, and in the context of, the relevant passages and other literary and historical features, we are pointed in that direction.[198]

Summary of Thoughts on Genesis 1

Genesis 1 has several mutually reinforcing features that lead us to conclude its implicit understanding of creation *ex nihilo*. These features include (1) the uniqueness of the Genesis creation account in comparison to other ANE epics, (2) the literary elegance and the structural and grammatical necessity of the absolute sense in Genesis 1:1, (3) the uniqueness

---

191. Ibid., 67.
192. Ibid., 72.
193. Walter Eichrodt, *Theology of the Old Testament*, vol. 2, trans. J. A. Baker (Philadelphia: Westminster, 1967), 101.
194. Ibid., 102.
195. Nahum M. Sarna, *Genesis*, JPS Torah Commentary (New York: Jewish Publication Society, 1989), 5. Harrison affirms that the phrase "the heavens and the earth" is a merism that indicates totality, not simply two antonymic elements. See Harrison, "Creation," in *The Zondervan Pictorial Encyclopedia of the Bible*, ed. Merrill C. Tenney (Grand Rapids: Zondervan, 1975), 1:1022; also Paul K. Jewett, *God, Creation, and Revelation* (Grand Rapids: Eerdmans, 1991), 457.
196. Keil and Delitzsch, *Commentary on the Old Testament*, 1:47.
197. Westermann, *Genesis*, 7.
198. Stek, "What Says the Scripture?" 221.

of *bārāʾ*, and (4) the creation of God by his word alone. Hence, we see emerging a strong cumulative case for creation *ex nihilo*.[199] In light of the entire fabric of Genesis 1, creation out of nothing is the only proper inference to draw.[200] No other conclusion can properly be secured.[201]

Is "Double Creation" Too Messy and Too Hellenistic?

The medieval Jewish commentator Ramban claims that the verb *bārāʾ* is the only possible verb that could express creation from absolute nothingness:

> The Holy One, blessed be He, created all things from absolute non-existence. Now we have no expression in the sacred language for bringing forth something from nothing other than the word *bārāʾ* [create].

Ramban goes on to say that that creation from absolute nothingness took place in stages. The first stage of God's creation from "total and absolute nothing" involved (1) *creating* or bringing forth a "substance

199. Walter Eichrodt notes three features of Genesis 1:1, the conjunction of which points us in the direction of—in fact, concretely depicts—creation out of nothing (*Theology of the Old Testament*, 2:101–6): the very opening absolute statement of Genesis 1:1; the fact that God creates by his *word*; and the use of *bārāʾ* in Genesis 1:1. Similarly, Thomas Mc-Comiskey writes: "The limitation of this word to divine activity indicates that the area of meaning delineated by the root [of *bārāʾ*] falls outside the sphere of human ability. Since the word never occurs with the object of the material, and since the primary emphasis of the word is on the newness of the created object, the word lends itself well to the concept of creation *ex nihilo*, although that concept is not necessarily inherent within the meaning of the word" (McComiskey, *"bārāʾ,"* 1:173). See also Jewett's helpful discussion in *God, Creation, and Revelation*, 455–67; and Schmidt, *"brʾ,* to create," 253–56. Arbez and Weisengoff remark that "the whole of Gen. 1 is permeated with the idea of the absolute transcendence of God and of the utter dependence of all being on God for its existence. The idea of a 'creatio ex nihilo' seems to be so logically bound up with the author's view of God that one can hardly refuse to see it in his opening statement" ("Exegetical Notes on Genesis 1:1–2," 144). Jewish writer Nahum Sarna captures our point nicely: "The Genesis narrative does contain intimations of such a concept. Precisely because of the indispensable importance of preexisting matter in the pagan cosmologies, the very absence of such mention here is highly significant. This conclusion is reinforced by the idea of creation by divine fiat without reference to any inert matter being present. Also, the repeated biblical emphasis upon God as the exclusive Creator would seem to rule out the possibility of preexistent matter. Finally, if *bārāʾ* is used only of God's [acts of] creation, it must be essentially distinct from human [acts of] creation. The ultimate distinction would be *creatio ex nihilo*, which has no human parallel and is thus utterly beyond all human comprehension" (*Genesis*, 5).

200. Mathews, *Genesis 1–11:26*, 141.

201. Ridderbos puts it plainly: "Genesis 1 teaches *creatio ex nihilo* = *Gen. i die* creatio ex nihilo *lehrt*" ("Genesis i 1 und 2," 259).

devoid of corporeality but having a power of potency" (the "primary matter," or *hylē*, in Greek thought). In the next stage, however, (2) God "did not *create* anything, but He *formed* and made things with [the *hylē*]."[202]

The idea that God created in two stages (creating "primary matter" and then forming it) brings us to a typical objection to such an approach (view 4). James Barr sees this understanding of "double creation" as "mistaken" because it implies that God (rather sloppily, in Barr's view) produced primordial matter and then later formed it into something orderly. Further, such a "double-creation" view apparently presupposes a Greek distinction between matter and form (although the Jewish Ramban himself adopts this view!).

Nevertheless, these charges of untidiness and of Hellenistic influence do not seem to be compelling. Regarding the "untidiness" problem, we see the Genesis text itself moving rather rapidly and pithily; thus, it does not address potential gaps that may emerge as we try to unpack the text. John E. Hartley, who views creation *ex nihilo* as biblical, observes that "only the brevity of the creation account creates this impression" of preexistent matter.[203] Creation out of nothing was not an issue, but was something taken for granted. To the Hebrew mind, it would have been unthinkable that anything could have existence independent of God unless God created it. As John Goldingay affirms, an OT thinker who handled the question, "Where did matter come from?" would no doubt declare, "Yhwh made it, of course."[204]

Second, plausible translations allowing for a double creation are not difficult to find. For example, E. J. Young offers a context-sensitive approach to Genesis 1:1–2—particularly with regard to the phrase *tōhû wābōhû*, "without form, and void" (KJV) or "desolate and uninhabitable"—that removes the apparent lack of neatness that Barr perceives in what he calls "double creation." According to Young:

> To determine the significance of [*tōhû*] in Genesis 1:2 is not particularly difficult. In Isaiah 45:18 it is used as a contrast to the phrase, "to be inhabited". According to this verse God did not create the earth for desolation, but rather to be inhabited. An earth of [*tōhû*], therefore, is an earth that cannot be inhabited. Such an earth has not fulfilled the purpose for which it was created; it is an earth created in vain, a desolate earth. If,

---

202. Ramban (Nachmanides), *Commentary on the Torah: Genesis*, trans. Charles B. Chavel (New York: Shiloh, 1971), 23.

203. Hartley, *Genesis*, 42.

204. John Goldingay, *Old Testament Theology*, volume 1, *Israel's Gospel* (Downers Grove, Ill.: InterVarsity, 2003), 77.

therefore, we translate [it] as "desolation," we shall probably be doing justice to the word.

Likewise, the similar sounding [bōhû] apparently signifies something uninhabitable, and we may well render it as "waste".[205]

Young comments that in Jeremiah 4:23, the combination of "desolation/uninhabitable" *(tōhû)* and "waste" *(bōhû)* harks back to Genesis 1:2, speaking of the land of Palestine after it had been decimated by the Babylonian invasion. At that time (ca. 587–86 BC) the promised land would become like Genesis 1:2—"a desolation and a waste," a place where human beings could not dwell: "It is that thought which is expressed in Genesis. The earth was in such a condition that [people] would have been unable to live thereon."[206]

The translation of the words *tōhû wābōhû* (Gen. 1:2) as "chaos" is unfortunate. But if one uses it, one must regard it, Young argues, as the "first stage in the formation of the present well-ordered earth" rather than as "what was confused and out of order," as though this state had been out of God's control.[207] In fact, there is no reason, given what we read in Genesis 1, why God could not have pronounced the condition described in Genesis 1:2 as "very good."[208] After all, the earth was not only uninhabitable in 1:2;[209] *it was in the same condition during the later days of creation:*

> Genesis 1:2 is the first picture of the created world that the Bible gives, and the purpose of the remainder of the chapter is to show how God brought this world from its primitive condition of desolation and waste to become an earth, fully equipped to receive man and to be his home. The earth was desolation and waste, but all was in God's hand and under his control; nothing was contrary to his design.[210]

Commenting on Isaiah 45:18 (which reflects this theme), John Oswalt remarks that chaos did not exist before God, nor did God bring a meaningless chaos into existence. Instead, "the preexistent God" created the world specifically for human habitation.[211]

205. Young, *Studies in Genesis 1*, 33–34.

206. Ibid., 34. See also Hasel on two-stage creation ("Recent Translations of Genesis 1:1," 165).

207. Young, *Studies in Genesis 1*, 38.

208. Ibid.

209. Ridderbos ("Genesis i 1 und 2," 233) translates it "wilderness and emptiness/ uninhabited [*Wüste und Leere*]."

210. Young, *Studies in Genesis 1*, 38.

211. John N. Oswalt, *Isaiah 40–66*, NICNT (Grand Rapids: Eerdmans, 1998), 218.

A similar two-stage perspective is taken by John Sailhamer, but with the following variation.[212] Genesis 1:1 refers to God's creation of the universe, and then 1:2 begins unfolding the preparation of the promised *land* (not "earth")—Eden, in which a garden was placed—the boundaries of which are literarily linked to the land God promised Abraham and his descendants (cf. Gen. 2:10–14; 15:18). God the Creator is identified as God the Covenant-Maker. What is held in common by scholars such as Young, Sailhamer, and also Kidner[213] is that there is an elegant, purposeful depiction of a two-step process to creation—not a clumsy, ad hoc one.

Similar things can be said about the "waters" in Genesis 1:2. The commentator U. Cassuto says that the "deep" is the "primeval World-Ocean," but it is not an eternally preexistent one. He insists that "it had not existed from time immemorial but was created by the will of God, and was ready to receive whatever form its Maker would be pleased to fashion for it."[214]

Much more could be said in response to Barr's charge that a two-stage creation is inelegant. As we have seen, this complaint can be easily countered.

Then what about Barr's second concern, that a two-step creative process apparently reflects *Hellenistic influences* (in which eternal, primal stuff is organized into an orderly cosmos)? Admittedly, we must clear away the confusion that comes with the LXX's rendering of Genesis 1:2 (*hē de gē ēn aoratos kai akataskeuastos = "And the earth was unseen/invisible and unformed"*). This translation of 1:2 clearly reflects a Hellenistic influence,[215] and English versions such as the KJV and RSV Hellenize the phrase *tōhû wābōhû* into "without form and void."

---

212. Sailhamer, *Genesis Unbound*, 247–49; see also idem, "Genesis," 41–43.

213. Commenting on Genesis 1:2, Kidner declares, "The whole process is creation" (*Genesis*, 45). See also Blocher, who takes this two-step view (*In the Beginning*, 64).

214. Cassuto, *Commentary on Genesis*, 24.

215. So Armin Schmitt: "Aus dieser Sicht ist es gut möglich, daß [*aoratos*] in Gen 1 2 platonisch beeinflußt ist. Auch [*akataskeuastos*] tendiert in diese Richtung = From this view it is very likely that [*aoratos* = unseen/invisible] in Gen. 1:2 is influenced by Platonism. [*Akataskeuastos* = unformed] also tends in this direction" ("Interpretation der Genesis aus hellenistischem Geist," *Zeitschrift für alttestamentliche Wissenschaft* 86 [1974]: 150). Even though the LXX takes Genesis 1:1 in an absolute state, the terms in 1:2 do not capture what the Hebrew expresses. Schmitt points out that these particular terms are "eine wesentliche Komponente der griechischen und speziell der platonishen Weltentstehungslehre, daß die Welt aus einem anfänglich ungeordneten Status in einen Zustand der Harmonie und Schönheit überführt wird = an essential component of the Greek and especially the Platonic doctrine of origins that the world was conveyed/transformed from an initially disordered status to a condition of harmony and beauty" (151). That said, this still does not rule out a two-stage creation from nothing.

Nevertheless, we should not infer that the translators assumed eternally preexistent matter.

Translating Genesis 1:2 in this way, however, has contributed to a somewhat Greek outlook for many Christians who think of the earth described as some amorphous mass. Yet these Hebrew terms, when taken in consideration of later biblical usage (Isa. 45:18; Jer. 4:23) that links back to Genesis 1:2, lead us to the better (and less-Hellenized) understanding of the land as being desolate and uninhabitable, "a desert and a wasteland," as Victor Hamilton translates it.[216]

Medieval Jewish interpreters, not influenced by the LXX, took this perspective as well.[217] Further reinforcing the point is the fact that later Greek versions of the LXX departed from a Platonic view of creation in favor of a more biblical one: Aquila translates the terms as "empty and nothing," and Symmachus as "fallow and undistinct."[218] Furthermore, our earliest Semitic (Palestinian) Targums, which are interpretive presentations of the Hebrew Bible, have "no trace of the concepts" found in the LXX.[219] For example, the Targum Neophiti I (no later than the third century AD and possibly pre-Christian) renders Genesis 1:2 as "desolate, without human beings or beast, and void of all cultivation of plants and of trees"—thus capturing Hebrew usage.

Therefore, there is no need to see Genesis 1:2 as referring to eternally preexistent matter. As Keil and Delitzsch offer, "'*And the earth was without form and void,*' not before, but when, or after God created it."[220] Indeed, there is nothing belonging to the composition of the universe (whether material or formal), which had an existence out of God before this divine act in the beginning.[221] Although some assert that Genesis 1:1 should be interpreted in light of Genesis 1:2, we argue that the reverse is true. And the fact that the Hebrew of 1:2 begins with a *wāw*-consecutive ["*and* the earth/land"] indicates the temporal priority of verse 1:1 to 1:2.[222] Lending further support to such an approach, as we will see, is the testimony of not only Jewish scholars such as Ramban

216. See discussion in Hamilton, *Genesis 1–17*, 108–9; echoing this is Mathews's extensive discussion in *Genesis 1–11:26*, 130–44.

217. Sailhamer, *Genesis Unbound*, 213–22, esp. 214.

218. Sailhamer, *The Pentateuch as Narrative*, 85 n.

219. Ibid.

220. Keil and Delitzsch, *Commentary on the Old Testament*, 1:47–48. John H. Walton, commenting on Genesis 1:2, says that the point here is that God is purposively directing and ordering his creation ("Creation," in *Dictionary of the Old Testament and Pentateuch*, ed. T. Desmond Alexander and David W. Baker [Downers Grove, Ill.: InterVarsity, 2003), 157.

221. Keil and Delitzsch, *Commentary on the Old Testament*, 1:47.

222. Ibid., 47–48.

but also early church fathers who stated or implied that God created in two stages.

Additional OT Texts Implying *Creatio ex Nihilo*

Having looked at Genesis 1:1, we now want to examine other OT passages that reinforce the idea of creation out of nothing. Here we see clearly the totalism and contingency of God's creation. Such a totalism is to be expected since, in the Hebrew mind, there was no other kind of phenomenological existence outside the creative activity of God.[223]

We have already recognized that the expression "the heavens and the earth" refers to "absolutely everything."[224] Hermann Sasse reports that the Hebrew OT has no word for "the universe," but uses "heaven and earth" instead.[225] Or sometimes *hakōl*—"the totality, everything, all"—is used, which is at times expanded to "the heavens and the earth, the sea, and all that is in them" (Exod. 20:11; cf. Ps. 24:1–2; Jer. 51:48).[226] Occasionally, the OT writers utilize the term "the all [*hakōl*]" to refer to everything or the totality—that is, all reality outside of God.[227] Unlike the Greeks, the Hebrews had no word for the cosmos; hence, the word *all* or *everything* is used (e.g., Isa. 44:24).[228] All things had a beginning, and God is their originator.

The clear implication of Yahweh's title "the first and the last" (Isa. 44:6)—or, as the NT puts it, "the Alpha and the Omega" (Rev. 1:8)—is that he is the ultimate originator and only eternal Being. Proverbs 8:22–26 states that before the depths were brought forth (i.e., the "deep" of Gen. 1:2), Wisdom was creating with God. Commenting on this passage, Richard J. Clifford states that "the basic elements of the universe did *not* exist. There were no cosmic waters [Prov. 8:24], no pillars of the earth, . . . and no habitable surface of the earth."[229]

223. Harrison, "Creation," 1:1023.
224. Von Rad, *Genesis*, 46.
225. Sasse, *"kosmos,"* in *TDNT,* 3:878.
226. Van Leeuwen, *"br>,"* 730.
227. Sasse, *"kosmos,"* 881.
228. George A. F. Knight, *Deutero-Isaiah: A Theological Commentary on Isaiah 40–55* (Nashville: Abingdon, 1965), 124.
229. Richard J. Clifford, *Proverbs: A Commentary* (Louisville: Westminster John Knox, 1999), 96. There is no good reason to take Roger N. Whybray's odd comment seriously: "['The depths'] is probably not an allusion to the primeval ocean . . . of Gen. 1:2 . . . but to the existing terrestrial ocean" (*Proverbs*, NCB [Grand Rapids: Eerdmans, 1994], 132). Given the linguistic similarity (*tĕhōmôt* in Prov. 8:24 and *tĕhôm* in Gen. 1:2) and theological backdrop assumed by the Wisdom writer, it is virtually certain that the primeval ocean *is* in view generally. Rather than taking seriously wording such as "before" or "when there

Nothing else besides the Creator existed—and this would preclude any preexistent stuff. Thus, the reference made in 2 Peter 3:5 to God's creating "from water" must take into account that the waters themselves were brought into existence by God. Hence, we should not read into such a passage some eternally existent "deep" based on Genesis 1:2, since God created the "deep" (Ps. 104:6; Prov. 8:24, 27–28). Neither should we see the "darkness" of Genesis 1:2 as eternal and uncreated, since God creates *both* darkness and light (Isa. 45:7).

In his Anchor Bible commentary, Michael Fox emphasizes Proverbs 8:24 revealing that the "waters" of Genesis 1:2 are part of the process of creation. Their formation is a step, or stage, in creation.[230] He observes similarity in language between Proverbs 8:25 ("Before the mountains were set down . . .") and Psalm 90:2 ("before the mountains were born, . . . from everlasting to everlasting you are God"), concluding: "Prov 8 starts from the indisputable commonplace that God existed before the start of time and ascribes the same precedence to wisdom."[231]

God's creating without the help of any preexisting material is suggested by the sequencing of passages in Psalm 104 and Proverbs 8. Thus Psalm 104:5–8 NIV declares:

> He set the earth on its foundations; it can never be moved. You covered it with the deep as with a garment; the waters stood above the mountains. But at your rebuke the waters fled, at the sound of your thunder they took to flight; they flowed over the mountains [as clouds], they went down into the valleys [as seas], to the place you assigned for them.

According to this passage, God established the earth (Gen. 1:1) and then covered it with waters. He did not simply create the earth out of some primeval sea. (In chapter 2 we shall look at 2 Peter 3:5, which indicates a two-stage creation rather than God's creating out of primordial chaos.)

Someone may object that these poetic passages are not laying out a specific sequence in chronological order. While we can appreciate this point, the overwhelming emphasis in the OT texts is on God's sovereignty and the totality of everything under his control. God not only shapes, but he creates. God brings into existence even those allegedly primordial elements. (As noted, Isa. 45:7 declares that part of Yahweh's creating activity is "forming light and creating darkness.") While we must be careful about seeing poetical texts as attempting to give a strict

---

was not," Leo G. Perdue makes a similar unsubstantiated assertion that creation here is not out of nothing (*Proverbs* [Louisville: Westminster John Knox, 2000], 144).

230. Michael V. Fox, *Proverbs 1–9*, AB 18A (New York: Doubleday, 2000), 282.
231. Ibid., 284.

chronology of creation events, we can still draw some firm conclusions, which serve as pointers to creation out of nothing. What seems clear from such passages is that everything that is not God has been brought into existence by God.

A passage that refers to "the beginning, before the world began" (Prov. 8:23b NIV), reads:

> When there were no depths I was brought forth,
> When there were no springs abounding with water.
> Before the mountains were settled,
> Before the hills I was brought forth.

Proverbs 8:24–25 NASB

Although some claim that Genesis 1:2 refers to an eternally existent primeval ocean of chaos from which God created (allegedly supported by 2 Peter 3:5), Proverbs 8 will have none of this. There simply were no oceans (or "depths/the deep") when Wisdom began to act creatively. There was not even the "first dust of the world" (8:26 NASB) when Wisdom worked creatively. Everything that exists independently of God/Wisdom had a distinct temporal origin. Derek Kidner writes of Proverbs 8: "Wisdom is both older than the universe, and fundamental to it. Not a speck of matter (26b), not a trace of order (29), came into existence but by wisdom."[232] Roland Murphy declares that the meaning of this passage is "clear": "[Wisdom] is . . . preexistent to anything else. . . . Wisdom was there before anything else."[233] John Goldingay observes that Proverbs 8 goes back "to a time when there was no matter out of which the world might be formed."[234]

Psalm 24:1–2 NIV speaks in sweeping terms about God's creation: "The earth is the LORD's and everything in it. . . . For he founded it on the seas." Or consider Psalm 146, where we read that the believers' hope is to be "in the LORD their God"—that is, the God "who made heaven and earth, the sea, and all that is in them." It is this God who "keeps faith forever" (Ps. 146:5–6 NRSV). In the various psalms in which creation is mentioned, God first creates an ordered cosmos for human habitation, and then he works out his redemptive plan through his people Israel. Creation is not the primary focus, but it serves as a backdrop for God's saving actions in human history.[235]

---

232. Derek Kidner, *Proverbs*, TOTC 15 (Downers Grove, Ill.: InterVarsity, 1964), 78.
233. Roland E. Murphy, *Proverbs*, WBC 22 (Nashville: Nelson, 1998), 52.
234. Goldingay, *Old Testament Theology*, 47.
235. See Stacy R. Obenhaus, "The Creation Faith of the Psalmists," *Trinity Journal* 21 (fall 2000): 131–42.

In addition, the notion of *creatio ex nihilo* is reinforced when Scripture declares the eternality and self-sufficiency of God in contrast to the transience of the finite created order. Psalm 102:25–27 (NIV) speaks to the enduring nature of God as opposed to the transience of the universe:

> In the beginning you laid the foundations of the earth,
>   and the heavens are the work of your hands.
> They will perish, but you remain;
>   they will all wear out like a garment.
> Like clothing you will change them
>   and they will be discarded.
> But you remain the same, and your years will never end.

Comments Leslie Allen, "Creator and creation are distinct: he is so much greater than they and must outlive them, as a man outlives his clothes. Unlike material things, Yahweh alone is immortal and immune from decay."[236]

We read something similar in Psalm 90:2 (NIV): "Before the mountains were born or you brought forth the earth and the world, from everlasting to everlasting you are God." Rendtorff infers from this passage (and Gen. 1:1), "Before the 'beginning,' there was nothing but God."[237] Thus, the God "who called forth creation out of nothing has power also to reduce it to nothing again."[238] So we read that God, unlike human beings or the universe, existed independently and without relation to anything else, and has the inherent power to endure without anything extraneous to his being. Unlike God, anything else could pass away. All this strongly suggests that God is essentially everlasting or enduring; all else is not. It would indeed contradict the mind-set of biblical writers to say to God, "From everlasting to everlasting, you are God—but matter exists alongside you from everlasting to everlasting"!

Implicit throughout Isaiah 40–48 is the supreme sovereignty and utter uniqueness of Yahweh in creation, besides whom there is no other god—or anything else—when he created: "I am the first and I am the last" (44:6 NIV; cf. 48:12); "I, the LORD, am the maker of all things" (44:24 NASB); "I am the LORD, and there is none else" (45:18 NASB; cf. 46:9). God's stupendous creative power is without analogy. God sets himself apart as "creator and author of all things"—not merely organizer or arranger.[239] As Wolfhart Pannenberg comments:

---

236. Leslie C. Allen, *Psalms 101–150*, WBC 21 (Waco: Word, 1983), 16.
237. Rendtorff, "Creation and Redemption in the Torah," 313.
238. Carl F. H. Henry, *God, Revelation, and Authority* 6 (Waco: Word, 1983), 122.
239. Knight, *Deutero-Isaiah*, 124.

[The OT] statements about creation in, e.g., Pss. 104:14–30; 139:13; 147:8f. refuse to limit the creative power of God by linking it with preexistent matter. Like the thought of creation by the Word in Gen. 1, they imply the unrestricted freedom of God's creative action that the phrase "creation out of nothing" would later express.[240]

Such freedom is unknown in the other ANE cosmogonies discussed earlier. In his book *The Religion of Israel*, Yehezkel Kaufman sees these cosmogonies and religions as utterly distinct from that of the Bible: "A divine will, sovereign and absolute, which governs all and is the cause of all being—such a conception is unknown" elsewhere—in addition to the fact that the God of the Bible is not limited by preexistent *Urstoff* or primeval powers.[241] It was not a matter of pure luck that primordial stuff just happened to exist so that God could create!

As we read the OT, we observe that there are simply *no* preexisting conditions to which God is subject; it is God's commanding word that brings creation into being.[242] Claus Westermann observes that (Deutero-)Isaiah's emphasis on God *alone* as the Creator and sole God, is by virtue of his being not only "greater and more powerful than all the rest" of Babylon's gods, but also "being the one who remains ('I am the first and the last')."[243]

What we have in the OT are various strands that draw out what is implied by the biblical text rather than stated straightforwardly (such as "creation out of nothing"). Israel was not so much concerned with the *ex nihilo* dimensions of creation as it was with the sovereignty of God over creation, of God's absolute rule without competition, of the power of God's word.[244] The ancient Hebrew writers were primarily *theologically* minded rather than *philosophically* minded. All of these features fit quite nicely with creation *ex nihilo* but do not fit creation *ex materia*. The assumption behind the OT writings was that creation did not need to be defended; it was not an article of faith because "there was simply no alternative."[245] That is, "there was no other reality than that established by God," and thus the Israelites "had no need expressly to *believe* that the world was created by God because that was the presupposition of their thinking."[246]

240. Pannenberg, *Systematic Theology*, 2:17.

241. Yehezkel Kaufman, *The Religion of Israel*, trans. M. Greenberg (London: Allen & Unwin, 1961), 21–22.

242. Foerster, *"ktizō,"* 1012; "God created everything (without precondition)": W. H. Schmidt, *"brʾ*, to create," 256.

243. Claus Westermann, *Isaiah 40–66* (Philadelphia: Westminster, 1969), 156.

244. See Brueggemann, *Theology of the Old Testament*, 158–59.

245. Westermann, *Creation*, 5.

246. Ibid.

The very merism of totality—"the heavens and the earth"—expresses *totality* rather than simple *organization*. To say that God merely *organized* does not do justice to what this merism expresses.

Conclusion

In this chapter, the cumulative case for creation *ex nihilo* in the OT has been presented. These varying intertwining strands furnish us with solid support for this doctrine's being assumed by OT writers.

Reading Genesis 1 in the ANE cosmogonical context provides the first strand of support. Genesis 1:1 stands out dramatically as a robust, monotheistic statement; God and creation are ontologically distinct and constitute all the reality there is.

Furthermore, Genesis 1:1 is an absolute statement, not a temporal clause. Its absoluteness offers strong support for creation *ex nihilo*. Indeed, the majority of scholars today recognize that this absolute reading is not only grammatically and contextually preferable; it is also aesthetically superior. The verb *bārā᾿* (in certain contexts) further undergirds the idea of creation *out of nothing*. Its unique association with God and his word, its lack of connection with anything material, and its utter novelty make it a fitting expression of the idea of creation *ex nihilo*.

Then we came to the question of the uninhabitable wasteland or so-called "primeval chaos" in Genesis 1:2. Even if there existed primal elements from which God created, we can simply affirm that they were not eternally existent, but were created by God *ex nihilo*. A two-stage creation, in which God creates his raw materials out of nothing (Gen. 1:1) and then shapes them into a cosmos (Gen. 1:2–31), is perfectly plausible. It is textually sound, hardly inelegant, and not at all "Hellenistic."

Finally, the contingency of the created order as well as the totalism expressed by the OT further attest to creation out of nothing. God created everything external to himself, which means that reality is constituted by God and creation. Without God, nothing else could exist. He must bring it into being, and he must sustain it in being. Creation out of nothing is thus taken for granted and strongly implied in the OT.

2

The New Testament Witness to *Creatio ex Nihilo*

Some scholars commonly claim that the biblical position on creation (whether *ex nihilo* or *ex materia*) is ambiguous. We have noted Gerhard May's suggestion in this regard. Yet the absence of scriptural analysis in May's book weakens his position.[1] If properly done, sound biblical exegesis refutes the notion that creation out of nothing is a mere theological invention of the late second century in response to heretical Gnostic doctrines and Middle Platonist ideas.

This is true not only for the OT witness but also for the NT witness. Indeed, the NT writers build on the worldview of the OT. For example, the believers in Acts 4:24 pray to God, who created heaven, earth, the sea, and everything in them—a sweeping statement that does not omit anything.[2] Markus Barth and Helmut Blanke declare that "the OT idea of creation" serves as a background to Paul's affirmations about creation in the New.[3] Brevard Childs affirms, "It is apparent that the

1. Gerhard May, *Creatio ex Nihilo: The Doctrine of "Creation out of Nothing" in Early Christian Thought*, trans. A. S. Worrall (Edinburgh: University of Edinburgh Press, 1994).

2. John S. Feinberg, *No One like Him: The Doctrine of God* (Wheaton, Ill.: Crossway Books, 2001), 554.

3. Markus Barth and Helmut Blanke, *Colossians*, AB 34B, trans. Astrid B. Beck (New York: Doubleday, 1994), 198.

Old Testament's understanding of God as Creator was simply assumed and largely taken for granted as true" by NT authors.[4] The NT writers believed that "the world was not eternal" and, Childs adds, that "God's creative power encompasses everything." It is aptly summarized in the phrase *creatio ex nihilo.*[5]

Citing Genesis 1:1 and the intertestamental reference of 2 Maccabees 7:28, Jenson affirms that NT writers and the primal church

> simply took over Jewish teaching. For her the doctrine of creation was received truth that did not need to be asserted, but functioned rather as warrant in asserting other things. Thus the absolute difference between Creator and creature is an automatic classification (Romans 1.25; Hebrews 4.3). "Creator" is simply equivalent to "God" (1 Peter 4.19), and "creature" is simply equivalent to "everything" (Romans 8.19–39; Colossians 1.23).[6]

Of course, the NT writers connected creation and Christology. In Christ's sharing the identity of God as the Creator of the universe (e.g., 1 Cor. 8:6)[7] and in light of Jesus' resurrection from the dead (which has been called the "eighth day of creation"), creation is now infused with the hope of restoration. Even so, the monotheism of the OT—with its rejection of an eternal dualism—is clear. As in the OT, the NT writers see God as the Creator of all, without whom there would be no reality distinct from him. The NT writers obviously build on the OT.

There is no neat transition from the Hebrew verb *bārā'* to the Greek. The Greek verbs for God's creative activity include *ktizō* (create) and its cognates, which tend to be used for divine activity, and *poieō* (make/create), which is used for both divine and human action. For example, referring to Genesis 1:27, Jesus speaks of the creation of man and woman, declaring that God *created/made* [*epoiēsen*] them male and female (Matt. 19:4; par. Mark 10:6). Yet the verb *poieō* refers to what is *man*-made as well (e.g., the tabernacle in the wilderness [Acts 7:44]). In the LXX itself, the verb *bārā'* is translated sometimes with *ktizein* (to create) and other times with *poiein* (to create, make)—unlike the later versions by Aquila, Symmachus, and Theodotion, which consistently use *ktizein.*[8]

---

4. Brevard S. Childs, *Biblical Theology of the Old and New Testaments* (Minneapolis: Fortress, 1992), 391.

5. Ibid.

6. Robert W. Jenson, "Aspects of a Doctrine of Creation," in *The Doctrine of Creation,* ed. Colin E. Gunton (Edinburgh: T & T Clark, 1997), 17.

7. See Richard Bauckham, *God Crucified: Monotheism and Christology in the New Testament* (Grand Rapids: Eerdmans, 1998).

8. Werner Foerster, *"ktizō," TDNT,* 3:1000–35; W. H. Schmidt, *"br',* to create," in *TLOT,* 1:256.

Despite what some scholars assert about Greek philosophical influence on Jewish thought, there is still, according to James D. G. Dunn, a "distinctively Jewish influence" in the "exclusive use of 'create/creation' for the act and fact of *divine* creation."[9] Steeped in the OT, NT writers such as Paul exhibit the same kind of exclusiveness in their use of the verb create, which contrasts with the "less discriminating usage of Greek thought."[10] The Greeks used a range of words for creation. G. Petzke notes that the NT and postbiblical Judaism follow the LXX in avoiding the term *dēmiourgos* (demiurge), "which was common in the surrounding world," for the "Creator."[11] For all the talk about Hellenistic philosophical influences on biblical writers, what is remarkable is that the word *dēmiourgos* (builder) appears only once in the NT (Heb. 11:10; used for God). As noted earlier, this term is altogether avoided in the LXX. By contrast, "creator [*ho ktisēs*]" is the preferred term in Scripture. But even in Hebrews 11:10—unlike Platonism—the word "builder" *(dēmiourgos)* does not suggest a lower status than that of Creator. Instead, NT writers such as Paul regularly affirm the "essentially Jewish conception of the cosmos."[12] This is further borne out by the fact that the stock Greek word for unformed matter—*hylē*—is found only once in the NT—without any reference to unformed matter. James 3:5b NASB reads, "Behold, how great a *forest* [or 'wood' = *hylēn*][13] is set aflame by such a small fire."

This chapter examines the key creation texts of the NT, which attest to the doctrine of creation out of nothing, and reveals that creation *ex materia* is indeed foreign to the biblical worldview.

John 1:3

All things came into being by him; and apart from him nothing came into being that has come into being. (NASB)

9. James D. G. Dunn, *The Theology of Paul the Apostle* (Grand Rapids: Eerdmans, 1998), 38.
10. Ibid.
11. G. Petzke, *"ktizō,"* in *Exegetical Dictionary of the New Testament*, vol. 2, ed. Horst Balz and Gerhard Schneider, trans. James W. Thompson (Grand Rapids: Eerdmans, 1991), 325.
12. Dunn, *Theology of Paul the Apostle*, 38.
13. Ralph P. Martin, *James*, WBC 48 (Waco: Word, 1988), 113. Cf. Walter Bauer, William F. Arndt, F. Wilbur Gingrich, and Frederick W. Danker, *A Greek-English Lexicon of the New Testament and Other Early Christian Literature*, 2d ed. (Chicago: University of Chicago Press, 1979), 836.

Referring to creation, John 1:3 utilizes sweeping and unexceptional language: "All things [*panta*]" came into being through the Word.[14] Rather than second-century theologians' moving away from an antimaterialistic Gnosticism and inventing creation out of nothing, Raymond Brown notes that here, within the biblical text itself, we see that "the material world has been created by God and is good."[15] The implication is that all things exist through God's agent, who is the originator of everything.[16] This is borne out by the fact that though the Word already *was (ēn)*, the creation *came to be (egeneto).*[17]

So when Scripture speaks of God's creation, there is an all-embracing nature to it.[18] Klaus Wengst points out the obvious: nothing out of all that exists is excluded.[19] Indeed, as Ernst Haenchen affirms, this passage rejects any proto-Gnosticism, in which the material world was evil.[20] Rudolf Schnackenburg observes that this text defends the goodness of all created things since, in the work of creation, everything owes its existence to God.[21]

Even Rudolf Bultmann, for all of his talk about Hellenistic influences on NT writers, declares that the scope of creation in John 1:3 refers to "everything that there is [*panta*]." This is an affirmation in the strongest words possible that "everything without exception" has been made by the Logos. The word *egeneto* (made, created) is a pure expression of the idea of creation, which excludes both *emanation* and any original

14. John here uses *panta* (not preceded by the definite article), which may point to everything as a totality, rather than the stock expression *ta panta* (all things), which might have pointed to all individual things (Leon Morris, *The Gospel according to John* [Grand Rapids: Eerdmans, 1971], 79 n.). See also the revised edition of this volume (1995).

15. Raymond E. Brown, *The Gospel according to John I–XII*, AB 29 (New York: Doubleday, 1966), 26. Brown wrongly asserts that John 1:1–18 "does not necessarily have the same theology as the Gospel" (see D. A. Carson's discussion on how John's prologue actually introduces the Gospel's major themes: *The Gospel according to John* [Grand Rapids: Eerdmans, 1991], 111–12). Yet Brown (6) makes plain that the word *egeneto* ("come into being") is used consistently to describe creation in the LXX in Genesis 1.

16. On the punctuation of John 1:1–3, see D. Moody Smith, *John*, ANTC (Nashville: Abingdon, 1999), 52–53; George R. Beasley-Murray, *John*, WBC 36 (Waco: Word, 1987), 2; R. E. Brown, *John I–XII*, 6.

17. Brown, *John I–XII*, 8.

18. For a survey of the biblical data regarding creation, see Karl Hermann Schelkle, *Theology of the New Testament*, vol. 1, trans. William A. Jurgens (Collegeville, Minn.: Liturgical Press, 1971), 3–61.

19. "Nichts von allem, was ist, ist ausgeschlossen" (Klaus Wengst, *Das Johannessevangelium*, vol. 1 [Stuttgart: Verlag W. Kohlhammer, 2000], 48).

20. "Für diese war die materielle Welt schlecht" (Ernst Haenchen, *Das Johannesevangelium: Ein Kommentar* [Tübingen: Mohr/Siebeck, 1980], 120).

21. Rudolf Schnackenburg, *The Gospel according to St. John*, vol. 1, trans. Kevin Smyth (New York: Herder & Herder, 1968), 238–39.

duality: "The creation is not the arrangement of a chaotic stuff, but is . . . *creatio ex nihilo.*"[22] John uses the sweeping, totalistic language typical of the biblical writers, who have "a natural habit of speaking as comprehensively as possible about Yahweh's creative power."[23]

Along these lines, Herman Ridderbos remarks:

> The emphatic position that "all things" has in vs. 3 and the addition that *nothing* is excepted from what has been made by the Word, therefore intend to express—against all speculations about the origin of the world that are in competition with this viewpoint—not only the absolute monotheistic idea of creation [i.e., *ex nihilo*], but even more the all-embracing significance of the incarnation of the Word.[24]

What John articulates is what is essential to Jewish/Christian monotheism: there are no intermediaries between God/Christ and the world.[25] All things were made *through him*—without any exception whatsoever.[26] Surely creation *ex nihilo* resonates from this text.

Romans 4:17

> [Abraham] is our father in the sight of God, in whom he believed—the God who gives life to the dead and calls things that are not as though they were. (NIV)

Commentator C. E. B. Cranfield declares, "There is little doubt that the reference is to God's *creatio ex nihilo.*"[27] This must be qualified, however. Douglas Moo notes that Paul has another intention here—although "Paul's language is quite close to this Jewish *creatio ex nihilo* tradition," and such language "would not be out of place in the context [of Rom. 4:17]."[28] According to Moo, Paul's point is broader than—but

22. Rudolf Bultmann, *The Gospel of John: A Commentary*, trans. G. R. Beasley-Murray et al. (Philadelphia: Westminster, 1971), 38.

23. Walter Eichrodt, *Theology of the Old Testament*, vol. 2, trans. J. A. Baker (Philadelphia: Westminster, 1967), 102.

24. Herman Ridderbos, *The Gospel of John: A Theological Commentary*, trans. John Vriend (Grand Rapids: Eerdmans, 1997), 36.

25. Barnabas Lindars, *The Gospel of John*, NCB (London: Oliphants, 1972), 84.

26. Rodney A. Whitacre, *John*, IVPNTC (Downers Grove, Ill.: InterVarsity, 1999), 51.

27. C. E. B. Cranfield, *A Critical and Exegetical Commentary on the Epistle to the Romans*, ICC, vol. 1 (Edinburgh: T & T Clark, 1975), 244. See also Childs, *Biblical Theology of the Old and New Testaments*, 391: "The theme akin to *creatio ex nihilo* is sounded in Rom. 4:17."

28. Douglas J. Moo, *The Epistle to the Romans*, NICNT (Grand Rapids: Eerdmans, 1996), 282.

also incorporates—creation *ex nihilo*. It would be misguided to say, "Romans 4:17 does not speak of creation out of nothing; therefore, no one should appeal to this text in support of this doctrine."

As in Genesis ("Let there be . . ."), Paul speaks of God who "calls" all things into being. Paul is, according to NT scholar James Dunn, operating from an undisputed "theological axiom."[29] That is, *there is no precondition to God's activity*—whether it concerns creation, resurrection, or granting a child to an elderly infertile couple. Where there is death, God brings to life; where there is barrenness, God makes fruitful; in the case of creation, where there is nothing, God brings something into existence. Everything that exists is wholly dependent upon God for its being and continued existence.

Dunn explains the relationship between Paul's understanding of creation and how Paul relates it to his point about redemption in Romans 4:17:

> Paul calls on this theological axiom not simply because it is a formula few if any of his readers would dispute, but because it clearly implies also the relationship which must pertain between this creator and his creation. As creator he creates without any precondition: he makes alive where there was only death, and *he calls into existence where there was nothing at all*. Consequently, that which has been created, made alive in this way, must be totally dependent on the creator, the life-giver, for its very existence and life. Expressed in such terms the statement provides the governing principle by which all God's relationships with humankind must be understood, including salvation and redemption. Unless God is inconsistent, the same principle will govern God's dealings as savior: he redeems as he creates, and he reckons righteous in the same way in which he makes alive. That is to say, his saving work depends on nothing in that which is saved; redemption, righteous-reckoning, is not contingent on any precondition on the part of the recipient; the dead cannot make terms, that which does not exist cannot place God under any obligation—which is to say that the individual or nation is dependent on the unconditional grace of God as much for covenant life as for created life. It was this total dependence on God for very existence itself which man forgot, [and] his rejection of that dependence which lies at the root of his malaise ([Rom.] 1:18–28).[30]

Along similar lines, theologian John Feinberg says that Paul's point goes beyond the question of whether or not God created from preexisting matter. Rather, the aforementioned "theological axiom" applies in

29. James D. G. Dunn, *Romans 1–8*, WBC 38A (Dallas: Word, 1988), 237.
30. Ibid.

this way: nothing exists apart from God's creating, and if this is true of all things, then creation *ex nihilo* follows naturally from this fact.[31]

Otfried Hofius points out that Paul is drawing on the common connection, made within the extrabiblical Jewish thought and literature of his day, between creation out of nothing and the resurrection of the dead.[32] Indeed, Hofius affirms that creation out of nothing in such passages "is not doubtful."[33] Werner Foerster warns that we should not take the *mē onta* (things which do not [yet] exist) as though in some sense they were *onta* (existing things).[34] We should take the verse in a straightforward way—that God calls forth what does not yet exist. Foerster infers from Romans 4:17 that everything that exists arises out of nothing, by God's Word.[35]

Commenting on this passage, Leon Morris asserts that the "things that are not" refer to "the nonexistence of the called before the call came. Paul is speaking of God as creating something out of nothing by his call."[36] Morris agrees with Moo, Dunn, and Feinberg in noting that Paul's thinking most certainly applies to the physical creation, even if he does not directly refer to it. Romans 4:17 suggests this broad principle that incorporates both creation and resurrection. Robert H. Mounce explains the biblical assumption expressed here and throughout Scripture: "By definition the Creator brings into existence all that is from that which never was. Anything less than that would be adaptation rather than creation."[37] Paul Achtemeier concurs, commenting that God will go to whatever lengths possible to fulfill his promises—even if this means creating something where before nothing at all had existed.[38]

---

31. Feinberg, *No One like Him*, 556.

32. For a more extensive discussion, see Otfried Hofius, "Die Gottesprädikationen Röm 4,17b," in *Paulusstudien II*, Wissenschaftliche Untersuchungen zum Neuen Testament 143 (Tübingen: Mohr/Siebeck, 2002), 58–61.

33. " . . . ist . . . nicht zweifelhaft" (Hofius, "Röm 4,17b," 60 n). Thanks to Peter Frick for pointing out Hofius's work on this passage.

34. Foerster, *"ktizō,"* 1010.

35. Ibid., 1010. In support of creation out of nothing, Foerster (ibid., 1029) also points to 2 Corinthians 4:6 (echoing Gen. 1:3), where God calls the light out of darkness, another reference to creation out of nothing by God's word. Hofius makes the connection with 2 Corinthians 1:9 as well ("Röm 4,17b," 59).

36. Leon Morris, *The Epistle to the Romans* (Grand Rapids: Eerdmans, 1988), 208–9.

37. Robert H. Mounce, *Romans*, NAC 27 (Nashville: Broadman & Holman, 1995), 128. Mounce notes here that the neuter plural participles in this passage may indeed suggest a "broader context" in which God does not speak of things "that do not exist as though they did" but rather "speaks the nonexistent into existence" (Heb. 11:3; 2 Peter 3:5). W. H. Schmidt also sees Romans 4:17 as supporting the idea of creation *ex nihilo* ("*br*ʾ, to create," 256), as does William P. Brown ("Creation," in *Eerdmans Dictionary of the Bible*, ed. David Noel Freedman [Grand Rapids: Eerdmans, 2000], 293).

38. Paul J. Achtemeier, *Romans*, Interpretation (Atlanta: John Knox, 1985), 82.

Ernst Käsemann notes the "full radicalness" of the doctrine of justification as "an anticipation of the resurrection of the dead."[39] This deserves to be called "creation out of nothing."[40] Just as God brought being from nonbeing, so here God also brings life where there was death, salvation where there was alienation. As Matthew Black observes, the context does indeed reflect that God is "able to revivify the dead, and create afresh out of nothing (cf. 2 Macc. 7:28)."[41] Pointing to Romans 4:17, Bernhard Anderson asserts that the sovereignty of God as Creator does indeed *entail* the doctrine of creation out of nothing.[42] Roman Catholic scholar Joseph Fitzmyer recognizes in this passage the promise to Abraham made by the all-powerful Creator God himself, who "can bring about all things."[43]

Of Paul's creation theology, Gottfried Nebe writes that "he does not allude to the way from chaos or disorder or unformed matter to order, like the well-known ideas of creation in the pagan ancient world or even in Hellenistic Judaism. But we see here, as in ancient Judaism and Hellenistic Judaism, the so-called *creatio ex nihilo*."[44] In relation to Romans 4:17, the basis of the *connection* between creation out of nothing and the resurrection of the dead is the greatness and power of God. Indeed, the universe's beginning and continued existence depend solely on God's creative power.[45]

Rather than thoroughly Hellenizing Paul (as did Rudolf Bultmann, who proclaimed, "Paul originated in Hellenistic Judaism"),[46] Nebe cautions that we observe how very Jewish is his thinking.[47] Again, Romans 4:17, even if it does not directly address creation out of nothing, certainly includes it.

Hebrews 11:3

> By faith we understand that the universe was formed at God's command, so that what is seen was not made out of what was visible. (NIV)

39. Ernst Käsemann, *Commentary on Romans* (Grand Rapids: Eerdmans, 1980), 123.
40. Ibid.
41. Matthew Black, *Romans*, NCB, 2d ed. (Grand Rapids: Eerdmans, 1973), 72.
42. B. W. Anderson, "Creation," *IDB*, 1:728. Anderson also points out that Hebrews 11:3 articulates creation *ex nihilo*.
43. Joseph A. Fitzmyer, *Romans*, AB 33 (New York: Doubleday, 1993), 383.
44. Gottfried Nebe, "Creation in Paul's Theology," in *Creation in Jewish and Christian Tradition*, ed. Henning Graf Reventlow and Yair Hoffman, JSOT Supplement Series 319 (Sheffield: Sheffield Academic Press, 2002), 116.
45. Ibid., 119.
46. Rudolf Bultmann, *Theology of the New Testament*, vol. 1, trans. K. Grobel (London: SCM Press, 1952), 187.
47. Nebe, "Creation in Paul's Theology," 119–20.

This passage (along with Rom. 4:17), Jaroslav Pelikan avers, "explicitly" teaches creation out of nothing.[48] Indeed, it is one of the most forceful affirmations of creation out of nothing in the NT, despite its being phrased in a somewhat negative way ("was not made [*mē . . . gegonenai*]") rather than only positively.

At God's command, the universe was formed, made complete, created (*katērtisthai;* 11:3a), but not from "things visible" (11:3b). The phrase *to mē ek phainomenōn* means, literally, "not from things that appear." Though the expression *ta phainomena* (visible things) was common in classical Greek literature, the word order of the phrase "not from anything observable [*to mē ek phainomenōn*]" here is unusual and somewhat ambiguous.[49] Thus, it is worth exploring in more detail—even though the two most viable alternatives strongly support creation out of nothing.

Craig Koester presents the following alternatives regarding how "things unseen" should be interpreted:[50]

View #1. Nothingness	God brought the universe out of nonexistence (the invisible).
View #2. Transcendent realm	This reflects the Hellenistic notion that the visible world is derived from an invisible world.
View #3. The power of God's word	What "cannot be seen" corresponds to the "word of God."

Koester is one commentator among many who discount view #2 as a plausible alternative. He notes that it is inadequate because Hebrews does not posit connections between heavenly patterns and earthly realities in any consistent way.[51] In Plato's thought God is an Artificer, or Architect, working with preexisting materials and shaping them into an orderly cosmos. A certain eternal dualism is presupposed—a view antithetical to monotheism. Moreover, there are sufficient worldview differences between the biblical faith and Hellenistic philosophy that view #2 is most likely not in view. William Lane claims that this passage, saying that the universe was not brought into being from anything observable, "would seem to exclude any influence from Platonic . . . cosmology."[52]

48. Jaroslav Pelikan, "Creation and Causality in the History of Christian Thought," in *Evolution after Darwin*, vol. 3, ed. Sol Tax and Charles Callender (Chicago: University of Chicago Press, 1960), 34.

49. William L. Lane, *Hebrews*, WBC 47B (Dallas: Word, 1991), 332.

50. See Craig Koester's comparisons of Platonic thought and that of the writer to the Hebrews (*Hebrews*, AB 36 [New York: Doubleday, 2001], 97–100). For example, according to Plato, *faith* belongs to a lower order; not so for the author of Hebrews.

51. Ibid., 474.

52. Lane, *Hebrews*, 332. Some will claim that the rare use of *dēmiourgos* (creator) or *technitēs* (architect) in Hebrews 11:10 is borrowed from Plato, who uses the term for human

As an aside, one could argue that even on view #2, *creatio ex nihilo* is hardly excluded since it is possible to speak of God's bringing about the world out of nothing, no material; he simply speaks, and a cosmos—ordered according to the Ideas or Forms in the divine Mind—is brought into being.

Let us explore the reasoning behind the selection of view #3 (i.e., the invisible power of God's word), which Koester affirms as "most viable."[53] In this view, what cannot be seen is the word of God.[54] One argument in favor of this alternative is that the chiastic (or crisscrossing) pattern within the text seems to bear this out. That is, the two halves of the verse are parallel in meaning and form a chiasmus:[55]

1 was fashioned [*katērtisthai*]	1' came into being [*gegonenai*]
2 the universe [*tous aiōnas*]	2' that which can be seen [*to blepomenon*]
3 by the word of God [*rhēmati theou*]	3' by what cannot be seen [*to mē ek phainomenōn*]

Thus, "what cannot be seen" appears to refer to the "word of God."[56]

Such an interpretation would certainly support creation out of nothing. In this passage, which reflects the thinking of Psalm 33:6 ("By the word of the LORD the heavens were made" [NRSV]), we read of the creative power of *rhēmati theou*—"the word/command of God." This harks back to Hebrews 1:2–3, where God's *Word*—namely, Christ—is the instrument by which God "created [*epoiēsen*] the universe" (REB). Paul Ellingworth argues that the phrase "by the word/command of God" would "conflict" with any idea that the visible world was made out of materials in the invisible world.[57]

---

artists or craftsmen in book 10 of his *Republic* (371a, 373c). In *Timaeus*, Plato uses it of the Maker *(poiētēs)* and Father of this universe. He speaks of the universe's Architect/Maker *(ho tektainomenos)* and Constructor *(dēmiourgos)*. This Demiurge imposes order and structure on the raw material of matter, into which he makes "all that was visible [*pan hoson ēn horaton*]" (*Timaeus* 28c–32c, 42e). Also, the Demiurge is the fashioner *(dēmiourgos)* of night and day (*Timaeus* 40c). Without giving any substantial evidence for his assertion, Harold Attridge asserts that "a Platonic cosmogonic model" lies behind the formulation of this verse (*Epistle to the Hebrews* [Philadelphia: Fortress, 1989], 316).

53. Koester, *Hebrews*, 474.

54. Ibid., 481.

55. Ibid.; cf. also Paul Ellingworth, *The Epistle to the Hebrews: A Commentary on the Greek Text*, NIGTC (Grand Rapids: Eerdmans, 1993), 569.

56. The preposition *ek/ex*, which can mean "out of," can also be translated *causally*, since it parallels "by the word of God." The sense then would be that the visible comes into existence *by* the invisible (Koester, *Hebrews*, 474).

57. Ellingworth, *Hebrews*, 569.

This reading is certainly possible. And although view #1 comes closest to our view, it still does not capture what the text says as the most natural reading. The writer of Hebrews is not stating in *positive* terms that the world was made from something not visible. Instead, he puts it *negatively:* the world was not made from anything visible. Here, much turns on how the negative *mē* is to be used, since there is an unusual word order. Lane points out two alternative possibilities:

(a) so that what is seen was brought into existence from what *cannot* be seen
(b) so that what is seen was *not* brought into being from anything that can be seen

Lane, not to mention (among others) Ronald Williamson and Philip E. Hughes,[58] opts for alternative (b). Lane points out that the negative *mē* usually occurs before the word or phrase that is negated, and here it is the entire clause ("so that what is seen was not brought into being from anything observable").[59] The negative *mē* properly modifies the whole infinitival clause *(eis to mē ek phainomenōn to blepomenon gegonenai)*, the *eis to* phrase having a final or purposive sense to it (so that).[60] The thrust of this clause is a denial of the world's having a visible source. Furthermore, the plural *phainomenōn* seems oddly conjoined to the singular "word of God [*rhēmati theou*]" (although it has been argued that the neuter plural could convey a singular idea).[61] Lane summarizes by saying that although Hebrews 11:3 does not state *creatio ex nihilo* in positive terms, but negatively: "it denies that the created universe originated from primal material or anything observable."[62]

That said, what alternatives (a) and (b) both affirm is a *creatio ex nihilo* understanding of creation.[63] The power of God's word, not relying on anything visible, brings forth visible effects. The visible world is

---

58. Ronald Williamson, *Philo and the Epistle to the Hebrews* (Leiden: Brill, 1970), 377–79; Philip Edgecumbe Hughes, *The Epistle to the Hebrews* (Grand Rapids: Eerdmans, 1977), 443.

59. Lane, *Hebrews*, 326–27. See also Hughes, *Hebrews*, 443.

60. See Maximilian Zerwick, *Biblical Greek* (Rome: Pontifical Institute, 1963), 122, §352.

61. Koester, *Hebrews*, 474.

62. Lane, *Hebrews*, 332.

63. C. F. D. Moule says that the reference in Hebrews 11:3 seems to be to creation *ex nihilo*, "the *visible* having come into being out of the *invisible.*" Moule adds, however, that the order of the negative *mē* before the preposition *ek*, "from" or "out of," is somewhat awkward grammatically (C. F. D. Moule, *An Idiom Book of New Testament Greek*, 2d ed. [Cambridge: University of Cambridge Press, 1959], 168).

without any visible antecedents.[64] The remarkably dynamic and infinitely powerful word of God brought the created order into existence.[65]

F. F. Bruce affirms that the visible universe "was not made out of equally visible [preexistent] raw material; it was called into being by divine power."[66] This biblical idea would have been wholly uncongenial to Greek thought.[67] George Wesley Buchanan also affirms that the author of Hebrews, despite his thorough familiarity with things Hellenistic, is not buying into a Platonic conception of creation. Williamson asserts that the writer of Hebrews is "deliberately setting out to expound a doctrine of Creation opposed to that of Plato."[68]

Hebrews is not concerned with preexisting chaotic stuff—nor even an invisible, intangible world, for that matter. The author is speaking neither of some eternal matter nor ideas in the mind of God, although this latter idea would certainly not undermine creation *ex nihilo*, but would even support it. Rather, the author's concern is with the *future* appearance of what was not present before God spoke.[69] He believes in a God who promises and whose word is true, which is what Hebrews 11 is addressing. Just as the creation attests to the power of God's word in bringing about a universe by his command, so also the faith of OT saints attests to the power of God's word in the miracles, wonders, and hardships they experienced.

As Donald Guthrie notes, "An unseen power was the effective causation of the phenomenal world."[70] Indeed, the author of Hebrews is not making a metaphysical point about different types of matter (visible vs. invisible) or that God created out of invisible matter rather than visible.[71] David deSilva sees the author's purpose in Hebrews 11:3 as being "merely to affirm that the material, visible cosmos came into being by means of causes beyond and above the realm of what can be experienced by the senses, the principal cause [of] which was 'the word of God.'"[72] In his book *The Theology of the Book of Hebrews*, Barnabas

64. Hughes, *Hebrews*, 443.
65. Ibid., 452.
66. F. F. Bruce, *The Epistle to the Hebrews*, rev. ed., NICNT (Grand Rapids, Eerdmans, 1990), 280.
67. Ibid., 281.
68. Ibid.
69. Koester, *Hebrews*, 184. Cf. Williamson, *Philo and Hebrews*, 50–51, 421–22. Williamson insists that if there is any similarity between Platonism and Hebrews on creation (a connection he considers "extremely doubtful"), any such "traces of Platonism" are "insubstantial" (50).
70. Donald Guthrie, *The Letter to the Hebrews* (Downers Grove, Ill.: InterVarsity, 1983), 227.
71. Feinberg, *No One Like Him*, 557.
72. David deSilva, *Perseverance in Gratitude: A Socio-Rhetorical Commentary on the Epistle to the Hebrews* (Grand Rapids: Eerdmans, 2000), 386.

Lindars declares it assumed that "the visible created order is the result of divine fiat (Gen. 1.3)."[73] What was in God's mind was spoken and brought into actuality.[74]

The very theme of Hebrews 11 is that of faith in the God whose word brings things into existence. Just as God can bring about the created world without the assistance of preexistent matter,[75] so we see that everything depends on God's word for its very existence and sustenance. It is this word of God that has sustained his people throughout history in the midst of distress and trouble because they "saw him who is invisible" (11:27 NIV) and were able to trust the God who promises.

Hebrews 1:3 declares that God sustains "all things"—expressing totalistic language again—by his powerful word. Just as God brought all things about at creation (Heb. 11:3; Gen. 1:1), so he continues to sustain them and give them their existence moment by moment. In both cases the source is the same—God's powerful word, which is essential to giving things their being as well as keeping them in existence.

Other New Testament Passages

For from him and through him and to him are all things.

Romans 11:36 NIV

For by him all things were created: things in heaven and on earth, visible and invisible, whether thrones or powers or rulers or authorities; all things were created by him and for him.

Colossians 1:16 NIV

Yet for us there is but one God, the Father, from whom all things came and for whom we live; and there is but one Lord, Jesus Christ, through whom all things came and through whom we live.

1 Corinthians 8:6 NIV

73. Barnabas Lindars, *The Theology of the Book of Hebrews* (Cambridge: Cambridge University Press, 1991), 110.

74. H. W. Montefiore declares that God is not merely the divine *Architect* but also the divine *Creator* (*The Epistle to the Hebrews* [London: A & C Black, 1964], 188). We do not deny that a two-stage creation—out of nothing, ultimately—may be in the mind of the author. Simon Kistemaker comments that God *first* "created the heavens and the earth" (Gen. 1:1) and "then proceeded to give structure and variety to a formless and empty earth" (*Exposition of the Epistle to the Hebrews* [Grand Rapids: Baker, 1984], 313).

75. Gareth L. Cockerill, *Hebrews: A Bible Commentary in the Wesleyan Tradition* (Indianapolis: Wesleyan Publishing House, 1999), 232.

The sweeping comprehensiveness of these passages ("all things") resembles the OT worldview—with the addition of the cosmic Christ's sharing in God's identity. The sum total of reality is comprised of God/ Christ and everything else (i.e., creation). Nothing is omitted.

According to Romans 11:36, "from [ek]" God and "through [dia] him and to [eis] him are all things [ta panta]." In light of such a sweeping statement, it would seem odd to say that from, through, and to him are all things—except primordial matter. Unoriginated matter would hardly fit in with such an assertion. Absolute creation makes the best sense of such comprehensive claims. It speaks with a totalism that God is "the source (ek), sustainer (dia), and goal (eis) of all things."[76] All things find their origin in God—not to mention their being sustained and directed by him.[77]

Some have suggested that this formulation in Romans 11:36 is akin to (and therefore influenced by) Stoicism. However, we must be careful not to succumb to parallelomania. As Thomas Schreiner rightly observes, "The parallels are superficial since such formulations must be interpreted in terms of the worldview of the author, and Stoicism and Pauline thought are obviously different."[78] For example, the Stoic conception of God was pantheistic, but Paul's understanding of God was personal and theistic.

Similarly, Paul's language in 1 Corinthians 8:6 speaks with the same comprehensiveness of "Reality = God/Christ + Creation." Scholars such as Richard Bauckham and James Dunn note that Paul splits the Shema of Deuteronomy 6:4 ("Hear, O Israel: The LORD our God, the LORD is one" [NIV]). Paul affirms that Jesus is identified with Yahweh as the "one Lord" of Deuteronomy 6:4, and both Jesus and the Father are seen as bringing about the created order.[79] Amazingly, the monotheistic Paul is making a dramatic pronouncement in "Christianizing" the Shema.[80] The ta panta (all things)—like "the heavens and the earth" of Genesis 1 and elsewhere in the OT—refers to everything, the universe.[81]

---

76. Moo, Romans, 743.

77. Mounce, Romans, 227.

78. Thomas R. Schreiner, Romans, BECNT (Grand Rapids: Baker, 1998), 637.

79. Dunn, Theology of Paul the Apostle, 268; and Bauckham, God Crucified, 38. Bauckham notes that what Paul does is reproduce the words of the statement about Yahweh and make them apply to both the Father and Christ. Paul is thus including Jesus in the divine identity, redefining monotheism as christological monotheism. Whereas the "one Lord" was applied to God in the Shema, it is now being applied to Christ. Thus, for Paul, the unique identity of the one God consists of the one God, the Father, and the one Lord, his Messiah. So Paul is not repudiating monotheism by simply associating Jesus with the one God, but he is including Jesus in this unique identity.

80. F. F. Bruce, 1 and 2 Corinthians, NCB (Grand Rapids: Eerdmans, 1971), 80.

81. Dunn, Theology of Paul the Apostle, 267.

Even the word "creation" *(ktisis)*, according to the second edition of the Bauer-Arndt-Gingrich-Danker Greek lexicon, has the sense of "the sum total of everything created," and this is borne out by the Creator-creation distinction made in Scripture (cf. Heb. 9:11 NIV: "not a part of this creation").[82] In the third edition, the word "create [*ktizō*]" is defined as "to bring something into existence."[83]

Colossians 1:16–17 speaks comprehensively as well when it declares that *all things* were created *in* and *through* Christ and *for* him. The totalistic merism in Genesis 1:1 ("the heavens and the earth") is expressed in the phrase "all things" *(ta panta)*. Stating that Christ has created things "in heaven and on earth"—which corresponds to or parallels[84] "things visible and invisible" *(ta horata kai ta aorata)*—indicates that these expressions "embrace everything, for there are no exceptions."[85] M. Barth and Blanke observe that "things visible and invisible" should *not* be understood in a Platonic sense of the realm of appearance as opposed to the realm of Ideas or Forms. Rather, in accordance with the Hebrew worldview (which had no word for "invisible"), we should translate such a passage as "what is seen and what is not seen."[86]

N. T. Wright declares that "all things" could be translated "the totality."[87] Not only this, but Christ is *before* all things. The implication is that there was a state of being in which Christ existed and the universe did not. As F. F. Bruce notes, "The words ['before all things'] not only declare [Christ's] temporal priority to the universe, but also suggest his primacy over it."[88] Herman Ridderbos under-

82. Bauer, Arndt, et al., *A Greek-English Lexicon of the New Testament*, 2d ed. (1979), 456.

83. Walter Bauer, William F. Arndt, F. Wilbur Gingrich, and Frederick W. Danker, *A Greek-English Lexicon of the New Testament and Other Early Christian Literature*, 3d ed. (Chicago: University of Chicago Press, 2000), 572.

84. Corresponds, that is, in chiastic fashion.

85. P. T. O'Brien, *Colossians, Philemon*, WBC 44 (Waco: Word, 1982), 46.

86. Barth and Blanke, *Colossians*, 200. They suggest the phrase "what is seen" is chiastically describing things "upon the earth" (1:15), and "what is not seen" would correspond to things "in the heavens." They also note that according to OT and NT perceptions, "it is not justifiable to characterize angels as "invisible" (Gen. 18:2; Josh. 5:13; Judg. 6:11–24; 13:3–7; Matt. 25:31; Luke 1:11–20, 26–38; 2:9–15; 24:4–7; Acts 10:30; 12:7; 27:23; 2 Thess. 1:7; et al.). O'Brien sees these invisible things (thrones, dominions, etc.) as hostile angel powers (*Colossians, Philemon*, 46). On such a view, if we see the things "unseen" as referring to thrones and dominions and principalities and powers, they still find their source and temporal origination in Christ.

87. N. T. Wright, *Colossians and Philemon*, TNTC (Grand Rapids: Eerdmans, 1986), 73.

88. E. K. Simpson and F. F. Bruce, *The Epistles of Paul to the Ephesians and to the Colossians*, NICNT (Grand Rapids: Eerdmans, 1957), 200. O'Brien also points out Christ's "temporal priority to the universe" (*Colossians, Philemon*, 47), as does Wright, *Colossians and Philemon*, 71 ("priority in both time and rank"; "the continuing temporal sense of the word is clear").

stands Colossians 1:17 to mean that "all things have their existence together" in Christ.[89]

M. Barth and Blanke stress that the totality (*ta panta*) refers to the "entire creation" (comparable to the Hebrew *kōl*, "all"): "In the viewpoint of [Colossians], *everything* that is not creator is represented as having been created."[90] What is expressed in Colossians 1:16 is in "striking contrast" to "Hellenistic statements" about the nature of creation.[91] In fact, as M. Barth notes in his Ephesians commentary, even though Paul makes use of Hellenistic diction, his reference to God's/Christ's creation and rulership over "all things" may well intend to cut right through the "maze of Hellenistic syncretism" to the monotheistic OT witness to creation.[92] Thus, the text of Colossians 1:16–17 suggests the following affirmations:[93] (1) Christ's creating (bringing all things into being) and (2) his sustaining them in being. The fact that in him "all things hold together" (1:17) emphasizes his sustaining "what he has brought into being."[94] Without such an activity, everything would disintegrate.[95] (3) All things (i.e., creation) reach their fulfillment or climax in Christ (compare 1:20); they are made *for* him.

We could refer to other portions of Scripture along these lines. Revelation 1:8 declares that the Lord is the "Alpha and the Omega." He is the one "who is, and who was, and who is to come" (NIV). (This, of course, echoes passages such as Isa. 41:4; 44:6; 48:12.) He is "from everlasting to everlasting" (Ps. 90:2 NIV). It is not God—and eternal matter—who is "from everlasting to everlasting." It is God, "who created all things" (Eph. 3:9 NIV). Indeed, "you created all things, and by your will they were created and have their being" (Rev. 4:11 NIV).

So the doctrinal formulation of creation out of nothing is, as Moltmann puts it, "unquestionably an apt paraphrase" of what Scripture means by "creation."[96] As Foerster notes, "Creation out of nothing by

89. Herman Ridderbos, *Paul: An Outline of His Theology*, trans. John Richard de Witt (Grand Rapids: Eerdmans, 1975), 83.

90. Barth and Blanke, *Colossians*, 199.

91. Ibid.

92. Markus Barth, *Ephesians*, AB 34 (Garden City, N.Y.: Doubleday, 1974), 178. See P. T. O'Brien, *The Letter to the Ephesians*, Pillar (Grand Rapids: Eerdmans, 1999), 60. In Ephesians, Paul speaks of two spheres—"things of the earth" and "the heavenlies/heavens," both of which are the realms of God's creation. Cf. "heavenlies/heavenly places" in 1:3, 10, 20; 2:6; 3:10; 6:12; cf. 3:15; 4:10; 6:9; "things on earth" in 1:10; 3:15; 4:9; 6:3. So whether they are things visible or invisible, God has created them all.

93. O'Brien, *Colossians, Philemon*, 47.

94. Ibid.

95. Ibid.

96. Jürgen Moltmann, *God in Creation: A New Theology of Creation and the Spirit of God*, trans. Margaret Kohl (San Francisco: Harper & Row, 1985), 74.

the Word explicitly or implicitly underlies the NT statements [regarding creation]."[97]

Is 2 Peter 3:5 a Problem Passage for *Creatio ex Nihilo?*

Long ago by God's word the heavens existed and the earth was formed out of water and by water. (NIV)

There were heavens and earth long ago, created by God's word out of water and with water. (REB)

We would be remiss in not mentioning this passage because it bears on the question of creation out of nothing. J. N. D. Kelly claims that 2 Peter is following the cosmology of the Genesis narrative (1:2), where water is allegedly the "sole existent" and the "elemental stuff out of which the universe was formed."[98] Is this so?

The commentator Charles Bigg notes, "There appears to be no trace of a Jewish belief that water was the prime element of which earth was made."[99] Rather than this being *creatio ex aquis,* 2 Peter is speaking more loosely when he uses the phrases "from [*ek*] water" and "by [*dia*] water."[100] Indeed, as Thomas Schreiner suggests, the syntax is complicated and unclear;[101] so we should proceed with caution. It would be difficult to maintain that the author believed that the universe was made literally *from water*—a view held by the ancient philosopher Thales of Miletus—since this is utterly contrary to the biblical worldview, in which God alone is enduring and everlasting. Since God is the Creator of all things outside himself, any eternal dualism is utterly unbiblical, of which Peter is well aware.

Thus, while the NIV renders this verse "long ago by God's word the heavens existed and the earth was formed out of water and by water," it is unlikely.[102] In light of Peter's thorough familiarity with Genesis 1, his use of "heavens and earth" in this portion of Scripture (cf. also v. 7:

---

97. Foerster, "*ktizō*," 1029.

98. J. N. D. Kelly, *The Epistles of Peter and of Jude* (Peabody, Mass.: Hendrickson, 1969), 358–59.

99. Charles Bigg, *A Critical and Exegetical Commentary on the Epistles of St. Peter and St. Jude,* ICC (New York: Scribners, 1903), 293. Bigg also claims that the *ex* (out of) seems to express "the material out of which the earth was made," but it is not clear whether Bigg intends this to be understood as creation out of nothing (in two stages) or not.

100. Richard J. Bauckham, *Jude, 2 Peter,* WBC 50 (Waco: Word, 1983), 297.

101. Thomas R. Schreiner, *1 and 2 Peter, Jude,* NAC 37 (Nashville: Broadman & Holman, 2003), 374.

102. Ibid.

"the present heavens and earth" [NIV]) follows the Genesis 1:1 use of this merism for totality. Thus, the NIV's rendering is unlikely since it breaks up this unity. The more natural reading would unite "the heavens" and "earth."

Unlike Thales's philosophical quest for "primal stuff," Peter is thinking of the creation story in Genesis 1. God organizes the waters he himself has brought into being, separating the waters above and below (1:6–8), and makes the dry land by gathering the water together (1:9): "On the basis of the Genesis account, then, Peter's assertion that God created the heavens and the earth 'out of water' does not seem far-fetched."[103]

C. F. D. Moule observes that the earth was created "from water and through water." That is, Peter may be referring to "continuous land arising out of and extending through water."[104] The preposition *through (dia)* with the genitive case, when used literally or spatially, could denote the idea of "extension through" (e.g., Mark 9:30: "journeying *through* Galilee").[105] And the phrase "by water" then could simply be an expansion of the first phrase "out of water." As we see in Genesis 1, "God used water as an instrument in his creation of the sky."[106]

This would imply a two-step creation process (already noted in the previous chapter) involving God's creating the universe and its elements. This is supported by the fact that the verb "formed [*synestōsa*]" is used rather than the verb *ktizein* (create).[107] In Proverbs 8:24, we read that "the deep" did not always exist. God creates the waters and then uses them in the process of creation. Thus, water is the *material* from which the sky is created and *instrument (dia)* to create the sky.[108] Thomas Schreiner proposes that when Peter says that the world was formed *ex hydatos* ("out of water"), he probably has in mind the emergence of the earth and sky from these waters.[109] The phrase *through [dia] water* refers, Schreiner claims, to God's using water as an instrument in forming the world.

What is Peter's point? He clearly wants to make a parallel by bridging two uses of water in the Pentateuch to point out that things *have changed* since the creation of the world. God spoke, using the division of water

---

103. Douglas J. Moo, *2 Peter, Jude*, NIV Application Commentary (Grand Rapids, Zondervan, 1997), 170.

104. Moule, *An Idiom Book*, 55.

105. The prepositional phrase here is *dia tēs Galilaias* (the same prepositional usage as in Matt. 12:43; John 4:4; Rom. 15:28; Heb. 11:29).

106. Moule, *An Idiom Book*, 55.

107. Edwin A. Blum, "2 Peter," in *Expositor's Bible Commentary*, ed. Frank E. Gaebelein (Grand Rapids: Zondervan, 1981), 285.

108. Moo, *2 Peter, Jude*, 170.

109. Schreiner, *1 and 2 Peter, Jude*, 376.

to create the sky, but he also used water to destroy the world—simply by his divine decree.[110]

Therefore, we must be careful of pressing the preposition *ek/ex* ("out of") too far. After all, the Scriptures reinforce that God is indeed the ultimate source of all things, and the preposition *ek* is often used in the NT to convey this (e.g., Rom. 11:36: "from [*ek*] him . . . are all things" [NIV]). M. Barth and Blanke state that whereas the Stoic Seneca might use "from [*ek/ex*] to refer to the material out of which something is produced, biblical writers such as Paul use it to designate the Creator.[111] M. Barth and Blanke point out that the prepositions used in 2 Peter 3:5 and in Paul's writings overlap in depicting God's creative activity; so we must be cautious about "dogmatic differentiations" as well as drawing Hellenistic connections that simply are not there.[112]

Given the loose and even "confusing"[113] use of prepositions in this passage, it is unwise to read into them some cosmological theory—especially when God's dividing the waters above and below in the creative process (Gen. 1) would suffice to account for this language, as Jerome Neyrey maintains.[114]

In addition, we must allow for Peter's rhetorical purposes: "One of the main reasons he introduces the idea of the world as being created 'by water' is to prepare for the parallel he will make in verse 6, where God destroys the world 'by water.' "[115] In verse 5, God creates the world (in the second of two stages, as we have seen) by his word; then in verse 7, God judges it "by the same word."[116] Thus we have a fitting parallel.[117] Thomas Schreiner notes this as well: "Perhaps Peter stresses water for rhetorical purposes since it is the agent of judgment in the next verse."

Jerome Neyrey reminds us of the important point of Peter's writing: to address conflict over "theodicy and theology."[118] That is, the issue with which 2 Peter deals "depends less on cosmological theory than the immediate crisis surrounding the various words of God in

---

110. Bauckham, *Jude, 2 Peter*, 302. In his commentary, Bauckham appears to accept the idea of ANE mythological influences on biblical writers. We have responded to this idea in the early part of chapter 1.

111. Barth and Blanke, *Colossians*, 197, 205.

112. Ibid., 199.

113. Jerome H. Neyrey, *2 Peter, Jude*, AB 37C (New York: Doubleday, 1993), 234.

114. Ibid.: "Genesis 1 describes how the dry land was separated 'out of' the waters above and below."

115. Moo, *2 Peter, Jude*, 170.

116. Ibid., 171.

117. Bo Ivar Reicke suggests *ex nihilo* creation in his comments on 2 Peter 3:5: God by his "all-powerful word" brings about "the first days" of the "original creation" (*The Epistles of James, Peter, and Jude*, AB 37 [Garden City, N.J.: Doubleday, 1964], 175).

118. Neyrey, *2 Peter, Jude*, 233.

the document."[119] Peter writes that "by means of God's word" (cf. Ps. 33:6, 9), God divided the primal waters, producing the skies above and the waters beneath. God not only brought the waters into existence; he also separated them into clouds and bodies of water on earth while bringing to completion the creation he had begun.

Pheme Perkins declares, "God's word was powerful enough to create all things and to bring earth out of destructive waters a second time after the flood."[120] So the alleged support this passage gives to God's creating out of eternally preexistent watery chaos is beside the point.[121]

Conclusion

This chapter has revealed that the NT mirrors the OT's understanding of creation. Apart from the important NT addition of the cosmic Christ, the Pantocrator, the same creation themes are reiterated: the sweeping totalistic picture of God as the Creator of all, and the fact of creation's contingency in contrast to God's self-existence. Passages such as John 1:3; Romans 4:17; and Hebrews 11:3—to name a few—present a forceful, even if implicit, belief in creation out of nothing. The 2 Peter 3:5 passage should not be taken as supporting creation *ex materia* since Genesis 1 suggests God's creation of everything (including the waters) and then later dividing them at the end of a two-stage process. Indeed, the cumulative weight of evidence from the OT and NT leads to a strong case for creation *ex nihilo*.

In the introduction, we pointed out the distinction between the *implicit* and the *ambiguous*. An argument can have great power—even though implicit. A father might tell a son, "Either I am mowing the lawn, or you will have to do it—and I'm not mowing the lawn." The father's point is far from ambiguous. Moreover, while it is implicit, it is quite forceful, and there is no question as to what he means.

When we apply this point to creation out of nothing, we affirm, "Either *creatio ex nihilo* is true, or God did not create everything. But the Scripture says that God created everything." When the Bible declares that God created everything, it implicitly affirms that *creatio ex nihilo* is true; the issue is not ambiguous. Or consider this: We saw that if matter is eternal and God could not create without it, this would be a limit upon

119. Ibid., 234.

120. Pheme Perkins, *First and Second Peter, James, and Jude*, Interpretation (Louisville: John Knox, 1995), 189.

121. Contra J. N. D. Kelly, *The Epistles of Peter and of Jude* (Peabody, Mass.: Hendrickson, 1969), 358–59.

God's power since it is by pure luck that matter happened to be around so that God could create. Therefore we can assert: "Either *creatio ex nihilo* is true, or God is not all-powerful. But God is truly all-powerful." Again, God's being all-powerful strongly suggests creation out of nothing. Though it is implicit in Scripture, it is not ambiguous.

Another notable point: even if the biblical evidence *were* ambiguous and the biblical writers took no position on this issue, the idea that God created from eternally preexisting matter *would not win by default.* Instead, this position has its own burden of proof to bear. We are not dealing with an either-or situation (in which *either* the Bible explicitly teaches creation out of nothing, *or* the creation *ex materia* view is true by default). A Mormon or a *true* panentheist such as Ian Barbour (not Peacocke or Moltmann) who might try to use Scripture to justify *ex materia* creation must deal contextually and exegetically with the biblical texts and offer positive evidence for this position. The view proposing creation from preexistent matter would not win even if the Bible were silent on the matter.

Happily, we have no need for that hypothesis.

3

The Extrabiblical Witness
to *Creatio ex Nihilo*

In light of the texts we have just examined, the exegetical evidence indeed points us toward creation *ex nihilo*. Although we must be careful not to place too much weight on just one line of evidence, a strong cumulative case can be made from Scripture for the assumed belief within the biblical worldview that God is the Author and Originator of all reality apart from himself. A perspective such as creation *ex materia* simply would not make sense to the biblical authors.

Despite this, scholars such as Ian Barbour claim that creation out of nothing is a postbiblical invention or innovation to defend God's goodness and absolute sovereignty over the world against "Gnostic ideas regarding matter as evil or as the product of an inferior deity."[1] As we have seen, Barbour believes that the Bible is not simply ambiguous about the nature of God's relationship to creation but actually asserts that God created from preexistent materials:

> Genesis portrays the creation of order from chaos, and . . . the *ex nihilo* doctrine was formulated later by the church fathers to defend theism

1. Ian G. Barbour, *Religion in an Age of Science*, The Gifford Lectures 1989–91 [i.e., 1990], vol. 1 (San Francisco: Harper & Row, 1990), 144.

against an ultimate dualism or a monistic pantheism. We still need to defend theism against alternative philosophies, but we can do so without reference to an absolute beginning.[2]

However, there is not only biblical—and as we shall see, scientific and philosophical—warrant for an absolute beginning. In this chapter it will become clear that the church fathers (and other relevant texts reflecting the biblical worldview) assume or imply a creation out of nothing. So let us move to the extrabiblical witness.

Are there indicators that the creation out of nothing—even if not explicitly stated or articulated—is assumed and can even be properly inferred from the relevant writings *prior to* the late second and early third centuries AD, after which theologians would forthrightly declare that *ex nihilo* creation is *the* biblical view? According to May and others, Christian thinkers in the late second century tried to *formulate* the doctrine of creation in response to Gnosticism (with its emphasis on emanations and matter as evil) and Middle Platonic thought (with its emphasis on eternally preexistent matter), resulting in an explicit and precise formulation of *creatio ex nihilo*.[3]

This is fine so far as it goes. But a key question begs to be answered: Was this (1) an innovation/invention, or was it (2) merely drawing out and making explicit what was implicit all along? We argue that the latter is the case. We insist that there is an organic continuity with the biblical tradition rather than an innovation or aberration from it.

Even apart from the biblical witness, which strongly implies creation out of nothing, there is extrabiblical evidence that reveals the very same assumption in the minds of many claiming adherence to the biblical writings. Rather than viewing creation out of nothing as a novel idea that emerged in the late second century, we see a remarkable linkage between Scripture and a continuous line of thought that threads itself through many extrabiblical Jewish and Christian writers.[4] Most of these hold to a two-stage view of creation out of nothing; all of them hold to the impossibility of matter's coexisting alongside God from eternity. Creation *ex nihilo*, embedded in their thinking, becomes increasingly overt.

---

2. Ibid., 144.

3. Gerhard May, *Creatio ex Nihilo: The Doctrine of "Creation out of Nothing" in Early Christian Thought*, trans. A. S. Worrall (Edinburgh: University of Edinburgh Press, 1994), 2.

4. Most of the citations (unless otherwise noted) are taken from James H. Charlesworth, ed., *The Old Testament Pseudepigrapha*, 2 vols. (Garden City, N.Y.: Doubleday, 1983–85); and Alexander Roberts, James Donaldson, et al., eds., *Ante-Nicene Fathers*, 10 vols. (1885–96; repr., Edinburgh: T & T Clark, 1989). Available online at www.ccel.org/fathers2/; R. H. Charles, *The Apocrypha and Pseudepigrapha of the Old Testament in English*, 2 vols. (Oxford: Clarendon, 1913).

The Jewish Witness

G. F. Moore writes in his work *Judaism* that Jewish monotheism during the first centuries of Christianity (the Tannaitic period) typically emphasized the *soleness* of God (as opposed to, say, polytheism).[5] To the Jewish mind, God in his essence is one, and multiplicity emerges through creation.[6] By definition, this understanding of God excludes any ontological dualism (such as the independent existence of primordial matter). Walter Dietrich makes the same observation that has characterized Jewish monotheism, that everything apart from Yahweh is creature: "There is only Yahweh and His creation."[7]

Moore observes that creation out of nothing versus creation out of eternal formless matter "did not excite discussion in the Palestinian schools, and there are few utterances that bear on it in any way."[8] And no wonder: metaphysical dualism was simply a foreign idea to monotheism.

This point should not diminish the fact that a number of relevant Jewish texts with a bearing on the doctrine of creation imply *ex nihilo* creation. These texts refute the idea that creation out of nothing was a Christian innovation at the end of the second century and show that it is implicit within the belief structure of Judaism.[9]

The Apocrypha and Pseudepigrapha

Second Maccabees 7:28

Many scholars have suggested that the intertestamental apocryphal book 2 Maccabees (second century BC–first century AD)[10] states the idea of *creatio ex nihilo* clearly and explicitly for the first time in Jewish

---

5. George Foot Moore, *Judaism in the First Centuries of the Christian Era: The Age of Tannaim*, vol. 1 (1927; repr., Peabody, Mass.: Hendrickson, 1997), 360–61.

6. We are not addressing the question of the Trinity, in which there is a threeness in divine persons necessarily united as the one God.

7. *"Alles, aber auch alles außer JHWH ist Kreatur. . . . Es gibt nur JHWH und seine Schöpfung"* (Walter Dietrich, "Über Werden und Wesen des biblischen Monotheismus: Religionsgeschichtliche und theologische Perspektiven," in *Ein Gott allein? JHWH-Verehrung und biblischer Monotheismus im Kontext der israelitschen und altorientalischen Religionsgeschichte*, ed. Walter Dietrich and Martin A. Klopfenstein, Orbis Biblicus et Orientalis 139 [Göttingen: Vandenhoeck & Ruprecht, 1994], 21).

8. Moore, *Judaism*, 1:381.

9. Ibid., 1:381–82, where Moore does cite *Rabban Gamaliel II*, whose teaching on creation is explored below.

10. The precise date is difficult to establish, but certain portions of it were written during the second century BC. The time when it reached its final form is unknown.

literature. Gerhard von Rad maintains that the conceptional formulation of creation *ex nihilo* is first found here.[11] Hans Schwarz concurs.[12] In this passage, a mother pleads with her son to willingly accept torture rather than recant his beliefs:

> I beg you, child, look at the sky and the earth; see all that is in them and realize that God made them out of nothing [*hoti ouk ex ontōn epoiēsen auta ho theos*], and that man comes into being in the same way. (NEB)

Earlier in this chapter (7:23) she says:

> It is the Creator of the universe who moulds man at his birth and plans the origin of all things. Therefore he, in his mercy, will give you back life and breath again, since now you put his laws above all thought of self. (NEB)

The critical phrase in 7:28 is "out of nothing." It could mean either (1) "from the non-existent" or (2) "from things which did not exist" (such as preexistent, amorphous matter or "nothingness").[13] Despite the arguments of Jonathan Goldstein that the latter could be intended (this idea of order coming from chaotic "nothingness" was a Greek one),[14] this does not seem likely. One author, J. C. O'Neill, refers to "Goldstein's ingenious reading"(!)[15] and offers strong arguments to undermine Goldstein's argument.[16] The Hebrew scholar Nahum Sarna observes, "This doctrine [of creation *ex nihilo*] seems to have been first articulated in the late Second Temple work, 2 Maccabees."[17] Otfried Hofius, who surveys the relevant Jewish literature around this time, declares that it is assumed here (as in other Jewish sources) that hope in the future resurrection

---

11. Gerhard von Rad, *Old Testament Theology*, vol. 1, trans. D. M. G. Stalker (New York: Harper & Row, 1962), 142 n; see also William Brown, "Creation," in *Eerdmans Dictionary of the Bible*, ed. Allen Myers et al. (Grand Rapids: Eerdmans, 2000), 293.

12. Hans Schwarz, *Creation* (Grand Rapids: Eerdmans, 2002), 172–73.

13. N. Joseph Torchia, *Creatio ex nihilo and the Theology of St. Augustine: The Anti-Manichean Polemic and Beyond* (New York: Peter Lang, 1999), 2.

14. See Jonathan A. Goldstein, *II Maccabees*, AB 41A (Garden City, N.Y.: Doubleday, 1983), 307–15. David deSilva follows Goldstein's line of reasoning in *Introducing the Apocrypha* (Grand Rapids: Baker, 2002), 140–41. Against this, see Otfried Hofius, "Die Gottesprädikationen Röm 4,17b," in *Paulusstudien II*, Wissenschaftliche Untersuchungen zum Neuen Testament 143 (Tübingen: Mohr/Siebeck, 2002), 58–61; see also J. C. O'Neill, "How Early Is the Doctrine of *Creatio ex Nihilo?*" *Journal of Theological Studies* 53, no. 2 (Oct. 2002): 449–53.

15. O'Neill, "How Early Is the Doctrine of *Creatio ex Nihilo?*" 452 n.

16. See O'Neill's rebuttal of Goldstein on 2 Macc. 7:28 ("How Early Is the Doctrine of *Creatio ex Nihilo?*" 449–53).

17. Nahum M. Sarna, *Genesis*, JPS Torah Commentary (New York: Jewish Publication Society, 1989), 5.

was grounded upon the creation of the world out of nothing[18]—the very connection made by Paul in Romans 4:17.[19]

Several points are in order. *First,* though the influence of Hellenism was pervasive, we must not infer that worldview distinctives among Palestinian Jews—such as the firm belief in the eternality of God alone—were thoroughly undermined at every point. At first glance, the apocryphal book Wisdom of Solomon (11:17) appears to posit a formless archmatter:[20] God created "out of formless matter [*ex amorphou hylēs*]" (NRSV). This may be true, but even here, we should proceed with caution. In Wisdom 1:14, there could be in view a two-stage creation: "he created all things [*ektisen . . . ta panta*] that they might have being [*to einai*]" (NEB). Wisdom 9:1 speaks of the "God of our fathers" who has "made all things by [his] word" (NEB). It is plausible to argue that the *hylē* (primal matter) out of which the cosmos was made was the uninhabited "earth [*gē*]," which was already created in Genesis 1:1. God shaped the world out of material he previously created.[21]

For the sake of argument, however, let us assume that Wisdom holds to this Greek hylomorphism (i.e., an eternally preexistent substrate is given form) and that a two-stage *ex nihilo* creation is completely excluded. We can still make a contrast here in that "the Palestinian [perspective] (II Macc. vii. 28) insists that all was made by God 'out of nothing.'"[22] According to Claus Westermann, the Jewish understanding of creation was that "the world as a whole can only be understood in the context of its coming into being."[23]

Westermann, who sees 2 Maccabees 7:28 as clearly affirming *creatio ex nihilo,* claims that it is no accident that this idea should arise in a Hellenistic setting in defense of a biblical worldview ("God created the heavens and the earth").[24] In Genesis 1:1, the idea of matter's preexisting

18. Hofius, "Röm 4,17b," 61: "Diese Hoffnung wird . . . auf die Erschaffung der Welt aus dem Nichts begründet." Hofius observes that creation out of nothing is assumed in various passages such as *Joseph and Aseneth* 12:2; cf. 20:7; 2 Maccabees 7:23, 28–29; 2 (Syriac Apocalypse of) Baruch 14:17; 21:4; 48:8; cf. *Apostolic Constitutions* 8.12.7.

19. Ibid., 61.

20. Kaufmann Kohler and Emil G. Hirsch, "Creation," in *Jewish Encyclopedia* (published 1901–06), available online at www.jewishencyclopedia.com/index.jsp. The article on creation is at www.jewishencyclopedia.com/view.jsp?artid=853&letter=C.

21. O'Neill, "How Early Is the Doctrine of *Creatio ex Nihilo?*" 455–56.

22. Kohler and Hirsch, "Creation."

23. Claus Westermann, *Creation,* trans. John J. Scullion (Philadelphia: Fortress, 1974), 36.

24. Westermann adds that some within Judaism did come to be influenced around this time to think of eternal formless matter before creation (cf. Wisdom 11:17), but again, if a two-stage creation is possible here, then this can be readily incorporated into a creation *ex nihilo* perspective (as Wisdom 1:14 seems to suggest).

creation was not in the thinking of the writer,[25] and this antidualistic thinking permeates the OT. O'Neill contends that despite common scholarly commendation of the fine reasoning of the mother of seven sons, "she is commonly not allowed to be theologian enough to deploy the doctrine of *creatio ex nihilo.*"[26]

Second, to say that God created both (1) the heaven and earth *and* (2) human beings from primordial matter is simply incorrect. It is not uncommon to hear people declare that, based on Genesis 2, God did not create human beings out of nothing, but rather out of the dust of the ground, which is not *ex nihilo.* It would be incorrect, however, to declare that human beings were made from eternally preexisting amorphous matter ("from things which did not exist," as 2 Macc. 7:28 puts it), as "the heavens and the earth" allegedly were. The dust of the ground was *already* created by God; the heavens and earth were created, and the dust of the ground is part of this creation. God had formed the dust of the earth, and thus man could not have been created "in the same way" as were the heavens and the earth. So "in the same way" refers to the very word and limitless power of God to create or bring into being what was not before.

Third, a very legitimate reading (and one used by Josephus and the early church fathers, as well as other Jewish exegetes) would be a *two-stage creation,* with the first stage created out of nothing. Then God would ultimately form or shape both (1) "the heavens and the earth" and (2) human beings from the substrate he had previously created *ex nihilo.*

Fourth, while the mother is not making a precise philosophical point, she is ascribing to God full sovereignty over creation, which would be compromised by a preexisting matter, eternally coeval with God. In his commentary on 2 Maccabees, John Bartlett declares that the point of the mother's declaration is this: if God can make the universe—and humankind in particular—*out of nothing,* then the mother (along with her child) may be sure that she will receive back her martyred offspring.[27] Xenophon (citing Socrates's eldest son Lamprocles) uses similar language to speak of children, who once did not exist but came into being by their parents—"whom parents cause to be out of nothing [*ek . . . ouk ontōn*]."[28] Where once there was no child, now there is a child. To assert that, "technically, children don't come from literally nothing" is to miss

25. Claus Westermann, *Genesis 1–11* (Minneapolis: Augsburg, 1984), 110.

26. O'Neill, "How Early Is the Doctrine of *Creatio ex Nihilo?*" 449.

27. John R. Bartlett, *The First and Second Books of the Maccabees* (Cambridge: Cambridge University Press, 1973), 276.

28. Xenophon, *Memorabilia* 2.2.3.

the point made by the mother in 2 Maccabees as well as by Lamprocles. What is in view is *absolute novelty*.[29] As we shall see below, early church fathers such as Theophilus of Antioch saw this text as clearly spelling out creation *ex nihilo*. Indeed, we can speak of a large number of scholars and exegetes who affirm that creation *ex nihilo* is found in this passage. For example, Bernhard Anderson sees the doctrine of *creatio ex nihilo* set forth here.[30] James Barr, too, sees this passage as a "deliberate expression" of creation out of nothing.[31] According to S. D. Luzzatto, God's creating out of nothing is first explicitly declared here.[32] In the *Oxford Companion to the Bible*, J. R. Porter also takes the view that creation out of nothing appears here.[33] Robert Oden Jr. comments in the *Anchor Bible Dictionary* that the formulation of creation *ex nihilo* first appears in postbiblical Judaism in 2 Maccabees 7:28.[34] Hermann Sasse admits this as well in another biblical dictionary.[35] In the *Theologische Realenzyklopädie*, we read that creation out of nothing is first set forth here.[36] Biblical scholar W. H. Schmidt agrees.[37] Another scholar, Craig A. Evans, notes in his work on

29. I follow O'Neill ("How Early Is the Doctrine of *Creatio ex Nihilo?*" 451). See his further argumentation in this essay.

30. Bernhard W. Anderson, *Contours of Old Testament Theology* (Minneapolis: Fortress, 1999), 87.

31. James Barr, "Was Everything That God Created Really Good? A Question in the First Verse of the Bible," in *God in the Fray*, ed. Tod Linafelt and Timothy K. Beal (Minneapolis: Fortress, 1998), 63.

32. S. D. Luzzatto, *The Book of Genesis: A Commentary by ShaDal* [S. D. Luzzatto], trans. Daniel A. Klein (Northvale, N.J.: Jason Aronson, 1998), 3.

33. J. R. Porter, "Creation," in *The Oxford Companion to the Bible*, ed. Bruce M. Metzger and Michael D. Coogan (New York: Oxford University Press, 1993), 140. Anglican priest and physicist John Polkinghorne sees 2 Maccabees 7:28 as the "earliest unequivocal statement of the idea of creation out of nothing." Nevertheless, he believes that Genesis 1 stresses at least "the dependence of all upon the sovereign will of God for its existence," which is "certainly consonant with the central significance of *creatio ex nihilo*" (*Reason and Reality* [Philadelphia: Trinity Press International, 1991], 72). Stanley Jaki sees this passage as containing "the first biblical appearance of the phrase 'creation out of nothing'" (*The Savior of Science* [Washington, D.C.: Regnery, 1988], 65).

34. Robert A. Oden Jr., "Cosmogony, Cosmology," in *ABD*, 1:1166.

35. Hermann Sasse, *"Kosmos,"* in *TDNT*, 3:878.

36. Reinhard G. Kratz and Hermann Spieckermann, *"Schöpfer/Schöpfung* II," in *Theologische Realenzyklopädie* 30, no. 1 (Berlin: Walter de Gruyter, 1998), 270. The authors allow for a double creation in Scripture. Even if there is chaos, this does not negate creation out of nothing. The context of the quotation reads, "This does not imply that the Hebrew Old Testament excludes from the outset a creation out of nothing, which is first mentioned in 2 Maccabees 7:28, but reveals the self-sufficiency and creative shaping of chaos = *Das impliziert nicht den dem hebräischen Alten Testament fremden Gedanken einer Schöpfung aus dem Nichts, die erst II Makk 7,28 belegt ist, schließt aber die Eigenmächtigkeit und schöpferische Selbstentfaltung des Chaos vorherein aus.*"

37. W. H. Schmidt, *"br*ʾ, to create," *TLOT*, 1:256.

noncanonical writings that 2 Maccabees 7:28 may be the first to teach that God created the universe out of nothing.[38] The list goes on.

Suffice it to say that no small number of well-respected scholars see creation out of nothing clearly expressed here.

JUBILEES

Jubilees was written in Hebrew by a Pharisee somewhere between 135 and 105 BC.[39] In this book, God is not only the Creator of an ordered universe but also brings into existence the allegedly primordial, chaotic elements of darkness and the deep. *Jubilees* 2:2 says:

> For on the first day He created the heavens which are above and the earth and *the waters* and all the spirits which serve before him—the angels of the presence, and the angels of sanctification, and the angels [of the spirit of fire, and the angels] of the spirit of the winds, and the angels of the spirit of the clouds, and of *darkness*, and of snow and of hail and of hoar frost, and the angels of the voices and of the thunder and of the lightning, and the angels of the spirits of cold and of heat, and of winter and of spring and of autumn and of summer, and of all the spirits of his creatures which are in the heavens and on the earth; [he created] *the abysses and the darkness*, eventide [and night], and the light, dawn and day, which He hath prepared in the knowledge of his heart. [emphasis added]

This implication of creation *ex nihilo* is further reinforced in 2:16, which makes clear that God created everything in six days—including the *darkness* and the *deep* mentioned in Genesis 1:2: "And He finished all his work on the sixth day—all that is in the heavens and on the earth, and in the seas and in the abysses, and in the light and in the darkness, and in everything."

To round things out toward the end of the chapter, we observe the comprehensiveness of God's creation. Indeed, nothing is excluded: "He created heaven and earth and everything that he created in six days" (2:25). Truly, God is "Creator of all" (2:31).

In *Jubilees*, we see that nothing is excluded from the sweep of God's creation. It appears that an eternal dualism of God and some preexistent matter would have been intolerable to the writer.

SECOND ENOCH

Second Enoch was written in the second or perhaps early third century by a Jew in Egypt. Some suggest the date may go back even to the

38. Craig A. Evans, *Noncanonical Writings and New Testament Interpretation* (Peabody, Mass.: Hendrickson, 1992), 17.
39. Ibid., 31.

late first century AD.[40] This work, too, reflects the doctrine of creation out of nothing in several places. In 24:1, the Lord summons Enoch to sit on his left with Gabriel. Enoch bows down to the Lord, who then tells him: "Enoch, beloved, all that you see, all things that are standing finished I tell to you even before the very beginning, all that I created from nonbeing, and visible things from invisible" (24:2).

Admittedly, there are some odd (and even bizarre) speculations offered in the account of creation in *2 Enoch*, but there is no dualism presupposed in this book. Any invisible entities are clearly created by God, who alone exists from eternity.

Before God created the "visible creation," he moved about among "invisible things" such as the sun, which moves "from east to west, and from west to east" (24:4). Clearly, the sun is part of the creation of God, as Genesis 1 makes clear. Indeed, "the invisible things" are not some eternally preexistent elements distinct from God. Rather, the sun is part of "all things" that God creates (24:5).

Indeed, we see in *2 Enoch* an apparent two-stage creation. First God makes "invisible things" (such as the sun). Then God makes "visible things," as in laying the earth's foundations: "But even the sun has peace in itself, while I found no peace, because I was creating all things, and I conceived the thought of placing foundations, and of creating visible creation" (24:5).

In the next chapter, God "commanded . . . that visible things should come down from invisible" (25:1). What is this invisible thing? It is the *adoil*—the light of creation ("above the light there is nothing else" [25:5]). God then commands: "Let the visible come out of you" (25:2). Again, while the language of this extrabiblical passage may strike us as rather odd, it expresses the belief that the light—whether invisible or visible—is a creation of God.

In chapter 26, God commands, "Let one of the invisible things come out solid and visible" (26:1). *Archas*—the spirit of creation—is called forth to make the foundation for lower things. In parallel to the light, there is "nothing else" below the darkness (26:4). Again, the suggestion is that *both* light and darkness are the creation of God; in chapter 27, the light and the darkness are separated. That light and darkness (which are "invisible") are God's creation is reinforced in 32:1: "I blessed all my creatures visible and invisible."

Unlike his creation (whether heavenly or earthly), which is transient, God alone is eternal, uncreated, and unchanging:

40. Ibid., 23.

All that you have understood, all that you have seen of heavenly things, all that you have seen on earth, and all that I have written in books by my great wisdom, all these things I have devised and created from the uppermost foundation to the lower and to the end, and there is no counselor nor inheritor to my creations. I am self-eternal, not made with hands, and without change. My thought is my counselor, my wisdom and my word are made, and my eyes observe all things how they stand here and tremble with terror. If I turn away my face, then all things will be destroyed. (33:2–5)

The self-existent God holds all things in being. The invisible God is the Maker of all things distinct from himself—whether visible or invisible: "All this he measured, with good measurement of hours, and fixed a measure by his wisdom, of the visible and the invisible. From the invisible he made all things visible, himself being invisible" (48:4–5).

Toward the end of *2 Enoch*, we read of Enoch speaking to his people of the comprehensiveness of God's creation. He did not create everything visible from some eternal, invisible substrate. He created *both* visible and invisible things: "Hear, my children, before that all creatures were created, the Lord created the visible and invisible things" (65:1). Even if "nothingness" or "the void" (as many Greeks believed) were an existing entity and thus not literally nothing, then God would have been the Creator of this as well as all things visible.

Thus, we observe here the ontological distinction between God and everything else (i.e., his creation). Further, creation is understood to have taken place in stages, in which God brings into existence all things and then forms them into an orderly universe.

JOSEPH AND ASENETH

The Jewish pseudepigraphal book *Joseph and Aseneth*, from around the first century AD and with language resembling that of the Dead Sea Scrolls,[41] contains a passage that also implies *creatio ex nihilo*. Indeed, it is strikingly similar to passages in *2 Enoch*, reflecting that God created everything, whether visible or invisible.

Aseneth, having thrown her idols out of the window and put on sackcloth for a week, addresses the God of Joseph:

Lord God of the ages,
who created all (things) and gave life (to them),
who gave breath of life to your whole creation,
who brought the invisible (things) out into the light,

---

41. James H. Charlesworth, *The Pseudepigrapha and Modern Research*, Septuagint and Cognate Studies 7 (Chico, Calif.: Scholars, 1981), 137.

who made the (things that) are and the (ones that) have an appearance
from the non-appearing and non-being,
who lifted up the heaven
and founded it on a firmament upon the back of the winds.
. . . .
For you, Lord, spoke and they were brought to life,
because your word, Lord, is life for all your creatures. (12:1–3)

Again, we read that God created all things and brought everything
into being. The sweeping comprehensiveness is difficult to avoid. As is
common in extrabiblical books such as this, God is the Maker of things
visible and invisible. It is God's powerful word that causes anything to
exist at all.

SECOND BARUCH/THE SYRIAC APOCALYPSE OF BARUCH

In the early second century, the Jewish author of 2 Baruch wrote to
encourage Diaspora Jews.[42] While doing so, he in various places expresses
an implicit belief in creation out of nothing.

In chapter 14, "our Creator" is being addressed. "When of old there
was no world with its inhabitants, you did devise and speak with a word,
and forthwith the works of creation stood before you" (14:17). We notice
here that, as with the NT, first there was nothing; God spoke; and then
creation came into being.

In 21:4, God is addressed once again: "O thou that hast made the
earth, . . . that hast fixed the firmament by the word [cf. Ps. 33:6], . . .
that hast called from the beginning of the world that which did not yet
exist." In his dissertation on 2 Baruch, Frederick James Murphy comments that *creatio ex nihilo* is being expressed here, indicating that the
present visible world is not eternal. It had a beginning.[43]

In chapter 48, the enduring power of God's word is seen—in contrast
to the temporal creation:

O my Lord, you summon the advent of the times,
And they stand before you;
You cause the power of the ages to pass away,
And they do not resist you. (48:2)

Verse 8 continues this emphasis on God's power:

And with a word you quicken that which was not,
And with mighty power you hold that which has not yet come.

42. Evans, *Noncanonical Writings*, 26.
43. Frederick James Murphy, *The Structure and Meaning of Second Baruch*, SBL Dissertation Series (Atlanta: Scholars Press, 1985), 43.

Indeed, in all of these passages, Werner Foerster observes, creation out of nothing is "plainly taught."[44]

Other Jewish Sources

JOSEPHUS

In his works, the first-century Jewish historian Josephus (ca. AD 38–100) describes God as "being himself one, uncreated, eternally unchanging."[45] Josephus uses the term *dēmiourgos* to refer to the "Creator of the universe [*dēmiourgos tōn holōn*]" and "the creator of universal being [*dēmiourgos tēs holēs*]."[46] In our chapter on the OT witness, we showed that a two-step (double) creation is not an implausible or inelegant reading of the creative process. Even in the NT (e.g., 2 Peter 3:5), a two-stage creation is quite possible.

Although strangely unnoticed in the scholarly discussion about creation *ex nihilo*, Josephus holds to two stages in creation—but ultimately with an absolute beginning. In his *Jewish Antiquities,* he declares that God first created everything/the universe ("In the beginning God created the heaven and the earth") and then completes the creation:

> In the beginning God created the heaven and the earth [*En archē ektisen ho theos ton ouranon kai tēn gēn*]; but when the earth did not come into sight, but was covered with thick darkness, and a wind moved upon its surface, God commanded that there should be light; and when that was made, he considered the whole mass/matter [*hylēn*], and separated the light and the darkness; the name he gave to one was *Night,* and the other he called *Day.*[47]

This text is identical to the LXX's rendering of Genesis 1:1, which Josephus reads as *absolute* rather than *construct.* Second, the clear implication is that although God created heaven and earth in the beginning, the creation moves forward in stages. God shapes the "mass" or "matter [*hylēn*]" that he has created. So God continues the creative process he initiated—the implication seems obvious—*ex nihilo.* Josephus sees God as originally bringing about the very materials used in the further creative process.

---

44. Werner Foerster mentions 2 Baruch 14:17; 21:4–8.; and 48:2–8 ("*ktizō,*" *TDNT,* 3:1017).
45. Josephus, *Against Apion* 2.16 (166–168).
46. Josephus, *Jewish Antiquities* 1.155; 1.272.
47. Ibid., 1.1.

DEAD SEA SCROLLS

The Dead Sea Scrolls (250 BC–AD 68) produced by the Qumran community present yet another set of Jewish writings in which an *ex nihilo* understanding of creation is assumed. For example, we see creation out of nothing assumed in the *Rule of the Community:*

> From the God of knowledge stems all there is and all there shall be. Before they existed he made all their plans, and when they came into being, they will execute all their works in compliance with his instructions, according to his glorious design without altering anything. (1QS 3.15–16)[48]

Gottfried Nebe sees this passage as supportive of creation *ex nihilo.* Here we find "the connection of creation by God and ontological terms and ideas [e.g., 'all there is . . . and shall be,' 'existed,' and 'came into being']."[49] Another quotation from the same scroll (1QS 11.11) echoes this same idea of God's absolute creation:

> By his knowledge everything shall come into being,
> and all that does exist
> he establishes with his calculations
> and nothing is done outside of him.

The Qumran writings notably stress God's absolute sovereignty: God creates for his own glory, and the very being of the universe originates from him. "[Without you] nothing is done, and nothing is known without your will" (1QH 9.8). Not only has God created everything physical, but the invisible realm of spirits as well: "You have fashioned every spirit" (1QH 9.20–31). In 1QH 9.14, even the "seas and deeps" and "everything which is in them" have been founded by the wisdom of God. This is reinforced in the "War Scroll," which declares that God created absolutely everything—the "earth," the "laws of its divisions," the "circle of the sea," the "reservoirs of the rivers," as well as "the chasm of the abyss" (1QM 10.13). Thus, the waters are not some primordial element uncreated by God.

One cannot escape the comprehensive scope of God's creation. Everything apart from God is creature. This totalistic emphasis is obvious in 1QS 3.15: "From the God of knowledge stems all there is and all there shall be."

48. Cited in Florentino García Martínez, *The Dead Sea Scrolls Translated,* 2d ed. (Leiden: Brill, 1996), 6. All other citations are taken from this translation.

49. Gottfried Nebe, "Creation in Paul's Theology," in *Creation in Jewish and Christian Tradition,* ed. Henning Graf Reventlow and Yair Hoffman, JSOT Supplement Series 319 (Sheffield: Sheffield Academic Press, 2002), 119 n.

This segment from 1QH 9 reinforces the theme of God's comprehensive creation:

> And in the wisdom of your knowledge
> you have determined their [humans'] course
> before they came to exist.
> And with [your approval] everything occurs
> And without you nothing occurs. (9.19–20)

God's creative action takes place by his wisdom (and power)—not from preexisting materials. Reading the *Psalms Scroll* (11Q5 26.9–15) praising the Creator, we see that God "established the dawn with the knowledge of his heart"; he "made the earth with his strength" and established "the world with his wisdom." "With his knowledge he spread out the heavens."[50] God's uncontested power in creation is strongly emphasized.[51] As Devorah Dimant states, "Creation is the materialization of the divine plan so establishing its total submission to God."[52] Again, we are pointed toward creation *ex nihilo* rather than away from it.

In light of all of these texts, Dead Sea Scrolls scholar Craig A. Evans concludes:[53]

> We should assume, unless there is good reason to think otherwise, that thinking at Qumran (touching the Godhead, eschatology, atonement, etc.) is pretty much mainstream Jewish. I see nothing in the Scrolls that deviates from the expressions found in the [above texts]. I think it highly probable that the men of Qumran believed in creation *ex nihilo*. The DSS texts [cited above] are quite compatible with this belief, even if they don't quite express it. Creation was not part of the debate that occasioned the emergence of the Qumran sect (understanding the covenant and the priesthood was—therefore they are talked about a lot); so it is not surprising that next to nothing is said about [creation].

The Dead Sea Scrolls, therefore, furnish us with further support for the belief that God and his creation are all the reality there are. *Ex nihilo* creation would have been assumed by the Qumran community.

50. For a brief discussion of the doctrine of creation in the Qumran texts, see Daniel J. Harrington, "Creation," in *Encyclopedia of the Dead Sea Scrolls*, 2 vols., ed. Lawrence H. Schiffman and James C. VanderKam (Oxford: Oxford University Press, 2000), 1:155–57.

51. Alex Deasley, *The Shape of Qumran Theology* (Carlisle: Paternoster, 2000), 161.

52. Devorah Dimant, "Qumran Sectarian Literature," in *Jewish Writings of the Second Temple Period*, vol. 2, ed. M. E. Stone, Compendia rerum judaicarum ad Novum Testamentum (Leiden: Brill, 1984), 533.

53. Personal correspondence, Nov. 2001.

THIRD MACCABEES

This book, sharing the flavor of 2 Maccabees, was written in the vicinity of Alexandria, Egypt, around the first century BC–first century AD.[54] As is typical, the comprehensiveness of creation language is quite apparent and in keeping with OT monotheism. For example, we read: "Lord, Lord, King of heaven and Ruler of all creation [*despota pasēs ktiseōs*]. . . . You who created all things and govern the whole world" (3 Macc. 2:2–3). Later in the chapter, God is called "the Ruler of all creation" and then the One who oversees "all things" and is the "first Father of all"—clearly "all" without exception (3 Macc. 2:7, 21).

While *3 Maccabees* presents minimal material about the subject at hand, what we do read fits quite well with the idea that God created everything. Nothing—except for God—is outside the realm of creation.

PHILO OF ALEXANDRIA

Philo (10 BC–AD 50) is something of an enigma, and there are scholars on both sides of the debate. As Gerhard May has written, "The debate on whether Philo of Alexandria already taught creation out of nothing seems to continue unabated."[55] The notable Philo scholar David T. Runia admits that the question of whether or not Philo subscribes to *creatio ex nihilo* is "one of the most controversial topics in Philonic studies, on which so far no consensus has emerged."[56] Some assert that Philo's thought was so steeped in Middle Platonic thought (especially through the *Timaeus*) that his view on creation ultimately entailed the eternal preexistence of primordial stuff, which God shaped into an orderly cosmos.[57] (Gerhard May himself believes, incorrectly, that Philo was following Stoic theory in his understanding of creation.)[58]

Philo, commenting on Genesis 1:27, writes, "You prepared a soul for him out of nonbeing." Gregory E. Sterling (who purports to follow Gerhard May's analysis) notes that this line appears to suggest that the soul was created *ex nihilo*. Yet he explains this passage (away?) as a "Christian redaction or [as a] formulaic expression that at an early date

54. Charlesworth, *Pseudepigrapha and Modern Research*, 149. It may have been written as early as the late second century BC. See H. Anderson, "3 Maccabees," in *Old Testament Pseudepigrapha* (ed. Charlesworth), 2:512.

55. May, *Creatio ex Nihilo*, viii–ix.

56. David T. Runia, *Philo of Alexandria: On the Creation of the Cosmos according to Moses*, Philo of Alexandria Commentary Series (Leiden: Brill, 2001), 152.

57. Gregory E. Sterling, "*Creatio Temporalis, Aeterna, vel Continua?* An Analysis of the Thought of Philo of Alexandria," *The Studia Philonica Annual* 4 (1992): 15–41.

58. May, *Creatio ex Nihilo*, 10 n. May makes this point regarding Philo's use of *ousia*, alleging that he borrowed from the Stoics. For a refutation, see O'Neill, "How Early Is the Doctrine of *Creatio ex Nihilo?*" 456–62.

expressed the distinctiveness of the biblical view of creation but did not signal the later Christian understanding of *creatio ex nihilo*."[59]

Other scholars such as Harry Wolfson,[60] Ronald Williamson,[61] Richard Sorabji,[62] J. C. O'Neill,[63] and James Barr[64] are of a different mind-set. In fact, they see Philo intentionally distancing his Mosaic thinking from that of "impious" thinkers. Thus we see Philo espousing creation out of nothing.

In book 2 of his *On the Creation of the World* (which Philo wrote around AD 30), he says:[65]

For some men, admiring the world itself rather than the Creator of the world [*ton kosmopoion*], have represented it as existing without any Maker, and eternal; and as impiously and falsely have represented God as existing in a state of complete inactivity, while it would have been right on the other hand to marvel at the might of God as the Creator and Father of all, and to admire the world in a degree not exceeding the bounds of moderation.

But Moses, who had early reached the very summits of philosophy, and who had learnt from the oracles of God the most numerous and important of the principles of nature, was well aware that it is indispensable that in all existing things there must be an active cause, and a passive subject; and that the active cause is the intellect of the universe, thoroughly unadulterated and thoroughly unmixed, superior to virtue and superior to science, superior even to abstract good or abstract beauty; while the passive subject is something inanimate and incapable of motion by any intrinsic power of its own, but having been set in motion, and fashioned, and endowed with life by the intellect, became transformed into that most perfect work, this world. *And those who describe it as being uncreated, do, without being aware of it, cut off the most useful and necessary of all the qualities which tend to produce piety, namely, providence: for reason proves that the Father and Creator has a care for that which has been created*; for a father is anxious for the life of his children, and a workman aims at the duration of his works, and employs every device imaginable to ward

59. Gregory E. Sterling, "Philo and Greek-Speaking Judaism," *The Studia Philonica Annual* 11 (1999): 17–18.

60. H. A. Wolfson, *Philo: Foundations of Religious Philosophy in Judaism, Christianity, and Islam*, 2 vols. (Cambridge: Harvard University Press, 1968).

61. Ronald Williamson, *Philo and the Epistle to the Hebrews* (Leiden: Brill, 1970).

62. Richard Sorabji, *Time, Creation, and the Continuum* (London: Duckworth, 1983).

63. O'Neill, "How Early Is the Doctrine of *Creatio ex Nihilo*?" 456–62.

64. Barr, "Was Everything That God Created Really Good?" 58. In this passage, Barr argues that Philo takes Genesis 1:1 to be absolute rather than construct, which, of course, strongly implies the doctrine of creation out of nothing.

65. This translation is from Oliver J. Thatcher, ed., *The Roman World*, vol. 3 of *The Library of Original Sources* (Milwaukee: University Research Extension, 1907) (emphasis added). Available online at www.fordham.edu/halsall/ancient/philo-creation.html.

off everything that is pernicious or injurious, and is desirous by every means in his power to provide everything which is useful or profitable for them. But with regard to that which has not been created, there is no feeling of interest as if it were his own in the breast of him who has not created it.

It is then a pernicious doctrine, and one for which no one should contend, to establish a system in this world, such as anarchy is in a city, so that it should have no superintendent, or regulator, or judge, by whom everything must be managed and governed.

But the great Moses, thinking that a thing which has not been created is as alien as possible from that which is visible before our eyes (for everything which is the subject of our senses exists in birth and in changes, and is not always in the same condition), has attributed eternity to that which is invisible and discerned only by our intellect as a kinsman and a brother, while of that which is the object of our external senses he had predicated generation as an appropriate description. Since, then, this world is visible and the object of our external senses, it follows of necessity that it must have been created [*genētos*]; on which account it was not without a wise purpose that he recorded its creation, giving a very venerable account of God. (2.7–12)

Philo scholar David T. Runia renders the italicized passage (above) thus:

> Those who declare that the cosmos is ungenerated are unaware that they are eliminating the most useful and indispensable of the contributions to piety, the (doctrine of) providence. Reason demands that the Father and Maker exercise care for that which has come into being.[66]

In our judgment, Philo repudiates the idea that anything apart from God can be ungenerated and eternal. Moreover, he self-consciously places himself under the authority of Moses, even if this runs counter to the philosophers. He goes on to speak of Moses, who considered what is ungenerated to be of a completely different order from what is visible. What is invisible and intelligible is assigned to "eternity"; what is sense-perceptible has a beginning.[67] There seems to be a two-step process of creation. Theologian Colin Gunton sees in Philo a "two stage creation" in which God first creates the intelligible world of Forms and then the material or sensible world.[68]

66. Philo, *On the Creation of the Cosmos* 2.9–10, §48. Translations of this work and further Philonic passages are from Runia, *Philo of Alexandria*, loc. cit.

67. Philo, *On the Creation of the Cosmos* 2.12, §49.

68. Colin E. Gunton, *The Triune Creator: A Historical and Systematic Study* (Grand Rapids: Eerdmans, 1998), 46.

This certainly is a sensible interpretation of Philo, who later even writes that God created invisible things before creating the visible:

First, therefore, the Maker made an incorporeal heaven and an invisible earth and a form of air and of the void. To the former he assigned the name darkness, since the air is black by nature, to the latter the name abyss, because the void is indeed full of depths and gaping.[69]

Indeed, the "abyss," "the void," and "darkness" are the "elements" mentioned in Genesis 1:2. They are not eternal elements, existing independently of the Creator. God creates them and then shapes these into a cosmos, ordering and separating and beautifying. Even if they are at first invisible, God is clearly the Creator at every stage.

Regarding the relationship of time to creation, Philo writes in the beginning of book 7 that time either came into existence in the beginning (Gen. 1:1) or after it. To say that time is older than the world is utterly inconsistent with philosophy.

At the end of *On the Creation of the World,* Philo presents five "vital lessons," of which we mention three:[70] The first is that "the divinity is and exists." Second, "God is one, on account of those who introduce polytheistic opinion." Third, "the cosmos has come into existence, on account of those who think it is ungenerated and eternal, attributing no superiority to God." What is obvious is Philo's fierce monotheism—that nothing can exist alongside the eternal and ungenerated God.

In the last paragraph of his work, Philo proclaims that "God is and exists, and that he who truly exists is one, and that he made the cosmos and made it unique, . . . similar to himself in respect of its being one."[71] Truly, it would seem odd to declare an eternal, preexistent matter that exists apart from God's begetting it. It is such a dualism that Philo rejects, given his monotheism. Indeed, Runia says that in places, Philo's position is "more coherent if coupled with the doctrine of *creatio ex nihilo.*"[72]

According to Harvard Philo scholar Harry Wolfson, Philo, on the basis of Scripture, distances himself from pure Platonism when he says that "neither before creation was there anything with God, nor, when the world had come into being, does anything take place with Him, for there is absolutely nothing which He needs."[73]

---

69. *On the Creation of the Cosmos* 6.29, 53. Thus, Philo later mentions that God expends the "available material"—that which he has earlier made—"for the genesis of the whole" (25.171, §§92–93).

70. Ibid., 25.171–72, §§92–93.

71. Ibid., 25.172, §93.

72. Runia, *Philo of Alexandria,* 159.

73. Wolfson, *Philo,* 1:172. See Harry A. Wolfson, "Plato's Pre-existent Matter in Patristic Philosophy," in *The Classical Tradition,* ed. Luitpold Wallach (Ithaca, N.Y.: Cornell University Press, 1966), 418.

Wolfson points out that Philo established three principles:

1. God alone is uncreated, whereas all other beings are created by God.
2. Nothing is coeternal with God.
3. Eternity means deity.[74]

As we shall see below, these "Philonic principles" were adopted by Christianity with the qualification that the divine Logos and Wisdom of God, the second person of the Trinity, coexisted with God as God from eternity.[75] Church fathers such as Justin, Theophilus, Basil, Tertullian, Irenaeus, and Augustine would uniformly hold to them without debate. In their minds, to say that something besides God is unbegotten is idolatrous or blasphemous.[76]

Hence, on the doctrine of creation, Philo does not sell out to Greek philosophy. Ronald Williamson asserts, "It is probable that Philo thought of the material out of which God fashioned the visible universe as created *ex nihilo* by God."[77] In his work on Philo, Wolfson takes pains to show how Philo differentiates his own viewpoint from Plato's *Timaeus* by holding that God created primordial matter *ex nihilo* before shaping it into an orderly creation.[78] Williamson concurs with Wolfson. While Philo interpreted Genesis 1 with Plato's *Timaeus* in mind (e.g., Philo's understanding of primordial matter [*hylē*] is the same as Plato's), the crucial point is that he *re*interpreted the *Timaeus* in light of "traditional Jewish belief in a creation *ex nihilo*."[79] According to Williamson, "It seems to me that Wolfson has proved his case."[80]

While we take care not to be dogmatic,[81] we have good reasons to see a creation *ex nihilo* in Philo. David Runia's own view is that "Philo does

74. Wolfson, "Plato's Pre-existent Matter," 414.
75. Ibid., 415. Within Christianity the idea was accepted that the Son was "eternally begotten" or "eternally generated." For a discussion of this, see John S. Feinberg, *No One Like Him: The Doctrine of God* (Wheaton, Ill.: Crossway Books, 2001), 485–92.
76. Tertullian claimed that because eternity is "a property of God, it will belong to God alone"; and "if another also shared in the possession, there would be as many gods as there were possessors of these properties of God" (*Against Hermogenes* 4). Basil states it pointedly: "If matter were uncreated, then it would from the very first be of a rank equal to that of God and would deserve the same veneration" (*Hexaemeron* 2.4). For similar comments from the church fathers, see below.
77. Williamson, *Philo and the Epistle to the Hebrews*, 375–76.
78. See Wolfson, *Philo*.
79. Williamson, *Philo and the Epistle to the Hebrews*, 374.
80. Ibid., 373.
81. For example, Thomas H. Tobin discusses varying interpretations of Philo's concept of creation in "Interpretations of the Creation of the World in Philo of Alexandria," in

not give a clear answer to the question of the origin of matter." Nevertheless, Runia asserts that "this view does not mean that Philo accepts matter as a principle next to God"—something he emphatically denies in *On the Creation of the World* 2.7–8.[82] Even Gerhard May admits, "When Philo postulates the pre-existence of matter, he in no way envisages it as an ontologically equal principle alongside God. There is no question with him of a specific dualism."[83]

In the *Jewish Encyclopedia*, Kohler and Hirsch acknowledge:

> Philo is not rigidly consistent. There are passages . . . from which a belief in the creation of matter out of nothing might be assumed. He speaks of matter as corruptible, and "corruptible" is, in his theory, a correlative of "created." . . . It was not matter, but form, that God praised as good, and acknowledged thus as His creative work. Yet Philo protests that God is "not a demiurge, but a creator." What before was not, He made.[84]

Moreover, this creation out of nothing has a temporal beginning. In a nice summary, Peter Frick makes a strong case for holding that Philo held to the universe's temporal beginning; God alone is eternal and unbegotten, and there was, in Philo's view, a time when the world was not since whatever begins is destructible (though God providentially sustains it in being).[85]

It seems, then, that we cannot dismiss this ancient Jewish author as an irrelevant witness to creation out of nothing. At present, Philo cannot be ruled out as another possible Jewish witness to the doctrine of creation out of nothing.[86] In fact, the claim that Philo just assumed the eternality of matter is actually *undermined* by his belief that God created the visible world out of the intangible and invisible world of Forms (presumably in his mind).[87] No preexisting matter is even used. In light of all this, the likelihood of creation out of nothing in Philo is indeed great.[88]

Creation in the Biblical Traditions, ed. Richard J. Clifford and John J. Collins, Catholic Biblical Quarterly Monograph Series 24 (Washington, D.C.: Catholic Biblical Association of America, 1992), 108–28.

82. Runia, *Philo of Alexandria*, 153.

83. May, *Creatio ex Nihilo*, 15.

84. For detailed documentation, see Kohler and Hirsch, "Creation."

85. Peter Frick, *Divine Providence in Philo of Alexandria* (Tübingen: Mohr Siebeck, 1999), 94–108.

86. Runia says that Philo could hold to a creation *ex nihilo* even if this creation did not happen in time (*Philo of Alexandria*, 156–62).

87. In *On the Creation of the World* 6, Philo writes that the archetypal (and invisible) model of the world comes from the mind or reason of God.

88. O'Neill, "How Early Is the Doctrine of *Creatio ex Nihilo*?" 459–60.

RABBAN GAMALIEL II

One first-century rabbi (who taught ca. AD 90–110), Rabban Gamaliel II, expresses the concept of creation in a dispute. A philosopher challenged him to think of God, who like a painter had preexistent materials at his disposal: "Your God was indeed a great artist, but he had good materials [unformed space/void, darkness, water, wind, and the deep] to help him." Gamaliel, wishing that this philosopher's spirit would burst (or "give up the ghost"),[89] declared, "All of them are explicitly described as having been created by him [and not as preexistent]."[90]

After an interchange between Jonathan Goldstein and David Winston, Goldstein (despite some recantations and adjustments of his position) strongly defends his reading of *creatio ex nihilo* in Gamaliel's statement over against Winston.[91] He affirms that "the patriarch Rabban Gamaliel asserted the doctrine [of creation *ex nihilo*] unambiguously, within a few decades after the destruction of the temple in 70 CE."[92]

Winston's arguments against that understanding are weak. In a later essay on monotheism (interacting with the Winston-Goldstein debate), Peter Hayman sides with Winston and—in a strange distortion—announces Goldstein's "conceding the weakness of his position."[93] But this is misleading. Among other errors,[94] Hayman fails to address the question of Rabban Gamaliel II, as Goldstein staunchly defends his interpretation and offers corrections to some of Winston's "untenable" arguments.

For instance, in response to Winston's claim that Gamaliel is objecting to the philosopher's suggestion of polytheism, not to eternal matter, Goldstein replies:

89. This translation is from Jonathan A. Goldstein in "Creation *ex nihilo*: Recantations and Restatements," *Journal of Jewish Studies* 38 (autumn 1987): 189.

90. Unformed space/void was formed by God (Isa. 45:7), as were darkness (Isa. 45:7), water (Ps. 148:4–5), wind (Amos 4:13), and the depths (Prov. 8:24, 28). This translation is from Jacob Neusner, *Confronting Creation* (Columbia: University of South Carolina Press, 1991), 41–42.

91. David Winston, "The Book of Wisdom's Theory of Cosmogony," *History of Religions* (1971): 185–202; Jonathan Goldstein, "The Origins of the Doctrine of Creation *Ex Nihilo*," *Journal of Jewish Studies* 35 (1984): 127–35; David Winston, "*Creation Ex Nihilo* Revisited: A Reply to Jonathan Goldstein," *Journal of Jewish Studies* 37 (1986): 88–92; and Goldstein, "Creation *ex nihilo*," 187–94.

92. Goldstein, "Creation *ex nihilo*," 187.

93. Peter Hayman, "Monotheism—A Misused Word in Jewish Studies," *Journal of Jewish Studies* 42 (1991): 3.

94. Richard Bauckham points out that Hayman overstates his case (*God Crucified: Monotheism and Christology in the New Testament* [Grand Rapids: Eerdmans, 1998], 18). See also idem, "First-Century Jewish Monotheism," *Journal for the Study of the New Testament* 71 (1998): 3–26; and idem, "Jesus, Worship of," in *ABD*, 3:812–19.

The philosopher compares God to a painter . . . working with pigments. . . . The pigments enter only as material use by the Painter. Nothing in the text suggests that the pigments have will and power. Winston stresses that the verb "help" . . . is ambiguous and can refer to active powers as well as inactive instruments. The ambiguity of the verb is unimportant because the nouns are unambiguous: we deal here with a Painter and with pigments. The passage can only be a protest against the doctrine of creation from pre-existent matter, not a protest against a theory that other active powers participated with God in creation.[95]

There is no good reason to deny what Goldstein first declared about Gamaliel's belief in creation *ex nihilo*—that it is "unequivocally" stated.[96]

Even Gerhard May himself sees in Gamaliel II a reference to creation out of nothing:

Gamaliel refutes this [philosopher's] scheme by pointing out that all the available primitive stuffs named by the philosopher are described in the Bible expressly as created by God. Gamaliel thus denies that Genesis 1:2 refers to unformed matter and thereby implicitly asserts *creatio ex nihilo*.[97]

Hence, despite the existence and influence of Middle Platonism during the time of all of these writings, we must resist the thesis that Platonic ideas were embedded in the minds of these Jews such that they saw the Bible and Platonism as one and the same. In addition, Jewish thought was preoccupied with the *theological* rather than the *philosophical*, with the God of the cosmos rather than with the cosmos itself, with the *creatio* rather than the *ex nihilo*.[98] The OT writers viewed natural phenomena primarily as pointers to God, who created them and whose glory was revealed through them. Even if belief in *creatio ex nihilo* was not expressed with philosophical precision, such a belief would not have been foreign to the faithful Hebrew (and early Christian) mentality.[99]

HELLENISTIC SYNAGOGAL PRAYERS

According to James Charlesworth, prayers found in the collection of ecclesiastical ordinances known as the *Apostolic Constitutions* were probably compiled in Syria by AD 380. Several scholars have recognized

95. See Goldstein, "Creation *ex nihilo*," 187, 189. See also O'Neill's comments on Winston in "How Early Is the Doctrine of *Creatio ex Nihilo*?" 461.

96. Goldstein, "Origins of the Doctrine of Creation *ex Nihilo*," 133.

97. May, *Creatio ex Nihilo*, 23.

98. For this point I am grateful to D. A. Carson, personal conversation, May 1994.

99. O'Neill declares that the doctrine of creation out of nothing was not merely implicit but was explicitly formulated in 2 Maccabees 7:28, in Philo, and in the Dead Sea Scrolls ("How Early Is the Doctrine of *Creatio ex Nihilo*?" 463).

that book 7 (and book 8) of the *Constitutions* contains prayers resembling the Jewish prayer book used in Diaspora Judaism, perhaps from around AD 150. These are known as the "Hellenistic Synagogal Prayers."[100]

Book 7 contains the typical Jewish blessing: "Blessed are you, O Lord, king of the ages who made everything."[101] A two-stage creation is presupposed in that God fashioned the world from "that which was unprepared."[102] In book 8, the sweep of creation—including the "un-prepared" materials—come into being from the eternal God: the "one who is truly God" is "the one who is before things that have been made, . . . the only one without origin, and without a beginning." The "eternal God" is the one through whom "all things" have been made. He is "first by nature and only one in being."[103] God alone is eternal; everything else comes about through him.

Although we must not press the dating too forcefully, we appear to have some basis for another relevant support for a Jewish source suggesting creation *ex nihilo*.

MEDIEVAL JEWISH EXEGETES

One might think bringing into the discussion the ideas of medieval Jewish thinkers is irrelevant to our discussion since this period of time is well past the era of formulating the doctrine of creation out of nothing by Christian theologians. But it is not uncommon to hear scholars call in these exegetes in the defense of creation *ex materia*, claiming that these exegetes did not believe in creation out of nothing. Though he sees *creatio ex nihilo* in Gamaliel II, Jonathan Goldstein is sometimes invoked on this front: "Medieval Jewish thinkers still held that the account of creation in Genesis could be interpreted to mean that God created from pre-existing formless matter."[104] Everett Fox, who translates Genesis 1:1

---

100. Charlesworth, "Hellenistic Synagogal Prayers," in *The Old Testament Pseudepigrapha*, 2:671–97, listing (on 671) the following scholars who maintained this view of borrowing/adapting from Jewish liturgy: K. Kohler, W. Bousset, and E. R. Goodenough (cf. 690 n).

101. *Apostolic Constitutions* 7.34.1. "Through Christ" is "clearly" a later interpolation: "King of the ages, who *through Christ* made everything" (Charlesworth, "Hellenistic Synagogal Prayers," 678 n).

102. *Apostolic Constitutions* 7.34.1.

103. *Apostolic Constitutions* 8.12.6, 8. May believes this section is a later Christian interpolation (*Creatio ex Nihilo*, 22 n). But Pseudepigrapha scholar James Charlesworth, among others, rejects the idea. At least the lack of consensus should preclude us from hastily dismissing creation *ex nihilo* from the text.

104. Goldstein, "Origins of the Doctrine of Creation *Ex Nihilo*," 127. Norbert M. Samuelson, *Judaism and the Doctrine of Creation* (Cambridge: Cambridge University Press, 1994), adopts this view but fails to take into account the subtleties suggested by Sailhamer (below).

as a construct ("At the beginning of God's creating of the heavens and the earth"), acknowledges, "I have followed several medieval commentators . . . in my rendition."[105]

However, when we view the question from another angle, a different picture comes into view. First, all the medieval Jewish exegetes (such as Rashbam, Ramban, Rambam, et al.) actually *uniformly* follow Rashi (Rabbi Shlomo Yitzchaki, 1040–1105) in *presupposing* creation out of nothing. How so? They assume, for example, that because water *already* exists in Genesis 1:2, this could not be absolute creation (i.e., out of nothing). That is, the creation described in 1:1 is not the first thing God creates. Rashi observes: "The text does not intend to point out the order of the *acts of* creation—to state that these (heaven and earth) were created first."[106] Thus one could easily understand Rashi to interpret divine creation as involving stages rather than merely one stage. Indeed, Ramban, a medieval Jewish exegete, did just that.

Ramban (Rabbi Moshe ben Nachman, thirteenth century), commenting on Genesis 1:1 (and referring to the specific phrasing: "In the beginning God created"), declares: "This is the root of faith, and he who does not believe in this and thinks the world was eternal denies the essential principle of the [Judaic] religion and has no Torah at all."[107] Ramban seems to speak for the other medieval Jewish exegetes in suggesting that any dualism allowing for the eternal coexistence of God and primordial matter is simply intolerable to the Jewish mind.

Rashi was the first, so far as we know, to read *bĕrēʾšîth* ("in the beginning") as construct ("in beginning") rather than absolute ("in the very beginning").[108] In his view, absolute creation took place *before* Genesis 1:1, and in Genesis 1 God is working with his own created materials to create further. Thus, it was not *grammatical* grounds that led Rashi to formulate *bĕrēʾšîth* as a construct but rather the subject matter in verse 2 (water).[109] Ibn Ezra, who followed Rashi in the "construct" view (with some variations), believed that God had *previously* created

105. *The Five Books of Moses*, Schocken Bible, vol. 1 (New York: Schocken, 2000), 13.

106. Rashi [Shlomo Yitzchaki], *The Pentateuch with Targum Onkelos, Haphtaroth, and Rashi's Commentary: Genesis*, trans. M. Rosenbaum and A. M. Silbermann (Jerusalem: A. M. Silbermann, 1929), 2.

107. Ramban (Nachmanides), *Commentary on the Torah: Genesis*, trans. Charles B. Chavel (New York: Shiloh, 1971), 17.

108. Rashi's comments on Genesis 1:1 are available in *Genesis*, vol. 1 of *The Pentateuch and Rashi's Commentary: A Linear Translation*, trans. Abraham Ben Isaiah and Benjamin Sharfman (Brooklyn: S. S. & R., 1949); see also Rashi, *Pentateuch with Targum Onkelos, Haphtaroth, and Rashi's Commentary*, 2: "The text does not intend to point out the order of the *acts of* creation—to state that these (heaven and earth) were created first."

109. Ironically, the failure to realize this important point has led some exegetes to follow Rashi and thus read Genesis 1:1 as construct. For example, see W. Gunther Plaut,

the water, which he then *later* used to create within selective aspects of the universe. But even Ibn Ezra declared that the verses of Genesis 1:1–2 "are to be so interpreted because Moses did not speak of the eternal world. . . . He spoke only of the transient world."[110] Neither Rashi nor Ibn Ezra believed the construct reading to be superior to the absolute one.[111]

Old Testament scholar John Sailhamer summarizes:

> Neither Rashi nor Ibn Ezra appears to have rejected the traditional view [of *bĕrēʾšîth* as absolute] on grammatical grounds, thinking the construct reading was the better reading. *Rather, they believed it was the only reading that would solve the apparent difficulty of the "water" in v. 2 not being accounted for in v. 1.* In fact, Ibn Ezra warned his readers not to be "astonished" at the suggestion of a construct before a verb, which suggests that he himself felt some difficulty in reading *bĕrēʾšîth* before a finite verb as a construct and that he anticipated the same reaction in his readers.
>
> Both Rashi and Ibn Ezra produced examples to show that a finite verb after a construct noun was permissible. Both the fact and the nature of their defense of their reading in 1:1 betrays their own uneasiness with such a reading.[112]

Hence, these medieval Jewish exegetes did not believe that God created out of eternally preexisting material. Rather, according to their thinking, God was the very originator of *any* finite materials he may have used to create in Genesis 1.

James Barr corroborates what Sailhamer has noted, stating that the reason some have favored a construct (rather than absolute) reading of Genesis 1:1 has been that Rashi endorsed such a view. Barr notices how the water in 1:2 came into being and comments: "Rashi's exegesis in this respect was not at all based on the linguistic characteristics of the text, but was a semi-allegorical attempt to deal with a theological problem: when and how was the water, later divided into two by the firmament, created?"[113]

Genesis: The Torah: A Modern Commentary (New York: Union of American Hebrew Congregations, 1974), 5 n.

110. Ibn Ezra, *Commentary on the Pentateuch: Genesis (Bereshit)*, vol. 1, trans. H. Norman Strickman and Arthur M. Silver (New York: Menorah Publishing, 1988), 30–31. Ezra notes that the eternal or invisible realm is the realm that the angels inhabit. At any rate, Ezra holds to a two-stage understanding of creation.

111. John Sailhamer, "Genesis," in the *Expositor's Bible Commentary*, vol. 2, ed. Frank Gaebelein (Grand Rapids: Zondervan, 1990), 22 (emphasis added). For further discussion, see Sailhamer's extensive note on 21–23.

112. Ibid., 22.

113. Barr, "Was Everything That God Created Really Good?" 58.

As cited earlier, the medieval commentator Ramban declares that the verb *bārā* alone can express the notion of creation from absolute nothingness:

> The Holy One, blessed be He, created all things from absolute non-existence. Now we have no expression in the sacred language for bringing forth something from nothing other than the word *bārā* (created).

He affirms that creation from absolute nothingness ("total and absolute nothing") took place in stages:

> Stage 1: *Creating* or bringing forth a "substance devoid of corporeality but having a power of potency"[114] (the "primary matter" or *hylē* of the Greeks).
>
> Stage 2: God "did not *create* anything, but He *formed* and made things with [primal matter = the *hylē*]."[115]

As Foerster comments, "In later Judaism, both in Rabb[inic] and pseudepigr[aphal] writings, it is clearly stated that God alone created the world by His Word, i.e., that He called it into existence from nothing."[116] He goes so far as to say that "the idea of a pre-existence of matter" was "alien" to rabbinic literature.[117]

In truth, it is extremely difficult to imagine how an un-Hellenized Hebrew would conclude from the biblical text that God and some unorganized matter (or chaos) coexisted from eternity. In the end we see a remarkable *continuity* among those who penned 2 Maccabees, the Dead Sea Scrolls, the LXX in later Jewish translations, the Semitic Targums, and various medieval Jewish commentators. Barr concurs, arguing that an absolute rendering of Genesis 1:1 is standard in these writings: "It is worth noting that no ancient Jewish sources—LXX, Targums, Jubilees, and (I think) Philo—show evidence" of following the construct reading—or even of "being influenced by it."[118]

Now, we move to the church fathers, whose testimony to creation out of nothing is quite evident, revealing that they faithfully adhered to the biblical tradition of creation out of nothing.

114. Ramban, *Commentary on the Torah: Genesis*, 23.
115. Ibid.
116. Foerster, *"ktizō,"* 1:1016.
117. Ibid., 1:1017.
118. Barr, "Was Everything That God Created Really Good?" 58.

The Witness of the Church Fathers

Philosophical Influence versus Terminological Borrowing?

It would be accurate to say that the Jewish and primal church's belief in creation out of nothing was not so much asserted as assumed.[119] In Acts 14:4–18, Paul maintains that Yahweh made heaven and earth and the sea and everything in them—in contrast to the pagan gods, which did not create and are unworthy of worship.[120] The NT adds this new feature—that creation is for the sake of Jesus Christ (Col. 1:15–20). To refer back to Jenson's citation from the last chapter, the primal church "simply took over Jewish teaching. For her the doctrine of creation was received truth that did not need to be asserted, but functioned rather as warrant in asserting other things."[121]

Jenson goes on, however, to speak of the post-apostolic church's continuity with OT and NT assumptions about creation in the context of nonbiblical cosmogonies: "Only in the course of the second century does creation again become an explicit matter of theology. Notoriously, this occurs in the church's confrontation with various philosophical or theological denials that the one responsible for this world can be the good God and Father of Jesus Christ."[122] This clash produced a spate of writing in which the doctrine of creation was hammered out and clarified. As Langdon Gilkey has observed, "It takes a heretic to make a theologian."[123] But even here, we must not forget that the implicit was being made explicit. We are not talking about a move from an *ambiguous* biblical text to *one of many possible interpretations* about creation.

This section explores briefly the question of philosophical influence versus terminological borrowing. Does the use of certain Platonic catchwords or common phrases by the earliest church fathers reveal a wholesale surrender to Platonic philosophy? Obviously, Middle Platonism serves as an important context for making sense of the church fathers and their apologetic and polemical task. Many scholars have misunderstood the patristic era, claiming that up until the late second and early third centuries, the church fathers and early apologists slavishly followed the Middle Platonic understanding of God's being the

119. Robert W. Jenson, *Systematic Theology: The Works of God,* vol. 2 (New York: Oxford University Press, 2000), 3.

120. Ibid., 2:4.

121. Robert W. Jenson, "Aspects of the Doctrine of Creation," in *The Doctrine of Creation,* ed. Colin E. Gunton (Edinburgh: T & T Clark, 1997), 17.

122. Ibid., 18.

123. Langdon Gilkey, *Maker of Heaven and Earth* (Garden City, N.J.: Doubleday, 1959), 44.

Artificer of eternally preexistent matter *(creatio ex materia)*. But the fathers' apologetic strategy bespeaks something different—terminological borrowing rather than philosophical surrender.

Jaroslav Pelikan reports that early Christian apologists were known to scour Plato's *Timaeus*, Homer's *Odyssey*, and Virgil's *Aeneid* to build bridges with pagan culture, to show that the Christian faith was not some innovation but was rooted in antiquity. At points they went overboard and succumbed to Hellenistic influences regarding divine impassibility (which tended to reduce God to a static, impassive entity) and the immortality of the soul[124] (but contrary to 1 Corinthians 15, which links immortality with the resurrection of the body). Nevertheless, to generalize by saying this was a wholesale sellout to Hellenism is just false.

With regard to creation, Plato's *Timaeus* was well known by thinkers of all stripes. The character Timaeus asserts that God brought order to (apparently) eternally preexistent matter:

> This is in the truest sense the origin of creation and of the world. . . .
> Wherefore also finding the whole visible sphere not at rest, but moving in
> an irregular and disorderly fashion, out of disorder [God] brought order,
> considering that this was in every way better than the other.[125]

It is alleged that the earliest Christian theologians simply could not shake off the profound influence of Greek philosophy.

We insist, however, that this Middle Platonic reading of patristic literature on creation is a mistake. Before looking at specific patristic texts, we cannot ignore two fundamental—but regularly overlooked—facts.

First, the patristic writers had a specific apologetic bent in their defense of the biblical worldview. While the apostolic Fathers of early Christianity wrote for the guidance and edification of Christians, the Greek apologists presented a more philosophical Christianity to the outside world of culture and science—a world of aggressive paganism. Thus, their work has a distinctively apologetic character. According to church historian Johannes Quasten, the second-century apologists had three objectives in mind:

---

124. Jaroslav Pelikan writes: "It is significant that Christian theologians customarily set down the doctrine of the impassibility of God, without bothering to provide very much biblical support or theological proof. . . . The concept of an entirely static God, with eminent reality, in relation to an entirely fluent world, with deficient reality—[is] a concept that came into Christian doctrine from Greek philosophy" (*The Christian Tradition,* vol. 1 of *The Emergence of the Catholic Tradition* [100–600], [Chicago: University of Chicago Press, 1971], 52–53).

125. Plato, *Timaeus* 30a, in Edith Hamilton and Huntington Cairns, eds., *Plato: The Collected Dialogues,* Bollingen Series 71 (Princeton: Princeton University Press, 1989), 1162.

1. They answered the charge that Christians were a danger to the state, asserting that Christians lived earnest and honorable lives.
2. They exposed the "absurdities and immoralities" of paganism and the "myths of its divinities," showing that the Christian has a correct understanding of God (monotheism) and the universe.
3. They showed that the arguments of philosophers only had human reason to rely upon, failing to come to truth (or truth unmixed with error). Christianity (through Christ, the divine Logos/Reason) is thus the divine philosophy.[126]

Quasten continues by saying that their effort was *not* a *Hellenization of Christianity* but rather a *Christianization of Hellenism*. While they may have used language familiar within their culture, the *content* of the apologists' theology "has been far less influenced by pagan philosophy than is sometimes asserted."[127]

Second, these writers frequently borrowed specific language, catch-phrases, and images from pagan literature to show that Christianity was not a novel religion but was rooted in antiquity. Jaroslav Pelikan has shown how these early theologians mined the Greco-Roman literature to find images of Christ and language that could be *discriminatingly* adapted to a Christian worldview, *mutatis mutandis*.

Regarding creation, we shall see, as Edwin Hatch explains, that early Christian theologians borrowed Greek Platonic language, which helped give "philosophical form" to the developed Christian doctrine of creation. They articulated the belief that God was "not merely the Architect of the universe, but its Source"; this belief had "probably been for a long time the unreasoned belief of Hebrew monotheism."[128]

It would be wise to take a case study of chapter 20 of Clement of Rome's *First Epistle to the Corinthians* (ca. AD 96).[129] Scholars in the past have claimed that it relies heavily upon Stoic philosophy, resulting in

---

126. Johannes Quasten, *Patrology*, vol. 1 (Westminster, Md.: Christian Classics, 1986), 186–87.

127. Ibid., 1:187.

128. Edwin Hatch, *The Influence of Greek Ideas and Usages upon the Christian Church* (London: Williams & Norgate, 1891), 197. Overall, Hatch *overplays* the influence of Greek thought on biblical doctrine and *overlooks* the deep Hebraic/OT influence on various NT texts and Christian doctrines.

129. In these comments on the alleged dependence of 1 Clement on Stoic philosophy, I rely on W. C. van Unnik, "Is 1 Clement 20 Purely Stoic?" *Vigiliae Christianae* 4 (1950): 181–89. The Stoic connection seems to be overstated (though nuanced) in Gregory E. Sterling, "Prepositional Metaphysics in Jewish Wisdom Speculation and Early Christian Liturgical Texts," *The Studia Philonica Annual* 9 (1997): 219–38.

the claim that Clement (d. 110) had been thoroughly Hellenized. Adolf von Harnack claimed that the framework of the letter is *"Hellenisch"*; another scholar declares it "wholly un-Jewish [*ganz unjüdisch*]" and "absolutely unoriental [*überhaupt unorientalisch*]."[130] But is this really the case?

The teachings of the *Stoa* root the orderly phenomena of this world in the pantheistic God. Through the orderliness of nature, human beings can infer that there is an organizing power behind it. But while 1 Clement's text certainly makes much reference to order and harmony, it would be a gross error to call Clement a Stoic. Indeed, there are remarkable *differences* between Clement and the Stoics. Clement sees order as established by God's *will* (cf. Ps. 33:9), which is not a pantheistic concept! Clement has in mind a *personal* Creator. In the passage below, note how Clement's emphasis is not on the goodness of the order and harmony, but how these are the result of God's will, which is *ganz jüdisch* and *orientalisch!*

> [1]The heavens, being put in motion *by His appointment*, are subject to him in peace; [2]night and day accomplish the course *ordered by Him*, in nothing hindering one another. [3]The sun and the moon and the dances of the stars *according to His appointment*, in harmony and without any violation of order, roll on the courses *appointed to them*. [4]The fruitful earth bringeth forth in due season, *according to His will*, abundant nourishment for men and beasts; nothing doubting, nor changing in anything from the things that are *decreed by Him*. [5]The unsearchable things of the abyss, and the secret ordinances of the lower parts of the earth, are held together *by the same command*. [6]The hollow of the vast sea, gathered together *by His hand* into its reservoirs, transgresseth not the bounds placed around it; but even as *He hath appointed to it*, so it doeth; [7]for He said, "Thus far shalt thou come, and thy waves shall be broken within thee." [8]The ocean, impassable to men, and the worlds that are beyond it, are governed *by the same commandments of their Master*. [9]The seasons of spring and summer, autumn and winter, in peace succeed one another. [10]The fixed stations of the winds, each in their due time, perform *their services* without offence. The ever-flowing fountains, made for enjoyment and health, offer their breasts without fail to sustain the lives of men. Even the smallest of animals come together in peace and harmony. [11]All these things *the great Creator and Master of all things hath appointed to be in peace and harmony*, doing good unto all things, but more especially unto us, who have fled for refuge to His mercies, through our Lord Jesus Christ, [12]to whom be glory and majesty for ever and ever. Amen. (Clement of Rome, *To the Corinthians 20*)

130. Both Harnack and Knopf are cited in van Unnik, "Is 1 Clement 20 Purely Stoic?" 183.

Curiously, scholars accusing Clement of succumbing to Greek philosophy ignore many *Palestinian-Jewish* sources that utilize this very language and idea of order *(taxis)*. For example, in *1 Enoch* 41:6–8, we read of the sun's path that moves "according to the commandment of the Lord of Spirits." In the *Testaments of the Patriarchs* (second century BC), the same language is used. The sun, moon, and stars do not change their "order." Similarly, the readers are exhorted: "So do ye change not the law of God in the disorderliness of your doings."[131] In the *Assumption of Moses* (probably first century AD), the "lights of heaven" are under God's direction; therefore those who obey "the commandments of God" will prosper (12:9–10). A final example comes from the *Psalms of Solomon* 18:12–14 (ca. 50 BC): God establishes the light of heaven to determine its seasons year after year, and they do not turn aside "from the way which He appointed [for] them."

Van Unnik observes:

> [These Jewish sources] all show the same ideas; the order in nature has been set by the commandment of God the Creator; the universe has been obedient and did not change the rules . . . ; therefore there is no curse in creation, and the universal order can be an example for men.[132]

He then goes on to draw this twofold conclusion. First, "the law in nature as an example for men is found both in [S]toic and [J]ewish literature. Influence from one side or the other seems very improbable." Second, regarding 1 Clement 20, "the tinge of Stoic language is unmistakable, but this conception of the universe is subjected to another, the biblical idea of God . . . ; the same conception and outlook is found among the Jews."[133]

With regard to the alleged Stoicism of Romans 11:36, we cited Schreiner, which aptly fits here: "The parallels are superficial since such formulations must be interpreted in terms of the worldview of the author, and Stoicism and biblical thought are obviously different."[134] This attribution of pagan influence on the church fathers is made repeatedly by scholars, but they fail to appreciate the remarkable worldview differences of the respective authors despite similarities in vocabulary. So before addressing the topic of creation out of nothing in the patristic/apologetic literature, we find it critical to point out these worldview considerations.

131. *Testament of Naphtali* 3.
132. Van Unnik, "Is 1 Clement 20 Purely Stoic?" 188.
133. Ibid., 189.
134. Thomas R. Schreiner, *Romans*, BECNT (Grand Rapids: Baker, 1998), 637.

The Unbegottenness of God and a Two-Stage ex Nihilo *Creation* in Patristic Writings

Scholars agree that with Irenaeus (who wrote in the latter part of the second century), the doctrine of *creatio ex nihilo* was well established. In expounding this belief, Irenaeus (ca. AD 130–200) argued that the world was not coeternal with God:

> But the things established are distinct from Him who has established them, and what [things] have been made from Him who has made them. For He is Himself uncreated, both without beginning and end, and lacking nothing. He is Himself sufficient for this very thing, existence; but the things which have been made by Him have received a beginning. . . . He indeed who made all things can alone, together with His Word, properly be termed God and Lord; but the things which have been made cannot have this term applied to them, neither should they justly assume that appellation which belongs to the Creator.[135]

The testimony of Irenaeus is simply the full elaboration upon the thoroughly biblical assumptions of the church fathers that preceded him. From the end of the first century onward, we do not see any deviation regarding the unbegottenness of God: God alone is unoriginated, unbegotten, uncorruptible; everything else is originated, begotten, and corruptible.

The earliest postbiblical theologians were remarkably consistent in affirming the following two beliefs: *First,* God and matter are not coeval. God, by his very nature, is ontologically distinct from matter. God is unbegotten *(agennētos)* and uncreated *(agenētos)* whereas everything else is begotten and created—including matter. Moreover, God is self-sufficient or "in need of nothing" *(adeētos).*[136] That is, contrary to Middle Platonic thought, there is no dualism of God and matter, and God needs no intermediary entities to create. This, of course, reflects the Bible's emphasis on the eternality and permanence of God and the transitory nature of all else, the created order, which requires God's power to sustain it in existence.

Second, God brought about the universe through a two-stage creation, first creating the very substrate itself and then shaping and ordering it into a cosmos. This two-stage creation threads its way throughout the early patristic theologians, running up to the early Augustine.[137] Even

135. Irenaeus, *Against Heresies* 3.20.3; cf. 2.10.4.
136. Cf. Acts 17:24.
137. N. Joseph Torchia, "Theories of Creation in the Second Century Apologists and Their Middle Platonic Background," *Studia Patristica* 26 (1993): 191–99. For a full-length

though creation *ex nihilo* is *assumed* by the ante-Nicene Fathers, it becomes more explicitly stated by the end of the second century. There is a clear building of one Father upon another till we get to Irenaeus, Tertullian, and Augustine, who reflect upon, and approve of, the views of their predecessors.[138]

As the church fathers encountered paganism, they drew upon the language of Plato for apologetic purposes. But as we saw with Clement's usage of OT language within a biblical worldview that resembled the Stoic emphasis on order, this was not a "Hellenization of Christianity" but rather a "Christianization of Hellenism." Even though these theologians may have used the language of Plato for apologetic purposes, they reveal that they are thinking independently of him.[139]

Patristic scholar Joseph Torchia rightly observes that the explicit doctrine of *creatio ex nihilo* emerged gradually in the church's encounter with paganism. Certain assumptions and presuppositions about divine creation came to be more finely tuned and expanded upon,[140] but to a man, they were convinced that the universe depended entirely upon God for its existence and its order and that God alone was eternal and unbegotten. Matter, on the other hand, was not. As Harvard classical scholar Harry A. Wolfson writes, "Whatever the Church Fathers may have believed with regard to Plato's conception of his pre-existent matter, all of them reject the creation of the world out of pre-existent uncreated matter, though some of them . . . admit its creation out of a pre-existent created matter."[141]

Much more is to be done with regard to the development of the doctrine of creation out of nothing, and we propose a way forward that avoids the "sudden-emergence" view of the doctrine. What we present below is an organic and more natural reading of the church fathers, recognizing the context of the developing creation-out-of-nothing doctrine. The later Christian theologians, who go to great lengths explicitly to defend creation out of nothing, are simply drawing out what is implicit in the biblical text and earlier Fathers: the underlying assumption of creation out of nothing.

---

discussion of this, see N. Joseph Torchia, *Creatio ex Nihilo and the Theology of St. Augustine: The Anti-Manichaean Polemic and Beyond*, series 7, no. 205 (New York: Peter Lang, 1999).

138. On this, see Harry A. Wolfson, "Patristic Arguments against the Eternity of the World," *Harvard Theological Review* 59 (1966): 351–67.

139. Torchia, "Theories of Creation," 197.

140. Torchia, *Creatio ex Nihilo and the Theology of St. Augustine*, 1, 4.

141. Wolfson, "Plato's Pre-existent Matter," 414.

Patristic and Other Ancient Christian Writings

ODES OF SOLOMON

The *Odes of Solomon* were composed in a time surrounding the turn of the first century AD (ca. 70–125); these odes are believed by some to be an early Christian hymnbook. They are not Jewish, but Jewish Christian, showing similarities with both the Dead Sea Scrolls and the Gospel of John.[142] They were probably originally written in Syriac,[143] although others claim they were first in Greek.[144] These odes were also likely influenced by the writing of *1 Enoch*.[145]

Again, we have indications of creation out of nothing, evidenced by the sweeping comprehensiveness of what God creates. God is the Creator of all reality outside himself:

> For all was manifest to you as God,
> and was set in order from the beginning before you.
> And you, O Lord, have made all. Hallelujah. (4:14–15)

Again:

> For he destroys whatever is foreign,
> and everything is of the Lord.
> For thus it has been from the beginning,
> and (will be) until the end.
> So that nothing will be contrary,
> and nothing will rise up against him. (6:3–5)

We see similar language in 16:18–19:

> And there is nothing outside of the Lord,
> because he was before anything came to be.
> And the worlds are by his word,
> And by the thought of his heart.

Lines such as "everything is of the Lord" and "there is nothing outside the Lord" strongly suggest opposition to any eternal dualism. Indeed, any alleged dualism of good (God) and evil in the *Odes* is only apparent,

---

142. Charlesworth, *Pseudepigrapha and Modern Research*, 189–90.

143. James Charlesworth, "Odes of Solomon," in *The Old Testament Pseudepigrapha* (ed. Charlesworth), 2:726–27.

144. W. Bauer makes this claim in "The Odes of Solomon," in *New Testament Apocrypha*, vol. 2, ed. Wilhelm Schneemelcher, trans. R. M. Wilson (Philadelphia: Westminster, 1964), 809.

145. Charlesworth, "Odes of Solomon," 732.

since the good spirit overcomes the evil and brings salvation to the faithful individual.[146] In the *Odes*, God alone is "incorruptible" (7:11; 9:4).

CLEMENT OF ROME

As we saw, Clement's *First Epistle to the Corinthians* (AD 96) asserted that God, by his command, ordered and arranged the universe. Without God, there would be no harmony whatsoever. While Clement does not speak to the question of creation out of nothing, he does refer to the creation in the totalistic language of the OT and NT: "All these things the great Creator and Master of all things hath appointed to be in peace and harmony, doing good unto all things, but more especially unto us, who have fled for refuge to His mercies, through our Lord Jesus Christ" (20.11).

He does borrow a term from Plato when speaking of God as "the Great Demiurge [*ho megas dēmiourgos*]" who orders the cosmos. This idea of God's arranging the universe is consistent with the biblical affirmation, and we should not assume that Clement could not resist the pull of Platonism. As with the similarities to Stoicism, he utilizes Platonic language to reinforce his emphasis, and in doing so he is thoroughly biblical.

THE SHEPHERD OF HERMAS

In the *Shepherd of Hermas* (ca. AD 150), the first command is to believe that

> God is one, who made all things and perfected them [*ho ta panta ktisas kai katartisas*], and made all things to be out of that which was not [*kai poiēsas ek tou mē ontos eis to einai ta panta*], and contains all things and is himself alone and uncontained [*kai panta chōrōn, monos de achērētos ōn*].[147]

Earlier in this work, a passage reads: "God, Who dwelleth in the heavens, and created out of nothing the things which are [*ktisas ek tou mē ontos ta onta*]" (Vision 1.1.6). Then later in the chapter, this majestic, sweeping statement is made:

> Behold, the God of Hosts, Who by His invisible and mighty power and by His great wisdom created the world, and by His glorious purpose clothed His creation with comeliness, and by His strong word fixed the heaven, and founded the earth upon the waters.[148]

146. Ibid., 730.
147. *Shepherd of Hermas*, Mandate 1.1.1.
148. *Shepherd*, Vision 1.1.6.

Then we read another sweeping statement that God "created all things, and set them in order, and endowed them with power."[149] With reference to the Son of God, we observe the absence of any dualism—that he is before all things and more ancient than his creation: "The Son of God is older than all His creation, so that He became the Father's adviser in His creation. Therefore also He is ancient."[150] Furthermore, the *Shepherd* affirms that the "holy pre-existent Spirit . . . created the whole creation."[151] This seems quite opposed to any preexistent matter existing alongside the Holy Spirit.

Commentator Carolyn Osiek asserts that Mandate 1 begins with a "very brief but quite significant introduction that affirms the centrality of monotheistic faith," citing Ephesians 3:9, where God is the "creator of all," and 2 Maccabees 7:28, where God creates "from nothing."[152]

Here we see the two emphases recognized earlier. First, *God and matter are not coeval* (God alone is unbegotten and everything else is not): "God . . . contains all things and is Himself alone and uncontained."[153] Surely this could not be said if there exists alongside God some primordial chaos. Second (and this is suggestive rather than definitive), *God brought about the universe through a two-stage creation* (creating the substrate itself and then ordering it into a cosmos): "God . . . made all things and perfected them." Perhaps there is an order of first bringing everything into existence and then ordering them.

It will not do (as Gerhard May does)[154] to urge that the *Shepherd* affirms nothing more than Middle Platonism in saying that God "made all things to be out of that which was not."[155] Indeed, in light of this reference, Denis Carroll comments that this is the first allusion to *creatio ex nihilo* in Christian literature.[156] Patristics scholar Eric Osborn asserts that creation *ex nihilo* is a consequence of monotheism, and it is "clearest in this passage," making it "fundamental to Christian belief."[157]

149. *Shepherd*, Parable 5.5.2.

150. *Shepherd*, Parable 9.12.2.

151. *Shepherd*, Parable 5.6.5.

152. Carolyn Osiek, *Shepherd of Hermas* (Minneapolis: Fortress, 1999), 103.

153. *Shepherd*, Mandate 1.1.1.

154. May, *Creatio ex Nihilo*, 27.

155. *Shepherd*, Mandate 1.1.1: *poiēsas ek tou mē ontos eis to einai ta panta*.

156. Denis Carroll, "Creation," in *The New Dictionary of Theology*, ed. Joseph Komanchak et al. (Wilmington, Del.: Michael Glazier, 1987), 249.

157. Eric Osborn, *The Emergence of Christian Theology* (Cambridge: Cambridge University Press, 1993), 122, 19.

DIDACHE

Although the *Didache* (by early second century AD) does not speak regarding creation out of nothing, we witness in it the *totalism* and *comprehensiveness* of the divine creation characteristic of the biblical writers: "Thou, Almighty Master [*despota pantokratōr*], didst create all things for Thy name's sake" (10.3). This passage sounds strikingly similar to the previously cited passage from 3 Maccabees 2:2–3: "Lord, Lord, King of heaven and Ruler of all creation [*despota pasēs ktiseōs*]. . . . You who created all things and govern the whole world."

POLYCARP

At his martyrdom, the Smyrnan bishop Polycarp (AD 69–155/6) reportedly prays:

> O Lord God Almighty, the Father of Thy beloved and blessed Son Jesus Christ, by whom we have received the knowledge of Thee, the God of angels and powers, and of all creation [*pasēs ktiseōs*], and of the whole race of righteous before thee, I give Thee thanks that Thou hast counted me worthy of this day and this hour, that I should have a part in the number of Thy martyrs.[158]

Polycarp articulates a sweeping totalism and apparently presupposes that what is not creature must be Creator. This language of God's creating everything *(pasēs ktiseōs)* is certainly consistent with the NT language as well as the church fathers. Indeed, Polycarp begins his *Epistle to the Philippians* (ca. AD 130) by describing God as the Pantocrator (*pantokratōr*), the Almighty.[159]

ARISTIDES

Aristides, whose writing goes back to as early as perhaps AD 125 (during the time of Hadrian), was an early Christian apologist who lived in Athens. Indeed, his work is the oldest of the Christian apologists, and the Greek text comes to us in the story of Barlaam and Joasaph (probably written by John of Damascus). We also have a Syriac text, which exhibits certain differences.[160]

What is significant is that he appears to hold implicitly to *creatio ex nihilo*. Such a belief is rooted in his understanding of God's nature:

---

158. *The Martyrdom of Polycarp* 14.
159. Polycarp, *Epistle to the Philippians*, opening greetings.
160. See May, *Creatio ex Nihilo*, 118–19.

Now when I say that [God] is "perfect," this means that there is not in him any defect, and he is not in need of anything, but all things are in need of him. And when I say that he is "without beginning," this means that everything which has a beginning has also an end, and that which has an end may be brought to an end. He has no name, for everything which has a name is kindred to things created. Form he has none, nor yet any union of members; for whatsoever possesses these is kindred to things fashioned. He is neither male nor female. The heavens do not limit him, but the heavens and all things, visible and invisible, receive their bounds from him. Adversary he has none, for there exists not any stronger than he.[161]

Aristides criticizes the idolatry of the Chaldeans (or Babylonians), who "worship the creation more than their Creator."[162] Aristides recognizes two categories—Creator and created. In his *Apology*, there is nothing in between. Even the waters themselves are a creation of God, used for the benefit of mankind.[163] The very "elements [*ta stoicheia*]" are "liable to ruin and change [*phtharta kai alloioumena*]," and they were "brought out of nothing [*ek tou mē ontos*] through the commandment of the true God."[164] God speaks, and they exist. Unlike these elements, God is "uncreated and imperishable."[165] Nevertheless, May unnecessarily cautions that we should not read too much into such a rendering: "Aristides means that the elements are created by God; but it does not appear from his book that he consciously distanced himself from the philosophical model of world-formation and creation."[166]

Yet Aristides makes a sweeping statement about the comprehensiveness of God's creation: nothing is excluded. In the Syriac version, we read: "For [Christians] know and trust in God, the Creator of heaven and of earth, in whom and from whom are all things."[167] The Greek rendering of this passage distinguishes between *creating* and merely *fashioning*. God is "the Creator and Fashioner of all things."

In critiquing man-made idols, Aristides writes:

If then it becomes us to admire a god which is seen and does not see, how much more praiseworthy is it that one should believe in a nature which is invisible and all-seeing? And if further it is fitting that one should ap-

161. Aristides, *Apology* 2 (Syriac).
162. Aristides, *Apol.* 3 (Greek).
163. Aristides, *Apol.* 5 (Syriac): "The waters were created for the use of man."
164. Aristides, *Apol.* 4 (Greek).
165. Aristides, *Apol.* 7 (Syriac).
166. May, *Creatio ex Nihilo*, 119–20.
167. Aristides, *Apol.* 15 (Syriac).

prove the handiworks of a craftsman, how much more is it fitting that one should glorify the Creator of the craftsman?[168]

Aristides claims that God is not merely an Artificer—a category into which humans would fit—but the Creator. As with Justin Martyr and those who follow him, Aristides holds that (1) there is an ontological distinction between Creator and creature—the former is imperishable, the latter is corruptible; and (2) God created in stages, first bringing into being the elements and then shaping them into a cosmos.

JUSTIN MARTYR

Many assume without question that Justin (AD 100–165) fully embraced a Middle Platonic cosmogony in which God creates out of eternally preexistent stuff. Justin's famous claim in the *First Apology* is that Plato (in the *Timaeus*) borrowed from Moses: "God by His Word created the whole world out of matter, of which Moses had already spoken."[169] In the same passage, he writes that "God changed shapeless matter and created the world [*hylēn amorphon ousan strepsanta ton theon kosmon poiēsai*]."[170] The word *strepsanta* appears to borrow language from the *Timaeus*, where the Demiurge creates the cosmos by placing the world soul into "rotation [*strepsanta*]."[171]

Earlier in Justin's *First Apology*, he writes, "God, in the beginning, in His goodness made [*dēmiourgēsai*] everything out of shapeless matter [*ex amorphou hylēs*] for the sake of men."[172] Justin declares that according to both Moses and Plato, "the whole cosmos came about from the substrates [*ek tēn hypokeimenōn*]," which was "first set forth by Moses and Plato."[173] Dare we even question that Justin's view was drenched in Platonism?

Again, remember the apologetic strategy that Justin and other church fathers utilized to show the antiquity of the Christian faith; it was not an innovation. Plato is, in fact, borrowing from Moses, thus revealing the superiority of the ancient Christian faith. After all, in his *First Apology* (ca. 155), Justin also claims that Plato borrows from Moses (the account of the bronze serpent) regarding the coming crucifixion of the Son of God! "The physiological discussion concerning the Son of God in the *Timaeus* of Plato, where he says, 'He placed him crosswise in the

168. Aristides, *Apol.* 14 (Syriac).
169. Justin, *First Apology* [*Apologia I pro Christianis*] 59.
170. Justin, *First Apol.* 59.
171. Plato, *Timaeus* 34A, B, 36E.
172. Justin, *First Apol.* 10.
173. Justin, *First Apol.* 59.

universe,' he borrowed in like manner from Moses."[174] Furthermore, Justin declares that Plato is indebted to the Hebrew prophets: "And let no one wonder that Plato should believe Moses regarding the eternity of God."[175]

Justin's strategy is like Paul's quoting pagans in Acts 17 ("we live and move and have our being" in God and are God's "offspring"), yet with a thoroughly OT-Jewish theology. Why should we think that Justin's use of Platonic catchwords compromises a biblical worldview?

Not only does Justin have an apologetic goal and strategy; he also utilizes biblical concepts in opposition to Platonic ones. The distinction between *concepts* and *words* or *formula* is critical. Osborn observes this regarding Justin's view of creation: "The concept of creation from nothing can be found without the formula [or words], and the formula can be found without the concept."[176] Accounts of creation, he urges, must be understood in the context of their total argument—a "conceptual" rather than "culinary" manner. Osborn, who has written a monograph on Justin,[177] asserts that we cannot isolate Justin's account of matter from the rest of his outlook, which includes God as the solely Unoriginated.[178] It is particularly noteworthy that Justin is concerned about destroying Marcion's dualistic heresy. So no wonder that Justin rejects any unbegotten competitor to God, who alone is *agennētos* (unbegotten). Osborn challenges Gerhard May's handling of Justin, charging him with a "fatal confusion of concepts with words."[179]

---

174. Justin, *First Apol.* 60.

175. Justin, *Dialogue with Trypho* [*Dialogus cum Tryphone Judaeo*] 26.

176. Eric Osborn, *Irenaeus of Lyons* (Cambridge: Cambridge University Press, 2001), 66.

177. Eric Osborn, *Justin Martyr* (Tübingen: Mohr/Siebeck, 1973).

178. See Osborn's discussion on God as the only unbegotten Being, in *Justin Martyr*, 46–49; see also 17–27. Matter, for Justin, is "never a second unbegotten entity beside the father. It is made by God" (48). See also Eric Osborn, *The Beginning of Christian Philosophy* (Cambridge: Cambridge University Press, 1981), 56–63, 124–29; Osborn, *Emergence of Christian Theology,* 19, 116–24, 154.

179. Osborn, *Irenaeus of Lyons,* 67 n. Osborn (66–67) cites May on Justin: "In his explicit statements about matter he *seems* to consider it an eternal, uncreated substratum of the cosmos. *One gets the impression* that for Justin the idea that the creation of the world must have resulted from matter given in advance was so self-evident that he saw no problem in it" (May, *Creatio ex Nihilo,* 124, Osborn's emphasis). And again: "So when Justin *presupposes* an *eternal* material as the stuff of creation, this conception simply has the function of how the creation of the world was possible; Justin obviously cannot but represent it as only the formation of a material substratum. Beyond that, the doctrine of uncreated matter plays no part in his thinking" (May, *Creatio ex Nihilo,* 125, Osborn's emphasis). Osborn shows how May slides from "seems to" and "gets the impression" to "presupposes." He adds, "May shows great integrity by leaving enough clues to challenge his argument and display the vitality of the problem" (Osborn, *Irenaeus of Lyons,* 67 n).

Upon closer scrutiny, Justin's worldview is quite biblical, not Platonic:

> I confess that I both boast and with all my strength strive to be found a Christian; not because the teachings of Plato are different from those of Christ, but because they are not in all respects similar, as neither are those of the others, Stoics, and poets, and historians. For each man spoke well in proportion to the share he had of the spermatic word. . . . Whatever things were rightly said among all men, are the property of us Christians.[180]

In fact, Justin distances himself from the Platonists with regard to creation. Unlike the traditional Middle Platonic worldview, Justin maintains that God and unformed matter are not coeternal. Elsewhere, he states that "God alone is unbegotten [*agennētos*]" and "incorruptible [*aphthartos*]," but "all things after Him are created."[181]

> For that which is unbegotten [*agennēton*] is similar to, equal to, and the same with that which is unbegotten; and neither in power nor in honour should the one be preferred to the other, and hence there are not many things which are unbegotten: for if there were some difference between them, you would not discover the cause of the difference, though you searched for it; but after letting the mind ever wander to infinity, you would at length, wearied out, take your stand on one Unbegotten [*epi henos stēse agennētou kamōn*], and say that this is the Cause of all.[182]

There are not two unbegotten entities (God and matter), but one—God alone. Justin tells Trypho (in AD 135): "There will be no other God, O Trypho, nor was there from eternity [*ēn ap' aiōnos*] any other existing . . . but He who made and disposed all this universe."[183] Unlike Plato's Demiurge (which fashions from whatever eternal *hylē* [primordial matter] is available), the true Creator is different. In his *Second Apology*, Justin writes of God, "the Father of all, who is unbegotten."[184] He is "the unbegotten and ineffable God."[185]

180. Justin, *Second Apology* [*Apologia II pro Christianis*] 13.
181. Justin, *Dialogue* 5.
182. Ibid.
183. Ibid., 11.
184. Justin, *2 Apol.* 6. We will not here address the question of the Word's procession from the Father; Justin refers to the Logos as "begotten" before the creation of the world (*2 Apol.* 6). Later in this work, Justin clarifies: "For next to God, we worship and love the Word who is from the unbegotten and ineffable God, since also He became man for our sakes, that becoming a partaker of our sufferings, He might also bring us healing" (*2 Apol.* 13).
185. Justin, *2 Apol.* 13.

In light of this very plausible *ex nihilo* understanding of Justin,[186] we see that he is actually correcting Plato in light of Scripture (as he does on other matters). Torchia writes, "From this standpoint, even a commitment to the idea of preexistent matter does not rule out a doctrine of creation *ex nihilo*. Indeed, God could have created matter prior to its formation or ordering."[187]

We have once again an implicit belief in creation out of nothing. Monotheism demands it.

ATHENAGORAS

Gerhard May charges that Athenagoras (d. AD 180, writing in the 170s) "shows himself more heavily dependent in his cosmology on the contemporary Platonist scheme of concepts than Justin."[188] May alleges that "Athenagoras understands the creation of the world unambiguously as the mere shaping of the unoriginate[d] matter," using the analogy of a potter's shaping clay.[189]

Again, we would disagree. Indeed, we set forth a more plausible and organic view. In the beginning of his *Plea for the Christians*, Athenagoras the Athenian addresses "the Emperors Marcus Aurelius Antoninus and Lucius Aurelius Commodus, conquerors of Armenia and Sarmatia, and more than all, philosophers." Athenagoras attempts to defend Christians against injustices and false charges of atheism, appealing in the process to various philosophers and poets and classical figures.

Even though Athenagoras speaks of God as the Shaper of the universe (as a potter shapes clay), this by no means excludes God as the Originator of that substrate. In the same section, Athenagoras makes clear that God alone is eternal—in contrast to all else: "So that, if we were to regard the various forms of matter as gods, we should seem to be without any sense of the true God, because we should be putting the things which are dissoluble and perishable [*ta lyta kai phtharta*] on a level with that which is eternal [*to aïdio*]."[190]

God's eternality is opposed to the noneternality of matter, as Athenagoras claims earlier in his *Plea:*

> But to us, who distinguish God from matter [*tēs hylēs*], and teach that matter is one thing and God another, and that they are separated by a wide

186. In light of additional research, this new position rejects the earlier view taken about Justin on preexistent matter (Copan, "Is *Creatio ex Nihilo* a Post-Biblical Invention?" 82–83); a two-stage creation is the more plausible view.
187. Torchia, "Theories of Creation," 194.
188. May, *Creatio ex Nihilo*, 137.
189. Cf. Athenagoras, *A Plea for the Christians* [*Legatio pro Christianis*] 15.
190. Ibid.

interval (for that the Deity is unbegotten [*agennēton*] and eternal [*aïdion*], to be beheld by the understanding and reason alone, while matter is created and perishable [*genētēn kai phthartēn*]), is it not absurd to apply the name of atheism? . . . But, since our doctrine acknowledges one God, the Maker of this universe [*tou pantos poiētēn*], who is Himself uncreated (for that which is does not come to be [*ginetai*], but that which is not [*to mē on*]) but has made all things by the Logos which is from Him, we are treated unreasonably in both respects, in that we are both defamed and persecuted.[191]

Unquestionably, matter is created and perishable; God is not.

In his *Plea*, Athenagoras makes ontological distinctions between matter and God—the created and the uncreated—as well as that which is and (in the context of idols made by humans) that which is not:

Because the multitude, who cannot distinguish between matter [*hylē*] and God, or see how great is the interval which lies between them, pray to idols made of matter, are we therefore, who do distinguish and separate the uncreated and the created [*to agenēton kai to genēton*], that which is [*to on*] and that which is not [*to ouk on*].[192]

In his other work, *On the Resurrection of the Dead*, Athenagoras connects creation and resurrection, declaring that God's "power is sufficient for the raising of dead bodies," which is shown by

the creation of these same bodies. For if, when they did not exist, He made at their first formation the bodies of men, and their original elements, He will, when they are dissolved, in whatever manner that may take place, raise them again with equal ease: for this, too, is equally possible to Him.[193]

It appears that God later shapes what he has brought about; he makes not only human bodies but also "their original elements." Here we have hints of a two-stage creation.

Joseph Torchia correctly observes what Justin Martyr and Athenagoras are explicating: "Such teachings clearly challenge any claim that these writers accepted the notion of a material substrate eternally coexisting with God."[194]

---

191. Ibid., 4.
192. Ibid., 15.
193. Athenagoras, *On the Resurrection of the Dead* 3. In chapter 11, Athenagoras writes, "If, then, by means of that which is by nature first and that which follows from it, each of the points investigated has been proved, it is very evident that the resurrection of dissolved bodies is a work which the Creator can perform, and can will, and such as is worthy of Him."
194. Torchia, "Theories of Creation," 194.

So again we see the twofold pattern continued in Athenagoras: (1) God and matter are not coeternal (apart from God, everything is corruptible); (2) God brought about the universe in two stages (since God alone is incorruptible, matter could not have been eternally preexistent; thus God must have first created corruptible matter and then shaped it accordingly, and this easily accounts for Athenagoras's reference to clay in the hands of the divine Potter).

TATIAN

Tatian, who wrote in the mid–second century (around AD 160), was a pupil of Justin. It quickly becomes apparent that the apple does not fall far from the tree. May claims that "Tatian is the first Christian theologian known to us who expressly advanced the proposition that matter was produced by God."[195] Unfortunately, May assumes that Tatian makes a theological jump, breaking from his Christian predecessors. Hubler does the same, declaring that it "was not until the last quarter of the second century that Justin's disciple, Tatian, formulated a teaching of *creatio ex nihilo*."[196]

There is a simpler and more plausible tack, recognizing continuity rather than discontinuity between Tatian and his teacher. As with Justin, Tatian uses Platonic language, but he articulates a view quite different from Plato. For example, Tatian, who clearly holds to creation out of nothing, declares that God is "the Demiurge/Framer of all [*tou pantōn dēmiourgou*]." We have here Platonic language, but without Platonism. After all, Tatian—echoing Justin's words—declares that matter was "generated [*gennētē*]" and "not generated by anyone else" except God. Tatian affirms that God is "without cause [*anarchos*]," and this is unlike "matter [*hē hylē*]."[197]

While it is difficult to be systematic in treating Tatian's teaching, his *Discourse to the Greeks (Oratio ad Graecos)* also speaks of two phases

---

195. May, *Creatio ex Nihilo*, 150.

196. James Noel Hubler, "Creatio ex Nihilo: Matter, Creation, and the Body in Classical and Christian Philosophy through Aquinas" (Ph.D. diss., University of Pennsylvania, 1995), 114. Even David Winston strains matters when he sees in *Discourse to the Greeks* [*Oratio ad Graecos*] 6 that Tatian describes the period before his birth as "a former state of nothingness [*ho mē palai*]," which Winston interprets as "a drop of semen" and thus "relative nothingness" rather than absolute ("Creation *ex Nihilo* Revisited," 89). But later, Tatian himself says, "Your assembly of many gods is nothing [*ouden esti*]" (*Orat.* 27), which sounds much like *utterly nonexistent!* So the context must determine whether "nothing" is used literally (as in the latter citation by Tatian) or more loosely (as in the former). As we can see from our analysis, given the context in which Tatian is speaking, he distinguishes between God (as unbegotten) and everything else (as begotten).

197. These citations are from Tatian's *Discourse to the Greeks* [*Oratio ad Graecos*] 5–6.

of creation. The first was the begetting of matter through the agency of the Logos (who is the beginning and begetter of the world), who "first created for Himself the necessary matter."[198] Indeed, even the invisible things were created by God.

> Our God did not begin to be in time: He alone is without beginning, and He Himself is the beginning of all things. God is a Spirit, not pervading matter, but the Maker of material spirits, and of the forms that are in matter; He is invisible, impalpable, being Himself the Father of both sensible and invisible things. Him we know from His creation, and apprehend His invisible power by His works.[199]

If matter were not itself created *ex nihilo* by God, then there would be something over which he lacked power, which contradicts his omnipotence. God existed alone and without any eternal matter. Tatian writes:

> God was in the beginning [*en archē*]; but the beginning, we have been taught, is the power of the Logos. For the Lord of the universe [*despotēs*], who is Himself the necessary ground of all being, inasmuch as no creature was yet in existence, was alone [*monos*]; but inasmuch as He was all power, Himself the necessary ground of things visible and invisible [*oratōn te kai aoratōn*], with Him were all things.[200]

The Logos, who was involved in creation, brought about the world, "having first created for Himself the necessary matter."[201] Matter must be ordered. Thus, even though Tatian uses Platonic language, he differentiates between matter that is *begotten* and matter that is then *ordered*. The matter that God first creates is "confused matter," which must be brought into "order."[202] Thus, Tatian rejects dualism in no uncertain terms: only God is eternal and without beginning. "For matter is not, like God, without beginning, nor, as having no beginning, is of equal power with God; it is begotten, and not produced by any other being, but brought into existence by the Framer of all things alone."[203]

In his discussion of creation, Tatian articulates what is in keeping with his predecessors: (1) Only God is eternal and unbegotten and "without beginning"—which is not true of matter. (2) Through the Logos, God "first created for Himself the necessary matter"—the first stage—and

198. Tatian, *Discourse* 4; cf. 5.
199. Ibid., 4.
200. Ibid., 5.
201. Ibid.
202. Ibid.
203. Ibid.

then ordered it into a cosmos. This two-step creation is nicely summarized in chapter 12 of his *Discourse to the Greeks:*

> The case stands thus: we can see that the whole structure of the world, and the whole creation, has been produced from matter, and the matter itself brought into existence by God; so that on the one hand it may be regarded as rude and unformed before it was separated into parts, and on the other as arranged in beauty and order after the separation was made.

THEOPHILUS OF ANTIOCH

Theophilus, writing around 180 (shortly after Tatian) to his pagan friend Autolycus, reveals that his first allegiance is to Scripture, even if it conflicts with Plato and those of his school. For instance, Theophilus cites Genesis 1:1, drawing on the absolute rendering of the LXX: "In the beginning God created heaven [*En archē epoiēsen ho theos ouranon*]." Theophilus criticizes Plato and his followers for holding that God is the uncreated "Father and Maker" of the universe while still holding to the eternality of the universe.

Theophilus first observes that some "philosophers of the Porch," such as Epicurus and Chrysippus, say that "there is no God at all." Others say that nature is eternal—that "all things are produced without external agency, and that the world is uncreated [*ton kosmon agenēton*]," thus eliminating the "providence of God." Still others maintain that God pervades all things.[204]

> But Plato and those of his school acknowledge indeed that God is uncreated [*agenēton*], and the Father and Maker [*patera kai poiētēn*] of all things; but then they maintain that matter [*hylēn*] as well as God is uncreated [*agenēton*], and aver that it is coeval with God [*isotheos*]. But if God is uncreated and matter uncreated, God is no longer, according to the Platonists, the Creator of all things, nor, so far as their opinions hold, is the monarchy [*monarchia*] of God established. And further, as God, because He is uncreated [*agenētos*], is also unalterable; so if matter, too, were uncreated [*agenētos*], it also would be unalterable, and equal to God; for that which is created is mutable and alterable, but that which is uncreated is immutable and unalterable.[205]

Hence, contrary to Plato, there is no dualism of God and matter. They are not coeval. There is an ontological distinction between the uncre-

---

204. Quotations in this paragraph are from Theophilus, *To Autolycus* [*Ad Autolycum*] 2.4.

205. Theophilus, *Auto.* 2.4.

ated God and created matter; the former is incorruptible, the latter is corruptible. Platonism ultimately denies the monarchy of God.

Though his point is clear enough, Theophilus drives his point home: To fashion a world out of preexistent material is relatively trivial. Humans make things from preexisting materials all the time. God's power is manifested in creating out of nothing at all.

> And what great thing is it if God made the world out of existent materials [*hyopkeimenēs hylēs*]? For even a human artist [*technitēs*], when he gets material from some one, makes of it what he pleases. But the power of God is manifested [*phaneroutai*] in this, that out of things that are not [*ex ouk ontōn*] He makes whatever He pleases; just as the bestowal of life and motion is the prerogative of no other than God alone. For even man makes indeed an image, but reason and breath, or feeling, he cannot give to what he has made. But God has this property in excess of what man can do, in that He makes a work, endowed with reason, life, sensation. As, therefore, in all these respects God is more powerful than man, so also in this; that out of things that are not [*ex ouk ontōn*] He creates and has created things that are, and whatever He pleases, as He pleases.²⁰⁶

Earlier, Theophilus declared that God is in a category by himself "without beginning [*anarchos*], because He is unbegotten."²⁰⁷ This sets him apart from created matter. In this paragraph, Theophilus speaks in sweeping terms to emphasize God's ontological distinctiveness. God is "before all things." Indeed, "all things God has made out of things that were not into things that are [*ta panta ho theos epoiēsen ex ouk ontōn eis to einai*]."²⁰⁸ Again, "the power of God is shown in this, that, first of all, He creates out of nothing [*ex ouk ontōn*], according to His will, the things that are made."²⁰⁹

Later in this text, Theophilus makes clear that his reliance is first upon "sacred Scripture," specifically, Genesis 1, which "at the outset" teaches that "matter [*hylē*], from which God made and fashioned [*pepoiēke kai dedēmiourgēken*] the world, was in some manner created, being produced by God."²¹⁰ Indeed, Theophilus makes specific mention of the OT and for support calls on both "Moses" (citing Gen. 1:2) as well as Solomon (citing Prov. 8:28–30).

206. Ibid.
207. Ibid., 1.4.
208. Ibid.
209. Ibid., 2.13.
210. Ibid., 2.10.

So the twofold pattern emerges once again: (1) Unlike matter, God alone is uncreated; and (2) God created in a two-step process by first creating the raw materials and then shaping them into a cosmos.

IRENAEUS, HIPPOLYTUS, PSEUDO-JUSTIN, ATHANASIUS, AND AUGUSTINE

As noted, there is wide agreement that with Irenaeus (ca. AD 130–ca. 200) the doctrine of *creatio ex nihilo* was well established. As did his predecessors, Irenaeus himself argued that the world was not coeternal with God:

> But the things established are distinct from Him who has established them, and what [things] have been made from Him who has made them. For He is Himself uncreated, both without beginning and end, and lacking nothing. He is Himself sufficient for this very thing, existence; but the things which have been made by Him have received a beginning. . . . He indeed who made all things can alone, together with His Word, properly be termed God and Lord; but the things which have been made cannot have this term applied to them, neither should they justly assume that appellation which belongs to the Creator.[211]

Unlike Theophilus (who divided the creation of matter and then its formation), Irenaeus held that the creation of matter and the shaping of the world are *two aspects* of one act by God, the King and Architect of the universe.[212]

Another important figure to consider is Hippolytus (d. ca. AD 236), who was probably a disciple of Irenaeus. This church father—yet again—follows the common twofold pattern commonly held by ante-Nicene fathers: (1) only God is unbegotten and eternal, all other reality being perishable and corruptible; (2) God creates all matter out of nothing in the first stage and then shapes it in the second.

Regarding the first point of God's sole unbegottenness, Hippolytus rejects the Platonic idea that matter is "an originating principle, and coeval with the Deity, and that in this respect the world is uncreated."[213] Matter is not characterized by "imperishableness" which "necessarily belongs to [literally, 'follows'] that which is uncreated."[214] Hippolytus not only rejects Platonic belief in the coeternality of matter as non-*Christian*, though. He claims it is non-*Jewish* as well. Hippolytus asserts that "all Jews" affirm

---

211. Irenaeus, *Against Heresies* 3.10.3; cf. 2.10.4.
212. Osborn, *Irenaeus of Lyons*, 69–70.
213. *Refutation of All Heresies [Refutatio Omnium Haeresium]* 8.10.
214. Ibid.

that there is one God, and that He is Creator and Lord of the universe: that
He has formed all these glorious works which had no previous existence;
and this, too, not out of any coeval substance that lay ready at hand, but
His Will—the efficient cause—was *to create*, and He did create.[215]

According to Hippolytus, the "first and only" God, who is "Creator and
Lord of all," had nothing "coeval" with himself—"not infinite chaos, nor
measureless water, nor solid earth, nor dense air, not warm fire, nor
refined spirit, nor the azure canopy of the stupendous firmament."[216]
God was "One, alone in Himself." Through the simple "exercise of His
will," he created everything, "which antecedently had no existence, except that He willed to make them."[217]

On the point of God's two-stage creation (ultimately out of nothing),
Hippolytus comments on Genesis 1:6–7, "On the first day God made
what He made out of nothing. But on the other days He did not make out
of nothing, but out of what He had made on the first day, by moulding
it according to His pleasure."[218] What God created "out of nothing" in
this first stage is considered (as the LXX of Gen. 1:2 puts it) "invisible"
and "formless." But then, in the second stage, "the Lord of all designed
to make the invisible visible." Even the invisible things that God creates
are made from no preexisting materials. In another work, *The Refutation of All Heresies*, Hippolytus declares that God brought into existence
the elements of "fire and spirit, water and earth, from which diverse
elements He proceeded to form His own creation."[219]

Thus the twofold pattern continues in the writings of Hippolytus,
who contests certain key ideas of Plato (and other ancient philosophers
and Gnostic thinkers); Hippolytus opposes them in these areas precisely
because he has *not* succumbed to Greek influences on this subject.

Pseudo-Justin (AD 220–300)[220] offers a critique of Plato's view of
creation in his *Hortatory Address to the Greeks*. In doing so, "Justin"
emphasizes that (1) only God is unbegotten (ruling out eternal matter)
and (2) God creates out of nothing in two stages.

> These expressions declare to those who can rightly understand them the
> death and destruction of the gods that have been brought into being. And
> I think it necessary to attend to this also, that Plato never names him the

---

215. Ibid., 9.25.
216. Ibid., 10.28.
217. Ibid.
218. *Exegetical Fragments from Various Books in Scripture* (on Gen. 1:6–7).
219. *Refutation* 10.28.
220. David T. Runia, "References to Philo from Josephus up to 1000 AD," *Studia
Philonica* 6 (1994): 114.

creator [*poiētēn*], but the fashioner [*dēmiourgon*] of the gods, although, in the opinion of Plato, there is considerable difference between these two. For the creator [*poiētēs*] creates the creature by his own capability and power, being in need of nothing else; but the fashioner [*dēmiourgos*] frames his production when he has received from matter [*ek tēs hylēs*] the capability for his work.[221]

"Justin" indicates that everything apart from God is inherently corruptible, appealing to Exodus 3:14, where God tells Moses, "I AM that I AM" (KJV):

> For those things which exist after God, or shall at any time exist, these have the nature of decay, and are such as may be blotted out and cease to exist; for God alone is unbegotten and incorruptible, and therefore He is God, but all other things after Him are created and corruptible. . . . He who is unbegotten [*agennēton*] is eternal, but that those that are begotten [*gennētous*] and made [*dēmiourgētos*] are generated and perish [*ginomenous kai apollymenous*].[222]

Here "Justin" is willing to express disagreement with Plato and even accuse him of contradiction. It is "Plato's opinion"—a mistaken one—that matter is "uncreated, and contemporary and coeval with the Maker."[223] Everything that is not-God is thus subject to corruption and annihilation. Thus, according to Torchia, "['Justin'] clearly rules out any possibility that matter could have existed from eternity: since God alone is unbegotten and incorruptible, matter had to be begotten in order to serve as the basis for creation."[224]

Furthermore, a double-creation view is evident in "Justin," the aforementioned pattern among many patristic writers. Besides God and matter not being coeternal (everything except for God is begotten and subject to corruption), God also brought about the universe in two stages (since God alone is incorruptible, matter could not have been eternally preexistent. Thus God must have first created corruptible matter and then shaped it accordingly). In referring to Genesis 1:1 in his *Hortatory Address to the Greeks* (regarding "the beginning of the creation of the world"), "Justin" follows the absolute (rather than construct) rendering

---

221. "Justin," *Hortatory Address to the Greeks* [*Cohortatio ad Graecos*] 22. Quasten, *Patrology*, 1:205, judges this work to be "pseudo-Justinian."

222. "Justin," *Hortatory Address* 22.

223. Ibid., 23, also stating: "For having formerly stated that he said that everything which is produced is perishable, [Plato] now introduces him saying the very opposite; and he does not see that it is thus absolutely impossible for him to escape the charge of falsehood."

224. Torchia, *Creatio ex Nihilo and the Theology of St. Augustine*, 7.

of the LXX: "For Moses wrote thus: 'In the beginning God created the heaven and the earth (*En archē epoiēsen ho theos ouranon kai tēn gēn*),' then the sun, and the moon, and the stars."[225]

To show continuity, we can go beyond Irenaeus and jump to Athanasius (AD 296–373). He uses the typical Platonic language when speaking of the Creator of the world as "Maker/Artificer [*dēmiourgos*]" or speaking of "(unformed) matter [*hylē*]." For example, he writes of "the creation of the universe, and of God its Artificer."[226] But, again, the vocabulary similar to Platonism hardly implies a capitulation to the Greeks. Instead, Athanasius shows that the Platonic worldview, to be adequate, must be supplemented with the idea of a Creator who is more than an Artificer, and with an understanding that matter is not eternal:

> Others take the view expressed by Plato, that giant among the Greeks. He said that God had made all things out of pre-existent and uncreated matter [*ek prohypokeimenēs kai agenētou hylēs*]. . . . How could God be called Maker and Artificer [*poiētēs kai dēmiourgos*] if His ability depended on some other cause, namely, on matter itself? If He only worked on existing matter and did not Himself bring matter into being, He would be not the Creator [*ktisēs*] but only a craftsman [*technitēs*].[227]

We move even further ahead, to Augustine (AD 354–430), who believes firmly in the doctrine of creation out of nothing.[228] He captures the Christian doctrine nicely when he argues that since God alone is Being, he willed to exist what formerly did not exist or had no being. Indeed, God is not a mere Shaper of formless and eternal primordial matter. He adds, "You did not work as a human craftsman does, making one thing out of something else as his mind directs. . . . Your Word alone created [heaven and earth]."[229] Yet Augustine declares that God shaped the matter that he had created out of nothing and shaped it into an orderly cosmos:

> Truly this earth was invisible and unformed and there was an inexpressibly profound abyss and there was an inexpressibly profound abyss above which there was no light since it had no form. Thou didst command it written that "darkness was on the face of the deep." What else is darkness except the absence of light? For if there had been light, where would it have been except by being over all, showing itself rising aloft and giving

225. "Justin," *Hortatory Address* 28.
226. Athanasius, *On the Incarnation of the Word* 1.4.
227. Ibid., 2.3–4.
228. See Torchia, *Creatio ex Nihilo and the Theology of St. Augustine.*
229. Augustine, *Confessions* 11.5.7.

light? Therefore, where there was no light as yet, why was it that dark-ness was present, unless it was that light was absent? Darkness, then, was heavy upon it, because the light from above was absent; just as there is silence where there is no sound. Therefore, why may I not consider the formlessness of matter—which Thou didst create without shapely form, from which to make this shapely world—as fittingly indicated to men by the phrase "the earth invisible and unformed"?[230]

This twofold emphasis we have repeatedly witnessed as a theme in the earlier church fathers, is apparent in Augustine's work, and this well after the doctrine of creation out of nothing was firmly established. Augustine stresses that (1) God alone is eternal; necessarily, nothing else can be. He also holds that (2) there is a two-stage creative process in which God creates matter *ex nihilo* ("which Thou didst create without shapely form") and then shapes it into a well-ordered cosmos ("from which to make this shapely world"). Again, we have remarkable continu-ity between Augustine and his predecessors, on whom he builds.

Conclusion

Joseph Torchia, discussing the views of the earliest of these writers, observes that in them "we find a well-defined ontological distinction between God and matter," and for each "God is the unbegotten, ultimate causal principle for everything which exists."[231] Thus, in a very impor-tant respect, even the church fathers who were steeped in Hellenism rejected the common belief that matter has eternally existed; instead, it is ontologically distinct from, but dependent upon, God. Only God is eternal. Matter cannot be. God is free and sovereign and is not limited to preexisting materials and physical laws in his creation. The universe is limited in duration.

The church fathers' formulation of the doctrine is simply in keeping with the biblical conception of God. *Only* a doctrine of creation out of nothing makes sense, given the biblical affirmation of God's sovereignty, freedom, eternality, and necessity. Eternal matter would compromise divine *sovereignty* or power since it would have existed from eternity, and God would have had no control over its existence. Preexisting mat-ter would have compromised divine *freedom*, allowing him no other option with regard to the material he was to use. Middle Platonism in-sists that God's only alternative was to create with primal matter. (Even

230. Ibid., 12.3–4.
231. Torchia, "Theories of Creation," 192.

here, one could offer the suggestion that since angelic beings and also human souls are intrinsically different from matter—which is spatially extended, has mass, and so on—and are essentially *immaterial*, then at least these entities would have to be created *ex nihilo*—without the use of eternally preexistent matter.)

Eusebius, while writing after AD 314, challenged those who believed that matter was eternally preexistent:

> [Tell] whether it does not follow from their argument that God by lucky chance found the substance unoriginate, without which, had it not been supplied to Him by its unoriginate character, He could have produced no work at all, but would have continued to be no Creator.[232]

Primordial chaos would also entail that something apart from God has inherent or necessary existence, leaving us with a dualism, alien to the biblical worldview. Indeed, as Harvard classical scholar Harry A. Wolfson states, apart from the influence of Plato and other classical Greek thinkers, there is nothing in Scripture that would have prompted early Christian theologians to contemplate the notion of preexistent matter.[233] But as the church confronted Gnosticism and Platonism, the situation changed.[234] Explicit statement, strong assertion, and rigorous defense of the biblical doctrine became necessary.

What was implicit, assumed, and embedded in the worldview of the biblical writers was that God was the author of everything, and that absolutely nothing apart from him could exist, except what he brought into existence. If asked, the biblical writers would have found utterly intolerable the eternal coexistence of God and primal matter. As we have seen, this was true of the early church fathers and other ancient witnesses.

Moreover, in their doctrinal battles with Gnostic and Middle Platonic thought, the church fathers did not, as some argue, use to their advantage a biblical ambiguity and then forge ahead with one of several possible interpretations of the biblical data. Instead, they made explicit the implicit. A finite time ago God created the universe out of absolutely nothing. Even if, in their words, both Jewish and Christian writers during the last two centuries BC and the first two centuries AD did not use the precise *words* "creation out of nothing," it is undeniable that the concept is in their worldview and writings.[235]

232. Eusebius, *Preparation for the Gospel* [*Praeparatio Evangelica*] 7.20.
233. Wolfson, "Plato's Preexistent Matter," 411. See also Wolfson, "Patristic Arguments against the Eternity of the World," 351–67.
234. Jenson, *Systematic Theology*, 2:4.
235. Thanks to Carl Mosser and Paul Owen for some very helpful references.

4

Understanding the Notion of *Creatio ex Nihilo*

I n the beginning God created the heavens and the earth" (Gen. 1:1 NIV/ RSV). With majestic simplicity the author of the opening chapter of Genesis thus differentiates his viewpoint, not only from the ancient creation myths of Israel's neighbors, but also effectively from pantheism (such as is found in religions like Vedanta Hinduism and Taoism), panentheism (whether of classical Neo-Platonist vintage or twentieth-century process theology), and polytheism (ranging from ancient paganism to contemporary Mormonism). We have seen that the biblical writers give us to understand that the universe had a temporal origin, and thus they imply *creatio ex nihilo* in the temporal sense that God brought the universe into being without any substratum or material cause at some point in the finite past.

Moreover, we have seen that the church fathers, though heavily influenced by Greek thought, dug in their heels concerning the doctrine of creation, sturdily insisting on the temporal creation of the universe *ex nihilo* in opposition to the prevailing Hellenistic doctrine of the eternity of matter. A tradition of robust argumentation against the past eternity of the world and in favor of *creatio ex nihilo*, issuing from the Alexandrian Christian theologian John Philoponus (d. 580?), continued for centuries in Islamic, Jewish, and Christian thought.

In 1215, the Catholic church promulgated temporal *creatio ex nihilo* as official church doctrine at the Fourth Lateran Council, declaring God to be "Creator of all things, visible and invisible, . . . who, by His almighty power, from the beginning of time has created both orders in the same way out of nothing."[1] This remarkable declaration not only affirms that God created everything outside himself without recourse to any material cause, but even that time itself had a beginning. The doctrine of creation is thus inherently bound up with temporal considerations and entails that God brought the universe into being at some point in the past without any antecedent or contemporaneous material cause.

At the same time, the Christian Scriptures also suggest that God is engaged in a sort of ongoing creation, sustaining the universe in being. Christ "reflects the glory of God and bears the very stamp of his nature, upholding the universe by his word of power" (Heb. 1:3 RSV). Although relatively infrequently attested in Scripture in comparison to the abundant references to God's original act of creation, the idea of continuing creation also came to constitute an important aspect of the doctrine of creation as well.

Indeed, for Thomas Aquinas this aspect becomes the core doctrine of creation. The question of whether the world's reception of being from God had a temporal commencement has for Aquinas only a secondary importance.[2] For Aquinas, creation is the immediate bestowal of being and as such belongs only to God, the universal principle of being; therefore, creation is *ex nihilo* in the sense that God's causing a creature to exist is without any intermediary. Even if that creature has existed from eternity, it is still created *ex nihilo* in the metaphysical sense that it receives its being immediately from God.

Creatio Originans and Creatio Continuans

Thus, God is conceived in Christian theology to be the cause of the world both in his initial act of bringing the universe into being and in

1. God is declared to be "creator omnium invisibilium et visibilium, spiritualium et corporalium, qui sua omnipotenti virtute simul ab initio temporis, utramque de nihilo condidit creaturam, spiritualem et corporalem" (Concilium Lateranense IV, *Constitutiones 1. De fide catholica*).

2. Thus, Aquinas, in his second and third ways of proving God's existence, argues for God as the first cause of all things, even while presupposing for the sake of argument the past eternity of the world (*Summa theologica* 1a.2.3). Or again, he affirms that *creatio ex nihilo* can be demonstrated, while at the same time admitting that the past temporal finitude of the world cannot be demonstrated, a position that is tenable only because he has "de-temporalized" the traditional doctrine of *creatio ex nihilo* (*Summa contra gentiles* 2.16, 32–38; cf. idem, *Summa theologica* 1a.45.1; 1a.4b.2). Though Aquinas discusses divine conservation, he does not differentiate it from creation (*Summa contra gentiles* 3.65; *Summa theologica* 1a.104.1).

his ongoing conservation of the world in being. These two actions have been traditionally classed as species of *creatio ex nihilo*: *creatio originans* and *creatio continuans*. While this is a handy rubric, it unfortunately quickly becomes problematic if pressed to technical precision, as Philip Quinn, one of the most important contemporary analysts working on this subject, has pointed out. In line with the traditional understanding of creation as involving a temporal origination, Quinn initially broached the following definitions,[3] where x is any contingent thing and t any instant of time (def. = definition):

D_1. At t God conserves x = $_{def.}$ x exists at t if and only if God at t brings it about that x exists at t

D_2. At t God creates x = $_{def.}$ God at t brings it about that x exists at t and there is no t' such that t' is before t and x exists at t'

D_3. God continuously creates x = $_{def.}$ for all t, x exists at t if and only if at t God creates x

Quinn points out, however, that these definitions entail a bizarre form of the philosophical doctrine called occasionalism, according to which no persisting things exist. For if continuous creation involves God's creating x at t, and if x's being created at t implies that x did not exist at a time earlier than t, then either t is the only moment of time there ever is, or else x does not endure from one moment of time to another. Instead, at every successive instant of time God creates a new individual thing, which, though it may look like x, is in fact numerically distinct from its chronological predecessor, so that personal identity over time and personal agency are precluded. So if we equate conservation with continuous creation, we are landed in occasionalism.

One can respond to this difficulty in one of two ways: either (1) by eliminating from the concept of creation any reference to a temporal beginning of existence, or else (2) by denying that conservation is properly a species of creation. Quinn initially chose the first solution, "de-temporalizing" creation so that it implies no beginning of existence:

D_4. At t God creates x = $_{def.}$ God at t brings it about that x exists at t

3. Philip L. Quinn, "Divine Conservation, Continuous Creation, and Human Action," in *The Existence and Nature of God*, ed. Alfred J. Freddoso (Notre Dame, Ind.: University of Notre Dame Press, 1983), 55–79.

In definition D_4, creation becomes indistinguishable from conservation: "At t God conserves x" means the same as "At t God creates x." We can now speak coherently of *creatio continuans:*

D_5. God continuously creates x = $_{def.}$ x is a persistent thing, and, for all t, if x exists at t, then at t God creates x

The definition of continuous creation thus becomes indistinguishable from the notion of continuous conservation.

This first way of solving the problem accords with Thomistic analysis. It also accommodates modern sensibilities, which bristle at the prospect of making empirical predictions on the basis of theology. Undoubtedly, the popularity of this solution among contemporary theologians has been largely due to these theologians' fear of a conflict with science. If the doctrine of creation involved an inherent reference to a beginning of the world, then theologians would risk the embarrassment of another Galileo-type case by making testable predictions about the origin of the universe. By denuding creation of any temporal reference, this first solution enables theologians to avoid the possibility of any such embarrassment by circumscribing the limits of their discipline to the safe harbor of metaphysics, removed from the realities of the physical, space-time world.[4]

Since the rise of modern theology with Friedrich Schleiermacher (1768–1834), the doctrine of *creatio originans* has thus been allowed to atrophy, while the doctrine of *creatio continuans* has assumed supremacy.[5] In Schleiermacher's analysis, the church has traditionally divided the fundamental relation of the world to God, that of absolute dependence, into two propositions: that the world was created and that the world is sustained. But there is no reason, he asserts, to retain this distinction, since it is linked to the Mosaic account of creation, the product of a

4. Good examples of such timorous theologians include Langdon Gilkey, *Maker of Heaven and Earth* (Garden City, N.Y.: Doubleday, 1959), 310–15; Ian Barbour, *Issues in Science and Religion* (New York: Harper & Row, 1966), 383–85; and Arthur Peacocke, *Creation and the World of Science* (Oxford: Clarendon, 1979), 78–79. By way of contrast, see Wolfhart Pannenberg, "Theological Questions to Scientists," in *The Sciences and Theology in the Twentieth Century*, ed. A. R. Peacocke, Oxford International Symposia (Stocksfield, U.K.: Oriel Press, 1981), 12; Ted Peters, "On Creating the Cosmos," in *Physics, Philosophy, and Theology: A Common Quest for Understanding*, ed. R. Russell, W. Stoeger, and G. Coyne (Vatican City: Vatican Observatory, 1988), 291; and Robert J. Russell, "Finite Creation without a Beginning: The Doctrine of Creation in Relation to Big Bang and Quantum Cosmologies," in *Quantum Cosmology and the Laws of Nature*, ed. R. J. Russell, N. Murphey, and C. J. Isham (Vatican City: Vatican Observatory, 1993), 303–10.

5. F. D. E. Schleiermacher, *The Christian Faith*, 2d ed., ed. H. R. MacIntosh and J. S. Stewart (Edinburgh: T & T Clark, 1928), 142–43, §36.1–2; 155, §41.

mythological age. The question of whether it is possible or necessary to conceive of God as existing apart from created things is a matter of indifference, since it has no bearing on the feeling of absolute dependence on God. Hence, the doctrine of *creatio originans* becomes an irrelevance. All that matters is that God continually sustains the world in being.

On the other hand, this first solution tends to compromise the teaching of Scripture and the church that a temporal beginning is, indeed, a vital element of the doctrine of creation. It is clear that the biblical authors' notion of creation is not some recondite metaphysical doctrine of ontological dependence, but involves the idea of a temporal origin of the thing that is created. The abundant references to creation as past and completed, while not precluding God's future creation of the world to come or specific creative acts in history, are alone sufficient to establish the point. Moreover, the church has so understood creation. By contrast, the first solution suppresses the temporal aspect of creation, thus leading to a depreciation of temporal *creatio ex nihilo*. One sees this devaluation in Quinn's own treatment:

> For God to create or conserve an individual at an instant is merely for him at that instant to bring about the existence of the individual at the instant. . . . Seen in this light, the question of whether the cosmos of contingent things was introduced into existence *ex nihilo* after a period of time when nothing contingent existed becomes relatively unimportant for theistic orthodoxy.[6]

This conclusion may be congenial to modern theologians. Yet the modern modus operandi of hermetically sealing off theology from science has tended to make theology itself somewhat irrelevant. This is all the more tragic because modern cosmology, which studies the large-scale structure and origin of the universe, has been strongly confirmatory of a doctrine of *creatio originans*. Moreover, since Quinn is offering us *definitions*, not mere explications, of divine creation, they must accord with our prephilosophical intuitions and language.[7]

There does seem to be an intuitive, conceptual distinction between creation and conservation, however, that is obscured by treating the latter as a species of creation. As John Duns Scotus observed,

6. Quinn, "Continuous Creation," 70, 74. Of course, it is no part of the doctrine of creation that the cosmos was created *in* time rather than *with* time. But Quinn means to downplay the importance of any sort of divine introduction of the cosmos into existence *ex nihilo*.

7. On definitions and explications, see Samuel Gorowitz et al., *Philosophical Analysis*, 3d ed. (New York: Random House, 1979), 135–40. Definitions offer us meanings of terms, while explications seek merely to analyze a concept.

Properly speaking, . . . it is only true to say that a creature is created at
the first moment (of its existence) and only after that moment is it conserved, for only then does its being have this order to itself as something
that was, as it were, there before. Because of these different conceptual
relationships implied by the words "create" and "conserve," it follows that
one does not apply to a thing when the other does.[8]

Rather than reinterpret creation in such a way as not to involve a time
at which a thing first begins to exist, we ought perhaps to treat *creatio
continuans* as a mere manner of speaking and try to distinguish creation
from conservation.

Creation and Conservation

In his more recent work Quinn pursues this second solution and attempts to differentiate between creation and conservation.[9] He offers
the following postulate and definitions:

A. Necessarily, for all x and t, if x exists at t, God willing that x exists at
    t brings about x existing at t.

D_6. God creates x at t = $_{def.}$ God willing that x exists at t brings about x
    existing at t, and there is no t' prior to t such that x exists at t'

D_7. God conserves x at t = $_{def.}$ God willing that x exists at t brings about
    x existing at t, and there is some t' prior to t such that x exists at t'

Unfortunately, both the postulate and definitions remain problematic.
First, in contrast to Quinn's original definitions, they construe divine
causation as a sort of state-state causation rather than as agent causation. That is to say, the causal relation is said to obtain between two
states of affairs rather than between God as an agent and his effects. In
Quinn's analysis, the *bringing about* relation is said to be a special relation of metaphysical causation that holds between the state of affairs
God willing that x exists at t and *x existing at t*.[10] Thus, Quinn says, "My

---

8. John Duns Scotus, *God and Creatures*, trans. E. Alluntis and A. Wolter (Princeton:
Princeton University Press, 1975), 276.
9. See Philip Quinn, "Creation, Conservation, and the Big Bang," in *Philosophical Problems of the Internal and External Worlds*, ed. John Earman, Allen I. Janis, Gerald J. Massey,
and Nicholas Rescher (Pittsburgh: University of Pittsburgh Press, 1993), 589–612; cf. idem,
"Divine Conservation, Secondary Causes, and Occasionalism," in *Divine and Human Action*,
ed. Thomas V. Morris (Ithaca, N.Y.: Cornell University Press, 1988), 50–73.
10. Quinn, "Secondary Causes," 52.

account of creation and conservation rests on the . . . assumption that there is a special two-place relation of divine bringing about defined on ordered pairs of states of affairs."[11] In Quinn's account, there are thus contingent states of affairs like *x existing at t* that are not brought about or metaphysically caused by God—which is incompatible with an adequate doctrine of creation.[12]

Second, even if we revert to the agent causation presupposed in D_2, Quinn's new definitions still fail to capture the essence of creation and conservation. Creation and conservation are distinguished in his account only by virtue of the accidental fact of *x*'s existing or not at a time prior to the time at which God brings it about that *x* exists. Quinn even takes it as a virtue of his account that creation and conservation are intrinsically the same: those who differentiate creation and conservation "seem to suppose that the kind of power required to create something *ex nihilo* is different from the sort of power needed merely to keep it from lapsing back into nonbeing once it has been created."[13] "But," according to Quinn, "the power and action involved in the bringing about are the same in both cases."[14] Accordingly, all that differentiates creation of *x* from conservation of *x* is the adventitious fact of *x*'s prior existence.[15]

Nevertheless, theologians who differentiate creation and conservation need not, as Quinn implies, find the intrinsic difference between them in the divine power and action. Rather, they may find the intrinsic difference between creation and conservation in the terminus of that action. Intuitively, creation involves God's bringing something into being, whereas conservation involves God's preserving something in

11. Quinn, "Big Bang," 596–97.
12. Hence, it is difficult to understand what Quinn means when he asserts, "According to this account, then, divine volition brings about the existence of every contingent individual at every instant at which it exists" (ibid., 597); this is precisely what his account does *not* state. If he allows that God's volition brings about the existence of individuals, then why define creation and conservation in terms of the superfluous state-state causation envisioned by Quinn?
13. Quinn, "Secondary Causes," 54.
14. Ibid., 55.
15. This is a common failing. Cf. similar assertions by Kvanvig and McCann: From the point of view of the creative act, "it is not even possible to distinguish God's bringing things to be from His sustaining them in existence" (Jonathan L. Kvanvig and Hugh J. McCann, "Divine Conservation and the Persistence of the World," in *Divine and Human Action* (ed. Morris), 49; God's "creating and conserving the world are, from the point of view of the act itself, indistinguishable, a seamless endeavor consistent with the divine simplicity . . . and responsible for every instant of the world's existence" (Hugh J. McCann, "Creation and Conservation," in *A Companion to Philosophy of Religion,* Blackwell Companions to Philosophy 8, ed. Philip L. Quinn and Charles Taliaferro [Oxford: Blackwell, 1997], 308). A similar tendency is evident in James F. Ross, "Creation," *Journal of Philosophy* 77 (1980): 614–19; and idem, "Creation II," in *Existence and Nature of God* (ed. Freddoso).

being. This distinction, which we shall explicate below, is obscured by Quinn's account, for it construes conservation as God's re-creation of some entity x at each successive instant of its existence.

Third, analyzing God's conservation of x, along Quinn's lines, as God's re-creation of x anew at each instant of x's existence, runs the risk of falling into the radical occasionalism of certain medieval Islamic theologians. Out of their desire to make God not only the Creator of the world but also its ground of being, they denied that the constituent atoms of things endure from one instant to another, holding instead that at every successive instant God creates them in new states of being.[16] The Islamic *mutakallimun* therefore denied the reality of secondary causation, leaving God as the sole cause of change.[17]

16. See Majid Fakhry, *Islamic Occasionalism and Its Critique by Averroës and Aquinas* (London: George Allen & Unwin, 1958), 30.

17. It is quite interesting to compare Kvanvig and McCann's development on this score with Quinn's. Quinn claims, "Because God can repeatedly create a single individual at every instant in a finite interval throughout which it persists, God can repeatedly create, or re-create, one and the same individual" (Quinn, "Continuous Creation," 76). But Kvanvig and McCann deny "that each of the things God creates somehow begins to exist *anew* at each moment of its duration. . . . Rather, what is intended is a view according to which each instant of the existence of any of God's creatures is as radically contingent as any other" (Kvanvig and McCann, "Divine Conservation," 15). They think that they are reaffirming Quinn's position, but his view is much more radical than the common claim that every instant of a creature's existence is equally contingent; this is evident from his affirmation that God's conservation of the same individual could be discontinuous. For Quinn, an individual is re-created anew at every instant at which it exists. McCann does not dispute that such continuous re-creation would preclude identity over time; instead, he attempts to block the inference from conservation to continual re-creation by denying that the world is "in any process of continually passing away and being re-created," with the emphasis on *process:* "there can be no process of the world's passing away, just as there can be none of its coming to be" (McCann, "Creation and Conservation," 307). But it is no part of Islamic occasionalism that ceasing to exist and being created are processes; quite the contrary. At each successive instant God creates e afresh, rather than acts upon e to preserve it from instant to instant. Thus, the absence of process is irrelevant to whether continual creation precludes identity over time. Kvanvig and McCann also affirm in their early work that secondary causes are operative in nature to produce changes in things (Kvanvig and McCann, "Divine Conservation," 16), but in their later article they argue that in fact there are no causal connections among things and events in the world because causation both over time and even at a time is impossible (Jonathan L. Kvanvig and Hugh J. McCann, "The Occasionalist Proselytizer: A Modified Catechism," in *Philosophy of Religion,* vol. 5 of *Philosophical Perspectives,* ed. James E. Tomberlin [Atascadero, Calif.: Ridgeway Publishing, 1991], 598–609). Perhaps they mean only to reaffirm their earlier position that secondary causes produce only changes in things, not their existence; but their arguments, if successful, seem to strike down any causal relations between creatures. They claim that they are not defending the view that there are no genuine interactions among creatures; but it is difficult to see what room is left in their account for such. When they say of the collision and acceleration of billiard balls, "It is simply a question of the things God creates being what they are rather than something else" (ibid., 611–12), this

There are actually two forms of occasionalism courted by Quinn: (1) the occasionalism implied by *creatio continuans* as originally defined, according to which similar but numerically distinct individual things are created at each successive instant; and (2) the occasionalism that affirms individual identity over time but denies the reality of causal relations between created things. Quinn insists that his account of *creatio continuans* avoids the first form because his definitions presuppose that x is a persistent thing. But is it even coherent to affirm that God creates a persistent entity anew at every instant? If at every t God creates *ex nihilo*, is it really x that exists at successive instants rather than a series of distinct but similar-looking things? Since there is no patient or object on which God acts in creation,[18] why should we say that the identical object is re-created at each instant out of nothing rather than a series of numerically distinct, but similar, objects?

This difficulty may be sharpened by noting that Quinn's definition D_7 allows that there may be temporal intervals separating the instants at which x exists. Not only does this feature of D_7 render it an inadequate definition of conservation (since intuitively each new beginning of x's existence represents creation, not conservation), but it also exacerbates one's doubts about x's identity over time in Quinn's account of conservation. Quinn dismisses the objection that God cannot create one and the same individual more than once and appeals to the doctrine of eschatological resurrection as positive support of his position.[19] But traditionally the identity of resurrected persons was vouchsafed by the doctrine of the intermediate state of the soul between bodily death and resurrection, or by God's using the remains of or the same material particles that constituted the mortal body. Apart from these doctrines it is quite difficult to see why a body created anew in the end time is the same person or body that lived and ceased to exist long before.[20]

Quinn also denies that his account of conservation implies type-2 occasionalism. He says this is because his state-state causation says nothing about whether or how events are brought about. For all we know from his account, events like x being F at t (where F designates some property) have causes only in the sense of being constantly conjoined and contiguous with certain other events, not in the sense of being

---

sounds very much like Islamic occasionalism. God creates things afresh in different states of being at each successive instant, and secondary causal relations become relations of mere conjunction and contiguity.

18. On the notion of a patient, see note 24 below.

19. Quinn, "Continuous Creation," 76.

20. For discussion, see Stephen T. Davis, *Risen Indeed* (Grand Rapids: Eerdmans, 1993), chap. 7.

brought about by God. Indeed, Quinn confesses that the empiricist in him inclines him toward such a position.[21]

Nevertheless, such a position seems both implausible and theologically unacceptable. For example, if fire brought near a ball of cotton does not blacken the cotton, but is merely part of an event regularly conjoined and contiguous with the event of the cotton's turning black, then the fire's being brought near the cotton is merely the occasion upon which the cotton turns black. So if God, then, does not turn the cotton black on such occasions, as Islamic occasionalists believed, then the cotton's turning black seems to be utterly mysterious and magical. This is not only incredible; it also impugns the providence of God.

Moreover, if God does conserve x at t, as Quinn agrees, then he must not only conserve x in abstraction, but x in its concrete particularity with all its properties.[22] God does not simply conserve the piece of cotton at t, but the blackened, smoldering piece of cotton at t. For the cotton to exist in all its particularity at t, God must bring about its existing with its properties. Therefore, conservation requires God to be a cause of x being F at t. If, then, natural causes are to be analyzed merely in terms of constant conjunction and contiguity of certain events, occasionalism follows, and God is the only real cause.

Quinn does entertain as well an account of causation according to which natural causes act to bring about their effects, just as God does. But he insists that such an account is compatible with his doctrine of conservation because that doctrine does not entail that God willing x is F at t brings about x being F at t. His account requires only that God willing x at t brings about x existing at t. But Quinn's attenuated account of conservation is incompatible with a robust doctrine of divine providence. For either God wills that x is F at t or not. If not, then God is utterly indifferent to what happens in the world, conserving it in being but not caring what happens in it—which denies God's providence.

Suppose, then, that God does will that x is F at t. Then his will is either directive or permissive. If his will is directive, then God is impotent, since on Quinn's account x being F at t is not brought about by God willing that x is F at t. But if God's will is merely permissive, then divine providence is again denied, since God does not directly will anything to happen.

The same point can be made in another way. Suppose that x being F at t brings about y being G at t^*. The latter state of affairs entails that y

21. Quinn, "Secondary Causes," 60.

22. On this point, see the extremely interesting piece by Alfred J. Freddoso, "God's General Concurrence with Secondary Causes: Why Conservation Is Not Enough," in *Philosophy of Religion* (ed. Tomberlin), 553–85.

exists at t^*, a state of affairs that, on Quinn's account, is brought about by God willing that y exists at t^*. Such a circumstance seems to preclude God's free choice not to will that y exists at t^*. Granted, x being F at t does not bring about God willing that y exists at t^*.[23] Still, given the efficacy of natural causes, God seems to have no choice but to will that y exists at t^*. Quinn, however, interprets this entailment in terms of divine concurrence: x being F at t cannot bring about its effect unless divine volition actively concurs in bringing about its effect at that time. But Quinn cannot mean that y being G at t^* is brought about both by x being F at t and God willing that y is G at t^* (which is what divine concurrence holds) because his account precludes this. Instead, he must mean that God wills that y exists at t^* because he knows what x being F at t will bring about, and he wills that its effect should be produced. In other words, he wills that y is G at t^*. The same goes for x being F at t; otherwise, he would not have willed that x exist at t.

On Quinn's account of concurrence, then, God does actively will the effects of natural causes, but his will is impotent, bringing about nothing in that respect. Not only does this impugn divine omnipotence, but it remains mysterious why God willing that y exists at t^* should be causally efficacious and yet his willing that y is G at t^* is not. Moreover, the same problem discussed above reappears in this account: to bring about y existing at t^*, God must bring about y existing with all its properties at t^*, so that conservation implies genuine divine concurrence: God's bringing about y being G at t^*.

It therefore seems that Quinn has not yet successfully captured the notions of creation and conservation. Can we improve upon his account?

Explicating Creation and Conservation

We intimated above that the intrinsic difference between creation and conservation is to be found, not in the divine power and action, but rather in the terminus of that action. Creation, we suggested, intuitively involves God's bringing something into being. Thus, if God creates some entity e (whether an individual or an event) at a time t (whether an in-

---

23. This is because *bringing about* is not closed under entailment: one may not be able to bring about things that are entailed by things that one can bring about. For example, we can bring it about that a rocket ship is painted red. The rocket's being painted red entails that the rocket ship exists. But being neither engineers nor wealthy, we do not have the power to bring it about that the rocket ship exists.

stant or finite interval), then e comes into being at t. We can explicate this last notion as follows:

> E$_1$. e comes into being at t if and only if (1) e exists at t, (2) t is the first time at which e exists, and (3) e's existing at t is a tensed fact.

Accordingly,

> E$_2$. God creates e at t if and only if God brings it about that e comes into being at t.

God's creating e involves e's coming into being, which is an absolute beginning of existence, not a transition of e from nonbeing into being. In creation there is no patient entity on which the agent acts to bring about its effect.[24] It follows that creation is not a type of change, since there is no enduring object that persists from one state to another.[25] Precisely for this reason conservation cannot be properly thought of as essentially the same as creation. For conservation does presuppose an object that is made to continue from one state to another. In creation God does not act on an object, but constitutes the object by his action. By contrast, in conservation God acts on an existent object to perpetuate its existence. This is the import of Scotus's remark that only in conservation does a creature "have this order to itself as something that was, as it were, there before." In conservation there is a patient entity on which the agent acts to produce its effect.

The doctrine of creation also involves an important metaphysical feature that is rarely appreciated (and is missed by Quinn's tenseless definitions): As clause 3 of E$_1$ implies, the doctrine commits one to a tensed or, in J. E. McTaggart's convenient terminology, an A-theory of time.[26] The key notion to be understood here is the idea of a "tensed fact."

First, let us say a word about what is meant by "fact." A fact may be defined as the state of affairs described by a true declarative sentence.

---

24. As noted by Alfred J. Freddoso, "Medieval Aristotelianism and the Case against Secondary Causation in Nature," in *Divine and Human Action* (ed. Morris), 79. For the scholastics, causation is a relation between substances (agents) who act on other substances (patients) to bring about states of affairs (effects). *Creatio ex nihilo* is atypical because in that case no patient is acted upon.

25. Aquinas, *Summa contra gentiles* 2.17.

26. J. Ellis McTaggart, "The Unreality of Time," *Mind* 17 (1908): 457–74; idem, *The Nature of Existence*, 2 vols., ed. C. D. Broad (Cambridge: Cambridge University Press, 1927), chap. 33. On A- versus B-theories of time, see Richard Gale, "The Static versus the Dynamic Temporal: Introduction," in *The Philosophy of Time*, ed. Richard M. Gale (New Jersey: Humanities Press, 1968), 65–85.

Thus, for example, while "Snow is white" and "Der Schnee ist weiß" are two different sentences, they both describe the same fact: snow's being white. Facts are features of reality, ways the world is.

Second, let us explain what we mean by a "tensed fact." We are all familiar with tense as it plays a role in language. In English we normally express tense by inflecting the verb of a sentence so as to express the past, present, or future tense, or by compounding verbs to express more complex tenses like the past perfect or the future perfect. Although most of our ordinary language is tensed, there are occasions on which we employ sentences that are grammatically in the present tense to express what are really tenseless truths.

For example, we say "Lady Macbeth commits suicide in Act V. scene v," "The glass breaks easily," "The area of a circle is πr^2," and "Centaurs have the body of a horse and the torso of a man." It is evident that the verbs in these sentences are really tenseless because it would be wrong-headed to replace them by the present tense equivalent of "is + (present participle)," for example, "is committing," "is breaking," and so forth. Such a substitution would render some of these sentences plainly false rather than true.

The function of tense is to locate something in relation to the present. This can be done not only by means of verbs, but also by means of temporal indexical expressions. Temporal indexical expressions include adverbial phrases (such as "today," "now," "three days ago"), adjectives (such as "past," "present," and "future"), prepositional phrases (such as "by next Saturday," "at present," "in yet two days' time"), and even nouns (as in "Today is Wednesday").

Such tensed expressions differ radically from expressions using clock times or dates, which are tenseless. "January 3, 1812" invariably refers to the same day, whether it is past, present, or future; whereas temporal indexical expressions like "yesterday," "today," or "tomorrow" depend upon the context of their utterance to determine what day is meant. Dates can therefore be employed in conjunction with tenseless verbs to locate things tenselessly in time.

For example, we can state, "In 1960 John Kennedy *pledges* to send a man to the moon before the end of the decade" (the italics being a stylistic convention to show that the verb is tenseless). This sentence expresses a tenseless fact and is therefore always true. Notice that even if one knew this truth, one would not know whether Kennedy has issued his pledge unless one also knew whether 1960 was past or future. By contrast, if we replaced the tenseless verb with the past-tensed verb "pledged," then we would know that the referenced event has happened. This tensed sentence would, however, not always be true: prior to 1960 it would be false. Prior to 1960 the tensed verb would have to be in the future tense, "will pledge," if the sentence is to be true. In contrast to tenseless sentences, then, tensed sentences serve to locate things in time relative to the present and so their truth-value may change in accord with the current date.

The salient point of all this is that in addition to tenseless facts, there also appear to be tensed facts. The information conveyed by a tensed sentence concerns not just tenseless facts, but also tensed facts as well, facts about how something is related to the present. Thus, what is a fact at one moment may not be a fact at another moment. As I write this sentence it is a fact that the United States has not yet invaded Iraq; by the time this book goes to press, that may no longer be a fact. Thus the body of tensed facts is constantly changing.

Now if there are tensed facts, then time itself is tensed: the moments of time are really past, present, or future, independently of our subjective experience of time. Tense is not merely a feature of human language and experience but is also an objective feature of reality. It is an objective fact, for example, that Columbus's voyage in 1492 is over; it is past. Therefore, 1492 is itself past, since the voyage was located at that time. The reality of tensed facts therefore entails a tensed theory of time, usually called an A-theory of time in the philosophical literature.

One of the implications of an A-theory of time is the objective reality of temporal becoming. As McTaggart showed, an A-theorist must, on pain of contradiction, also be a presentist, that is to say, he must hold to the metaphysical primacy of the present. The past and future do not exist; only the present is real. Things come into existence and go out of existence. Things that are real exist wholly in the present and endure through time from one present moment to the next. Thus, on an A-theory of time there is a dynamism about reality, a constant becoming of reality in time.

By contrast, on a tenseless or B-theory of time, as McTaggart called it, there really are no tensed facts. The factual content of sentences containing tensed verbs and temporal indexicals includes only the tenseless locations (dates, clock times) and tenseless relations (earlier than, simultaneous with, and later than) of events. Linguistic tense is an egocentric feature of language users. It serves only to express the subjective perspective of the user. Thus, there is no objective truth about what is now happening, for "now" serves merely to designate the perspective of the person making the tensed judgment. Every person at every time in the four-dimensional space-time universe regards his time as "now" and others as "past" or "future." But in objective reality there is no "now" in the world. Everything just exists tenselessly.

Hence, according to the B-theory of time, all things and events in time are equally existent. If there were no minds, there would be no past, present, or future. There would be just the four-dimensional space-time universe existing *en bloc*. It therefore follows that there is no temporal becoming. Temporal becoming is an illusion of human consciousness. Nothing in the space-time block ever comes into being or goes out of being, nor does the space-time block as a whole come into being or pass away. The space-time block universe is *intrinsically* temporal: it has an internal dimension that, by virtue of its ordering relations (earlier/later than), is time. But the whole block universe is *extrinsically* timeless in that it is not embedded in some higher dimension (a hyper–space-time). In a theistic view, it coexists timelessly with God.[27]

It is evident why we say that *creatio ex nihilo* entails an A-theory of time. A robust doctrine of creation involves the dual affirmations that God brought the universe into being out of nothing at some moment in the finite past and the affirmation that he thereafter sustains it in being moment by moment. But the B-theorist cannot seriously make the first affirmation. On a B-theory of time, God is the Creator of the universe in the sense that the whole block universe and everything in it depends on God for its existence. God by a single timeless act makes it exist. By the same act he causes all events to happen and things to exist at their tenseless temporal locations.

The B-theorist's affirmation that God brought the universe into being out of nothing at some moment in the finite past can at best mean that God tenselessly sustains the universe in being and that there is (tenselessly) a moment that is separated from any other moment of time by a finite interval of time and before which no moment of comparable duration exists. All that this adds to Schleiermacher's doctrine of absolute dependence is that the tenselessly existing block universe has a front edge. It has a beginning only in the sense that a yardstick has a beginning. There is in the actual world no state of affairs of God existing alone and without the space-time universe. God never really brings the universe into being; as a whole it coexists timelessly with him.

Brian Leftow, whose theory of divine eternity entails a B-theory of time, admits as much:

> So if God is timeless and the world or time exists, there is no phase of His life during which He is without a world or time or has not yet decided to create them, even if the world or time had a beginning.
>
> . . . God need not *begin* to do anything, then, in order to create a world with a beginning. That action that from temporal perspectives is God's beginning time and the universe, is in eternity just the timeless obtaining

27. For an assessment of these rival theories of time, see William Lane Craig, *Time and Eternity* (Wheaton: Crossway, 2001).

of a causal dependence or sustaining relation between God and a world
whose time has a first moment.
. . . He timelessly coexists with His creatures.[28]

Leftow never addresses the theological objection that such an emascu-
lated doctrine of *creatio ex nihilo* does not do justice to the biblical data.
The Scriptures give us clearly to understand that God and the universe
do not timelessly coexist, but that the actual world includes a state of
affairs that is God's existing alone, without the universe.[29]

Hence, clause 3 in E_1 represents a necessary feature of the doctrine
of creation. In the absence of clause 3, God's creation of the universe *ex
nihilo* could be interpreted along tenseless lines to require merely the
finitude of time in the *earlier than* direction. Such a doctrine would be
a pale shadow of the biblical doctrine of creation.

Having explicated the notion of creation, let us turn to an account
of divine conservation. The fundamental difference between creation
and conservation, as we have seen, lies in the fact that in conservation,
as opposed to creation, there is presupposed a patient entity on which
God acts. Intuitively, conservation involves God's preservation of that
entity in being over time. A fundamental flaw in Quinn's definitions of
conservation is that he construes it as instantaneous. Not only does this
subvert the meaning of "conservation," but it spawns counterintuitive
results as well.

For example, in Quinn's D_7 an individual thing that exists only for
an instant is not conserved because it fails to exist at a *prior* time; but
intuitively, we should say that the reason it is not conserved is because
it fails to persist until a *later* time. Or again, an individual thing that

---

28. Brian Leftow, *Time and Eternity,* Cornell Studies in Philosophy of Religion (Ithaca,
N.Y.: Cornell University Press, 1991), 290–91, 310; cf. 322, where he affirms that God is
eternally incarnate in Christ. Cf. also 239, where he affirms that in eternity events are
"frozen" in an array of B-series positions. See also Yates's chapter on timeless creation
in John C. Yates, *The Timelessness of God* (Lanham, Md.: University Press of America,
1990), 131–63.

29. Another theological problem facing the B-theory concerns the problem of evil. On the
B-theory of time, evil is never really vanquished from the world: It exists just as sturdily as
ever at its various locations in space-time, even if those locations are all earlier than some
point in cosmic time (for example, judgment day). On this view, creation is never really
purged of evil; at most it can be said that evil only infects those parts of creation that are
earlier than certain other events. But the stain is indelible. What this implies for events
such as the crucifixion and resurrection of Christ is very troubling. In a sense, Christ hangs
permanently on the cross, for the dreadful events of AD 30 never fade away or transpire.
The victory of the resurrection becomes a hollow triumph, for the spatio-temporal parts of
Jesus that were crucified and buried remain dying and dead and are never raised to new
life. It is unclear how we can say with Paul, "Death is swallowed up in victory!" (1 Cor.
15:55 RSV), when death is never really done away with on a B-theory of time.

exists merely for an instant is, on D_7, conserved so long as it also existed at a single, remote, prior instant, a scenario that intuitively has nothing to do with conservation. Or again, an individual thing that exists for only a finite time but lacks a first instant of existence is, on Quinn's account, conserved, but never created. By mere definition that would rule out the universe's having existed for only a finite time but lacking a first instant of existence, as is the case in certain cosmological models—unless one is prepared to abandon the doctrine that the universe has been created.

All this serves to underline the fact that conservation ought to be understood in terms of God's preserving some entity e from one moment of its existence to another. A crucial insight into conservation is that unlike creation, it does involve transition and therefore cannot occur at an instant. We may therefore provide the following explication of divine conservation:

> E_3. God conserves e if and only if God acts upon e to bring about e's enduring from t until some $t^* > t$ through every subinterval of the interval $t \rightarrow t^*$

In this light the statement that creating and conserving the world are, with respect to the act itself, indistinguishable is misleading. For creating and conserving cannot be adequately analyzed with respect to the act alone but involve relations to the object of the act. The act itself (the causing of existence) may be the same in both cases, but in one case it may be instantaneous and presupposes no prior object, whereas in the other case it occurs over an interval and does involve a prior object.

We have seen that the concept of creation is an inherently tensed concept. What about conservation? At first blush this notion would seem to be much more amenable to a B-theoretical, tenseless construal. God can be conceived to act tenselessly on e to sustain it from t_1 to t_2. But a moment's reflection reveals this construal to be problematic. What if e exists only at t? Or what if e is the whole, four-dimensional space-time block? In neither case can God be said to conserve e, according to our definition, for in neither case does e persist from one moment to another. Yet in a tenseless view of time God is the source of being for such entities and therefore in some sense sustains them.

Even more fundamentally, the need for a conserving cause of e to enable e to persist from t to t^* presupposes an A-theory of time. For the account of temporal persistence given by the B-theory of time does not involve the notion of e's enduring from one moment to another at all. B-theorists typically claim that objects that appear to us to be three-dimensional are in reality four-dimensional objects, extended in time as well as in space. The three-dimensional object we see is just a slice or part of a greater four-dimensional object. Things thus have three-dimensional spatio-temporal parts. For example, the Jimmy Carter we see is really just a part of the four-dimensional Jimmy Carter. Jimmy Carter today is not the same man who once was president. Both of them are parts of the four-dimensional Carter, and they obviously are not the same part.

Thus, the spatio-temporal parts of a four-dimensional object are not identical, since they are different parts and have different properties. Therefore, neither four-dimensional objects nor their parts endure through time, since time is one of the internal dimensions of such objects. In order to characterize the way in which four-dimensional objects are extended in time, philosophers have said that such objects "perdure" rather than endure. Because objects on a B-theory of time do not endure through time but are fixed at their tenseless temporal locations, it is impossible for them to be conserved in being. Yet they in some sense are dependent upon God for their tenseless existence.

Similarly, if we countenance timeless, abstract objects like numbers, sets, and universals in our ontology, then God must be the source of their being as well. In their case there is properly speaking no conservation, no preserving them in existence from one moment to another, since some of them, at least, exist timelessly. The existence of such atemporal entities would seem to necessitate a third category of creation not contemplated by the classical theologians, since they admitted no timeless entities apart from God.

We therefore propose, in order to accommodate would-be B-theorists and Platonists, a third type of dependency relation in which creatures might stand to God, what we might, on the pattern of *creatio originans* and *creatio continuans*, call, as a *façon de parler* (manner of speaking), *creatio stans*, a sort of static creation. *Creatio stans* would be the relation appropriate to a B-theory of time. We can use "sustenance" as the technical term for such divine action and explicate it as follows:

E4. God sustains *e* if and only if either *e* exists tenselessly at *t* or *e* exists timelessly, and God brings it about that *e* exists.

Of course, if we are A-theorists and non-Platonists, then we shall, like the classical theologians, have no need for a doctrine of sustenance so defined.[30]

---

30. Nevertheless, such a relation might be employed by theologians wanting to affirm the eternal generation of the Son from the Father.

Like creation, the very idea of conservation in being thus implies an A-theory of time, according to which temporal becoming is real and moments of time do elapse. Conservation of an entity is necessary if that entity, unlike the moment at which it exists, is not to lapse into nonbeing. On a B-theory of time, no such lapse occurs and no entity endures from one moment to another, so that conservation is unnecessary, indeed, excluded. Instead, on such a theory God is engaged in sustaining the four-dimensional universe as a whole and every entity in it in being, whether that entity has a temporal extension or exists merely at an instant. Thus, even conservation requires an A-theory of time.

Conclusion

Scripture and tradition conceive of God as both the Creator and the Conserver of the world, the former having reference to his initial act of bringing the universe into being out of nothing, and the latter referring to his preservation of the world in being from one moment to another. The widespread tendency among scholars to conflate these two actions on God's part flouts the witness of Scripture and the church, has heightened the sense of theology's irrelevance to the real world, and runs roughshod over important philosophical differences between the two. Creation is distinct from conservation in that creation does not presuppose a patient entity but involves God's bringing something into being; conservation does presuppose a patient entity and involves God's acting on it to preserve it from one moment to another. Both these notions imply an A-theory of time and a metaphysic of objective temporal becoming.

5

Creatio ex Nihilo
and Abstract Objects

I n the prologue of the Gospel of John, the evangelist presents a vision of the cosmic Christ, the Creator of all things: "In the beginning was the Word, and the Word was with God, and the Word was God. He was in the beginning with God. All things came into being through him, and without him not one thing came into being" (John 1:1–3a RSV/NRSV). The evangelist gives us to understand that God through his Word is responsible for the existence of literally everything other than, or external to, God himself. Apart from God, everything existent belongs to the creaturely realm, the class of things that have come into being *(genēta)*, and so owes its existence to God's creative Word or Reason *(logos)*, who is later identified as Christ (John 1:14–18).

Such a doctrine of divine creation can be straightforwardly applied to spatio-temporal entities, and we shall later see that there is, in fact, rather good empirical evidence for the creation of all such entities *ex nihilo*. If God at some point in the finite past brought space and time (or at least space) into being, then anything existing wholly in space or time has likewise come into being. Philosophically, there seems to be no conceptual difficulty in holding that every spatio-temporal entity has come into being and was created by God in the sense explicated in chapter 4.

But ever since Plato, philosophers and, subsequently, theologians have struggled to relate the doctrine of creation to a quite different class of entities, known in contemporary parlance as *abstract objects*. Usually contrasted with concrete objects, such abstract entities include things like numbers, sets, and other mathematical entities, propositions, and properties. Persons who believe that such entities really exist are usually called Platonists or realists; people who deny the existence of any such entities are variously known as anti-Platonists, anti-realists, or nominalists.[1]

It is notoriously difficult to explain just what an abstract object is. How does it differ from a concrete object? Contemporary philosophers are tempted to take concrete objects to be coextensive with material objects, but that inclination is a result of their naturalism or physicalism, not any conceptual necessity with respect to concrete objects. If souls or angels exist, they fall into the class of concrete objects, not abstract objects, even though they are immaterial entities. It is frequently asserted that concrete objects are spatio-temporal objects and that therefore any existing entity that is not spatio-temporal is an abstract object. But again, this cannot be right, for God, if he exists, is usually taken to transcend space and time and yet is a paradigm of a concrete object, being a personal agent who effects things in the world.

So what differentiates an abstract from a concrete object? We have seen that God, though immaterial and not spatio-temporal, would be classed by everyone as a concrete object in view of his being a personal causal agent. Perhaps that provides a clue to the distinction between concrete and abstract entities. It is virtually universally agreed that abstract objects, if they exist, are causally impotent: they do not stand in causal relations. Numbers, for example, do not effect anything. More than that, their causal impotence seems to be an essential feature of abstract objects. Thus the number seven does not just happen by accident to lack all causal relations; there is no possible world in which seven could effect something. This essential causal impotence serves to distinguish abstract objects from entities that just happen to be causally isolated in our world, but which could have had effects, and from

1. This nomenclature can be misleading: there are versions of anti-Platonism that are realist in nature, identifying mathematical entities, for example, with marks on paper or concrete objects. For good surveys of the options, see Stewart Shapiro, *Thinking about Mathematics: The Philosophy of Mathematics* (Oxford: Oxford University Press, 2000); and Hugh Lehman, *Introduction to the Philosophy of Mathematics*, APQ Library of Philosophy (Totowa, N.J.: Rowman & Littlefield, 1979). On properties, see D. M. Armstrong, *Universals and Scientific Realism*, 2 vols. (Cambridge: Cambridge University Press, 1978); and James Porter Moreland, *Universals*, Central Problems of Philosophy (Chesham, Bucks, U.K.: Acumen, 2001).

God, who could have refrained from creating and so have stood in no causal relations.[2]

The essential causal impotence of abstract objects implies that they have no causal powers whatsoever. They are utterly effete. This fact entails that they are unextended and immaterial, lest they come into contact with other objects and so affect them. It is less clear that they must also not be spatio-temporal and therefore immutable. Numbers certainly seem to be non-spatio-temporal and immutable, but for propositions the story may be quite different.

A proposition is the information content expressed by a declarative sentence. Propositions have contingent properties, like *being true* or *being false*. Many philosophers would say that propositions, unlike sentences, have no tense and so have their truth-values immutably, even if contingently. Propositions thus exist beyond space and time. But other philosophers disagree, arguing that the propositions expressed by tensed sentences can change their truth-value. For example, the proposition expressed by the sentence "George W. Bush is the president of the United States" was false during the Clinton presidency but became true in 2001 at Bush's inauguration. Such propositions are therefore not immutable and must exist in time, if not in space.

Or again, the story concerning properties also seems different from that of numbers. Properties raise the age-old dispute concerning what medieval thinkers called universals. For unlike particulars, properties do not seem to be confined to a specific place. For example, if we have two balls existing at the same time, they each occupy a distinct spatial location. If they occupied exactly the same space-time points, then we should have, not two balls, but one ball. But properties are often construed to be different. For suppose the two balls have the same shape. In that case, they each have the same property, *being spherical*. They cannot be said to have different properties in this respect, or they would differ in shape, which *ex hypothesi* they do not. Thus, the same property exists at the same time in two distinct spatial locations.

Moreover, the property exists wholly in those two places simultaneously. That is precisely why properties are called universals. If they really exist, they have, at least on the usual account, the bizarre property of existing wholly in two distinct places at the same time. But in that case, properties do seem to exist in space and time. Even if we try to avoid this conclusion by saying that properties themselves are not spatio-

2. Even on the Thomistic account of God, according to which God as an absolutely simple entity has no real relations with creatures, it remains the case that creatures do have real relations to God and so are effected by him, which would be impossible if God were an abstract object.

temporal, but that their instantiations or instances are in space and time, we still seem saddled with saying that properties can acquire and lose the property of *being exemplified*. In other words they are mutable with respect to exemplification, just as propositions are with respect to truth-value. Thus, properties also seem to be temporal entities.

While all abstract objects are causally impotent and immaterial, some of them have potentialities and are arguably even mutable and temporal in their being. Such objects, if they exist, are extremely queer entities, and we might well still find ourselves unclear as to what these things really are.

One final feature of abstract objects that requires mention is their necessary existence. This is not a distinguishing feature of abstract objects, for God is traditionally conceived to possess necessary existence, and yet he is a concrete entity. But unlike all nondivine concrete objects, abstract objects are usually taken to exist in all possible worlds.[3] For example, even if there were no universe at all, it would still be the case that there exist three persons in the Godhead and that there is one God. But if those numbers exist, then it seems that all the other numbers must exist as well. For those numbers are what they are by virtue of the places they occupy in the mathematical structure that constitutes the natural number series. Thus, it would still be the case that $3 - 1 = 2$, $3 + 1 = 4$, $3 + 2 = 5$, and so on.

As for propositions, if no world existed, the same propositions would still seem to exist but in many cases with different truth-values. For example, propositions implying the existence of any concrete object other than God would all be false. Propositions broadly logically necessary would still be true; for example, "Everything that has a shape has a size." Finally, properties, Platonistically conceived, do not depend on their being exemplified. If there happened to be no orange objects in the world or no hexagonal figures, for example, the properties of *being orange* or *being hexagonal* would still exist and could be exemplified.

---

3. The picture is not entirely clear, however. For what about sets, which are usually taken to be paradigm examples of abstract objects? If there were no universe, would the set of U.S. presidents still exist? Someone might say that it would, but that it would be an empty set. But such an answer is based on a misunderstanding. Mathematicians take sets to have their members essentially. Thus, sets that have different members are different sets. Sets are defined to have their members essentially and in this respect differ from mere collections or groups. So the set of U.S. presidents cannot have, say, forty-three members in the actual world and no members in another world. But then the set of U.S. presidents does not seem to have necessary existence. In worlds in which there are no U.S. presidents, that set of objects does not exist. Indeed, it is unclear what is even designated by "the set of U.S. presidents" in this context, since in different worlds there are different sets of U.S. presidents. Only in worlds in which the same U.S. presidents exist would the same set of U.S. presidents exist. Thus, sets, if they exist, would seem to be an exception to the rule that abstract objects have necessary existence.

Thus, if there were no universe at all, the being of these abstract properties would seem to be unaffected. Therefore, if abstract objects exist, they seem to be metaphysically necessary beings.

Do abstract objects exist, then, as Platonism claims? On the contemporary scene, there are principally two arguments lodged against Platonism and one argument in its favor. The two objections usually urged against Platonism are (1) the epistemological objection and (2) the uniqueness objection.[4] The major consideration weighing in for Platonism is the indispensability argument.[5]

The epistemological objection springs from the causal isolation of abstract objects. If such objects exist, they are causally unrelated to concrete objects like ourselves. Indeed, some of them, at least, do not even exist in space and time. But then, such objects seem to be epistemically inaccessible for us, for no information about them can pass from them to us. Hence, if Platonism were correct, human beings could have no mathematical knowledge. Since we do, in fact, have such knowledge, Platonism must be false.

The uniqueness objection is based on the insight that the only mathematically relevant properties of the natural numbers are their structural properties: properties having to do with the positions they occupy in a certain ordinal structure (a structure whose elements are ordered first, second, third, and so on). The internal properties of numbers are irrelevant to mathematics; only their relational properties rooted in that ordinal structure matter. Hence, any series of abstract objects exhibiting that ordinal structure satisfies the basic axioms of arithmetic. There does not seem to be anything metaphysically special about any of these sequences of abstract objects that would set one of them apart as *the* unique series of natural numbers. But if Platonism is true, there is a unique sequence of abstract objects that is the natural numbers. Therefore, Platonism is false.

The only major consideration in favor of Platonism is based on one apparently overriding fact about abstract objects: They are indispensable. For this reason even naturalists, whose physicalistic ontology does not comfortably accommodate such nonnatural entities as abstract objects,[6]

---

4. Paul Benacerraf in two seminal papers initiated the discussion of these two issues. See Paul Benacerraf, "What Numbers Could Not Be," *Philosophical Review* 74 (1965): 47–73; and idem, "Mathematical Truth," *Journal of Philosophy* 70 (1973): 661–79.

5. The seminal papers here are W. V. O. Quine, "On What There Is," in W. V. O. Quine, *From a Logical Point of View* (Cambridge: Harvard University Press, 1980), 1–19; and Hilary Putnam, "The Philosophy of Logic," in Hilary Putnam, *Mathematics, Matter, and Method* (New York: Cambridge University Press, 1975), 323–57.

6. See J. P. Moreland, "Naturalism and the Ontological Status of Properties," in *Naturalism: A Critical Analysis*, ed. William Lane Craig and J. P. Moreland, Routledge Studies in Twentieth-Century Philosophy 5 (London: Routledge, 2000), 67–109.

will often reluctantly embrace their reality. Platonism is alleged to be implied by the truth of mathematics, for example. Lest anyone claim that perhaps our mathematical theories are not really true, it is pointed out that these theories are indispensable to our scientific knowledge of the world. Thus, to deny the truth of Platonism is to deny science and to land us finally in skepticism.

Whether Platonists can successfully defeat the two principal objections lodged against their view may remain a moot question here. Instead, our concern is one that is scarcely ever broached in the literature: that Platonism is theologically untenable. If this objection is correct, then it will defeat all forms of Platonism, even versions crafted to avoid the epistemological and uniqueness objections.

In contemporary discussion, the question of Platonism's theological acceptability has been raised by Alvin Plantinga in his 1980 Aquinas Lecture "Does God Have a Nature?" at Marquette University.[7] Sharp-sighted critics have observed, however, that Plantinga misconstrued the theological challenge to traditional theism posed by Platonism.[8] Plantinga argued that the chief difficulty presented by Platonism for traditional theism is the challenge it poses to divine sovereignty: if Platonism is true, abstract objects lie outside God's control. Therefore, Plantinga dismisses nominalism as irrelevant to the discussion, since even if there are no such things as the properties of *being red* and *being colored*, for example, it nevertheless remains necessarily true that whatever is red is colored, and God can do nothing to make it otherwise.

Plantinga is therefore led into chasing rabbits (howbeit interesting and important ones!) down the trail of universal possibilism, the doctrine that there are no necessary truths. In the end he opts for a conception of divine sovereignty that does not require everything to be within God's control. He leaves unanswered the question of whether the existence of abstract objects depends upon, or can be explained by, God's nature or activity—which is surely the central question.

We may—and should—endorse an analysis of omnipotence that does not entail universal possibilism,[9] but the central theological problem

7. Alvin Plantinga, *Does God Have a Nature?* (Milwaukee: Marquette University Press, 1980).

8. See, e.g., Alfred J. Freddoso, critical notice of *Does God Have a Nature?* by Alvin Plantinga, *Christian Scholar's Review* 12 (1983): 78–82. Cf. Christopher Menzel, "Theism, Platonism, and the Metaphysics of Mathematics," in *Christian Theism and the Problems of Philosophy*, Library of Religious Philosophy 5 (Notre Dame, Ind.: University of Notre Dame Press, 1990), 209.

9. See Thomas Flint and Alfred Freddoso, "Maximal Power," in *The Existence and Nature of God*, ed. Alfred J. Freddoso (Notre Dame, Ind.: Notre Dame University Press, 1983), 81–113.

posed by Platonism remains unrelieved. The chief theological failing of Platonism, and therefore the reason it is unacceptable to orthodox theists, is that Platonism is incompatible with the doctrine of *creatio ex nihilo* and so fundamentally compromises divine aseity. For Platonism posits infinite realms of being that are metaphysically necessary and uncreated by God. The physical universe, which has been created by God, is an infinitesimal triviality utterly dwarfed by the unspeakable quantity of uncreated beings. To appreciate in some measure the vastness of the realms of uncreated being postulated by Platonism, consider the set theoretical hierarchy alone, as displayed in figure 1.

Of course, the existence of any entities independent of God is incompatible with *creatio ex nihilo*, but the profligacy of Platonism in this respect truly takes away one's breath. Moreover, the metaphysical pluralism entailed by Platonism's denial of *creatio ex nihilo* robs God of his aseity. The divine attribute of existing *a se* (from himself) is traditionally understood to be a unique perfection of God, the *ens realissimum* (ultimate reality). God alone exists self-sufficiently and independently of all things. All other beings exist *ab alio* (from another) and are contingent in their being. By contrast, Platonism posits endless infinities of infinities of beings, each of which exists *a se*, not *ab alio*. God himself is reduced to but one being among many.

A consistent Christian theist, then, cannot be a Platonist. But that implies that he must answer the Platonist's indispensability argument if he is rationally to reject Platonism. When the challenge posed by Platonism is thus correctly understood, we see that nominalism, far from being irrelevant, lies at the very heart of the debate, whereas doctrines of divine simplicity and universal possibilism, which preoccupied Plantinga, become of secondary importance. But nominalism is not the only alternative available to anti-Platonists. In what follows we shall briefly consider three major options that have been defended by anti-Platonists in the current debate.

Absolute Creationism

The alternative requiring the least adjustment to the ontology of Platonism is absolute creationism, as suggested by certain remarks by Thomas Morris and Christopher Menzel.[10] This view is a modified Pla-

10. Thomas V. Morris and Christopher Menzel, "Absolute Creation," in Thomas V. Morris, *Anselmian Explorations* (Notre Dame, Ind.: University of Notre Dame Press, 1987), 161–78. In all fairness, it should be said that Morris and Menzel present their view as an updated version of the Augustinian theory of divine ideas and, hence, as a version of

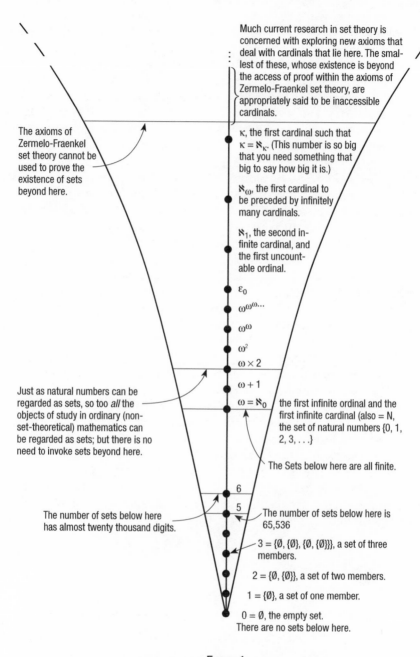

Much current research in set theory is concerned with exploring new axioms that deal with cardinals that lie here. The smallest of these, whose existence is beyond the access of proof within the axioms of Zermelo-Fraenkel set theory, are appropriately said to be inaccessible cardinals.

The axioms of Zermelo-Fraenkel set theory cannot be used to prove the existence of sets beyond here.

κ, the first cardinal such that $\kappa = \aleph_\kappa$. (This number is so big that you need something that big to say how big it is.)

$\aleph_\omega$, the first cardinal to be preceded by infinitely many cardinals.

$\aleph_1$, the second infinite cardinal, and the first uncountable ordinal.

ε_0

$\omega^{\omega^{\omega \cdots}}$

ω^ω

ω^2

$\omega \times 2$

$\omega + 1$

Just as natural numbers can be regarded as sets, so too *all* the objects of study in ordinary (non-set-theoretical) mathematics can be regarded as sets; but there is no need to invoke sets beyond here.

$\omega = \aleph_0$ — the first infinite ordinal and the first infinite cardinal (also = N, the set of natural numbers {0, 1, 2, 3, . . .}

The Sets below here are all finite.

6

The number of sets below here has almost twenty thousand digits.

5

The number of sets below here is 65,536

$3 = \{\emptyset, \{\emptyset\}, \{\emptyset, \{\emptyset\}\}\}$, a set of three members.

$2 = \{\emptyset, \{\emptyset\}\}$, a set of two members.

$1 = \{\emptyset\}$, a set of one member.

$0 = \emptyset$, the empty set. There are no sets below here.

FIGURE 1

The set theoretical hierarchy, starting at zero and proceeding up through the natural numbers to transfinite numbers. (Adapted from A. W. Moore, *The Infinite* [London: Routledge, 1990], 157.)

tonism, akin to the ancient Jewish philosopher Philo's position, which accepts the full pantheon of abstract objects but regards them, like concrete objects, as created beings. Since they, like concrete objects, depend upon God for their existence, God's aseity is preserved and *creatio ex nihilo* remains uncompromised.

Such a view requires two caveats. First, the creation of such abstract objects is eternal. God does not at any time bring the realm of abstract objects into being. Instead, they are coeternal with God, existing in a relation of absolute ontological dependence upon him. Second, God's creation of abstract objects is most plausibly taken to be necessary. The absolute creationist is not saddled with the absurd consequences of universal possibilism. God's freedom with respect to creation concerns the realm of concrete objects, which he could have refrained from creating. But the realm of abstract objects flows nonvoluntaristically from the nature or being of God himself.

Two principal difficulties arise for absolute creationism, the first troublesome and the second truly serious. *First,* modified Platonism misconstrues either the scope or nature of creation. If we think of abstract objects as part of the order of dependent beings existing external to God, then the scope of *creatio ex nihilo* becomes minuscule. For as we have argued, a biblically robust doctrine of creation involves God's bringing into being the objects of his creative activity and thereby implies a temporal beginning of existence of created things. But on the proposed view, the realm of dependent beings, with the exception of concrete objects, exists coeternally with God. Hence, scarcely anything, relatively speaking, is created *ex nihilo* by God. The overwhelming bulk of things is merely sustained in being but not, properly speaking, created by God.

If, to avoid this difficulty, we expand the meaning of creation so as to make any dependent being the object of God's creation, then we have radically subverted God's freedom with respect to creating. In orthodox Christian thought creation is seen as the freely willed act of God. He does not create by a necessity of nature, and there are possible worlds

---

what we (below) call conceptualism. Nevertheless, although that is their intention, they continue to speak of the products of God's intellectual activity as abstract entities, which suggests the interpretation that abstract objects are created things external to God and caused by divine intellectual activity. Cf. Christopher Menzel's remarks in his "God and Mathematical Objects," in *Mathematics in a Postmodern Age,* ed. Russell W. Howell and W. James Bradley (Grand Rapids: Eerdmans, 2001), 71, 73: "We can view abstract objects as created in precisely the same sense in which concrete, contingent things are created. . . . Divine [intellective] activity is thus causally efficacious: the abstract objects that exist at any given moment, as products of God's mental life, exist *because* God is thinking them; which is just to say that God creates them."

in which God refrains from creation and so exists alone. But absolute creationism robs God of his freedom with regard to creating. His freedom is restricted to creation of the tiny realm of concrete objects alone. The vast majority of being flows from him with an inexorable necessity independent of his will. Thus, the ontology of modified Platonism is incompatible with the doctrine of *creatio ex nihilo,* attenuating either God's freedom or the scope of creation.

Second, the more serious problem with absolute creationism is that it appears to be logically incoherent. On this view all abstract objects, including properties, are created by God. But then what about God's own properties? Does God create his own properties? To deny that he does do so introduces an ad hoc selectivity concerning what properties are or are not created by God (especially evident with respect to properties shared by contingent beings) and is in any case inconsistent with absolute creationism. But to maintain that God does create his own properties pulls us into a vicious circle: in order to create various properties, God must already possess those properties. For example, in order to create the property *being powerful,* God must already possess the property *being powerful.* The "already" here obviously concerns a logical or explanatory priority, not a chronological priority, since God's creation of properties is said to be eternal. One is thus ensnared in a vicious explanatory circle.

Does the absolute creationist have any way of escape from this vicious circularity? Morris and Menzel more or less bite the bullet on this score, simply insisting without argument that the circularity is not vicious. They give the analogy of a materialization machine that is able to create things *ex nihilo* and so creates new parts for itself as old parts wear out. But this analogy fails to capture the circularity involved in absolute creationism. For the machine's new parts are not explanatorily prior to themselves; explanatorily prior to the machine's creation of new parts is its possession of former parts.

A better analogy of the circularity involved in God's creating his own properties is the case of the time traveler who journeys back in time to deliver the plans for building a time machine to himself at a younger age. On reaching adulthood, he then uses the plans he received to build the time machine and then goes back in time to deliver the plans to himself—a circularity that is truly vicious! Morris and Menzel say nothing to defeat the charge that explanatorily prior to creating certain properties, God must already have those very properties in order to create them—which is incoherent.[11]

---

11. In his later piece "God and Mathematical Objects," 70–71, Menzel seems altogether oblivious to the difficulty, casting "the coherence problem" as merely the incompatibility of

Certain theists have sought to avoid the vicious circularity that threatens modified Platonism by embracing the doctrine of divine simplicity. According to that doctrine, God is not in any way composed. In particular, he transcends the distinction between a thing and its properties. Rather, God is identical to his properties, and all his properties are identical with one another. Thus, we should affirm with respect to God that omniscience = omnipotence = holiness = omnipresence = eternality = God. The doctrine of divine simplicity is said to avoid the vicious circularity attending absolute creationism because God does not create his own properties; instead, he just is his own properties. Hence, there is no state of affairs explanatorily prior to God's being omniscient, omnipotent, and so forth. God just exists necessarily as a simple being identical with his own nature.[12]

The problem with recourse to divine simplicity to rescue absolute creationism is that the doctrine of divine simplicity is just as difficult to maintain as is modified Platonism. For example, to say that God does not have distinct properties seems patently false: omnipotence is not the same property as goodness, for a being may have one and not the other. It might be said that God's omnipotence and goodness,

---

abstract objects' eternal existence and creation's involving a temporal beginning, a problem that he solves by redefining creation to mean God's sustaining something in being.

12. See Eleonore Stump, critical notice of *Does God Have a Nature?* by Alvin Plantinga, *Thomist* 47 (1983): 622; Brian Leftow, "Is God an Abstract Object?" *Noûs* 24 (1990): 581–98; Richard Brian Davis, *The Metaphysics of Theism and Modality*, American University Studies, series V, vol. 189 (New York: Peter Lang, 2001), chap. 4. Leftow argues that orthodox theists have no choice but to adopt the doctrine that God is identical to his essence. For, necessarily, God creates and maintains in existence whatever is not identical with himself. Therefore, if there are any properties essential to God's nature, such properties must be identical to God himself, since God cannot create his own nature. Leftow thinks it would be intolerable to deny that there are some properties essential to God's nature. For, minimally, God has the essential property of *creating and maintaining in existence whatever is not identical with himself*. If we deny that, then God's nature exists independent of God and God depends on it for the properties that are essential to being God.

In so arguing, however, Leftow begs the question against his anti-Platonist colleagues. For Leftow just assumes that if God creates and maintains in existence everything not identical with himself, then there is, that is to say, there exists, a property *creating and maintaining*, etc. He simply assumes that if God does not create and conserve his essential properties, then—absent divine simplicity—they exist independent of him. That begs the question in favor of Platonism against its antirealist detractors. Anti-Platonists who reject divine simplicity do not deny that God is necessarily omnipotent, omniscient, and so forth or that, necessarily, he creates and maintains in existence everything not identical with himself. Instead, they reject the inference that there are therefore abstract entities or objects such as *being omniscient*, or *being omnipotent*, or *creating and maintaining*, etc. Leftow's claim that theists committed to a robust doctrine of creation and conservation have no choice but to embrace the identity of God and his essence is therefore plainly question-begging.

as manifestations of a single divine property, differ in our conception only as, say, "the morning star" and "the evening star" have different senses but both refer to the same reality, Venus. But this response is inadequate. For *being the morning star* and *being the evening star* are distinct properties, both possessed by Venus; the same entity has these two distinct properties. In the same way, being omnipotent and being good are not different senses for the same property (as are, say, *being even* and *being divisible by two*) but are clearly distinct properties. Even if God has both properties in virtue of being in the same intrinsic state, he nonetheless has both of these different properties.

Or again, for the modified Platonist to say that God is his essence seems to make God into a property, which is incompatible with his being a living, concrete being. Medieval thinkers such as Thomas Aquinas avoided this untoward implication because they did not think of essences or natures as abstract objects but as concrete constituents of things.[13] But on the present view essences are properties, construed as abstract objects. All God's properties are said to be identical with one another, and God is said to be identical to the single, simple property that is his essence. But if God just is omnipotence and is goodness and is omniscience and so on, then God is not a substance and, in particular, not a personal agent.

It does no good to try to escape this conclusion by saying that God is his particular instance of these properties, for that would be to turn God into an abstract particular, to make him this goodness or this omnipotence. Nor will it do to say that God's being identical with his essence will simply force us to revise our concept of what a property is like. For we clearly grasp some of the essential characteristics of properties and of abstract objects in general, so as to be able confidently to assert that anything that is a personal agent just is not a property. The doctrine that God is any sort of abstract object is theologically and philosophically untenable, for such abstractions cannot be the Creator and sustainer of the universe as God is.

Moreover, if God is not distinct from his essence, then God cannot know or do anything different from what he knows and does. He can have no contingent knowledge or action, for everything about him is essential to him.[14] But in that case all modal distinctions collapse and everything becomes necessary. Since "God knows that *p*" is logically equivalent to

---

13. See the quite helpful article by Nicholas Wolterstorff, "Divine Simplicity," in *Philosophy of Religion*, ed. James E. Tomberlin, Philosophical Perspectives 5 (Atascadero, Calif.: Ridgeview Publishing, 1991), 531–52.

14. Leftow wants to hold that although God is identical with his essential attributes and they with each other, God nevertheless does possess contingent properties as well,

"*p* is true," the necessity of the former entails the necessity of the latter. Thus, divine simplicity leads to an extreme fatalism, according to which everything that happens does so with logical necessity.

It might be said that Aquinas could escape this unwelcome conclusion by his doctrine that God stands in no real relations to creatures. As a simple being, God transcends all the Aristotelian distinctions among substance and accidents, and since relations are one type of accident, God has no relational properties and stands in no real relations to things outside himself. Things stand in real relations to God, but the situation is not symmetrical: God's relations to creatures are just in our minds, not in reality. Thus, God is perfectly similar in all logically possible worlds that we can imagine. But in some worlds either different creatures stand in relation to God, or no creatures at all exist and are related to God. Thus, the same simple cognitive state counts as knowledge of one conjunction of propositions in one world and another conjunction of propositions in another world. Similarly, in one world the same act of power (which, according to the doctrine of divine simplicity, just is the divine being) has effects really related to it in the form of creatures, and in another world has no such effects.

But Aquinas's doctrine only serves to make divine simplicity more incredible. For it is incomprehensible how the same cognitive state can be knowledge that "I exist alone" in one world and that "I have created myriads of creatures" in another. Moreover, what God knows is still different, even if God's cognitive state is the same; and since God is his knowledge, contingency is introduced into God. It is equally unintelligible why a universe of creatures should exist in some worlds and not in others if God's act of power is the same across worlds. The reason cannot be found in God, since he is absolutely the same. Neither can the reason be found in creatures themselves, for the reason must be explanatorily prior to the existence of creatures. Thus, to contend that God stands in no real relations to things is to make the existence or nonexistence of creatures in various possible worlds independent of God and utterly mysterious.

Finally, to say that God's essence just is his existence seems wholly obscure, since then in God's case, no entity exists; there is just the ex-

---

with which he is not identical, since if the world were different, God's intrinsic state of knowledge would likewise be different (Leftow, "God an Abstract Object?" 595). In this case, divine simplicity has been abandoned, and one will have to say that God creates his own contingent properties. But then incoherence threatens. For consider the property *having contingent properties*. This property cannot be contingently possessed by God because in any possible world God will have some knowledge state and, hence, some contingent properties. So this property must be essential to God and, hence, identical with him. But then, explanatorily prior to his creating contingent properties, God must already possess contingent properties—which is incoherent.

isting itself without any subject. Things exist; but it is unintelligible to say that *exists* just exists.

In short, we have powerful reasons to reject the doctrine of divine simplicity and along with it the claim that God can create all properties other than those that we conceive to belong to his simple essence.

It therefore seems that the vicious circularity that threatens modified Platonism cannot be plausibly avoided by recourse to divine simplicity. Unless absolute creationists find some better solution to this problem, their attempt to modify Platonism in order to bring it into harmony with Christian doctrine seems to be an abortive strategy.

Fictionalism

Philosophical discussions of abstract objects seem to have an air of unreality about them. Certainly, things like brown dogs and big elephants exist; but are there really things like the brownness of the dog or the bigness of the elephant that also exist? It might be said that we see the dog's brownness. But while we definitely see the brown dog, we do not see its brownness, insofar as this is a Platonic universal, since properties are abstract objects and are therefore unextended and do not reflect photons. Brownness is thus, curiously, not itself brown. But then, how does being partly composed of, or standing in relation to, a colorless abstract object make an otherwise colorless dog brown?

Similarly, we may all agree that we have three apples on the table and that if we place two more apples there, five apples will be on the table. But does three itself actually exist? Are there things like two and five that exist independently of any concrete objects that they number? It is hard to resist the suspicion that we are being tricked by our linguistic practices into reifying linguistic expressions, which, while perhaps unavoidable, do not really refer to any existing things.

That is exactly the contention of fictionalism, which views abstract objects as more-or-less useful fictions. Sentences like "2 + 2 = 4" are like statements concerning fictional characters, such as "Santa Claus lives at the North Pole." Such sentences fail to refer to anything because they have vacuous terms in them. Because they thus fail to correspond to reality, they are literally false or at least truth valueless. Since there is no such person as Santa Claus, he cannot literally live at the North Pole. Since there are no such things as two and four, it is not literally true that four is the sum of two twos.

What is true to say, however, is that Santa Claus lives at the North Pole according to the usual story of Santa Claus; he does not, according to that story, make his home in East Peoria. Similarly, it is true to say that 2 + 2 = 4 according to the standard account of mathematics. This saves the fictionalist from the embarrassment of stating flatly that "2 + 2 = 4" is false, for he agrees that such a statement is true in the standard model of arithmetic. But he denies that that model corresponds to any independent reality. It is a mistake to think that mathematical practice commits us to the literal truth of mathematical theories, for the ontological question concerning the reality of mathematical objects is a philosophical question that mathematics does not itself address. At most, our practice commits us to holding that certain statements are true according to the standard account in the relevant area.

If the fictionalist is right, then the challenge posed by Platonism to *creatio ex nihilo* and to divine aseity is immediately dissolved. For then there are no abstract objects. Therefore, God alone exists *a se*, and he creates everything distinct from himself *ex nihilo*.

The chief difficulty facing fictionalism is the indispensability argument for Platonism. If mathematical statements are mere fictions, then why are they so useful, and why can we not get along without them in coming to know our world?

In his penetrating defense of fictionalism,[15] Mark Balaguer observes that two routes are open for responding to this objection. One route, taken by Hartry Field, is to challenge the assumption that mathematics is indispensable for science and to provide a nominalized science in its place. Although Balaguer disagrees with the consensus view that Field's nominalization program is a failure, he nevertheless prefers to concede that mathematics is inextricably woven into empirical science and to explain this from a fictionalist perspective. The second route, adopted by Balaguer, is to show that, however indispensable mathematics may be for scientific practice, it contributes nothing of content to our knowledge of the world, and its applicability is no better explained by Platonism.

Balaguer advocates what he calls nominalistic scientific realism, the view that the nominalistic content of empirical science is for the most part true, though its Platonistic content is fictional. This view is supported by the causal isolation of abstract objects. If, *per impossibile*, all the abstract objects in the mathematical realm were to disappear, there would be no effect on the physical world. Therefore, even if all mathematical objects disappeared, the nominalistic content of science

15. Mark Balaguer, *Platonism and Anti-Platonism in Mathematics* (New York: Oxford University Press, 1998), part 2. See idem, "A Theory of Mathematical Correctness and Mathematical Truth," *Pacific Philosophical Quarterly* 82 (2001): 87–114.

would remain true. This is simply to reiterate that abstract objects are causally inert.

"The idea behind the [indispensability] argument is actually very counterintuitive," muses Balaguer. "The idea here is that in order to believe that the physical world has the nature that empirical science assigns to it, I have to believe that there are causally inert mathematical objects, existing outside of spacetime."[16] This idea is inherently implausible. So why speak of mathematical entities at all? The answer, says Balaguer, is that empirical theories use mathematical object language to construct a theoretical apparatus or descriptive framework in which to make assertions about the physical world.

For example, when we say of some physical system S that "S is 40° Celsius," the number 40 serves merely as a convenient way of describing S's temperature state. By correlating different temperature states with different numbers, the Celsius scale permits us to use numerals as names of temperature states. The empirical structure of the temperature states can be represented by the mathematical structure of the real number line because they have the same structure. Thus, the Platonistic content of science is something that science says incidentally in its effort to say what it really wants to say—what is contained in its nominalistic content.

Balaguer does not explain why mathematics is applicable to the physical world or why it is indispensable in empirical science. He merely argues that its applicability and indispensability do not imply its literal truth. But he observes that neither can the Platonist answer such "why" questions. The truth of mathematical theories does not guarantee their relevance; so Platonists are faced with the question of why mathematical objects, existing outside of space-time and causally isolated, have any relevance to physical theory. The indispensability argument is really "a challenge to people who deny that mathematics is about causally efficacious, empirical objects to account for the relevance of mathematics to empirical science."[17] That challenge is even more pressing for the Platonist than for the fictionalist.

The challenge to explain the applicability of mathematics to the world brings to mind Plato's account of creation in the *Timaeus*. God looks to the Forms as the patterns on which to model the physical universe. Although such an account is inconsistent with a robust doctrine of *creatio ex nihilo*, it does solve the applicability/indispensability problem. Because God has fashioned the world on the model of certain mathematical forms, mathematics is inherent in any accurate description of

16. Balaguer, *Platonism and Anti-Platonism*, 136.
17. Ibid., 111.

the world. But a similar account is available to the fictionalist. God may have employed certain mathematical fictions to serve as a blueprint for his construction of the physical universe, and hence those fictions are useful as a descriptive framework for our empirical science.

Thus, when Balaguer asserts that "the real number line is relevant to length ascriptions because physical objects are ordered with respect to 'longer than' just as real numbers are ordered with respect to 'greater than,'"[18] the theist will attribute this homomorphic structuring to God's design. The applicability of mathematics to the empirical world is therefore not a problem for the theist, be he a Platonist or a fictionalist. The fictionalist, moreover, may grant the indispensability of mathematics to empirical science as a descriptive aid, but he will insist that such indispensability does not warrant the conclusion that abstract mathematical objects actually exist.

What about propositions? How will the fictionalist deal with them? In a recent article Balaguer has extended his fictionalist analysis of mathematical objects to take in propositions as well.[19] He observes that the chief reason Platonists give for thinking that propositions exist is the indispensability argument. They claim that in sentences containing "that" clauses, such as "Balaguer believes that there are no good arguments for Platonism," or "Balaguer admits that mathematical sentences are scientifically indispensable," the "that" clause is a referring expression picking out some object. Moreover, the most plausible referents for such expressions are propositions, rather than, say, sentences, thoughts, or what have you. Accordingly, propositions are indispensable objects of our various attitudes.

In response to this argument Balaguer defends what he calls semantic fictionalism. He agrees with the Platonist that, semantically, "believes" is a two-place relation involving a subject and an object of the subject's attitude. But he denies that, metaphysically, believing is a two-place relation. Instead, having a belief is a nonrelational property of the believer. Hence, Balaguer agrees with the Platonist's semantic analysis of sentences containing "that" clauses: such clauses are referring expressions. He agrees, moreover, that the most plausible candidate for the referents of such expressions is, indeed, propositions.

But since fictionalism denies that there are any such entities as propositions, it follows that, according to the semantic fictionalist, "that" clauses are vacuous because they fail to refer. Therefore, there are no true sentences containing "that" clauses—they are all either false or else

18. Ibid., 144.
19. Mark Balaguer, "Attitudes with Propositions," *Philosophy and Phenomenological Research* 58 (1998): 805–26.

have no truth-value. Nevertheless, such sentences are useful fictions, and there is no reason to try to excise them from our discourse.

Balaguer acknowledges that it might seem crazy to hold that there are no true sentences containing "that" clauses. But he is not denying that we have beliefs, fears, hopes, and other attitudes usually taken to have propositions as their objects. When Balaguer claims that a sentence like "Jones believes that George Bush is president" is not true, he is not denying that Jones has such a belief, but rather that Jones is related to some abstract object by the *believes* relation. His strategy for rendering this claim plausible parallels that of the mathematical fictionalist. There is a nominalistic content of "Jones believes that George W. Bush is president" that is causally isolated from, and therefore independent of, any purported Platonistic content concerning a proposition. Because abstract objects are causally inert, a proposition, even if it exists, does nothing to determine Jones's belief state. When Jones believes that George W. Bush is president, there is a certain concrete state of his soul/brain that is utterly unaffected by any abstract objects like propositions. So even if there were no propositions, if they were all to vanish, Jones would still be in the same belief state and therefore still have the same beliefs that he does.

Platonistic talk of propositions, like talk of mathematical objects, is merely a descriptive convenience that makes it easier to say what we want to say about the physical world. When we say that Jones believes that George W. Bush is president, we employ such a referring expression to pick out a proposition as an easy way of expressing the belief state Jones is in. Just as the physical structure of temperature states can be represented by the mathematical structure of the real number line, so also the concrete structure of a person's belief states can be expressed by the logico-linguistic structure of propositions. But if Platonistic talk is just a descriptive aid, then its semantic indispensability gives no grounds for thinking that it is not, strictly speaking, fictional, since fictions can aid descriptions as easily as truths. So long as this is understood, the semantic fictionalist sees no need whatsoever of trying to purge our language of such useful fictions.

Although Balaguer does not mention it, one can envision how the fictionalist program might be extended to include property fictionalism as well. Properties, construed as abstract objects (universals), are causally isolated from, and hence have no effect upon, how the physical world is. The fictionalist can agree that many of our statements involve referring expressions that putatively pick out universals, for example, "Brilliance is no excuse for laziness." It is not clear that all property ascriptions must be taken to involve reference to universals. For example, "The couch is red" may not seem to commit one to the existence of an abstract object like redness but merely to the observed, particular redness of the couch. Be that as it may, however, the fictional- ist will maintain that all sentences that do contain referring expressions putatively picking out universals have vacuous terms. Since they thus fail to refer, the relevant sentences are not true. Nevertheless, there is a nominalistic content to such sentences that is true even though the Platonistic content is fictional. Therefore, such sentences remain useful fictions. Although property talk is deeply embedded in our language and may even be indispensable for describing how the physical world is, such talk does not commit us to the existence of abstract objects. The way the physical world is is causally independent of the existence of abstract objects, and our descriptive statements employ a fictional Platonistic framework to describe the way the world is.

Interestingly, property fictionalism, in answer to Plantinga's question "Does God Have a Nature?" entails that God does not have a nature in the modern sense of an abstract essence existing external to himself and to which he stands in the relation of *exemplification*. But such a denial is entirely consistent with God's having a nature in the scholastic sense of an internal constituent answering to the definitional question "What is it?"[20]

Moreover, even if God does not have a nature in either of these senses, fictionalism does not imply that God could have failed to be omnipotent, omniscient, holy, and so forth. Just as a figure would not be a triangle if it lacked three angles, so a being would not be God if that being were morally flawed or ignorant of certain truths or incapable of doing certain actions. That is why, it will be recalled, Plantinga thought that nominal- ism was irrelevant to the question, inasmuch as God on the nominalistic view will still be unable to control necessary truths, such as *God is holy*. Thus, the Christian fictionalist will think of God's concrete condition as accurately described by the Platonist's ascription of various proper- ties to God, but the fictionalist will not construe these properties to be instances of independently existing, abstract universals.

Fictionalism, then, is compatible with divine aseity and *creatio ex nihilo*, since it rejects the existence of any abstract objects, making it a

---

20. On this distinction, see Wolterstorff, "Divine Simplicity," 531–52. Wolterstorff calls scholastic theories "constituent" ontologies in contrast to the "relational" ontologies of modern theories.

It is noteworthy that the standard Christian view of universals, which reached its high point in medieval Scholasticism, did not affirm that natures exist as Platonic entities but as concrete objects, being universal only as ideas in the mind. For a contemporary defense of what he calls "immanent realism" about properties, a constituent ontology wholly compatible with divine aseity and *creatio ex nihilo*, see D. M. Armstrong, *Universals: An Opinionated Introduction* (Boulder, Colo.: Westview Press, 1989), chaps. 6–7.

theologically attractive option. Is fictionalism a philosophically tenable option? We are not prepared to pronounce judgment on this controversial question. Undoubtedly, the greatest stumbling block to embracing fictionalism is its denial of the truth of so many statements that seem obviously true. One must steel oneself to affirm with a straight face that it is false, or at least not true, that "4 is divisible by 2," that "Jones believes that ____," or that "these two balls have the same shape."

The fictionalist, however, does not simply deny the truth of such statements and leave it at that. He affirms that "four is divisible by two" is true in our standard theory of arithmetic, that Jones is in the belief state that we describe via the useful fiction of propositional objects of belief, and that the physical state of the two balls is as we describe using the fiction of abstract universals. Such affirmations are much less jarring than the flat denials.

Moreover, there are ways for the antirealist to maintain a nominalist position without embracing fictionalism. For, as J. Azzouni points out, the fictionalist strategy tacitly assumes Quine's criterion for ontological commitment.[21] On Quine's view, if one's best scientific theory requires existential quantification over certain entities, then one is ontologically committed to such entities.[22] That is to say, if one must use the existential quantifier "∃" (read as "There is . . .") in the symbolization in first-order logic of the appropriately regimented sentences of one's best scientific theory, then the entities quantified over do actually exist. Thus, Quine's criterion, while not telling us directly what exists, informs us what exists if a certain theory is true. It tells us what ontological commitments a theory has.

Now if one does not believe that abstract objects exist, one can try to so regiment one's theoretical discourse as to avoid having to quantify over abstract objects. Field pursues this strategy of trying to interpret talk of abstract objects in such a way as to avoid being ontologically committed to them. An alternate strategy is to admit that one's discourse does, in fact, commit one to the existence of such entities and to deny that such discourse is literally true. The fictionalist strategy implicitly accepts Quine's criterion of ontological commitment, for apart from such an assumption there is no reason to regard sentences quantifying over abstract objects as false. Absent Quine's criterion, one could regard such statements as true but just shrug off talk of abstract objects as forcing no ontological commitments.

21. J. Azzouni, "On 'On What There Is,'" *Pacific Philosophical Quarterly* 79 (1998): 1–18.

22. W. V. O. Quine, "On What There Is," in *From a Logical Point of View*, 2d ed. (Cambridge: Harvard University Press, 1980), 1–19.

In point of fact, there is no compelling reason to accept Quine's criterion of ontological commitment. There is no basis for investing the existential quantifier with the sort of ontological force that Quine ascribes to it. It may seem odd to assert that "There is a prime number between six and eight" while denying that numbers exist, but the expression "there is" need not be taken to commit us to the actual existence of the object quantified over. Azzouni observes:

> A good case can be made that physicists, and other scientists too, usually regard *their* employment of mathematics to be ontologically neutral. Despite the (indispensable) use of quantification over mathematical entities to formulate scientific theories, and to make empirical inferences, mathematical talk is taken to be *true* even though, simultaneously, it isn't taken to be about anything "real." This gives powerful intuitive evidence that *some* uses of the ordinary language "there is" (e.g., in the context of applied mathematics) *do not* carry ontological weight.[23]

Indeed, we think there is good reason not to regard the existential quantifier as the key to ontology. For example, the language of logic is an artificial language that abstracts from all tense. A sentence such as "Trilobites flourished in the Paleozoic sea" requires existential quantification over trilobites, so that we are ontologically committed to the existence of trilobites. But then we seemed forced either to say that trilobites presently exist, which we know to be false, or to adopt Quine's four-dimensional ontology. According to Quine, there is no ontological distinction between past, present, and future entities, an ontology that we have very good reasons to reject (not least being its incompatibility with the doctrine of *creatio ex nihilo*).[24] Hence, ontological commitments should not be read off the existential quantifier.

Azzouni observes that it is well known that the existential quantifier can play two different roles that sometimes come apart, indicating ontological commitment or indicating the admissibility of a logical rule of inference.[25] When someone says, "There are infinitely many prime

---

23. Azzouni, "On 'On What There Is,'" 4.

24. One can finesse the quantification of tensed sentences by conjoining with the existential quantifier a tense logical operator in whose scope the quantifier lies. But this is an implicit rejection of Quine's use of the simple quantifier as the key to ontological commitment. Indeed, use of higher order logic or modal logic in symbolizing the regimented sentences of a scientific theory will undermine the perspicuity of Quine's criterion. For a discussion of the failings of a four-dimensional ontology, see William Lane Craig, *The Tenseless Theory of Time: A Critical Examination*, Synthese Library 294 (Dordrecht: Kluwer Academic Publishers, 2000).

25. J. Azzouni, "Applied Mathematics, Existential Commitment and the Quine-Putnam Indispensability Thesis," *Philosophia Mathematica* 5 (1997): 193–209.

numbers," and then adds, "But there really aren't such things as numbers," he is not speaking incoherently but shifting from one role of the quantifier to another. Azzouni suggests that we abandon the role of the quantifier indicating ontological commitment in favor of a predicate like "is real." Ontological commitment (determined by causal efficacy) would be indicated not merely by saying that there is a certain thing but, in addition, that that thing is real.

Nor is that the end of the story. For even if one agrees with Quine that the existential quantifier "∃" does provide the key to the ontological commitments of a theory, what ontological commitments a theory has will depend upon our interpretation of "∃." Logicians distinguish between the *objectual* and the *substitutional* interpretation of the existential quantifier. According to the objectual interpretation, an existentially quantified sentence (like "There are wolves in Yellowstone National Park") is true if and only if there is some object that has the property predicated of it. Objectual quantification thus involves use of referential terms that ostensibly pick out some referent in the world. On the other hand, on the substitutional interpretation, an existentially quantified sentence is true if and only if a true sentence can be formed by substituting terms for the variable associated with "∃." Substitutional quantification thus does not involve reference to objects in the world. Therefore, only the objectual interpretation, as opposed to the substitutional interpretation, involves one in ontological commitments as a result of true existentially quantified statements. Quine recognizes this but rejects the substitutional interpretation because it eliminates reference altogether. But, as Dale Gottlieb explains, the anti-realist need not maintain that every use of existential quantification is substitutional.[26] He may justify its use in the special case of quantification over abstract objects in view of the almost magical ontological consequences that would result from an objectual interpretation. In order to prove that we are ontologically committed by the existentially quantified statements of our theory to some entity, it must be shown not only that the logical form of such statements is indispensable but also that the quantifiers cannot be interpreted substitutionally, which is, in Gottlieb's judgment, "almost impossible to establish."[27]

Rejection of Quine's criterion for ontological commitment permits the antirealist to maintain skepticism about the existence of abstract

---

26. Dale Gottlieb, *Ontological Economy: Substitutional Quantification and Mathematics,* Clarendon Library of Logic and Philosophy (Oxford: Oxford University Press, 1980), 53–54.

27. Ibid., 50.

objects without embracing fictionalism. Azzouni lays down two conditions for a nonfictionalist nominalism:

> Once one *refuses* to take Quine's criterion for granted, and provided one can show that some significant difference exists between kinds of posits in a scientific theory, one can deny that the existential commitments of a scientific theory are equally justified *ontologically* despite our presupposing the truth of *all* the sentences in such a theory.[28]

The antirealist may reject Quine's criterion due to its evident inadequacy and want of probative grounds. In so doing, the antirealist may show a significant difference between the abstract and concrete posits of a scientific theory on the basis of the former's causal isolation from and, hence, irrelevance to the empirical realm. Therefore, one adroitly avoids the dilemma of denying the truth of some of the theory's sentences or else abandoning antirealism.

Whether in its fictionalist or nonfictionalist guise, a nominalist perspective on the challenge posed by Platonism to divine aseity and *creatio ex nihilo* merits further exploration by Christian thinkers.

Conceptualism

Historically, the mainstream Christian position in response to the challenge of Platonism has been conceptualism, not fictionalism. The seminal figure for Christian conceptualism was Augustine, who transposed the Platonic realm of Forms or Ideas into the divine mind, so that they literally become ideas of God. "As for these reasons *(rationes)*, they must be thought to exist nowhere but in the very mind of the Creator," he wrote. "For it would be sacrilegious to suppose that he was looking at something placed outside himself when he created in accord with it what he did create."[29] Augustine thereby rejects Plato's account of creation in favor of an exemplarist account of creation that is consistent with divine aseity. Medieval thinkers who wrestled with the problem of universals, from Boethius through Ockham, all adopted versions of Augustine's conceptualism. Universals were construed to have an ideal existence, not to be independently existing abstract objects.

On the contemporary scene, Philip Kitcher has defended a view of mathematical reality that is suggestive for the philosopher of religion.[30]

---

28. Azzouni, "On 'On What There Is,'" 6.
29. Augustine, *De diversis quaestionibus* 46.2.21–32.
30. Philip Kitcher, *The Nature of Mathematical Knowledge* (Oxford: Oxford University Press, 1983), chap. 6.

Like the fictionalist, Kitcher takes the referring expressions in mathematical statements to be vacuous, since there are no abstract objects. But rather than regard mathematical statements as therefore untrue, Kitcher construes them as idealizations grounded in our experience of the world, which are, as such, stipulated by us to be true and are, accordingly, vacuously true.

Mathematical statements have the same status as the laws of ideal gases. For example, the Boyle-Charles law that relates the volume, temperature, and pressure of a gas is false with respect to any actual gas, but it does describe the behavior of an ideal gas. The law is true in virtue of the definition of an ideal gas. The stipulation of the characteristics of an ideal gas, Kitcher explains, is warranted by our experience of actual gases, which approximately satisfy the conditions laid down in the Boyle-Charles law. We know from experience that the behavior of actual gases approximates the behavior of an ideal gas. Hence, we are led to abstract from certain features of actual situations and to introduce the notion of an ideal gas in order to describe how actual gases would behave in the absence of complicating factors. Thus, ideal gas laws, though true by stipulation, are nonetheless useful in understanding the actual physical world.

Kitcher similarly views mathematical statements as idealizations rooted in the concrete structures of the physical world and our activities as agents. Central to Kitcher's approach is replacing abstract objects as the subject of mathematics with various kinds of mathematical activities that agents perform. Arithmetic, for example, describes those structural features of the world in virtue of which we are able to segregate and recombine objects. Set theory describes collecting and ordering activities of agents.

Now Kitcher recognizes that no actual agents carry out all the operations described by mathematics. The relation between mathematics and the actual operations of human agents parallels the relation between the laws of ideal gases and the behavior of actual gases. Mathematics is an idealizing theory of our actual operations. Thus mathematical statements are true in virtue of stipulations that we set down, specifying conditions that, while actually satisfied by nothing at all, are approximately satisfied by operations we perform. Since mathematical statements are idealizations abstracted from the world of empirical experience, the mystery of the applicability of mathematics to the world is resolved.

Kitcher's view becomes especially interesting for the theist when he remarks, "We may personify the idealization, by thinking of arithmetic as describing the constructive output of an ideal subject."[31] Similarly, in

---

31. Ibid., 109.

set theory we can replace talk of the successive formation of collections with talk of the iterated collecting activity of an ideal mathematical subject.[32] Kitcher emphasizes that his view involves no commitment to the actual existence of an ideal subject.[33] Statements of arithmetic, he reminds us, are vacuously true, like the statements of ideal gas theory. They are distinguished from pointless and uninteresting vacuously true statements by the fact that the stipulations about the ideal subject's activities abstract from the accidental limitations of human agents. The truths of mathematics are not to be construed as descriptions of the actual activities of some person.

Precisely for this reason Balaguer charges that Kitcher's view collapses back into fictionalism.[34] Kitcher's version of arithmetic is vacuous because it is about the activities of an ideal agent, and there is no ideal agent. In Kitcher's view statements such as "There is a prime number between six and eight" or "The set of all primes exists" are simply false. Balaguer insists that fictionalists can say the same thing that Kitcher says concerning the applicability of mathematics: First, we arrive at mathematical theories by reflecting upon certain structural features of the physical world, extending them, and abstracting from their particularities. Second, our mathematical theories are applicable to empirical science because they describe certain idealized (nonexistent) structures that are partially and imperfectly instantiated in the physical world.

But what if such an ideal agent actually does exist? In that case, the referring expressions in mathematical statements would not be vacuous but would describe actual operations performed by that agent. And, of course, it is precisely in the existence of such an omniscient, omnipotent Mind that the Christian theist believes. If God exists, then Kitcher's view is transformed into a sort of theistic constructivism, according to which mathematical structures are constituted by God's mental activities of collecting and ordering.

32. Ibid., 131.
33. Ibid., 117; cf. 142.
34. Balaguer, *Platonism and Anti-Platonism*, 107–9. Cf. Menzel's misgivings: "A problem with most all constructivist accounts—both 'strict,' intuitionist accounts as well as 'looser,' classically based accounts such as those of Kitcher and Chihara—is: What, exactly, is an idealization, the *mere possibility* of a construction? And for whom is the construction possible? For us? For possible humans? For an ideal agent of some ilk? And how do such idealizations serve as the subject matter of mathematics? How, in particular, can mathematical statements be *true* if these idealizations do not exist in any sense? How can an existentially quantified statement be true in virtue of the mere possibility of an idealized construction that has not in fact ever been carried out?" (Menzel, "God and Mathematical Objects," 93).

Such a position has been defended by Christopher Menzel, who takes properties, relations, and propositions (PRPs) to be "the contents of a certain kind of divine intellective activity in which God, by his nature, is essentially engaged. To grasp a PRP, then, . . . is to grasp a product of the divine intellect, a divine idea."[35] Menzel offers a reductive analysis of numbers, according to which numbers are properties of sets, and takes sets to be the products of a collecting activity on God's part. In order to avoid various paradoxes, such as God's collecting all propositions into a set, Menzel enunciates a sort of divine logicism, according to which there exists a logical hierarchy in God's mind, at different levels of which various sets and PRPs are constructed.

At the most basic level of this divine logicism are concrete objects and logically simple properties and relations, the latter being presumably ideas in the divine mind. The next level up consists of all the entities on the lowest level plus all the sets that can be formed of them, and all the new PRPs that can be formed by applying logical operations to the entities of the lowest level. The third level is similarly constructed from the entities of the second level, and so on, ad infinitum. Such a hierarchical ordering of God's constructive activity prevents paradoxical entities like the set of all propositions from appearing, since no level will include all the propositions there are.

If we are to distinguish conceptualism from what we have called absolute creationism, then the products of divine intellectual activity must not be taken to be abstract objects existing external to God but rather as somehow existing in the divine consciousness. Hence, numbers, sets, properties, and so forth are not created beings but God's own concepts. In Menzel's view, there exists a sort of atemporal explanatory hierarchy among God's concepts, which comprises all supposedly abstract objects.

The great advantage of conceptualism is that it gives us the literal truth of standard mathematics, of ascriptions of propositional beliefs, and of property statements. Moreover, it is immune to many of the traditional objections to psychologism, which replaces abstract objects with concepts of human persons. For example, it has resources for solving the applicability problem, since God can construct the world in such a way that its concrete structures are isomorphic with the mathematical

35. Christopher Menzel, "Theism, Platonism, and the Metaphysics of Mathematics," in *Christian Theism and the Problems of Philosophy*, ed. Michael D. Beaty, Library of Religious Philosophy 5 (Notre Dame: University of Notre Dame Press, 1990), 209–10; see further Menzel, "God and Mathematical Objects," 93: "The idealized constructions that mathematics is about are in fact actual in the divine intellect, and hence . . . the objects of mathematics can be identified with divine constructions—God's collectings and God's concomitant concepts."

CREATIO EX NIHILO AND ABSTRACT OBJECTS193

structures conceived by him. Because God is omniscient, there is no problem with his conceiving numbers or performing operations that no human being has thought of or performed. For the same reason, there is no problem in talking about, say, all the real numbers, even though no human being can conceive of them all. Accounting for mathematical error, despite the plurality of human conceptions, is unproblematic, since God's conceptions are the standard for human conceptions. Finally, even if no human being existed, it would still be true that 2 + 2 = 4, since God exists necessarily with such a conception.

Furthermore, conceptualism seems to avoid the vicious circularity facing absolute creationism. Properties, in the sense of universals, are mental abstractions. Explanatorily prior to the abstraction of its properties, a concrete object does not exist as a characterless nothing, a bare particular, so to speak, but as an object replete with its various particularities. So, explanatorily prior to God's conceiving various properties, God exists as a concrete object that is omnipotent, omniscient, holy, eternal, and so forth. God at that moment is able to form the conception of, say, *omnipotence*, so that in a posterior explanatory moment, the universal property *omnipotence* exists as a divine idea. God's being omnipotent is not a matter of his exemplifying a property, since the property is only an idea that does not exist until God conceives it. So there is no explanatory circle in conceptualism.

Nevertheless, the conceptualist scenario is not entirely rosy. For one thing, conceptualism has the disadvantage of proposing a semantics for abstract object talk that is at odds with the prima facie semantics of such statements. Rather than taking the referring expressions of such statements at face value as attempting to pick out abstract objects, we must reinterpret them in a nonstandard way to be in fact referring to God's ideas. While this objection does have force, it is not in the final analysis a very powerful objection, however, since for one thousand years conceptualism was the standard analysis given to such talk. Furthermore, it can be argued that fictionalism, while preserving standard semantics, is less plausible than conceptualism, given that God exists.

A more serious misgiving concerns the ontological status of the divine ideas.[36] For if we take the divine ideas appealed to in the theory as

---

36. Ockham proffered both versions of conceptualism sketched in the text. The version that takes an idea to be an actual thought he called the *intellectio* theory; the version that takes an idea to be a mere concept he called the *fictum* theory. See William of Ockham, *Ordinatio* 2.8, in *Five Texts on the Medieval Problem of Universals*, ed. and trans. Paul Vincent Spade (Indianapolis: Hackett, 1994), 218–30. See further Marilyn McCord Adams, "Universals in the Early Fourteenth Century," in *The Cambridge History of Later Medieval Philosophy*, ed. Norman Kretzmann, Anthony Kenny, and Jan Pinborg (Cam-

literally thoughts that God has or mental activities he performs, then such thoughts and activities are particulars, not universals. But then it becomes quite unclear as to how property exemplification is supposed to work. If *redness* is a thought in God's mind, what does it mean to say that a fire truck, for example, stands in the *exemplifies* relation to that particular thought? How can that particular be multiply exemplified, since the whole point of construing properties as universals was supposed to be their ability to be multiply exemplified?

Suppose we are led to abandon the modern idea of property exemplification in favor of the scholastic notion of properties as existing in concrete particulars. In that case we are led to wonder how God's thought, as a particular, can exist in anything except God's own mind. Construing universals as particular thoughts in God's mind might fit well with the Platonic notion of the Ideas as models for, rather than constituents of, concrete objects, but such an exemplarist view faces problems of its own. For example, humility is not itself humble, nor is quickness itself quick.

Moreover, what about sets? If sets are really particular entities formed by God's collecting activity, then how do we have any access to such sets?[37] When I collect into a unity all the pens on my desk, that set is not identical, it seems, with the set constituted by God's collecting activity. Since we have two collectings and since sets are God's particular collectings, the "set" I form is not identical to the set of all pens on my desk. But if sets are determined by membership, how could they not be identical, since they have the same members?

Suppose instead that we take numbers, properties, and so on to be, not particular thoughts in God's mind, but pure concepts, the sort of things that are the intentional objects of thought. In that case, since these concepts are genuinely universal in content, particular qualities could more plausibly be said to be instantiations of what God is thinking of. Hence, substances characterized by such property instances could

---

bridge: Cambridge University Press, 1982), 436–39; and idem, *William Ockham*, 2 vols., Publications in Medieval Studies 26 (Notre Dame, Ind.: University of Notre Dame Press, 1987), 1:73–106.

37. Menzel responds to this difficulty by arguing, "What we do when we construct a set or form a concept is *like* what God does. Hence, our set-like constructions and concepts are like his. We thereby gain basic knowledge of mathematical objects in virtue of knowledge of our own perceptions and concepts, and of their similarity to those in the divine mind" (Menzel, "God and Abstract Objects," 94). But if our collectings are not God's collectings, then we do not in fact have knowledge of real sets but only set-like constructions. If we say that we do grasp the same sets as God, then we seem to have given up on conceptualism and reverted to thinking of sets as distinct from, rather than identical with, collecting operations.

be said to stand in a relation of exemplification to God's concepts. Sets could be said to be conceptual collectings carried out by any intellect. God's conceptual collectings would serve only to guarantee that sets unconceived by human beings also exist and, perhaps, serve as the standard for which collectings count as bona fide sets as opposed to paradoxical collections.

A further interesting feature of such a conceptualism is that it could be made to accord with another scholastic doctrine: the unicity of the divine ideas in the simplicity of God's intellect. We could hold that God's knowledge of all truth is via a simple intuition, and that we finite knowers represent to ourselves what God knows in terms of propositional beliefs. Similarly, God could form all sets via a single collecting activity that we represent to ourselves as a hierarchical ordering of multiple activities. Such a model of divine cognition would enable us to avoid having to posit an actual infinitude of divine cognitions. We could also avoid positing the extraordinarily bizarre thought life that God must continually maintain, according to the view that the set-theoretical hierarchy and all other concepts are actual thoughts in God's consciousness.

The fictionalist, however, might contend that such a conceptualism does not differ essentially from fictionalism. For the fictionalist agrees that we can have abstract objects as the intentional objects of our thoughts. We can have thoughts about the number 2 or the property of *being pusillanimous* just as we can have thoughts about Santa Claus. But the fact remains that there are no actual entities in the world corresponding to those concepts. Thus, if abstract objects are no more than intentional objects of the divine intellect, statements implying their actual existence are, in the end, false—at least if we accept Quine's criterion of ontological commitment.

Conclusion

The age-old dispute over universals has been rekindled in our day in debates over Platonism and anti-Platonism and over divine aseity. We are not prepared to pronounce judgment on which solution is the most plausible account available to theists. Much creative work is being done and remains to be done on God's relationship to so-called abstract objects. In our view, some sort of nominalist or conceptualist account seems to be the most promising solution. So long as some such account seems plausible, the doctrines of divine aseity and *creatio ex nihilo* need not be compromised to accommodate the metaphysical pluralism entailed by Platonism.

6

Philosophical Arguments
for *Creatio ex Nihilo*

The church fathers, as we have seen, despite their reliance on Greek philosophical thought for the enunciation of Christian doctrine, refused to compromise the Hebraic doctrine of *creatio ex nihilo* in deference to the Aristotelian doctrine of the eternity of matter. Because Aristotle had not merely asserted but argued for the eternity of the world, Christian theologians could not rest content with citing biblical proof texts for the Judaeo-Christian view; they also engaged Greek thinkers in philosophical discussion of their competing paradigms.

The last great champion of *creatio ex nihilo* prior to the advent of Islam was the Alexandrian Aristotelian commentator John Philoponus, who in his works *Against Aristotle* and *On the Eternity of the World against Proclus* initiated a tradition of argumentation for *creatio ex nihilo* based on the impossibility of an infinite past. This tradition was subsequently enriched by medieval Muslim and Jewish theologians and then transmitted back into Christian scholastic theology.[1] Any person who rejects

---

1. John Philoponus, *Against Aristotle, on the Eternity of the World*, trans. Christian Wildberg (London: Duckworth, 1987); and John Philoponus and Simplicius, *Place, Void, and Eternity*, trans. David Furley and Christian Wildberg (Ithaca, N.Y.: Cornell University Press, 1991). For an exposition of the argument in its historical context, see William Lane Craig, *The Cosmological Argument from Plato to Leibniz* (London: Macmillan, 1980); Harry A.

the doctrine of *creatio ex nihilo* cannot responsibly ignore this tradition but must respond substantively to such thinkers as al-Ghazali, Saadia ben Gaon, Bonaventure, and their modern counterparts.

In his book *al-Iqtisad fi'l-i'tiqad*, the great medieval Muslim theologian al-Ghazali (1058–1111) presented the following simple syllogism in support of the existence of a Creator: "Every being which begins has a cause for its beginning; now the world is a being which begins; therefore, it possesses a cause for its beginning."[2] On the basis of philosophical arguments against the existence of an infinite, temporal regress of past events, al-Ghazali sought to demonstrate that the universe began to exist. Contemporary interest in the argument arises largely out of the startling empirical evidence of astrophysical cosmology for a beginning of space and time.

We may formulate an argument for *creatio ex nihilo* on the basis of the following four premises:

1. The temporal series of past, physical events either had a beginning or is beginningless.
2. If the temporal series of past, physical events had a beginning, the beginning was either caused or uncaused.
3. The temporal series of past, physical events is not beginningless.
4. The beginning was not uncaused.

The argument has two stages. First, from 1 and 3 it follows logically that

5. The temporal series of past, physical events had a beginning.

Wolfson, "Patristic Arguments against the Eternity of the World," *Harvard Theological Review* 59 (1966): 354–67; idem, *The Philosophy of the Kalam*, Structure and Growth of Philosophic Systems from Plato to Spinoza 4 (Cambridge: Harvard University Press, 1976); H. A. Davidson, *Proofs for Eternity, Creation, and the Existence of God in Medieval Islamic and Jewish Philosophy* (New York: Oxford University Press, 1987); and Richard C. Dales, *Medieval Discussions of the Eternity of the World*, Brill's Studies in Intellectual History 18 (Leiden: Brill, 1990). There is another tradition of argumentation for *creatio ex nihilo* in a nontemporal sense, initiated by such church fathers as Tatian and Tertullian, which appeals to divine omnipotence. If matter were not itself created *ex nihilo* by God, then there would be something over which he lacked power, which contradicts his omnipotence. Despite the force of this line of argument on behalf of *creatio ex nihilo*, we have chosen to focus on temporal *creatio ex nihilo* because a biblically and philosophically robust doctrine of *creatio ex nihilo* requires a temporal origin of the universe.

2. [Abu Hamid] al-Ghazali, *al-Iqtisad fi'l-i'tiqad* (*The Middle Path in Theology*), ed. I. A. Çubukçu and H. Atay (Ankara: University of Ankara Press [Nur Matbaasi], 1962), 15–16.

This is a beginning before which there are no temporal, physical events and therefore represents an absolute beginning. The first stage of the argument thus demonstrates the *ex nihilo* aspect of the doctrine. Next, from 2 and 5 it follows logically that

6. The beginning was either caused or uncaused.

And 4 and 6 logically imply

7. The beginning was caused.

Thus, the second stage of the argument goes to prove the *creatio* aspect of the doctrine.

The argument is obviously logically valid, and so the question of its soundness devolves to the truth of its four premises. Now premises 1 and 2 are necessarily true, since they have the form of the Law of Excluded Middle: p or not-p. Premise 4 has not traditionally been a matter of dispute. Since something cannot come into being uncaused out of nothing, it was generally agreed that if the universe did begin to exist, then it must have been created by a transcendent cause. So the dispute has focused on premise 3.

To assess the truth of premise 3, it will be helpful to define some terms. By a "physical event," we mean any change occurring within the space-time universe. Since any change takes time, there are no instantaneous events. Neither could there be an infinitely slow event, since such an "event" would in reality be a changeless state. Therefore, any event will have a finite, nonzero duration. In order that all the events comprising the temporal series of past events be of equal duration, we arbitrarily stipulate some event as our standard.

Taking as our point of departure the present standard event, we consider any series of such standard events ordered according to the relation *earlier than*. The question is whether this series of events had a beginning or not. By a "beginning," one means a first standard event. It is therefore not relevant whether the temporal series had a beginning point (a first temporal instant). The question is whether there was in the past an event occupying a nonzero, finite temporal interval that was absolutely first, not preceded by any equal interval.

What reason is there to accept the crucial third premise, that the temporal series of past, physical events is not beginningless? This premise may be supported by both deductive and inductive arguments from metaphysics and physics.

Argument from the Impossibility of an Actual Infinite

The first argument we shall consider is the argument based on the impossibility of the existence of an actual infinite. While potential infinites can exist, no actual infinite can exist, for the real existence of an actually infinite number of things would entail absurdities. Because an actually infinite number of things cannot exist, the series of past events must be finite in number and, hence, the temporal series of past, physical events is not beginningless. We may formulate the argument as follows:

1. An actual infinite cannot exist.
2. An infinite temporal regress of events is an actual infinite.
3. Therefore, an infinite temporal regress of events cannot exist.

Since an infinite temporal regress of events cannot exist, the temporal series of past, physical events must have had a beginning. Let us examine more closely each of the two premises.

1. *An actual infinite cannot exist.* In order to understand this premise, we need to differentiate clearly between an actual infinite and a potential infinite. By an actual infinite, one means any collection having at a time t a number of definite and discrete members that is greater than any natural number 0, 1, 2, 3, . . . An infinite set in standard Zermelo-Fraenkel axiomatic set theory is defined as any set R having a proper subset that is equivalent to R. A proper subset is a subset that does not exhaust all the members of the original set: at least one member of the original set is not also a member of the subset. Two sets are said to be equivalent if the members of one set can be related to the members of the other set in a one-to-one correspondence: a single member of one set corresponds to a single member of the other set, and vice versa. This convention is called the principle of correspondence. Equivalent sets are regarded as having the same number of members.

Thus, an infinite set is one in which the whole set has the same number of members as a proper part. The symbol representing the number of members in an infinite set is the Hebrew letter *aleph*: $\aleph$. A null subscript $\aleph_0$ indicates that $\aleph_0$ is the lowest of the transfinite cardinal numbers. The notion of an actual infinite is to be contrasted with a potential infinite, which is any collection having at any time t a number of definite and discrete members equal to some natural number, but which over time increases endlessly toward infinity as a limit. The symbol used to represent such an indefinite quantity is called a lemniscate: ∞.

When we say that an actually infinite number of things cannot exist, we use "exist" to mean "have extramental existence," or "be instantiated in the real world." When we refer to a beginningless series of events, we mean by an "event" any of the changes that we have stipulated to belong to the class of standard events. The question is whether this series of events is comprised of an actually infinite number of events or not. If not, then since the universe is not distinct from the series of past, physical events, the universe must have had a beginning, in the sense of a first standard event.

Premise 1 asserts, then, that an actual infinite cannot exist in the real, spatio-temporal world. It is usually alleged that this sort of argument has been invalidated by Georg Cantor's work on the actual infinite and by subsequent developments in set theory. But this allegation misconstrues the nature of both Cantor's system and modern set theory, for the argument does not in fact contradict a single tenet of either. The reason is this: Cantor's system and set theory may be taken to be simply a universe of discourse, a mathematical system based on certain adopted axioms and conventions.

The argument's defender may hold that while the actual infinite may be a fruitful and consistent concept within the postulated universe of discourse, it cannot be transposed into the spatio-temporal world, for this would involve counterintuitive absurdities. We are quite happy to grant the coherence and consistency of infinite set theory and transfinite arithmetic, while denying that the actual infinite can exist in reality. Some philosophers of mathematics (for example, the intuitionists) do go so far as to deny the legitimacy of the actual infinite even in the mathematical realm, allowing only potential infinites to exist, and they may well be right. But our argument does not require so strong a thesis as the impossibility of the mathematical infinite. It is the real existence of the actual infinite that we question.

Perhaps the best way to support this premise is by way of thought experiments that illustrate the various absurdities that would result if an actual infinite were to be instantiated in the real world. An example is the famous Hilbert's Hotel, a product of the mind of the great German mathematician David Hilbert.[3] Let us first imagine a hotel with a finite number of rooms. Suppose, furthermore, that all the rooms are full. When a new guest arrives asking for a room, the proprietor apologizes, "Sorry, all the rooms are full," and the new guest is turned away.

Now let us imagine a hotel with an infinite number of rooms, and suppose once more that all the rooms are full. There is not a single vacant room throughout the entire infinite hotel. Now suppose a new guest shows up, asking for a room. "But of course!" says the proprietor, and he immediately shifts the person in room 1 into room 2, the person in

---

3. The story of Hilbert's Hotel is related in George Gamow, *One, Two, Three, Infinity* (London: Macmillan, 1946), 17.

room 2 into room 3, the person in room 3 into room 4, and so on, out to infinity. As a result of these room changes, room 1 now becomes vacant, so the new guest gratefully checks in. But remember, before he arrived, all the rooms were full! Equally curious, according to the mathematicians, there are now no more persons in the hotel than there were before: the number is just infinite. But how can this be? The proprietor just added the new guest's name to the register and gave him his keys—how can there not be one more person in the hotel than before?

The situation becomes even stranger. Suppose an infinity of new guests show up at the desk, each asking for a room. "Of course, of course!" says the proprietor, and he proceeds to shift the person in room 1 into room 2, the person in room 2 into room 4, the person in room 3 into room 6, and so on, out to infinity, always putting each occupant into the room numbered twice his previous room's number. Because any natural number multiplied by two always equals an even number, all the guests wind up in even-numbered rooms. As a result, all the odd-numbered rooms become vacant, and the infinity of new guests is easily accommodated. And yet, before they came, all the rooms were full! And again, strangely enough, the number of guests in the hotel is the same after the infinity of new guests check in as before, even though there were as many new guests as old guests. In fact, the proprietor could repeat this process *infinitely many times*, and yet there would never be one single person more in the hotel than before.

Hilbert's Hotel, however, is even stranger than the German mathematician made it out to be. Suppose some of the guests start to check out. Suppose the guest in room 1 departs. Is there not now one less person in the hotel? Not according to the mathematicians—but just ask the housekeeping staff! Suppose the guests in rooms 1, 3, 5, . . . check out. In this case an infinite number of people have left the hotel, but according to the mathematicians, there are no fewer people in the hotel—but don't talk to the people in housekeeping! In fact, we could have every other guest check out of the hotel and repeat this process infinitely many times, and yet there would never be any fewer people in the hotel.

Suppose the proprietor does not like having a half-empty hotel (it looks bad for business). No matter! By shifting occupants as before, but in reverse order, he transforms his half-vacant hotel into one that is jammed to the gills. One might think that by these maneuvers the proprietor could always keep this strange hotel fully occupied. But one would be wrong. For suppose that the persons in rooms 4, 5, 6, . . . checked out. At a single stroke the hotel would be virtually emptied, the guest register reduced to but three names, and the infinite converted to finitude. And yet it would remain true that the *same* number of guests checked out this time as when the guests in rooms 1, 3, 5, . . . checked out! Can anyone believe that such a hotel could exist in reality?

Hilbert's Hotel is absurd. Since nothing hangs on the illustration's involving a hotel, the above sorts of absurdities show in general that it is impossible for an actually infinite number of things to exist. There is just no way to avoid these absurdities once we admit the possibility of the existence of an actual infinite. Laypeople sometimes react to such absurdities as Hilbert's Hotel by saying that these absurdities result because we really do not understand the nature of infinity. But this attitude is simply mistaken. Infinite set theory is a highly developed and well-understood branch of mathematics. Hence, these absurdities can be seen to result precisely because we *do* understand the notion of a collection with an actually infinite number of members.

What is the logical structure of the argument here? The proponent of the argument has two options open to him. On the one hand, he could argue: If an actual infinite were to exist, then the principle of correspondence would be valid with respect to it. And if an actual infinite were to exist and the principle of correspondence were to be valid with respect to it, then the various counterintuitive situations would result. Therefore, if an actual infinite were to exist, the various counterintuitive situations would result. (This argument has the valid inference form: $A \square \rightarrow B$; $A \& B \square \rightarrow C$; $\therefore A \square \rightarrow C$). But because these situations are absurd and so really impossible ($\neg \Diamond C$), it follows that the existence of an actual infinite is impossible ($\therefore \neg \Diamond A$).

On the other hand, the proponent of the argument might call into question the premise that if an actual infinite were to exist, then the principle of correspondence would be valid with respect to it. There is no reason to think that the principle is universally valid. It is merely a convention adopted in infinite set theory. Now, necessarily, if an actual infinite were to exist, then either the principle of correspondence or Euclid's maxim that "The whole is greater than its part" would apply to it ($\square [A \square \rightarrow B \vee C]$). But the application of either of these two principles to an actual infinite results in counterintuitive absurdities. Hence, it is plausible that if the existence of an actual infinite were possible, then if an actual infinite were to exist, neither of these two principles would be valid with respect to it ($\Diamond A \square \rightarrow \neg[A \square \rightarrow B \vee C]$). It therefore follows that the existence of an actual infinite is impossible ($\therefore \neg \Diamond A$), since the counterfactual "If an actual infinite were to exist, then neither principle would be valid with respect to it" is necessarily false.

These considerations also show how superficial J. L. Mackie's response to this premise is.[4] He thinks that the absurdities are resolved by not-

4. John L. Mackie, *The Miracle of Theism* (Oxford: Clarendon, 1982), 93.

ing that for infinite groups the axiom that the whole is greater than its part does not hold, as it does for finite groups. But far from being the solution, this is precisely the problem. Because in infinite set theory this axiom is denied, one gets all sorts of absurdities, like Hilbert's Hotel, when one tries to translate that theory into reality. Mackie's response does nothing to prove that the envisioned situations are not absurd, but only serves to reiterate, in effect, that if an actual infinite were to exist and the principle of correspondence were valid with respect to it, then the relevant situations would result, which is not in dispute. Moreover, the contradictions that result when guests check out of the hotel are not even prima facie resolved by Mackie's analysis. (In transfinite arithmetic, inverse operations of subtraction and division are prohibited because they lead to contradictions; but in reality, one cannot stop people from checking out of the hotel if they so desire!)

Sometimes it is said that we can find counterexamples to the claim that an actually infinite number of things cannot exist, so that premise 1 must be false. For example, Walter Sinnott-Armstrong asserts:

> Actual infinites also abound in the physical world. To see one, just wave your hand. When your hand moves a foot, it goes through an infinite number of intervening segments: half, then half of that, and so on. It also travels for half the time, then half of that, and so on. . . . We cannot measure or distinguish all of these spatial and temporal segments, but that does not show that they do not actually exist. The areas of space and periods of time really exist regardless of our limitations and actions. When you think them through, such simple thought experiments are enough to reveal actual infinities "in the real world."[5]

The defender of the argument may reply that this objection confuses a potential infinite with an actual infinite. While one can continue to divide any distance for as long as one wants, such a series is merely potentially infinite, in that infinity serves as a limit that one endlessly approaches but never reaches. If one thinks of a geometrical line as existing logically prior to any points that one may care to specify on it rather than as a construction built up out of points (itself a paradoxical notion),[6] then one's ability to specify certain points, like the halfway point along a certain distance, does not imply that such points actually exist independently of our specification of them. If one assumes that any distance is *already* composed out of an actually infinite number of

5. Walter Sinnott-Armstrong and William Lane Craig, *God? A Debate between a Christian and an Atheist* (Oxford: Oxford University Press, 2003), 43.

6. See William Lane Craig, critical notice of *Time, Creation, and the Continuum*, by Richard Sorabji, *International Philosophical Quarterly* 25 (1985): 319–26.

points, then one is begging the question. The objector is assuming what he is supposed to prove, that there is a clear counterexample to the claim that an actually infinite number of things cannot exist.

Some critics have charged that the Aristotelian position that only potential, but no actual, infinites exist in reality is incoherent because a potential infinite presupposes an actual infinite. For example, Rudy Rucker claims that there must be a "definite class of possibilities" that is actually infinite in order for the mathematical intuitionist to regard the natural number series as potentially infinite through repetition of certain mathematical operations.[7] Similarly, Richard Sorabji asserts that Aristotle's view of the potentially infinite divisibility of a line entails that there is an actually infinite number of positions at which the line could be divided.[8]

If this line of argument were successful, it would, indeed, be a *tour de force*, since it would show mathematical thought from Aristotle to Gauss to be, not merely mistaken or incomplete, but incoherent in this respect. But the objection does not seem to be successful. The claim that a physical distance is, say, potentially infinitely divisible does not entail that the distance is potentially divisible *here* and *here* and *here* and . . . Potential infinite divisibility (the property of being susceptible of division without end) does not entail actual infinite divisibility (the property of being composed of an infinite number of points where divisions can be made). The argument that it does have such an entailment seems to be guilty of a modal operator shift, invalidly inferring from the true claim

1. Possibly, there is some point at which *x* is divided

to the claim

2. There is some point at which *x* is possibly divided.

It is therefore coherent to maintain that a physical distance is potentially infinitely divisible without holding that there are an infinite number of positions where it could be divided.

It is sometimes thought that the existence of abstract objects like numbers provides a decisive counterexample to the claim that an actual infinite cannot exist. But we see no reason to accept this counterexample:

7. Rudolf v. B. Rucker, "The Actual Infinite," *Speculations in Science and Technology* 3 (1980): 66.

8. Richard Sorabji, *Time, Creation, and the Continuum* (Ithaca, N.Y.: Cornell University Press, 1983), 210–13, 322–24.

it begs the question by assuming Platonism or realism to be true. But why make this assumption? In order to defeat this counterexample, all the defender of the argument has to do is deny that realism has been shown to be true. In other words, the burden of proof rests on the objector to prove that realism is true before his counterexample can even be launched.

A conceptualist understanding of abstract objects combined with the simplicity of God's cognition is at least a tenable alternative to Platonism. Indeed, historically, this has been the mainstream theistic tradition, from Boethius through Ockham. In fact, theists had better hope that there is such an alternative to Platonism. As we have seen, the latter entails a metaphysical pluralism that leaves God as but one being among an unimaginable plenitude of beings existing independent of him, in contradiction to divine aseity and the doctrine of *creatio ex nihilo*.

In response to the absurdities springing from performing inverse operations with infinite quantities, David Yandell has insisted that subtraction of infinite quantities does not yield contradictions. He writes:

> Subtracting the even positive integers from the set of positive integers leaves an infinite set, the odd positive integers. Subtracting all of the positive integers greater than 40 from the set of positive integers leaves a finite (forty-membered) set. Subtracting all of the positive integers from the set of positive integers leaves one with the null set. But none of these subtractions could possibly lead to any other conclusion than each leads to. This alleged contradictory feature of the infinite seems not to generate any actual contradictions.[9]

Yandell has missed the point of the argument. It is, of course, true that every time one subtracts all the even numbers from all the natural numbers, one gets all the odd numbers, which are infinite in quantity. But that is not where the contradiction is alleged to lie. Instead, the contradiction lies in the fact that one can subtract equal quantities from equal quantities and arrive at different answers. For example, if we subtract all the even numbers from all the natural numbers, we get an infinity of numbers; and if we subtract all the numbers greater than three from all the natural numbers, we get only four numbers. Yet in both cases we subtracted the *identical number* of numbers from the *identical number* of numbers and yet did not arrive at an identical result. In fact one can subtract equal quantities from equal quantities and get any quantity between zero and infinity as the remainder. For this

---

9. David Yandell, "Response: Commentary on the Craig-Flew Debate," in *The Existence of God*, ed. Stan Wallace (Aldershot, Hampshire, U.K.: Ashgate, 2003), 132.

reason subtraction and division are simply prohibited with transfinite numbers—an arbitrary stipulation that has no force in the nonmathematical realm of reality.

Wesley Morriston would subvert the argument by calling into question what he takes to be its crucial assumption: that inverse arithmetical operations like subtraction can be performed on any actually existing collection of things. He summarizes the argument as follows:

> Craig appears to be assuming that certain familiar arithmetical operations can be performed on the number of elements in any legitimate set. Given this assumption, perhaps we can see what the "contradiction" is supposed to be. Let m = the number of books in our infinite library, n = the number of odd-numbered books, and o = the number of books numbered 4 or higher. Then perhaps Craig's argument goes like this:
> $(m - n)$ = infinity, whereas $(m - o)$ = 4.
> But,
> $n = o$ (since both n and o are infinite)
> It follows that we get inconsistent results subtracting the same number from m.[10]

Indeed! So what is wrong with this argument? Morriston proceeds:

> Or do we? If we say that $(m - n)$ = infinity, but that $(m - o)$ = 4, we are not actually subtracting *numbers* at all. What we are doing instead is imagining various subsets of books in our infinite library being "removed" from the library, and then determining the cardinality of the subset that "remains."[11]

This curious assertion is flatly self-contradictory, for Morriston stipulated above: "Let m = the *number* of books in our infinite library . . . and o the *number* of books numbered 4 or higher." So we clearly are subtracting numbers.

What Morriston apparently wants to say is that in checking books out of the library, we are not performing arithmetical operations on abstract objects like numbers but are manipulating collections of concrete objects that can be counted. Well and good; how does the objection proceed from there? Morriston continues, "When the set of books, $\{4, 5, 6, . . .\}$, is 'removed,' $\{0, 1, 2, 3\}$ 'remains.' Its cardinality is 4. When $\{1, 3, 5, . . . \}$ is 'removed,' $\{0, 2, 4, . . . \}$ 'remains'. Its cardinality is $\aleph_0$. There is no logical inconsistency so far."[12] Ah, but there is! For we have subtracted

10. Wes Morriston, "Craig on the Actual Infinite," *Religious Studies* 38 (2002): 151.
11. Ibid., emphasis added.
12. Ibid.

identical quantities from identical quantities and found nonidentical remainders. The fact that we are subtracting quantities of concrete objects (books) rather than quantities of abstract objects (numbers) does nothing to avert the contradiction.

Morriston nevertheless presses on: "But what if we insist on subtracting the numbers, n and o, respectively, from m? Even then, we will not get inconsistent results. For no matter how $(\aleph_0 - \aleph_0)$ is defined, both $(m - n)$ and $(m - o)$ will produce exactly the same 'remainder,' since m, n, and o just are $\aleph_0$."[13] Here Morriston reverts to thinking about performing arithmetical operations on abstract objects. His claim seems to be that if we define $\aleph_0 - \aleph_0$ to specify a particular number, then no inconsistency results. Even if this claim were true, it would purchase consistency only at the price of the truth of arithmetic. For example, suppose we define $\aleph_0 - \aleph_0 = 3$. In that case, $m - n = 3$, or in other words, all the natural numbers minus all the odd numbers leaves three numbers: there are only three even numbers. Or again, $m - m = 3$, or in other words all the natural numbers minus all the natural numbers leaves three left over, which leaves one wondering which numbers these could possibly be. Or again, $o - m = 3$, or in other words, all the numbers greater than or equal to four minus all the natural numbers leaves three numbers—which seems absurd.

In any case, it is evident that contradiction would ensue from such a stipulation. Suppose, on the pattern of any natural number subtracted from itself, we stipulate that $\aleph_0 - \aleph_0 = 0$. Let $p =$ the number of the even natural numbers. By definition, $m - p = n$. So $\aleph_0 - p = n$. But $\aleph_0 - p = 0$, since $p = \aleph_0$. So $n = 0$. But $n = \aleph_0$. So $\aleph_0 = 0$, which is a contradiction.

Morriston recognizes that $\aleph_0 - \aleph_0$ is undefined in transfinite arithmetic; but, reverting to the concrete realm, he demands, "Why should we accept Craig's assumption that ordinary subtraction *must* apply to the number of elements in *any* set that can be instantiated in 'the real world'?"[14] In our judgment, Craig makes no such assumption. On the contrary, as an anti-Platonist, Craig is more than willing to recognize that certain mathematical operations may be inapplicable to the real world. For example, suppose we have three books on the desk in front of us. Mathematically speaking, it is perfectly acceptable to subtract a larger quantity from a smaller quantity, for example, $3 - 5 = -2$. But such an operation makes no sense with respect to the collection of books before us, since there are no such things as negative books. With respect to books, unlike numbers, only smaller or equal quantities can be subtracted from a particular quantity.

13. Ibid., 151–52.
14. Ibid., 152.

Now perhaps Morriston believes that actually infinite collections are like this. Perhaps he thinks that we cannot subtract various quantities of books from an infinite collection of books. But this seems clearly false. If the books in an infinite library are numbered, then we can subtract books by simply checking out the books corresponding to various numbers and removing them from the library. Morriston protests, "If a person 'checks out' one or more books, he does indeed remove them from the library—but he is not 'subtracting' them in the arithmetical sense."[15]

One cannot help but wonder what sense Morriston is talking about. In arithmetic, subtraction consists in the diminution of a given quantity (the minuend) by another quantity (the subtrahend) to yield another quantity (the difference or remainder), which, when added to the subtrahend, gives the minuend as a sum.[16] This appears to be precisely what is going on when one removes various quantities of books from the quantity of books shelved in the library. If Morriston doubts that this is what subtraction of books involves, we invite him to answer the following question: If there were only a finite number of books on the shelves, how else would one subtract books from the library than by removing them? Morriston would surely not deny that if a library houses two million books, and one million books are then checked out of the library, there remain one million books still on the shelves.

Morriston proceeds: "Even if ordinary arithmetical subtraction is undefined for transfinite numbers, it does not follow that physically removing books from an infinite library is similarly 'undefined', much less that removing books from it is impossible."[17] This statement is bewildering, since our argument is predicated on the assumption that it *is* possible to remove books from the infinite library (or for guests to check out of a hotel). And does Morriston think that the physical removal of infinite quantities of books from an infinite library is defined? If so, we should like to know what it is. Zero? Three? Ten trillion and one? Infinity? Any such answer is absurd. Suppose we define the removal of an infinite quantity of books from an infinite quantity of books to be zero. Now suppose we remove all the odd-numbered books. Accordingly, there are zero books left. But then, what happened to all the even-numbered books? How did they disappear?

15. Ibid.

16. Consult any mathematical dictionary, such as Robert W. Marks, *The New Mathematics Dictionary and Handbook* (New York: Bantam Books, 1964), 146; Glen James and Robert C. James, eds., *Mathematics Dictionary*, 4th ed. (New York: Van Nostrand Reinhold Co., 1976), 369–70; and Christopher Morris, ed., *Academic Press Dictionary of Science and Technology* (London: Academic Press, 1992), 2126.

17. Morriston, "Craig on the Actual Infinite," 152.

Or does Morriston mean that there just is no determinate quantity of books remaining after such an operation? That seems clearly false, for if we remove all the books numbered 4 or greater, it is easy to see how many books are left. There they are on the shelf—just count them! If we remove all the odd-numbered books, then the principle of correspondence requires that the number of books remaining is infinite. Morriston shows no inclination to deny the truth of that principle; indeed, if one were to do so, the whole theory of the actual infinite would collapse. The problem posed by inverse arithmetical operations is not that they fail to yield determinate results, but that the results are contradictory.

Morriston concludes: "What follows is only that, since subtraction is undefined for infinite quantities, we cannot automatically assume that the number of books is smaller after some of them have been removed. That is indeed a characteristic of the actual infinite, but it is hardly a 'logical contradiction.'"[18] Morriston seems to have lost his way, for no one has ever claimed that it is characteristic of the actual infinite that subtraction of a given quantity from an infinite quantity gives a remainder smaller than the minuend (think of the odd-numbered books being removed from the library). Instead, the contradiction lies in this: one can subtract exactly *the same number* of items from *the same number* of items and find nonidentical remainders as a result.

Thus, we seem to have good reason to accept the first premise of the argument: an actual infinite cannot exist.[19]

2. *An infinite temporal regress of events is an actual infinite.* This second premise seems rather obvious. If the universe never began to exist, then prior to the present event there have existed an actually infinite number of previous events.

As we say, this seems obvious. Nevertheless, some critics of the argument have denied premise 2, claiming that the past is a potential infinite only. Swinburne, for example, admits that it makes little sense to think that the past could have an end but no beginning, but he advises that we avoid this puzzle by numbering the events of the past by beginning in the present and proceeding to count backward in time.[20] In this way the past is converted from a series with no beginning but an end into a series with a beginning but no end—which is unobjectionable.

18. Ibid.

19. Laypeople frequently ask if God, therefore, cannot be infinite. The question is based on a misunderstanding. When we speak of the infinity of God, we are not using the word in a mathematical sense to refer to an aggregate of an infinite number of finite parts. God's infinity is, as it were, qualitative, not quantitative. It means that God is metaphysically necessary, morally perfect, omnipotent, omniscient, eternal, and so on.

20. Richard Swinburne, *Space and Time*, 2d ed. (New York: St. Martin's Press, 1981), 298–99.

Swinburne's solution is clearly wrongheaded. In order for the past to be a mere potential infinite, it would have to be finite, but growing in a backward direction, which contradicts the nature of time and becoming. Swinburne confuses the mental regress of counting with the real progress of time itself. The direction of time itself is from past to future, so that if the series of, for example, past seconds is beginningless, then an actually infinite number of seconds have elapsed.

3. *Therefore, an infinite temporal regress of events cannot exist.* If the above two premises are true, then this conclusion follows logically. The series of past events must be finite and have a beginning. Hence, the temporal series of past, physical events is not beginningless.

Argument from the Impossibility of Forming an Actually Infinite Collection of Things by Successive Addition

The second argument is independent of the foregoing argument, for it does not deny that an actually infinite number of things can exist. It rather denies that a collection containing an actually infinite number of things can be *formed* by adding one member after another. If an actual infinite cannot be formed by successive addition, then the series of past events must be finite, since that series is formed by successive addition of one event after another in time. This argument, too, can be formulated in three steps:

1. The series of events in time is a collection formed by successive addition.
2. A collection formed by successive addition cannot be actually infinite.
3. Therefore, the series of events in time cannot be actually infinite.

Since the series of events in time cannot be actually infinite, the temporal series of past, physical events cannot be beginningless. Let us take a closer look at each of the two premises.

1. *The series of events in time is a collection formed by successive addition.* This may seem rather obvious. The past did not spring into being whole and entire but was formed sequentially, one event occurring after another. Such sequential formation involves the *addition* of one element after another. Although we may *think* of the past by subtracting events from the present, as when we say that an event occurred ten years ago, it is nonetheless clear that the series of events is *formed* by addition of one event after another. We must be careful not to confuse the realms

of thought and reality. Although we sometimes speak of a "temporal regress" of events, this can be misleading, for the events themselves are not regressing in time; our thoughts regress in time as we mentally survey past events. But the series of events is itself progressing in time: the collection of all past events grows progressively larger with each passing moment. Thus, in reality an infinite past would be an infinite temporal progress of events with no beginning and with its end in the present.

As obvious as premise 1 might seem, however, it does presuppose the truth of an A-theory of time.[21] Since B-theorists reject the reality of temporal becoming, they deny that the past series of events was formed by successive addition. All times exist tenselessly, and there is no lapse of time. So this premise would not be accepted by partisans of the B-theory of time. But since *creatio ex nihilo* presupposes an A-theory of time anyway, as we have seen, we are not here asking any who are open to that doctrine to believe anything that they must not already be prepared to believe in order to accept that doctrine. In other words, anyone who would reject premise 1 on grounds of a B-theory of time would not accept *creatio ex nihilo* anyhow, regardless of the present argument.

In any case, moreover, there are good reasons to think that the B-theory of time is mistaken and that temporal becoming is real.[22] Time is dynamic, and therefore the past has been formed sequentially, one moment elapsing after another. If the past is infinite and God is in time, then God has lived through an infinite number of past temporal intervals, one after another, to arrive at today. But such a traversal of the infinite past, we shall argue, is absurd.

2. A collection formed by successive addition cannot be actually infinite. This is the crucial premise. Sometimes this is called the impossibility of counting to infinity or the impossibility of traversing the infinite. This impossibility has nothing to do with the amount of time available: no matter how much time one has available, an actual infinite cannot be so formed. For no matter how many numbers one counts or how many steps one takes, one can always add one more number or take one more step before arriving at infinity.

Now, someone might admit that an infinite collection cannot be formed by beginning at a point and adding members. But he might claim that an infinite collection could be formed by never beginning but

<hr />

21. Recall the discussion of the A- and B-theories of time in chapter 4.

22. See William Lane Craig, *The Tensed Theory of Time: A Critical Examination*, Synthese Library 293 (Dordrecht: Kluwer Academic Publishers, 2000); and idem, *The Tenseless Theory of Time: A Critical Examination*, Synthese Library 294 (Dordrecht: Kluwer Academic Publishers, 2000). For a semipopular treatment, see William Lane Craig, *Time and Eternity: Exploring God's Relationship to Time* (Wheaton: Crossway, 2001).

by ending at a point after having added one member after another from eternity. But this method seems even more unbelievable than the first method. If one cannot count *to* infinity, how can one count down *from* infinity? If one cannot traverse the infinite by moving in one direction, how can one traverse it by moving in the opposite direction?

Indeed, the idea of a beginningless temporal series of events ending in the present seems absurd. Consider one illustration: Tristram Shandy, in the novel by Laurence Sterne, writes his autobiography so slowly that it takes him a whole year to record the events of a single day. According to Bertrand Russell, if Tristram Shandy were immortal, then the entire book could be completed, since by the principle of correspondence, one year would correspond to each day, and both are infinite.[23] Russell's assertion is wholly untenable, however, since the future is in reality a potential infinite only. Though he write forever, Tristram Shandy would only get farther and farther behind; instead of finishing his autobiography, he would progressively approach a state in which he would be *infinitely* far behind. But he would never reach such a state because the years and, hence, the days of his life would always be finite in number, though indefinitely increasing.

But let us turn the story around: Suppose Tristram Shandy has been writing from eternity past at the rate of recording one day per year of writing. Should not Tristram Shandy now be infinitely far behind? For if he has lived for an infinite number of years, Tristram Shandy has recorded an equally infinite number of past days. Given the thoroughness of his autobiography, these days are all consecutive days. At any point in the past or present, therefore, Tristram Shandy has recorded a beginningless, infinite series of consecutive days. But now the question inevitably arises: *Which* days are these? Where in the temporal series of events are the days recorded by Tristram Shandy at any given point?

The answer can only be that they are days infinitely distant from the present. For there is no day on which Tristram Shandy is writing that is finitely distant from the last recorded day. This may be seen through an incisive analysis of the Tristram Shandy paradox given by Robin Small.[24] He points out that if Tristram Shandy has been writing for one year's time, then the most recent day he could have recorded is one year ago. But if he has been writing for two years, then he could not have recorded that day only one year past. For since his intention is to record *consecutive* days of his life, the most recent day he could have

23. Bertrand Russell, *The Principles of Mathematics*, 2d ed. (London: Allen & Unwin, 1937), 358–59.

24. Robin Small, "Tristram Shandy's Last Page," *British Journal for the Philosophy of Science* 37 (1986): 214–15.

recorded is the day immediately after a day at least two years ago. This is because it takes a year to record a day, so that to record two days he must have two years. Similarly, if he has been writing three years, then the most recent day recorded could be no more recent than two days after three years ago. In other words, the longer he has written, the further behind he has fallen. In fact, the recession into the past of the most recent recordable day can be plotted according to the formula (present date − n years of writing) + n − 1 days.

But what happens if Tristram Shandy has, *ex hypothesi*, been writing for an infinite number of years? The most recent day of his autobiography recedes to infinity, that is to say, to a day infinitely distant from the present. Nowhere in the past at a finite distance from the present can we find a recorded day, for by now Tristram Shandy is infinitely far behind. The beginningless, infinite series of days that he has recorded are days lying at an infinite temporal distance from the present. But there is no way to traverse the temporal interval from an infinitely distant event to the present, or more technically, for an event that was once present to recede to an infinite temporal distance. Since the task of writing one's autobiography at the rate of one year for each day seems obviously coherent, what follows from the Tristram Shandy story is that an infinite series of past events is absurd.

Mackie's objections to this premise are off the target.[25] He thinks that the argument illicitly assumes an infinitely distant starting point in the past and then pronounces it impossible to travel from that point to today. If we take the notion of infinity "seriously," he says, we must say that in the infinite past there would be no starting point whatever, not even an infinitely distant one. Yet from any given point in the past, there is only a finite distance to the present.

We know of no proponent of the argument who assumed that there was an infinitely distant starting point in the past. On the contrary, the beginningless character of the series of past events only serves to underscore the difficulty of its formation by successive addition. The fact that there is no beginning at all, not even an infinitely distant one, makes the problem worse, not better. It is thus not the proponent of the argument who fails to take infinity seriously. To say that the infinite past could have been formed by adding one member after another is like saying that someone has just succeeded in writing down all the negative numbers, ending at −1.

And, we may ask, how is Mackie's point that from any given moment in the past there is only a finite distance to the present even relevant to the issue? The defender of the argument could agree to this without

25. Mackie, *Miracle of Theism*, 93.

batting an eye. For the issue is how the *whole* series can be formed, not a finite portion of it. Does Mackie think that because every *finite* segment of the series can be formed by successive addition, the whole *infinite* series can be so formed? That is as logically fallacious as saying that because every part of an elephant is light in weight, the whole elephant is light in weight. Mackie's point is therefore irrelevant. It thus seems that this premise of the argument remains undefeated by his objections.

But now a deeper absurdity bursts into view. Even if every recorded past event did lie at only a finite distance from the present, still, if the series of past events is actually infinite, we could ask: Why did Tristram Shandy not finish his autobiography yesterday or the day before, since by then an infinite series of events had already elapsed? No matter how far along the series of past events one regresses, Tristram Shandy would have already completed his autobiography. Therefore, at no point in the infinite series of past events could he be finishing the book. We could never look over Tristram Shandy's shoulder to see if he were now writing the last page. For at any point an actually infinite sequence of events would have transpired, and the book would have already been completed. Thus, at no time in eternity will we find Tristram Shandy writing—which is absurd, since we supposed him to be writing from eternity. And at no point will he finish the book—which is equally absurd, because for the book to be completed, he must at some point have finished it.

David Conway and Richard Sorabji have, however, disputed this argument, maintaining that there is no reason to think that Tristram Shandy would at any point have already finished and, hence, that the successive formation of a temporal series of order type ω^* ($\ldots$, -3, -2, -1, 0) is impossible.[26] Since one of us has elsewhere commented briefly on Sorabji's remarks,[27] we shall restrict our discussion to Conway's objection.

Conway's perplexity with this version of the Tristram Shandy paradox stems largely, we think, from his incorrect rendering of it. In his analysis, the nub of the argument lies in the conditional

A. If an infinite number of pages had been written by yesterday, then Tristram Shandy will have finished by yesterday.

26. David A. Conway, "'It Would Have Happened Already': On One Argument for a First Cause," *Analysis* 44 (1984): 159–66; and Sorabji, *Time, Creation, and the Continuum*, 222.
27. See Craig, critical notice of *Time, Creation, and the Continuum*, 319–26.

But Conway's conditional is quite ambiguous, and the arguments that he suggests in support of it have no apparent relevance to the reasoning behind the Tristram Shandy paradox. Instead, the conditional at the heart of this version of the paradox is something more like this:

> B. If Tristram Shandy would have finished his book by today, then he would have finished it by yesterday,

and the truth of this conditional would seem to be guaranteed by the principle of correspondence. It is on the basis of this principle that the defender of the infinite past seeks to justify the intuitively impossible feat of someone's counting down all the negative numbers and ending at –1. Since the negative numbers can be put into a one-to-one correspondence with the series of, say, past hours, someone counting from eternity would have completed his countdown. But by the same token, Tristram Shandy at any point in the past should have already completed his book, since by then a one-to-one correspondence exists between, say, each page of writing and a past hour. In this version of the story, having infinite time does seem to be a sufficient condition of finishing the job. Having had infinite time, Tristram Shandy should have already completed his task.

Such reasoning in support of the finitude of the past and the beginning of the universe is not mere armchair cosmology. P. C. W. Davies, for example, utilizes this reasoning in explaining two profound implications of the thermodynamic properties of the universe:

> The first is that the universe will eventually die, wallowing, as it were, in its own entropy. This is known among physicists as the "heat death" of the universe. The second is that the universe cannot have existed for ever, otherwise it would have reached its equilibrium end state an infinite time ago. Conclusion: the universe did not always exist.[28]

The second of these implications is a clear application of the reasoning that underlies the "deeper absurdity" revealed by the Tristram Shandy paradox. Even if the universe had infinite energy, it would in infinite time come to equilibrium. Since at any point in the past infinite time has elapsed, a beginningless universe would have already reached equilibrium, or as Davies puts it, it would have reached equilibrium an infinite time ago. Therefore, the universe began to exist, *quod erat demonstrandum.*[29]

28. Paul Davies, *God and the New Physics* (New York: Simon & Schuster, 1983), 11.
29. See the similar reasoning of John Barrow and Frank J. Tipler, *The Anthropic Cosmological Principle* (Oxford: Clarendon, 1986), 601–8, against steady state cosmologies on

These illustrations reveal the absurdities involved in trying to form an actually infinite collection of things by successive addition. Hence, set theory has been purged of all temporal concepts; as Russell says, "Classes which are infinite are given all at once by the defining properties of their members, so that there is no question of 'completion' or of 'successive synthesis.'"[30] The only way an actual infinite could come to exist in the real world would be by being created all at once, simply in a moment. It would be a hopeless undertaking to try to form it by adding one member after another.

3. *Therefore, the series of events in time cannot be actually infinite.* Given the truth of the premises, the conclusion logically follows. If the universe did not begin to exist a finite time ago, then the present moment would never arrive. But obviously it has arrived. Therefore, we know that the universe is finite in the past and that the temporal series of past, physical events is not beginningless.

Conclusion

We have argued that the impossibility of the existence of an actual infinite implies that the temporal series of past, physical events is not beginningless. Even if an actual infinite could exist, the impossibility of forming this infinite by successive addition implies that the temporal series of past, physical events is not beginningless. We may now turn to the empirical confirmation of this argument.

---

the ground that any event that would have happened by now would have already happened before now if the past were infinite.

30. Bertrand Russell, *Our Knowledge of the External World*, 2d ed. (New York: W. W. Norton, 1929), 170.

7

Scientific Evidence for *Creatio ex Nihilo*

From time immemorial men have turned their gaze toward the heavens and wondered. Both cosmology and philosophy trace their roots to the wonder felt by the ancient Greeks as they contemplated the cosmos. According to Aristotle:

> It is owing to their wonder that men both now begin and at first began to philosophize; they wondered originally at the obvious difficulties, then advanced little by little and stated difficulties about the greater matters, *e.g.*, about the phenomena of the moon and those of the sun and the stars, and about the origin of the universe.[1]

Aristotle himself postulated God as the source of the order and motion in the cosmos. But Aristotle's God did not create the universe or even act as an efficient cause in introducing order into it. Rather, his eternal Unmoved Mover acts merely as a final cause of the order of the universe by serving as the object of desire for the souls of the heavenly spheres

1. Aristotle, *Metaphysics* 982b.10–15.

enraptured by him. Their desire for God gives rise to the eternal rotary motion of the spheres, which in turn produces the motions we observe in the sublunary world. Like God himself, matter, of which all physical substances are composed, is eternal and uncreated and underlies the eternal process of generation and corruption undergone by things in the sublunary realm. In its large-scale structure the universe has remained unchanged from all eternity.

The medieval schoolmen substituted angelic Intelligences for Aristotle's self-moving souls as the engines of motion of the spheres and denied the Hellenistic doctrine of the eternality of the world, but they did not question Aristotle's view of an unchanging large-scale cosmos. Even with the demise of Aristotelian physics in the scientific revolution completed by Isaac Newton, the assumption of a static universe remained unchallenged. Although Newton himself believed that God had created the world, the universe described by his physics was to all appearances eternal.

For that reason Pierre-Simon de Laplace, when queried by Napoleon about the absence of God from his system of the world, could reply, "Sire, I have no need of that hypothesis." Given Newton's immutable laws and the knowledge of the present position and velocity of every particle in the universe, Laplace boasted that he could retrodict or predict the exact state of the universe at any other time. The unspoken assumption, of course, was that the universe is immemorial and everlasting in its existence.

The assumption that the universe was never created was only further reinforced by Helmholtz's statement in the nineteenth century of the laws of the conservation of matter and energy. Since matter and energy can be neither created nor destroyed, there must have always been and will always be a universe: the universe is temporally infinite in the past and the future. To be sure, there were already clues in pre-relativistic physics that there was something wrong with the prevailing assumption of an eternal, static cosmos. One example is Olbers's Paradox of why the night sky is dark rather than aflame with light if an infinity of stars has existed from eternity past. Another is the second law of thermodynamics, which seems to imply that the universe, if it has existed from eternity, ought to lie moribund in a state of equilibrium. But these niggling worries could not overturn what was everywhere taken for granted: that the universe as a whole has existed and will exist unchanged forever.

By sharp contrast, there is today considerable scientific evidence that the universe is not eternal in the past but had an absolute origin a finite time ago. In this chapter we shall review two broad lines of evidence that point to this astonishing conclusion.

The Expansion of the Universe

Tremors of the impending upheaval that would demolish the old cosmology were first felt in 1917, when Albert Einstein made a cosmological application of his newly discovered gravitational theory, the general theory of relativity (GR).[2] Einstein assumed that the universe is homogeneous and isotropic and that it exists in a steady state, with a constant mean mass density and a constant curvature of space. To his chagrin, however, he found that GR would not permit such a model of the universe unless he introduced into his gravitational field equations a certain "fudge factor" Λ to counterbalance the gravitational effect of matter and so ensure a static universe.

Einstein's static universe was balanced on a razor's edge, however, and the least perturbation—even the transport of matter from one part of the universe to another—would cause the universe either to implode or to expand. By taking this feature of Einstein's model seriously, the Russian mathematician Alexander Friedman and the Belgian astronomer Georges Lemaître in the 1920s were independently able to formulate solutions to the field equations that predicted an expanding universe.[3]

The monumental significance of the Friedman-Lemaître model lay in its historization of the universe. As one commentator has remarked, up to this time the idea of the expansion of the universe "was absolutely beyond comprehension. Throughout all of human history the universe was regarded as fixed and immutable, and the idea that it might actually be changing was inconceivable."[4] But if the Friedman-Lemaître model were correct, the universe could no longer be adequately treated as a static entity existing, in effect, timelessly. Instead, the universe has a history, and time will not be a matter of indifference for our investigation of the cosmos.

In 1929 the American astronomer Edwin Hubble's measurements of the red-shift in the optical spectra of light from distant galaxies,[5] taken to indicate a universal recessional motion of the light sources in the

2. Albert Einstein, "Cosmological Considerations on the General Theory of Relativity," in *The Principle of Relativity*, trans. W. Perrett and J. B. Jefferey (New York: Dover Publications, 1952), 177–88.

3. A. Friedman, "Über die Krümmung des Raumes," *Zeitschrift für Physik* 10 (1922): 377–86; and G. Lemaître, "Un univers homogène de masse constante et de rayon croissant, rendant compte de la vitesse radiale des nébuleuses extragalactiques," *Annales de la Société scientifique de Bruxelles* 47 (1927): 49–59.

4. Gregory L. Naber, *Spacetime and Singularities: An Introduction* (Cambridge: Cambridge University Press, 1988), 126–27.

5. E. Hubble, "A Relation between Distance and Radial Velocity among Extra-galactic Nebulae," *Proceedings of the National Academy of Sciences* 15 (1929): 168–73.

line of sight, provided a dramatic verification of the Friedman-Lemaî-tre model. Incredibly, what Hubble had discovered was the isotropic expansion of the universe predicted by Friedman and Lemaître on the basis of Einstein's GR. It was a veritable turning point in the history of science. "Of all the great predictions that science has ever made over the centuries," exclaims John Wheeler, "was there ever one greater than this, to predict, and predict correctly, and predict against all expectation a phenomenon so fantastic as the expansion of the universe?"[6]

The Standard Big Bang Model

According to the Friedman-Lemaître model, as time proceeds, the distances separating galactic masses become greater. It is important to understand that as a GR-based theory, the model does not describe the expansion of the material content of the universe into a preexisting, empty, Newtonian space, but rather the expansion of space itself. The ideal particles of the cosmological fluid constituted by the matter and energy of the universe are conceived to be at rest with respect to space, but to recede progressively from one another as space itself expands or stretches, just as buttons glued to the surface of a balloon would recede from one another as the balloon inflates.

As the universe expands, it becomes less and less dense. This has the astonishing implication that as one reverses the expansion and extrapolates backward in time, the universe becomes progressively denser until one arrives at a state of infinite density at some point in the finite past. This state represents a singularity at which the space-time curvature, along with temperature, pressure, and density, becomes infinite. It therefore constitutes an edge or boundary to space-time itself. P. C. W. Davies comments:

> If we extrapolate this prediction to its extreme, we reach a point when all distances in the universe have shrunk to zero. An initial cosmological singularity therefore forms a past temporal extremity to the universe. We cannot continue physical reasoning, or even the concept of spacetime, through such an extremity. For this reason most cosmologists think of the initial singularity as the beginning of the universe. On this view the big bang represents the creation event; the creation not only of all the matter and energy in the universe, but also of spacetime itself.[7]

6. John A. Wheeler, "Beyond the Hole," in *Some Strangeness in the Proportion,* ed. Harry Woolf (Reading, Mass.: Addison-Wesley, 1980), 354.
7. P. C. W. Davies, "Spacetime Singularities in Cosmology," in *The Study of Time III,* ed. J. T. Fraser (New York: Springer Verlag, 1978), 78–79.

The term "big bang," originally a derisive expression coined by Fred Hoyle to characterize the beginning of the universe predicted by the Friedman-Lemaître model, is thus potentially misleading. It might lead us to mistakenly try to visualize the expansion from the outside (even though there is no "outside," just as there is no "before" with respect to the big bang).[8]

The standard big bang model, as the Friedman-Lemaître model came to be called, thus describes a universe that is not eternal in the past, but which came into being a finite time ago. Moreover—and this deserves underscoring—the origin it posits is an absolute origin *ex nihilo*. For not only all matter and energy, but space and time themselves, come into being at the initial cosmological singularity. As Barrow and Tipler emphasize, "At this singularity, space and time came into existence; literally nothing existed before the singularity, so, if the Universe originated at such a singularity, we would truly have a creation *ex nihilo*."[9] Thus, we may graphically represent space-time on the standard model as a cone (fig. 2).

In such a model the universe originates *ex nihilo* in the sense that at the initial singularity it is true that there is no earlier space-time point, or it is false that something existed prior to the singularity.

Now such a conclusion is profoundly disturbing for anyone who ponders it. For the question cannot be suppressed: Why did the universe come into being? Quentin Smith observes, "It belongs analytically to the concept of the cosmological singularity that it is not the effect of prior physical events. The definition of a singularity . . . entails that it

---

8. Gott, Gunn, Schramm, and Tinsley write, "The universe began from a state of infinite density about one Hubble time ago. Space and time were created in that event and so was all the matter in the universe. It is not meaningful to ask what happened before the big bang; it is somewhat like asking what is north of the North Pole. Similarly, it is not sensible to ask where the big bang took place. The point-universe was not an object isolated in space; it was the entire universe, and so the only answer can be that the big bang happened everywhere" (J. Richard Gott III, James E. Gunn, David N. Schramm, and Beatrice M. Tinsley, "Will the Universe Expand Forever?" *Scientific American* [Mar. 1976]: 65). The Hubble time is the time since the singularity if the rate of expansion has been constant. The singularity is a point only in the sense that the distance between any two points in the singularity is zero. Anyone who thinks there must be a place in the universe where the big bang occurred still has not grasped that it is space itself that is expanding; it is the two-dimensional *surface* of an inflating balloon that is analogous to three-dimensional space. The spherical surface has no center and so no location where the expansion begins. The analogy of the North Pole with the beginning of time should not be pressed, since the North Pole is not an edge to the surface of the globe; the beginning of time is more like the apex of a cone. But the idea is that just as one cannot go further north than the North Pole, so one cannot go further back than the initial singularity.

9. John Barrow and Frank Tipler, *The Anthropic Cosmological Principle* (Oxford: Clarendon, 1986), 442.

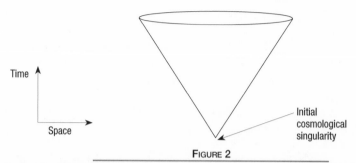

FIGURE 2

Conical Representation of Standard Model Space-Time. Space and time begin at the initial
cosmological singularity, before which literally nothing exists.

is *impossible to extend the spacetime manifold beyond the singularity.*
. . . This rules out the idea that the singularity is an effect of some prior
natural process."[10] Smith recognizes that the question that then remains
is whether the big bang might not be plausibly regarded as the result of
a supernatural cause. Otherwise, one must say that the universe simply
sprang into being uncaused out of absolutely nothing. Hence, in the words
of one astrophysical team, "The problem of the origin involves a certain
metaphysical aspect which may be either appealing or revolting."[11]

The Steady State Model

Revolted by the stark metaphysical alternatives presented by an
absolute beginning of the universe, certain theorists have been under-
standably eager to subvert the standard big bang model and restore
an eternal universe. Sir Fred Hoyle, for example, could countenance
neither an uncaused nor a supernaturally caused origin of the universe.
With respect to the singularity, he wrote, "This most peculiar situation
is taken by many astronomers to represent *the origin of the universe.*
The universe is supposed to have begun at this particular time. From
where? The usual answer, surely an unsatisfactory one, is: from nothing!"[12] Equally unsatisfactory was the postulation of a supernatural
cause. Noting that some accept happily the universe's absolute beginning, Hoyle complained:

10. Quentin Smith, "The Uncaused Beginning of the Universe," in William Lane Craig
and Quentin Smith, *Theism, Atheism, and Big Bang Cosmology* (Oxford: Clarendon, 1993),
120.
11. Hubert Reeves, Jean Audouze, William A. Fowler, and David N. Schramm, "On the
Origin of Light Elements," *Astrophysical Journal* 179 (1973): 912.
12. Fred Hoyle, *Astronomy Today* (London: Heinemann, 1975), 165.

To many people this thought process seems highly satisfactory because a "something" outside physics can then be introduced at $\tau = 0$. By a semantic maneuver, the word "something" is then replaced by "god," except that the first letter becomes a capital, God, in order to warn us that we must not carry the enquiry any further.[13]

To Hoyle's credit, he did carry the inquiry further by helping to formulate the first competitor to the standard big bang model. In 1948 Hoyle, together with Hermann Bondi and Thomas Gold, broached the steady state model of the universe.[14] According to this theory, the universe is in a state of isotropic cosmic expansion, but as the galaxies recede, new matter is drawn into being *ex nihilo* in the voids created by the galactic recession (fig. 3).

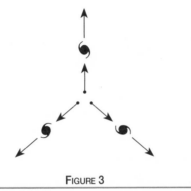

FIGURE 3

Steady State Model. As the galaxies mutually recede, new matter comes into existence to replace them. The universe thus constantly renews itself and so never began to exist.

The expansion of the universe in the steady state model can be compared to a rubber sheet with buttons glued to it: as the sheet is stretched and the buttons separate, new buttons come into being in the voids created by the recession of the previously existing buttons. Thus, the condition of the sheet remains constant over time, and no beginning of the process need be posited. If one extrapolates the expansion of the universe back in time, the density of the universe never increases because the matter and energy simply vanish as the galaxies mutually approach!

13. Fred Hoyle, *Astronomy and Cosmology: A Modern Course* (San Francisco: W. H. Freeman, 1975), 658.

14. H. Bondi and T. Gold, "The Steady State Theory of the Expanding Universe," *Monthly Notices of the Royal Astronomical Society* 108 (1948): 252–70; and F. Hoyle, "A New Model for the Expanding Universe," *Monthly Notices of the Royal Astronomical Society* 108 (1948): 372–82.

The steady state theory never secured a single piece of experimental verification; its appeal was purely metaphysical.[15] The discovery of progressively more radio galaxies at ever greater distances undermined the theory by showing that in the past the universe was significantly different than it is today, thus contradicting the notion of a steady state of the universe. Instead, it became increasingly evident that the universe had an evolutionary history.

The decisive refutation of the steady state model came with two discoveries that constituted, in addition to the galactic red-shift, the most significant evidence for the big bang theory: the cosmogonic nucleosynthesis of the light elements and the microwave background radiation. Although the heavy elements were synthesized in the stellar furnaces, stellar nucleosynthesis could not manufacture the abundant light elements such as helium and deuterium. These could only have been created in the extreme conditions present in the first moment of the big bang.

In 1965 a serendipitous discovery revealed the existence of a cosmic background radiation predicted in the 1940s by George Gamow on the basis of the standard model. This radiation, now shifted into the microwave region of the spectrum, consists of photons emitted during a very hot and dense phase of the universe. In the minds of almost all cosmologists, the cosmic background radiation decisively discredited the steady state model.

Oscillating Models

The standard big bang model was based on the assumptions of homogeneity and isotropy. In the 1960s and 1970s some cosmologists suggested that by denying homogeneity and isotropy, one might be able to craft an oscillating model of the universe and thus avert the absolute beginning predicted by the standard model.[16] If the internal gravitational pull of

15. As Jaki points out, Hoyle and his colleagues were inspired by "openly anti-theological, or rather anti-Christian motivations" (Stanley L. Jaki, *Science and Creation* [Edinburgh: Scottish Academic, 1974], 347). Martin Rees recalls his mentor Dennis Sciama's dogged commitment to the steady state model: "For him, as for its inventors, it had a deep philosophical appeal—the universe existed, from everlasting to everlasting, in a uniquely self-consistent state. When conflicting evidence emerged, Sciama therefore sought a loophole (even an unlikely seeming one) rather as a defense lawyer clutches at any argument to rebut the prosecution case" (Martin Rees, *Before the Beginning*, with a foreword by Stephen Hawking [Reading, Mass.: Addison-Wesley, 1997], 41). The phrase "from everlasting to everlasting" is the psalmist's description of God (Ps. 90:2 NIV/RSV). Rees gives a good account of the discoveries leading to the demise of the steady state model.

16. See, e.g., E. M. Lifschitz and I. M. Khalatnikov, "Investigations in Relativist Cosmology," *Advances in Physics* 12 (1963): 207.

the mass of the universe were able to overcome the force of its expansion, then the expansion could be reversed into a cosmic contraction, a big crunch. If the universe were not homogeneous and isotropic, then the collapsing universe might not coalesce at a point, but the material contents of the universe might pass by one another, so that the universe would appear to bounce back from the contraction into a new expansion phase. If this process could be repeated indefinitely, then an absolute beginning of the universe might be avoided (fig. 4).

Radius of the universe

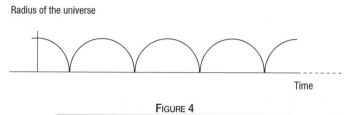

Time

FIGURE 4

Oscillating Model. Each expansion phase is preceded and succeeded by a contraction phase, so that the universe in concertina-like fashion exists beginninglessly and endlessly.

Such a theory is extraordinarily speculative, but again there were metaphysical motivations for adopting this model.[17] The prospects of the oscillating model were severely dimmed in 1970, however, by Roger Penrose and Stephen Hawking's formulation of the singularity theorems that bear their names.[18] The theorems disclosed that under very generalized conditions an initial cosmological singularity is inevitable, even for inhomogeneous and non-isotropic universes. Reflecting on the impact of this discovery, Hawking notes that the Hawking-Penrose singularity theorems "led to the abandonment of attempts (mainly by the Russians)

17. As evident from the sentiments expressed by John Gribbin: "The biggest problem with the Big Bang theory of the origin of the universe is philosophical—perhaps even theological—what was there before the bang? This problem alone was sufficient to give a great initial impetus to the Steady State theory; but with that theory now sadly in conflict with the observations, the best way round this initial difficulty is provided by a model in which the universe expands from a singularity, collapses back again, and repeats the cycle indefinitely" (John Gribbin, "Oscillating Universe Bounces Back," *Nature* 259 [1976]: 15). Scientists not infrequently misexpress the difficulty posed by the beginning of the universe as the question of what existed before the big bang (which invites the easy response that there was no "before"). The real question concerns the causal conditions of this event, why the universe exists rather than nothing.

18. R. Penrose, "Gravitational Collapse and Space-Time Singularities," *Physical Review Letters* 14 (1965): 57–59; S. W. Hawking and R. Penrose, "Space-Time Singularities," in *The Large-Scale Structure of Space-Time*, ed. S. W. Hawking and G. F. R. Ellis (Cambridge: Cambridge University Press, 1973), 266.

to argue that there was a previous contracting phase and a nonsingular bounce into expansion. Instead, almost everyone now believes that the universe, and time itself, had a beginning at the big bang."[19]

Despite the fact that no space-time trajectory can be extended through a singularity, the oscillating model exhibited a stubborn persistence. Two further strikes were lodged against it. First, there are no known physics that would cause a collapsing universe to bounce back to a new expansion. If, in defiance of the Hawking-Penrose singularity theorems, the universe rebounds, this is predicated upon a physics that is completely unknown. Physics predicts that a universe in a state of gravitational self-collapse would not rebound like a basketball dropped to the floor, but instead land like a lump of clay.[20]

Second, the observational evidence indicates that the mean mass density of the universe is insufficient to generate enough gravitational attraction to halt and reverse the expansion. In January of 1998 astronomical teams from Princeton, Yale, the Lawrence Berkeley National Laboratory, and the Harvard-Smithsonian Astrophysics Institute reported at the American Astronomical Society meeting that their various tests all show that "the universe will expand forever."[21] A spokesman for the Harvard-Smithsonian team stated that they were now at least 95 percent certain that "the density of matter is insufficient to halt the expansion of the universe."[22]

Indeed, in an unexpected development, the tests suggest that far from decelerating, the expansion actually seems to be accelerating. The cosmic acceleration has been directly measured through observations of several hundred Type Ia supernovae and is independently implied by more recent experiments on the cosmic microwave radiation background (the Boomerang, DASI, and Maxima experiments), which detected density variations in the background indicative of a flat space-time geometry, and most recently by data released in 2003 gathered from the Wilkinson Microwave Anisotropy Probe and compared with the galactic map of the Sloan Digital Sky Survey. These observations suggest that the universe is composed of only 4 percent ordinary, luminous matter, 23 percent non-luminous, invisible matter, and a whopping 73 percent mysterious, so-called "dark energy." It is this last, dominating factor that is driving

19. Stephen Hawking and Roger Penrose, *The Nature of Space and Time*, The Isaac Newton Institute Series of Lectures (Princeton: Princeton University Press, 1996), 20.

20. Alan Guth and Mark Sher, "The Impossibility of a Bouncing Universe," *Nature* 302 (1983): 505–6; and Sidney A. Bludman, "Thermodynamics and the End of a Closed Universe," *Nature* 308 (1984): 319–22.

21. Associated Press news release, 9 Jan. 1998.

22. Ibid. See also James Glanz, "Astronomers See a Cosmic Antigravity Force at Work," *Science* 279 (27 Feb. 1998): 1298–99.

the universe apart with ever-increasing speed. Whether this factor is to be understood as a positive value cosmological constant or a strange new energy field or something else altogether is not yet understood, but the conclusion that the expansion of the universe is speeding up rather than slowing down "now seems inescapable."[23] This cosmic acceleration is independent of the density of the universe and is incompatible with a cosmic re-contraction, as predicted by oscillating models.

Although such difficulties were well known, proponents of the oscillating model tenaciously clung to it until a new alternative to the standard model emerged during the 1970s.[24] Looking back, quantum cosmologist Christopher Isham muses:

> Perhaps the best argument in favor of the thesis that the Big Bang supports theism is the obvious unease with which it is greeted by some atheist physicists. At times this has led to scientific ideas, such as continuous creation or an oscillating universe, being advanced with a tenacity which so exceeds their intrinsic worth that one can only suspect the operation of psychological forces lying very much deeper than the usual academic desire of a theorist to support his/her theory.[25]

The oscillating model drew its life from its avoidance of an absolute beginning of the universe. But once other models became available that claimed to offer the same benefit, the oscillating model sank into oblivion under the weight of its own deficiencies.

Vacuum Fluctuation Models

Cosmologists realized that a physical description of the universe prior to the Planck time (10^{-43} second after the big bang singularity) would require the introduction of quantum physics in addition to GR. On the quantum level so-called virtual particles are thought to arise due to fluctuations in the energy locked up in the vacuum, particles that the Heisenberg indeterminacy principle allows to exist for a fleeting mo-

23. Sean Carroll et al., "Is Cosmic Speed-Up Due to New Gravitational Physics?" http://arXiv:astro-ph/0306438v2 (10 July 2003) at http://xxx.1an1.gov/abs/astro-ph/0306438 (2003).

24. One thinks, for example, of the late Carl Sagan on his *Cosmos* television series propounding this model and reading from Hindu scriptures about cyclical Brahman years to illustrate the oscillating universe, but with nary a hint to his viewers about the difficulties attending this model.

25. Christopher Isham, "Creation of the Universe as a Quantum Process," in *Physics, Philosophy, and Theology: A Common Quest for Understanding*, ed. R. J. Russell, W. R. Stoeger, and G. V. Coyne (Vatican City: Vatican Observatory, 1988), 378.

ment before dissolving back into the vacuum. In 1973 Edward Tryon speculated on whether the universe might not be a long-lived virtual particle, whose total energy is zero, born out of the primordial vacuum.[26] This seemingly bizarre speculation gave rise to a new generation of cosmogonic theories that we may call vacuum fluctuation models.

These vacuum fluctuation models were closely related to an adjustment to the standard model known as inflation. In an attempt to explain—or explain away, depending on one's viewpoint—the astonishing large-scale homogeneity and isotropy of the universe, certain theorists proposed that between 10^{-35} and 10^{-33} sec after the big bang singularity, the universe underwent a phase of superrapid, or inflationary, expansion that served to push the inhomogeneities out beyond our event horizon.[27] Prior to the inflationary era the universe was merely empty space, or a vacuum, and the material universe was born when the vacuum energy was converted into matter via a quantum mechanical phase transition.

In most inflationary models, as one extrapolates backward in time, beyond the Planck time, the universe continues to shrink down to the initial singularity. But in vacuum fluctuation models, it is hypothesized that prior to inflation the universe-as-a-whole was not expanding. This universe-as-a-whole is a primordial vacuum that exists eternally in a steady state. Throughout this vacuum subatomic energy fluctuations constantly occur, by means of which matter is created and mini-universes are born (fig. 5).

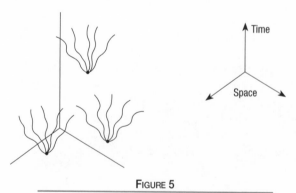

FIGURE 5

Vacuum Fluctuation Models. Within the vacuum of the wider universe, fluctuations occur that grow into mini-universes. Ours is but one of these, and its relative beginning does not imply a beginning for the universe-as-a-whole.

26. Edward Tryon, "Is the Universe a Vacuum Fluctuation?" *Nature* 246 (1973): 396–97.

27. A. Guth, "Inflationary Universe: A Possible Solution to the Horizon and Flatness Problems," *Physical Review D* 23 (1981): 247–56.

Our expanding universe is but one of an indefinite number of mini-universes conceived within the womb of the greater universe-as-a-whole. Thus, the beginning of our universe does not represent an absolute beginning, but merely a change in the eternal, uncaused universe-as-a-whole.

Though still bandied about in the popular press, vacuum fluctuation models did not outlive the decade of the 1980s. Not only were there theoretical problems with the production mechanisms of matter, but these models faced a deep internal incoherence.[28] According to such models, it is impossible to specify precisely when and where a fluctuation will occur in the primordial vacuum that will then grow into a universe. Within any finite interval of time there is a positive probability of such a fluctuation occurring at any point in space. Thus, given infinite past time, universes will eventually be spawned at *every* point in the primordial vacuum, and as they expand, they will begin to collide and coalesce with one another. Thus, given infinite past time, we should by now be observing an infinitely old universe, not a relatively young one.

One theorist tried to avoid this problem by stipulating that fluctuations in the primordial vacuum only occur infinitely far apart, so that each mini-universe has infinite room in which to expand.[29] Not only was such a scenario unacceptably ad hoc, but it does not even solve the problem. For given infinite past time, each of the infinite regions of the vacuum will have spawned an open (ever-expanding) universe that by now will have entirely filled that region, with the result that all of the individual mini-universes would have coalesced.

Isham has called this problem "fairly lethal" to vacuum fluctuation models and says that therefore they "have not found wide acceptance."[30] About the only way to avert the problem would be to postulate an expansion of the primordial vacuum itself; but then we are right back to the absolute origin implied by the standard big bang model. According to Isham, these models were therefore "jettisoned twenty years ago" and "nothing much" has been done with them since.[31]

28. See Isham, "Creation of the Universe," 385–87.

29. J. R. Gott III, "Creation of Open Universes from de Sitter Space," *Nature* 295 (1982): 304–7.

30. Christopher Isham, "Space, Time, and Quantum Cosmology" (paper presented at the conference "God, Time, and Modern Physics," Mar. 1990).

31. Christopher Isham, "Quantum Cosmology and the Origin of the Universe" (lecture presented at the conference "Cosmos and Creation," Cambridge University, 14 July 1994).

Chaotic Inflationary Model

Inflation also forms the context for the next alternative we shall consider: the chaotic inflationary model. Inflationary theory has not only been criticized as unduly "metaphysical"; it has also been crippled by various physical problems (such as getting inflation to transition to the current expansion). We have seen come and go the old inflationary theory and the new inflationary theory, both of which are now dead. By 1997 Alan Guth could count over fifty competing inflationary models in the scientific literature.

One of the most fertile of the inflation theorists has been the Russian cosmologist Andrei Linde, who champions his chaotic inflationary model.[32] According to cosmologist Robert Brandenberger, "Linde's chaotic inflation scenario is . . . the only viable inflationary model in the sense that it is not plagued with internal inconsistencies (as 'old inflation' and 'new inflation' are)."[33] In Linde's model, inflation *never* ends: each inflating domain of the universe, when it reaches a certain volume, gives rise via inflation to another domain, and so on, ad infinitum (fig. 6).

FIGURE 6

Chaotic Inflationary Model. The wider universe produces via inflation separate domains that continue to recede from one another as the wider space expands.

Linde's model thus has an infinite future. But Linde is troubled at the prospect of an absolute beginning. He writes, "The most difficult aspect of this problem is not the existence of the singularity itself, but the question of what was *before* the singularity. . . . This problem lies somewhere at the boundary between physics and metaphysics."[34] Linde therefore

---

32. See, e.g., A. D. Linde, "The Inflationary Universe," *Reports on Progress in Physics* 47 (1984): 925–86; and idem, "Chaotic Inflation," *Physics Letters B* 129 (1983): 177–81.
33. Robert Brandenberger, personal communication.
34. Linde, "Inflationary Universe," 976.

proposes that chaotic inflation is not only endless, but also beginning-less. Every domain in the universe is the product of inflation in another domain, so that the singularity is averted and with it as well the question of what came before (or more accurately, what caused it).

In 1994, however, Arvind Borde and Alexander Vilenkin showed that a universe eternally inflating toward the future cannot be geodesically complete in the past. There must have existed at some point in the in-definite past an initial singularity:

> A model in which the inflationary phase has no end . . . naturally leads to this question: Can this model also be extended to the infinite past, avoid-ing in this way the problem of the initial singularity?
>
> . . . This is in fact not possible in future-eternal inflationary spacetimes as long as they obey some reasonable physical conditions: such models must necessarily possess initial singularities.
>
> . . . The fact that inflationary spacetimes are past incomplete forces one to address the question of what, if anything, came before.[35]

In his response, Linde concurs with the conclusion of Borde and Vilen-kin: there must have been a big bang singularity at some point in the past.[36] Therefore inflationary models, like their predecessors, failed to avert the beginning predicted by the standard model.

Quantum Gravity Models

At the close of their analysis of Linde's chaotic inflationary model, Borde and Vilenkin say with respect to Linde's metaphysical question, "The most promising way to deal with this problem is probably to treat the Universe quantum mechanically and describe it by a wave function rather than by a classical spacetime."[37] They thereby allude to the next class of models that we shall discuss, quantum gravity models. Vilenkin and, more famously, James Hartle and Stephen Hawking have proposed models of the universe that Vilenkin candidly calls exercises in "meta-physical cosmology."[38]

35. A. Borde and A. Vilenkin, "Eternal Inflation and the Initial Singularity," *Physical Review Letters* 72 (1994): 3305, 3307.

36. Andrei Linde, Dmitri Linde, and Arthur Mezhlumian, "From the Big Bang Theory to the Theory of a Stationary Universe," *Physical Review D* 49 (1994): 1783–1826.

37. Borde and Vilenkin, "Eternal Inflation," 3307.

38. A. Vilenkin, "Birth of Inflationary Universes," *Physical Review D* 27 (1983): 2854. See J. Hartle and S. Hawking, "Wave Function of the Universe," *Physical Review D* 28 (1983): 2960–75; and A. Vilenkin, "Creation of the Universe from Nothing," *Physical Letters B* 117 (1982): 25–28.

In his best-selling popularization of his theory, Hawking even reveals an explicitly theological orientation. He concedes that in the standard model one could legitimately identify the big bang singularity as the instant at which God created the universe.[39] Indeed, he thinks that a number of attempts to avoid the big bang were probably motivated by the feeling that a beginning of time "smacks of divine intervention."[40] He sees his own model as preferable to the standard model because there would be no edge of space-time at which one "would have to appeal to God or some new law."[41] As we shall see, he is not at all reluctant to draw theological conclusions on the basis of his model.

Both the Hartle-Hawking and the Vilenkin models eliminate the initial singularity by transforming the conical hypersurface of classical space-time into a smooth, curved hypersurface having no edge (fig. 7).

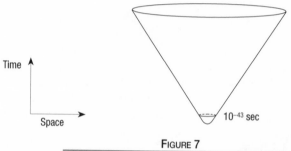

Time

Space

10^{-43} sec

FIGURE 7

Quantum Gravity Model. In the Hartle-Hawking version, space-time is "rounded off" prior to the Planck time, so that although the past is finite, there is no edge or beginning point.

This is accomplished by the introduction of imaginary numbers (multiples of $\sqrt{-1}$) for the time variable in Einstein's gravitational equations, which effectively eliminates the singularity. Hawking sees profound theological implications in the model:

> The idea that space and time may form a closed surface without boundary . . . has profound implications for the role of God in the affairs of the universe. . . . So long as the universe had a beginning, we could suppose it had a creator. But if the universe is really completely self-contained, having no boundary or edge, it would have neither beginning nor end. What place, then, for a creator?[42]

39. Stephen Hawking, *A Brief History of Time* (New York: Bantam Books, 1988), 9.
40. Ibid., 46.
41. Ibid., 136.
42. Ibid., 140–41.

Hawking does not deny the existence of God, but he does think his model eliminates the need for a Creator of the universe.

The key to assessing this theological claim is the physical interpretation of quantum gravity models. By positing a finite, imaginary time on a closed surface prior to the Planck time rather than an infinite time on an open surface, such models actually seem to support, rather than undercut, the idea that time had a beginning. Such theories, if successful, enable us to model the beginning of the universe without an initial singularity involving infinite density, temperature, pressure, and so on. As Barrow points out, "This type of quantum universe has not always existed; it comes into being just as the classical cosmologies could, but it does not start at a Big Bang where physical quantities are infinite. . . ."[43] Barrow points out that such models are "often described as giving a picture of 'creation out of nothing,'" the only caveat being that in this case "there is no definite . . . point of creation."[44]

Hartle-Hawking themselves construe their model as giving "the amplitude for the Universe to appear from nothing," and Hawking has asserted that according to the model the universe "would quite literally be created out of nothing: not just out of the vacuum, but out of absolutely nothing at all, because there is nothing outside the universe."[45] Similarly, Vilenkin claims that his model describes the creation of the universe "from literally *nothing*."[46] Taken at face value, these statements entail the beginning of the universe.

Hawking presumably therefore means to include himself when he asserts that "almost everyone now believes that the universe, and time itself, had a beginning at the big bang."[47] Hawking's statement quoted above concerning the theological implications of his model must therefore be understood to mean that on such models there are no beginning or ending *points*. But having a beginning does not entail having a beginning point. Even in the standard model, theorists sometimes "cut out" the initial singular point without thinking that therefore space-time no longer begins to exist and so the problem of the origin of the universe is thereby resolved. Time begins to exist just in case, for any finite temporal interval, there are only a finite number of equal temporal intervals earlier than it. That condition is fulfilled for quantum gravity models as well as for the standard model.

43. John D. Barrow, *Theories of Everything* (Oxford: Clarendon, 1991), 68.
44. Ibid., 67–68.
45. Hartle and Hawking, "Wave Function of the Universe," 2961; Hawking and Penrose, *Nature of Space and Time*, 85.
46. Vilenkin, "Creation of the Universe," 26.
47. Hawking and Penrose, *Nature of Space and Time*, 20.

Nor should we think that, by giving the amplitude for the universe to appear from nothing, quantum cosmologists have eliminated the need for a Creator. That probability is conditional upon several choices that only the Creator could make (such as selecting the wave function of the universe) and is dubiously applied to absolute nothingness.[48] Thus, quantum gravity models, like the standard model, imply the beginning of the universe.

Perhaps it will be said that such an interpretation of quantum gravity models fails to take seriously the notion of "imaginary time." Introducing imaginary numbers for the time variable in Einstein's equation has the peculiar effect of making the time dimension indistinguishable from space. But in that case, the imaginary time regime prior to the Planck time is not a space-time at all, but a Euclidean four-dimensional space. Construed realistically, such a four-space would be evacuated of all temporal becoming and would simply exist timelessly. Thus, Vilenkin characterizes this regime as a "state in which all our basic notions of space, time, energy, entropy, etc., lose their meaning."[49] Hawking describes it as "completely self-contained and not affected by anything outside itself. It would be neither created nor destroyed. It would just BE."[50]

The question that arises for this construal of the model is whether such an interpretation is meant to be taken realistically or instrumentally. On this score, there can be little doubt that the use of imaginary quantities for time is a mere mathematical device without ontological significance. First, there is no intelligible physical interpretation of imaginary time on offer. What, for example, would it mean to speak of the lapse of an imaginary second or of a physical object's enduring through two imaginary minutes? Second, time is metaphysically distinct from space, its moments being ordered by an *earlier than* relation that does not similarly order points in space. But this essential difference is obscured by imaginary time. Thus, "imaginary time" is most plausibly construed as a mathematical *Hilfsmittel* (expedient).

Barrow observes, "Physicists have often carried out this 'change time into space' procedure as a useful trick for doing certain problems in ordinary quantum mechanics, although they did not imagine that time was *really* like space. At the end of the calculation, they just swop back into

---

48. See William Lane Craig, "Hartle-Hawking Cosmology and Atheism," *Analysis* 57 (1997): 291–95. With respect to determining the wave function of the universe, Bryce DeWitt says, "Here the physicist must play God" (B. DeWitt, "Quantum Gravity," *Scientific American* 249 [1983]: 120).

49. Vilenkin, "Birth of Inflationary Universes," 2851.

50. Hawking, *Brief History of Time*, 136.

the usual interpretation of there being one dimension of time and three . . . dimensions of . . . space."[51] In his model, Hawking simply declines to reconvert to real numbers. If we do, then the singularity reappears. Hawking admits, "Only if we could picture the universe in terms of imaginary time would there be no singularities. . . . When one goes back to the real time in which we live, however, there will still appear to be singularities."[52] Hawking's model is thus a way of redescribing a universe with a singular beginning point in such a way that that singularity is transformed away; but such a redescription is not realist in character.

Remarkably, Hawking has more recently stated explicitly that he interprets the Hartle-Hawking model non-realistically. He confesses, "I'm a positivist. . . . I don't demand that a theory correspond to reality because I don't know what it [reality] is."[53] Still more extreme, "I take the positivist viewpoint that a physical theory is just a mathematical model and that it is meaningless to ask whether it corresponds to reality."[54] In assessing the worth of a theory, "All I'm concerned with is that the theory should predict the results of measurements."[55]

The clearest example of Hawking's instrumentalism is his combination of an electron quantum tunneling in Euclidean space (with time being imaginary) and an electron/positron pair accelerating away from each other in Minkowski space-time.[56] This analysis is directly analogous to the Hartle-Hawking cosmological model; and yet no one would construe vacuum particle pair creation as literally the result of an electron transitioning out of a timelessly existing four-space into our classical space-time. It is just an alternative description employing imaginary numbers rather than real numbers.

Significantly, the use of imaginary quantities for time is an inherent feature of *all* quantum gravity models.[57] This precludes their being construed realistically as accounts of the origin of the space-time universe in a timelessly existing four-space. Instead, they are ways of modeling the real beginning of the universe *ex nihilo* in such a way as to not involve a

51. Barrow, *Theories of Everything*, 66–67.

52. Hawking, *Brief History of Time*, 138–39.

53. Hawking and Penrose, *Nature of Space and Time*, 121.

54. Ibid., 3–4. Cf. Hawking's comment, "I . . . am a positivist who believes that physical theories are just mathematical models we construct, and that it is meaningless to ask if they correspond to reality, just whether they predict observations" (Stephen Hawking, "The Objections of an Unashamed Positivist," in *The Large, the Small, and the Human*, by Roger Penrose [Cambridge: Cambridge University Press, 1997], 169).

55. Hawking and Penrose, *Nature of Space and Time*, 121; cf. 4.

56. Ibid., 53–55.

57. As pointed out by Christopher Isham, "Quantum Theories of the Creation of the Universe," in *Quantum Cosmology and the Laws of Nature*, ed. R. J. Russell, N. Murphey, and C. J. Isham (Vatican City: Vatican Observatory, 1993), 56.

singularity. What brought the universe into being remains unexplained in such accounts.

Moreover, we are not without positive reasons for affirming the reality of the singular origin of space-time postulated by the standard model. John Barrow has rightly cautioned: "One should be wary of the fact that many of the studies of quantum cosmology are motivated by the desire to avoid an initial singularity of infinite density, so they tend to focus on quantum cosmologies that avoid a singularity at the expense of those that might contain one."[58] As we shall see, the initial cosmological singularity may be a virtual thermodynamical necessity. But whether it was at a singular point or not, the fact that the universe began to exist remains a prediction of any realistic interpretation of quantum gravity models.

Ekpyrotic Models

We come finally to the extreme edge of cosmological speculation: string cosmology. These models are based on an alternative to the standard quark model of elementary particle physics. So-called string theory (or M-theory) conceives of the fundamental building blocks of matter to be, not particles like quarks, but tiny vibrating strings of energy. String theory is so complicated and embryonic in its development that all its equations have not yet even been stated, much less solved. But that has not deterred some cosmologists from trying to craft cosmological models based on concepts of string theory to try to avert the beginning predicted by standard big bang cosmology.

The most celebrated of these scenarios in the popular press has been the so-called ekpyrotic scenario championed by Paul Steinhardt.[59] In the most recent revision, the cyclic ekpyrotic scenario, we are asked to envision two three-dimensional membranes (or "branes," for short) existing in a five-dimensional space-time. One of these branes is our universe. These two branes are said to be in an eternal cycle in which they approach each other, collide, and retreat again from each other. It is the collision of the other brane with ours that causes the expansion of our universe. With each collision, the expansion is renewed. Thus, even though our three-dimensional universe is expanding, it never had a beginning (fig. 8).

58. John D. Barrow, *The Origin of the Universe* (New York: Basic Books, HarperCollins, 1994), 113.

59. See feynman.princeton.edu/~steinh/.

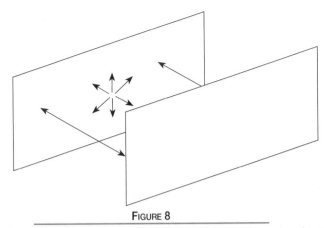

FIGURE 8

Cyclic Ekpyrotic Model. Two three-dimensional membranes in an eternal cycle of approach, collision, and retreat. With each collision the expansion of our universe is reinvigorated.

Apart from its speculative nature, however, the ekpyrotic scenario is plagued with problems.[60] For example, the Horava-Witten version of string theory on which the scenario is based requires that the brane on which we live have a positive tension. But in the ekpyrotic scenario it has a negative tension in contradiction to the theory. Attempts to rectify this have been unsuccessful.

Second, the model requires an extraordinary amount of ad hoc fine tuning. For example, the two branes have to be so perfectly aligned that even at a distance of 10^{30} greater than the space between them, they cannot deviate from being parallel by more than 10^{-60}. There is no explanation for this extraordinary setup.

Third, the collapsing and retreating branes are the equivalent of a four-dimensional universe that goes through an eternal cycle of contractions and expansions. In this sense, the cyclic ekpyrotic model is just the old oscillating model writ large in five dimensions. As such, it faces exactly the same problem as the original: there is no way for the universe to pass through a singularity at the end of each cycle to begin a new cycle and no physics to cause a nonsingular bounce.

Finally, even if the branes could bounce back, there is no means for the physical information in one cycle to be carried through to the next

60. See especially Gary Felder, Andret Frolov, Lev Kaufman, and Andrei Linde, "Cosmology with Negative Potentials," http://aXiv:hep-th/0202017v2 (16 Feb. 2002); http://eprints.osti.gov/cgi-bin/dexpldcgi?qry2062780997;4 and the therein-cited literature, particularly the studies by David Lyth.

cycle. Hence, the ekpyrotic scenario has been unable to deliver on its promises to explain the large-scale structure of the observable universe. These are just some of the problems afflicting the model. It is no wonder that Andrei Linde has recently complained that while the cyclic ekpyrotic scenario is "very popular among journalists," it has remained "rather unpopular among scientists."[61]

But let all that pass. Perhaps all these problems can be somehow solved. The more important point is that it turns out that, like the chaotic inflationary model, the cyclic ekpyrotic scenario cannot be eternal in the past. In September of 2001 Borde and Vilenkin, in cooperation with Alan Guth, were able to generalize their earlier results on inflationary models in such a way as to extend their conclusion to other models. Specifically, they state, "Our argument can be straightforwardly extended to cosmology in higher dimensions," specifically, brane-cosmology.[62] According to Vilenkin, "It follows from our theorem that the cyclic universe is past-incomplete."[63] This means that the need for an initial singularity has not been eliminated. Therefore, such a universe cannot be past-eternal.

Summary regarding Cosmogonic Theories

With each successive failure of alternative cosmogonic theories to avoid the absolute beginning of the universe predicted by the standard model, that prediction has been corroborated. It can be confidently said that, with regard to the standard big bang model, no cosmogonic model has been as repeatedly verified in its predictions, as corroborated by attempts at its falsification, as concordant with empirical discoveries, and as philosophically coherent.

Of course, in view of the metaphysical issues raised by the prospect of a beginning of the universe, we may be confident that the quest to avert such a beginning will continue unabated. Such efforts are to be encouraged. We have no reason to think that such attempts at falsification of the prediction of the standard model will result in anything other than further confirmation of its prediction of a beginning. Scientific evidence is always provisional; yet in this case there can be little doubt where the evidence points.

61. Andrei Linde, "Cyclic Universe Runs into Criticism," *Physics World* (June 2002): 8.

62. Arvind Borde, Alan Guth, and Alexander Vilenkin, "Inflation Is Not Past-Eternal," http://arXiv:gr-qc/0110012v1 (1 Oct. 2001): 4. The article has been updated as of January 2003 (http://arXiv.org/abs/gr-qc/0110012).

63. Alexander Vilenkin, personal communication.

The Thermodynamics of the Universe

If this were not enough, there is a second inductive argument for the beginning of the universe based on the evidence of thermodynamics. According to the second law of thermodynamics, processes taking place in a closed system always tend toward a state of equilibrium. For example, if we had a bottle containing a sealed vacuum, and we introduced into it some molecules of gas, the gas would spread itself out evenly throughout the bottle. It would be virtually impossible for the molecules to retreat, for example, into one corner of the bottle and remain there.

This is why, when we walk into a room, the air in the room never separates suddenly into oxygen at one end and nitrogen at the other. It is also why, when we step into the bath, we may be confident that it will be an even temperature instead of frozen solid at one end and boiling at the other. It is clear that life would not be possible in a world not governed by the second law of thermodynamics.

Our interest in the law is what happens when it is applied to the universe as a whole. The universe is, on a naturalistic view, a gigantic closed system, since it is everything there is and nothing is outside it. What this seems to imply, then, is that, given enough time, the universe and all its processes will run down, and the entire universe will come to equilibrium. This is known as the heat death of the universe. Once the universe reaches this state, no further change is possible. The universe is dead.

The question that this implication of the second law inevitably forces upon us is the following: *If, given enough time, the universe will reach heat death, then why is it not in a state of heat death now, if it has existed forever, from eternity?* If the universe did not begin to exist, then it should now be in a state of equilibrium. Like a ticking clock, it should by now have run down. Since it has not yet run down, this implies, in the words of one baffled scientist, "In some way the universe must have been *wound up.*"[64]

As alluded to earlier, nineteenth-century physicists were already aware of this conundrum. The German scientist Ludwig Boltzmann offered a daring proposal in order to explain why we do not find the universe in a state of "heat death" or thermodynamic equilibrium.[65] Boltzmann hypothesized that the universe as a whole *does*, in fact, exist in an equilibrium state, but that over time fluctuations in the energy level occur

---

64. Richard Schlegel, "Time and Thermodynamics," in *The Voices of Time*, ed. J. T. Fraser (London: Penguin, 1968), 511.

65. Ludwig Boltzmann, *Lectures on Gas Theory*, trans. Stephen G. Brush (Berkeley: University of California Press, 1964), 446–48, §90.

here and there throughout the universe, so that by chance alone there will be isolated regions where disequilibrium exists. Boltzmann referred to these isolated regions as "worlds." We should not be surprised to see our world in a highly improbable disequilibrium state, he maintained, since in the ensemble of all worlds, there must exist by chance alone certain worlds in disequilibrium, and ours just happens to be one of these.

The problem with Boltzmann's daring many-worlds hypothesis is that if our world were merely a fluctuation in a sea of diffuse energy, then it is overwhelmingly more probable that we should be observing a much tinier region of disequilibrium than we do. In order for us to exist, a smaller fluctuation, even one that produced our world instantaneously by an enormous accident, is inestimably more probable than a progressive decline in entropy over fifteen billion years to fashion the world we see.

In fact, Boltzmann's hypothesis, if adopted, would force us to regard the past as illusory. Things would have the mere appearance of age, with the stars and planets being illusory, mere "pictures" as it were, since that sort of world is vastly more probable given a state of overall equilibrium than a world with genuine, temporally and spatially distant events. Therefore, Boltzmann's many worlds hypothesis has been universally rejected by the scientific community, and the present disequilibrium is usually taken to be just a result of the initial low entropy condition mysteriously obtaining at the beginning of the universe.

The failure of Boltzmann's hypothesis forces us to take seriously questions of physical eschatology. Today eschatology is no longer merely a branch of theology; instead, it has become a field of cosmology. Just as cosmogony studies the origin of the universe, so physical eschatology studies its end. In contemporary cosmological eschatology, there are two possible types of heat death for the universe. If the universe will eventually recontract, it will die a "hot" death. Beatrice Tinsley describes such a state:

If the average density of matter in the universe is great enough, the mutual gravitational attraction between bodies will eventually slow the expansion to a halt. The universe will then contract and collapse into a hot fireball. There is no known physical mechanism that could reverse a catastrophic big crunch. Apparently, if the universe becomes dense enough, it is in for a hot death.[66]

66. Beatrice Tinsley, "From Big Bang to Eternity?" *Natural History Magazine* (Oct. 1975): 103.

If the universe is fated to recontraction, then as it contracts the stars gain energy, causing them to burn more rapidly so that they finally explode or evaporate. As everything in the universe grows closer together, the black holes begin to gobble up everything around them, and eventually begin themselves to coalesce. In time, "all the black holes finally coalesce into one large black hole that is coextensive with the universe,"[67] from which the universe will never reemerge.

But suppose, as is more likely, that the universe will expand forever. Tinsley describes the fate of this universe:

> If the universe has a low density, its death will be cold. It will expand forever at a slower and slower rate. Galaxies will turn all of their gas into stars, and the stars will burn out. Our own sun will become a cold, dead remnant, floating among the corpses of other stars in an increasingly isolated Milky Way.[68]

At 10^{30} years the universe will consist of 90 percent dead stars, 9 percent supermassive black holes formed by the collapse of galaxies, and 1 percent atomic matter, mainly hydrogen. Elementary particle physics suggests that thereafter protons will decay into electrons and positrons, so that space will be filled with a rarefied gas so thin that the distance between an electron and a positron will be about the size of the present galaxy.

Then at 10^{100} years, some scientists believe that the black holes themselves will dissipate by a strange effect predicted by quantum mechanics. The mass and energy associated with a black hole so warp space that they are said to create a "tunnel" or "worm-hole" through which the mass and energy are ejected into another region of space. As the mass of a black hole decreases, its energy loss accelerates, so that it is eventually dissipated into radiation and elementary particles. Eventually all black holes will completely evaporate, and all the matter in the ever-expanding universe will be reduced to a thin gas of elementary particles and radiation. Equilibrium will prevail throughout, and the entire universe will be in its final state, from which no change will occur.

Davies, an expert in the physics of temporally asymmetrical processes, reports:

> Today, few cosmologists doubt that the universe, at least as we know it, did have an origin at a finite moment in the past. The alternative—that the universe has always existed in one form or another—runs into a rather

67. Duane Dicus et al., "The Future of the Universe," *Scientific American* (Mar. 1983): 99.

68. Tinsley, "Big Bang," 105.

basic paradox. The sun and stars cannot keep burning forever: sooner or later they will run out of fuel and die.

The same is true of all irreversible physical processes; the stock of energy available in the universe to drive them is finite, and cannot last for eternity. This is an example of the so-called second law of thermodynamics, which, applied to the entire cosmos, predicts that it is stuck on a one-way slide of degeneration and decay towards a final state of maximum entropy, or disorder. As this final state has not yet been reached, it follows that the universe cannot have existed for an infinite time.[69]

Davies concludes, "The universe can't have existed forever. We know there must have been an absolute beginning a finite time ago."[70]

Some theorists have tried to escape this conclusion by adopting an oscillating model of the universe that never reaches a final state of equilibrium (recall fig. 4). But wholly apart from the aforementioned physical and observational difficulties confronting such a model, the thermodynamic properties of this model imply the very beginning of the universe that its proponents have sought to avoid. For entropy is conserved from cycle to cycle in such a model, which has the effect of generating larger and longer oscillations with each successive cycle (fig. 9).

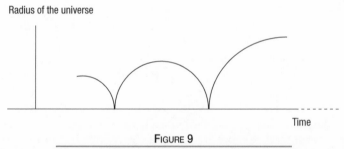

Radius of the universe

Time

FIGURE 9

Oscillating Model with Entropy Increase. Due to the conservation of entropy, each successive oscillation has a larger radius and longer expansion time.

As one scientific team explains, "The effect of entropy production will be to enlarge the cosmic scale, from cycle to cycle. . . . Thus, looking back in time, each cycle generated less entropy, had a smaller cycle time, and had a smaller cycle expansion factor than the cycle that

69. Paul Davies, "The Big Bang—and Before" (paper presented at the Thomas Aquinas College Lecture Series, Thomas Aquinas College, Santa Paula, Calif., Mar. 2002).

70. Paul Davies, "The Big Questions: In the Beginning," ABC Science Online, interview with Phillip Adams, http://aca.mq.edu.au/PaulDavies/pdavies.html.

followed it."[71] Thus, as one traces the oscillations back in time, they become progressively smaller until one reaches a first and smallest oscillation. Zeldovich and Novikov therefore conclude, "The multicycle model has an infinite future, but only a finite past."[72] In fact, astronomer Joseph Silk estimates that, on the basis of current entropy levels, the universe cannot have gone through more than one hundred previous oscillations.[73]

Even if this difficulty were avoided,[74] a universe oscillating from eternity past would require an infinitely precise tuning of initial conditions in order to perdure through an infinite number of successive bounces. A universe rebounding from a single, infinitely long contraction is, if entropy increases during the contracting phase, thermodynamically untenable and incompatible with the initial low entropy condition of our expanding phase. Postulating an entropy decrease during the contracting phase in order to escape this problem would require us to postulate inexplicably special low entropy conditions at the time of the bounce in the life of an infinitely evolving universe. Such a low entropy condition at the beginning of the expansion is more plausibly accounted for by the presence of a singularity or some sort of quantum creation event.

Indeed, thermodynamics may provide good reasons for affirming the reality of the singular origin of space-time postulated by the standard model. Roger Penrose, one of the greatest mathematical physicists of our time, states, "I have gradually come around to the view that it is actually misguided to ask that the space-time singularities of classical relativity should disappear when standard techniques of quantum (field) theory are applied to them."[75] For if the initial cosmological singularity is removed, then "we should have lost what seems to me to be the best chance we have of explaining the mystery of the second law of thermodynamics."[76]

What Penrose has in mind is the remarkable fact that, as one goes back in time, the entropy of the universe steadily decreases. Just how unusual this is can be demonstrated by means of the Bekenstein-Hawking

71. Duane Dicus et al., "Effects of Proton Decay on the Cosmological Future," *Astrophysical Journal* 252 (1982): 1, 8.

72. I. D. Novikov and Ya. B. Zeldovich, "Physical Processes near Cosmological Singularities," *Annual Review of Astronomy and Astrophysics* 11 (1973): 401–2.

73. Joseph Silk, *The Big Bang*, 2d ed. (San Francisco: W. H. Freeman, 1989), 311–12.

74. See D. Hochberg, C. Molina-Paris, and M. Visser, "Tolman Wormholes Violate the Strong Energy Condition," *Physical Review D* 59 (1999).

75. Roger Penrose, "Some Remarks on Gravity and Quantum Mechanics," in *Quantum Structure of Space and Time*, ed. M. J. Duff and C. J. Isham (Cambridge: Cambridge University Press, 1982), 4.

76. Ibid., 5.

formula for the entropy of a stationary black hole. The total observed entropy of the universe is 10^{88}. Since there are around 10^{80} baryons in the universe, the observed entropy per baryon must be regarded as extremely small. By contrast, in a collapsing universe the entropy would be 10^{123} near the end. Comparison of these two numbers reveals how absurdly small 10^{88} is compared to what it might have been. Thus, the structure of the big bang must have been severely constrained in order that thermodynamics as we know it should have arisen.

So how is this special initial condition to be explained? According to Penrose, we need the initial cosmological singularity, conjoined with the Weyl curvature hypothesis, according to which initial singularities (as opposed to final singularities) must have vanishing Weyl curvature.[77] In standard models, the big bang does possess vanishing Weyl curvature. The geometrical constraints on the initial geometry have the effect of producing a state of very low entropy. So the entropy in the gravitational field starts at zero at the big bang and gradually increases through gravitational clumping. The Weyl curvature hypothesis thus has the time asymmetric character necessary to explain the second law of thermodynamics.

By contrast, the Hartle-Hawking model "is very far from being an explanation of the fact that past singularities have small Weyl curvature whereas future singularities have large Weyl curvature."[78] On Hawking's time symmetrical theory, we should have white holes spewing out material, in contradiction to the Weyl curvature hypothesis, the second law of thermodynamics, and probably also observation.[79] Penrose supplies the following figure to illustrate the difference (see fig. 10). If we remove the initial cosmological singularity, we render the Weyl curvature hypothesis irrelevant, and "we should be back where we were in our attempts to understand the origin of the second law."[80]

Could the special initial geometry have arisen sheerly by chance in the absence of a cosmic singularity? Penrose's answer is decisive: "Had there not been any constraining principles (such as the Weyl curvature hypothesis), the Bekenstein-Hawking formula would tell us that the probability of such a 'special' geometry arising by chance is at least as small as about one part in $10^{1000B(3/2)}$, where B is the present baryon number of the universe [~10^{80}]."[81] Thus Penrose calculates that, aiming

---

77. Weyl curvature is the curvature of space-time that is not due to the presence of matter and is described by the Weyl tensor. Space-time curvature due to matter is described by the Ricci tensor. Together they make up the Riemann tensor giving the metric for space-time.

78. Hawking and Penrose, *Nature of Space and Time*, 129.

79. Ibid., 130.

80. Penrose, "Remarks on Gravity," 5.

81. Ibid.

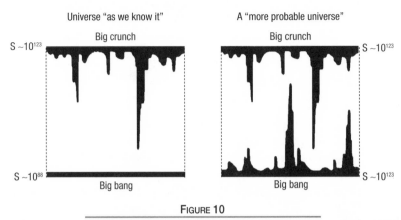

Universe "as we know it"   A "more probable universe"

FIGURE 10

Contrast between the universe "as we know it" (for convenience, assumed to be closed) with a "more probable universe." In both cases the big crunch is a high entropy (~10^{123}), complicated, unconstrained singularity. For the left-hand picture, the big bang is a low entropy ($\leq 10^{88}$), highly constrained, initial singularity; for the right-hand picture, it is an unconstrained, much more probable big bang. The "stalactites" represent singularities of black holes, while the "stalagmites" represent singularities of white holes.

at a phase space whose regions represent the likelihood of various possible configurations of the universe, "the accuracy of the Creator's aim" would have to have been one part in $10^{10^{(123)}}$ in order for our universe to exist.[82] He comments, "I cannot even recall seeing anything else in physics whose accuracy is known to approach, even remotely, a figure like one part in $10^{10^{(123)}}$."[83] Thus, the initial cosmological singularity may be a virtual thermodynamical necessity.

Thus, whether one adopts a recontracting model, an ever-expanding model, or an oscillating model, thermodynamics implies that the universe had a beginning. In a certain respect, this evidence of thermodynamics is even more impressive than the evidence afforded by the expansion of the universe. It is certainly true that an accurate physical description of the universe prior to the Planck time remains unknown and perhaps always will remain unknown, thereby affording room for speculations aimed at averting the origin of time and space implied by the expanding cosmos. Yet no such uncertainty attends the laws of thermodynamics and their application. Indeed, thermodynamics is so well established that this field is virtually a closed science.

82. Roger Penrose, "Time-Asymmetry and Quantum Gravity," in *Quantum Gravity 2*, ed. C. J. Isham, R. Penrose, and D. W. Sciama (Oxford: Clarendon, 1981), 249; cf. Hawking and Penrose, *Nature of Space and Time*, 34–35.

83. Penrose, "Time-Asymmetry," 249.

Even though we may not like it, concludes Davies, we must say on the basis of the thermodynamic properties of the universe that the universe's energy was somehow simply "put in" at the creation as an initial condition.[84] Prior to the creation, says Davies, the universe simply did not exist.

Conclusion

We therefore have two independent scientific confirmations of the philosophical arguments examined in chapter 6, leading to the conclusion that the temporal series of past, physical events is not beginningless. First, the expansion of the universe implies that the universe had a beginning. Second, thermodynamics shows that the universe began to exist. Because these lines of evidence are independent and mutually reinforcing, the confirmation they supply for a beginning of the universe is all the stronger. At a minimum we can say confidently that those who believe in the doctrine of *creatio ex nihilo* will not find themselves contradicted by the empirical evidence of contemporary cosmology but on the contrary will be fully in line with it.

84. P. C. W. Davies, *The Physics of Time Asymmetry* (London: Surrey University Press, 1974), 104.

8

Naturalistic Alternatives
to *Creatio ex Nihilo*

The fact that the universe is not eternal but had a beginning implies that the universe is not necessary in its existence and therefore has its ground in a transcendent being. The only way of avoiding this conclusion would be to deny that whatever begins to exist has a cause of its existence, that is, to claim that the universe simply sprang into being uncaused out of nothing. Reflecting upon the current situation, P. C. W. Davies muses:

> "What caused the big bang?" . . . One might consider some supernatural force, some agency beyond space and time as being responsible for the big bang, or one might prefer to regard the big bang as an event without a cause. It seems to me that we don't have too much choice. Either . . . something outside of the physical world . . . or . . . an event without a cause.[1]

The question, then, is whether a spontaneous origination of the universe out of nothing is as plausible or more plausible than the creation of the universe out of nothing by a transcendent cause.

---

1. Paul Davies, "The Birth of the Cosmos," in *God, Cosmos, Nature, and Creativity*, ed. Jill Gready (Edinburgh: Scottish Academic Press, 1995), 8–9.

A Self-Created Universe?

In a recent article in the *Physical Review,* J. Richard Gott and Li-Xin Li have sought to elude this dilemma by defending the extraordinary hypothesis that *the universe created itself.* They recognize that "the question of first-cause has been troubling to philosophers and scientists alike for over two thousand years." Modern scientists have, like Aristotle, found models of the universe attractive that involve the universe's sempiternal existence, since in this way "one would not have to ask what caused it to come into being."[2] "Now that it is apparent that our universe began in a big bang explosion," however, "models with a finite beginning have taken precedence" and "the question of what happened before the big bang arises."[3]

Gott and Li-Xin observe that inflation seemed to be "a very promising answer, but as Borde and Vilenkin have shown, the inflationary state preceding the big bang could not have been infinite in duration—it must have had a beginning also. Where did it come from? Ultimately, the difficult question seems to be how to make something out of nothing."[4] Gott and Li-Xin, however, suggest instead that we should ask whether anything in the laws of physics would prevent the universe from creating itself.

Noting that general relativity allows for the possibility of closed timelike curves, they hypothesize that as we trace the history of the universe back through an original inflationary state, we encounter a region of closed timelike curves prior to inflation. According to one possible scenario, a metastable vacuum inflates, producing an infinite number of (big-bang-type) bubble universes. In many of these a number of bubbles of metastable vacuum are created at late times by high energy events. These bubbles usually collapse and form black holes, but occasionally one will tunnel to create an expanding, metastable vacuum or baby universe. One of these expanding, metastable vacuum baby universes "turns out to be the original inflating metastable vacuum we began with" (fig. 11). Gott and Li-Xin conclude that "the laws of physics may allow the universe to be its own mother."[5]

Now we may leave it to the physicists to assess Gott and Li-Xin's claim that the laws of physics permit such a scenario, as well as the question of whether there are nonlawlike physical facts that contradict it. For the Gott–Li-Xin hypothesis raises fundamental metaphysical issues

2. J. Richard Gott III and Li-Xin Li, "Can the Universe Create Itself?" *Physical Review D* 58, no. 2 (1998): 023501–1.
3. Ibid.
4. Ibid.
5. Ibid.

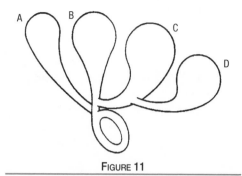

FIGURE 11

Self-creating Universe. Four inflating baby universes are shown. Universes A and D have not created any baby universes. Universe C has created universe D. Universe B has created three universes: A, C, and itself, B. The torus-shaped region at the bottom is a region of closed timelike curves. Such a universe neither arose from a singularity nor tunneled from nothing, but it created itself.

about the nature of time that, we think, render their hypothesis either metaphysically impossible or else superfluous.

We have seen that philosophers have distinguished two different views about the nature of time, which have been called the A- and the B-theories of time.[6] According to the A-theory, temporal moments may be classed as past, present, and future, and only that moment which is present exists. Past moments and the things or events that occupy them have passed away and no longer exist; future moments, things, and events have not yet come to be and so do not yet exist. In the A-theory of time things come into and go out of being, and thus temporal becoming is a real and objective feature of reality.

By contrast, on the B-theory of time the distinction between past, present, and future is a subjective illusion of human consciousness. All things or events in time are equally real and existent, and moments, things, and events merely stand to one another in tenseless relations of *earlier than, simultaneous with,* or *later than.* Nothing ever comes into being or goes out of being, and temporal becoming is an illusion.

All instances of causal influence over the past—whether we are talking about closed timelike curves, time travel, tachyonic anti-telephones, or whatever—presuppose the truth of the B-theory of time.[7] For clearly

6. See chap. 4; for a helpful introduction to these two competing perspectives, see Richard M. Gale, "The Static versus the Dynamic Temporal: Introduction," in *The Philosophy of Time: A Collection of Essays,* ed. Richard M. Gale (New Jersey: Humanities Press, 1968), 65–85.

7. See the discussion in William Lane Craig, *Divine Foreknowledge and Human Freedom: The Coherence of Theism I: Omniscience,* Studies in Intellectual History 19 (Leiden: E. J. Brill, 1990), 150–56.

on the A-theory of time, at the time at which the effect is present, the cause is future and therefore literally nonexistent. Thus, the effect just comes into being from nothing. Not only does this scenario seem absurd, but it also reduces to the first horn of Davies's dilemma with respect to the origin of the universe. The universe just came uncaused from nothing.

Thus the Gott–Li-Xin hypothesis presupposes the B-theory of time. But if one presupposes such a view of time, then Gott and Li-Xin's hypothesis becomes superfluous. For, as we have seen, in a B-theory of time the universe never truly comes into being at all.[8] The whole four-dimensional space-time manifold just exists tenselessly, and the universe has a beginning only in the sense that a meterstick has a beginning prior to the first centimeter. Although the space-time manifold is intrinsically temporal in that one of its four dimensions is time, nonetheless it is extrinsically timeless: it does not exist in an embedding hypertime but exists tenselessly, neither coming into being nor going out of being. The four-dimensional space-time manifold is in this latter sense eternal. Hence, there is no need for the device of causal loops or closed timelike curves at the beginning to explain how it came into being.

Given the truth of the A-theory of time, the idea that the universe is self-created, that it brought itself into being via closed timelike curves, is either metaphysically impossible or else reduces to the notion that the universe sprang into existence uncaused out of nothing. Thus, we seem to be stuck with Davies's dilemma: the beginning of the universe is either an event without a cause or the result of a supernatural agency.

The Supernaturalistic Alternative

Suppose we go the route of postulating some causal agency beyond space and time as being responsible for the origin of the universe. A conceptual analysis of what properties must be possessed by such an

8. This is the salient point of Grünbaum's critique of the inference to a First Cause of the origin of the universe (Adolf Grünbaum, "A New Critique of Theological Interpretations of Physical Cosmology," *British Journal for the Philosophy of Science* 51 [2000]: 1–43). As a B-theorist, Grünbaum does not believe that the universe ever came into being, even if it had a first temporal interval. As he elsewhere writes, "Coming *into* being (or 'becoming') is *not* a property of *physical* events themselves but only of human or conscious awareness of these events" ("The Anisotropy of Time," in *The Nature of Time*, ed. T. Gold [Ithaca, N.Y.: Cornell University Press, 1967], 153). What Grünbaum fails to see, however, is that the claim that an absolute beginning of the universe entails that the universe came into being is rooted not in the presupposition of the so-called spontaneity of nothingness but in an A-theory of time.

ultramundane cause enables us to recover a striking number of the traditional divine attributes. As the cause of space and time, this entity must transcend space and time and therefore exist atemporally and nonspatially, at least sans the universe. This transcendent cause must therefore be changeless and immaterial, since timelessness entails changelessness, and changelessness implies immateriality. Such a cause must be beginningless and uncaused, at least in the sense of lacking any antecedent causal conditions. Ockham's razor will shave away further causes, since we should not multiply causes beyond necessity. This entity must be unimaginably powerful, since it created the universe out of nothing.

Finally and most strikingly, such a transcendent cause is plausibly regarded as personal. As Richard Swinburne points out, there are two types of causal explanation: scientific explanations in terms of laws and initial conditions, and personal explanations in terms of agents and their volitions.[9] A first state of the universe cannot have a scientific explanation, since there is nothing before it, and therefore it can be accounted for only in terms of a personal explanation.

Moreover, the personhood of the cause of the universe is implied by its timelessness and immateriality, since the only entities we know of that can possess such properties are either minds or abstract objects, and abstract objects do not stand in causal relations. Therefore, the transcendent cause of the origin of the universe must be of the order of mind.

This same conclusion is also implied by the origin of a temporal effect from a timeless cause. For if the cause of the universe were an impersonal set of necessary and sufficient conditions, it could not exist without its effect. The only way for the cause to be timeless and changeless but for its effect to originate *de novo* a finite time ago is for the cause to be a personal agent who freely chooses to bring about an effect without antecedent determining conditions. A finite time ago a Creator endowed with free will could have acted to bring the world into being at that moment. In this way, God could exist changelessly and eternally sans the universe but choose to create the world at a first moment of time.

By "choose" one need not mean that the Creator changes his mind about the decision to create, but that he freely and eternally intends to create a world with a beginning. By exercising his causal power, he brings it about that a world with a temporal beginning comes to exist. So the cause is eternal, but the effect is not. In this way, then, it is possible for the temporal universe to have come to exist from an eternal

9. Richard Swinburne, *The Existence of God,* rev. ed. (Oxford: Clarendon, 1991), 32–48.

cause: through the free will of a personal Creator. Thus, we are brought, not merely to a transcendent cause of the universe, but to its personal Creator.

The Naturalistic Alternative

The non-theist will, of course, be extremely loath to take on board such metaphysical baggage. But consider the naturalistic alternative to creation: that the universe came into being uncaused out of nothing. That seems to be metaphysically absurd. The naturalist philosopher of science Bernulf Kanitscheider remonstrates, "If taken seriously, the initial singularity is in head-on collision with the most successful onto-logical commitment that was a guiding line of research since Epicurus and Lucretius": *out of nothing nothing comes.* Kanitscheider calls this "a metaphysical hypothesis which has proved so fruitful in every corner of science that we are surely well-advised to try as hard as we can to eschew processes of absolute origin."[10]

Mario Bunge thinks that an absolute origin of the universe "would be unscientific, for science abides by the principles that nothing comes out of nothing or turns into nothingness, . . . and that everything hap-pens according to law rather than miracles."[11] On the basis of the first principle, Bunge, like Kanitscheider, rejects the view that the universe came into being uncaused out of nothing. On the basis of the second principle, he thinks to reject theism. But while the principle that *out of nothing nothing comes* is a first principle of metaphysics as well as sci-ence, there is no incompatibility between being a theist metaphysically and a methodological naturalist scientifically. Moreover, even method-ological naturalism is far from unchallengeable.[12] It is difficult to see

10. Bernulf Kanitscheider, "Does Physical Cosmology Transcend the Limits of Natural-istic Reasoning?" in *Studies on Mario Bunge's "Treatise,"* ed. Paul Weingartner and G. J. W. Doen (Amsterdam: Rodopi, 1990), 344.

11. Mario Bunge, *Philosophy of Science and Technology,* Part 1: *Formal and Physical Sciences,* vol. 7 of *Treatise on Basic Philosophy,* Epistemology and Methodology 3 (Dor-drecht: D. Reidel, 1985), 238–39.

12. See the very interesting recent discussions about the warrant for methodological naturalism in science, e.g., Paul de Vries, "Naturalism in the Natural Sciences: A Christian Perspective," *Christian Scholar's Review* 15 (1986): 388–96; Alvin Plantinga, Howard J. Van Till, Pattle Pun, and Ernan McMullin, "Symposium: Evolution and the Bible," *Christian Scholar's Review* 21 (1991): 8–109; William Hasker, "Evolution and Alvin Plantinga," *Per-spectives on Science and Christian Faith* 44 (1992): 150–62; Alvin Plantinga, "On Rejecting the Theory of Common Ancestry: A Reply to Hasker," *Perspectives on Science and Chris-tian Faith* 44 (1992): 258–63; idem, "Methodological Naturalism" (paper presented at the symposium "Knowing God, Christ, and Nature in the Post-Positivistic Era," University of

how any sensible person, particularly the naturalist, can think that the universe just sprang into existence uncaused out of nothing.

It has therefore been remarkable to observe in recent years the number of non-theists who, under the force of the evidence for an absolute beginning of the universe, have embraced the view that the universe is a surd contingent, something that popped into existence uncaused, out of nothing. Quentin Smith declares, "The fact of the matter is that the most reasonable belief is that we came from nothing, by nothing, and for nothing."[13] Rather than posit a cause of the origin of the universe, Smith advises, "We should instead acknowledge our foundation in nothingness and feel awe at the marvelous fact that we have a chance to participate briefly in this incredible sunburst that interrupts without reason the reign of nonbeing."[14]

Sometimes attempts are made to render this remarkable hypothesis more plausible, but these are usually not very impressive. Consider, for example, Peter Atkins's account of the origin of the universe:

> Now we go back in time beyond the moment of creation, to when there was no time, and to where there was no space. . . . In the beginning there was nothing. . . . By chance there was a fluctuation, and a set of points, emerging from nothing, . . . defined a time. . . . From absolute nothing, absolutely without intervention, there came into being rudimentary existence. . . . Yet the line of time collapsed, and the incipient universe evaporated, for time alone is not rich enough for existence. Time and space emerged elsewhere, but they too crumbled back into their own dust, the coalescence of opposites, or simply nothing. Patterns emerged again, and again, and again. Each time the pattern formed a time, and through their patterning into time, the

---

Notre Dame, 14–17 Apr. 1993); J. P. Moreland, "Theistic Science and Methodological Naturalism," in *The Creation Hypothesis,* ed. J. P. Moreland (Downers Grove, Ill.: InterVarsity, 1994), 41–66; and J. P. Moreland, Stephen C. Meyer, and Richard H. Bube, "Conceptual Problems and the Scientific Status of Creation Science: A Discussion," *Perspectives on Science and Christian Faith* 46 (1994): 2–25.

13. Quentin Smith, "The Uncaused Beginning of the Universe," in William Lane Craig and Quentin Smith, *Theism, Atheism, and Big Bang Cosmology* (Oxford: Clarendon, 1993), 135. Elsewhere he has written, "[This world] exists nonnecessarily, improbably, and causelessly. It exists *for absolutely no reason at all.* . . . The impact of this captivated realization upon me is overwhelming. I am completely stunned. I take a few dazed steps in the dark meadow, and fall among the flowers. I lie stupefied, whirling without comprehension in this world through numberless worlds other than this one" (Quentin Smith, *The Felt Meanings of the World* [Lafayette, Ind.: Purdue University Press, 1986], 300–301). In *Theism, Atheism, and Big Bang Cosmology,* Smith claimed that the universe came into being uncaused out of nothing at the Planck time; but he has since recanted that position under the realization that the whole field of quantum cosmology is then the investigation of a complete fiction!

14. Smith, "Uncaused Beginning of the Universe," 135.

points induced their own existence. . . . Sometimes chance patterned points
into a space as well as a time. . . . Then, by chance, there came about our
fluctuation. Points came into existence by constituting time but, this time,
in this pattern time was accompanied by three dimensions of space. . . .
With them comes stability, later elements, and still later elephants.[15]

This account is so obviously incoherent in postulating time before time
and so confused in its reification of mathematical entities that we may
rightly dismiss it as the pseudo-scientific drivel that it is.[16]

John Gribbin asserts that the origin of the universe from nothing
presents no problem, since the positive energy associated with mass
is precisely offset by the negative energy associated with gravitation.
Hence, in the case of the origin of the universe, we have "not something
for nothing, after all, but *nothing* for nothing."[17] He thus commits himself to the absurd position that nothing exists (not even he himself!).
At best, the fact that the universe contains counterbalancing amounts
of positive and negative energy could show that the universe need not
have a material cause; but it does nothing to obviate the need for an
efficient cause. As Isham puts it, there is still the "need for ontic seed-
ing" to produce the positive and negative energy, even if on balance it is
naught.[18] That is why the quantum vacuum was needed as a substratum
in cosmogonic theories postulating such a process.

More often, naturalistic thinkers have sought to commend their view
either by attacking the causal principle "Whatever begins to exist has a
cause," or else by arguing for the implausibility or incoherence of the
existence of a cause of the universe. Attacks on the causal principle are
usually based on an appeal to quantum indeterminacy. For example,
virtual particles are sometimes said to constitute a counterexample to the
principle because they spring uncaused from the quantum mechanical
vacuum. Wholly apart from the disputed question as to whether virtual
particles really exist at all,[19] the central point to be understood here is

15. Peter W. Atkins, *Creation Revisited* (New York: W. H. Freeman, 1992), 129,
149–51.

16. John Leslie asks incredulously, "How could such nonsense have been churned
out by the author of *Physical Chemistry*, a superb textbook?" (John Leslie, "Is It All Quite
Simple?" *Times Literary Supplement*, 29 Jan. 1993, 3). For a good critique of Atkins, see
Keith Ward, *God, Chance, and Necessity* (Oxford: One World, 1996), chap. 1.

17. John Gribbin, *In Search of the Big Bang* (New York: Bantam Books, 1986), 374.

18. Christopher Isham, "Quantum Cosmology and the Origin of the Universe" (lecture
presented at the conference "Cosmos and Creation," Cambridge University, 14 July 1994),
8.

19. See Robert Weingard, "Do Virtual Particles Exist?" in *Proceedings of the Philosophy
of Science Association*, 2 vols., ed. Peter Asquith and Thomas Nichols (East Lansing, Mich.:
Philosophy of Science Association, 1982), 1:235–42.

that the quantum vacuum on which they depend for their existence is not nothing.

For that reason statements frequently made with respect to vacuum fluctuation models—that "the universe quantum tunneled into being out of nothing," or that "nothingness is unstable" to fluctuations that grow into universes, or that "the universe is a free lunch" because in this case "we got something for nothing"—cannot be taken seriously. They treat nothing as though it were something, a sort of substance possessing properties and governed by the laws of quantum physics. In fact, such statements turn out to be just rhetorical flourishes that no informed scientist takes literally. The quantum vacuum, which underlies all of space-time reality, is a fluctuating sea of energy. Because the vacuum is a physical entity existing in space and time, vacuum fluctuation models did not envision a genuine origin of the universe out of nothing, as Kanitscheider emphasizes:

> The violent microstructure of the vacuum has been used in attempts to explain the origin of the universe as a long-lived vacuum fluctuation. But some authors have connected with this legitimate speculations [sic] far-reaching metaphysical claims, or at most they couched their mathematics in a highly misleading language, when they maintained "the creation of the universe out of nothing." . . .
>
> From the philosophical point of view it is essential to note that the foregoing is far from being a spontaneous generation of everything from naught, but the origin of that embryonic bubble is really a causal process leading from a primordial substratum with a rich physical structure to a materialized substratum of the vacuum. Admittedly this process is not deterministic; it includes that weak kind of causal dependence peculiar to every quantum mechanical process.[20]

Thus, quantum physics does not serve to rebut the principle that whatever begins to exist has a cause.

It is not surprising that naturalists should attack the notion of a cause for the universe, since they reject supranatural realities independently of their motivation to justify an uncaused origin of the universe from nothing. Sometimes these critiques may be easily dismissed. For example, metaphysician John Post obviously begs the question when he claims that there cannot be a cause for the origin of the universe, since "by definition the universe contains everything there is or ever was or will be."[21] Again, it is an obvious non sequitur when Post infers

20. Kanitscheider, "Does Physical Cosmology Transcend?" 346–47.

21. John Post, *Metaphysics: A Contemporary Introduction* (New York: Paragon House, 1991), 85.

that because "the singularity cannot be caused by some earlier *natural* event or process," therefore "the universe has an uncaused beginning," and "it seems [that] contemporary physical cosmology cannot be cited in support of the idea of a *divine* cause or creator of the universe."[22]

On the other hand, Smith realizes that the metaphysician must take seriously the "more difficult question" of "whether or not the singularity or the Big Bang probably is an effect of a supernatural cause, God."[23] What problems, then, are there with a supernaturalist perspective? Adolf Grünbaum has argued vigorously against what he styles "the New Creation Argument" for a supernatural cause of the origin of the universe.[24] His critique is based on the fundamental assumption that causal priority implies temporal priority. Since there were no instants of time prior to the big bang, it follows that the big bang cannot have a cause.[25]

The supernaturalist has a number of options for dealing with this objection. One option is to hold that the transcendent personal cause of the universe is causally, but not temporally, prior to the big bang event, such that his act of causing the universe to begin to exist is simultaneous, or coincident, with its beginning to exist. Grünbaum provides no justification for his assumption that causal priority implies temporal priority. Discussions of causal directionality deal routinely with cases in which cause and effect are simultaneous. A supernaturalist could hold that the Creator sans the universe exists changelessly and hence timelessly and, at the big bang singularity, created the universe, along with time and space. For the Creator sans the universe, there simply is no time because there are no events of any sort; time begins with the first event, at the moment of creation.

The time of the first event would be not only the first time at which the universe exists, but also, technically, the first time at which God exists, since sans the universe God exists timelessly.[26] The moment of creation

---

22. Ibid., 87.

23. Smith, "Uncaused Beginning of the Universe," 120.

24. Adolf Grünbaum, "The Pseudo-Problem of Creation in Physical Cosmology," *Philosophy of Science* 56 (1989): 373–94. For a response, see William Lane Craig, "The Origin and Creation of the Universe: A Reply to Adolf Grünbaum," *British Journal for the Philosophy of Science* 43 (1992): 233–40.

25. Adolf Grünbaum, "Creation as a Pseudo-Explanation in Current Physical Cosmology," *Erkenntnis* 35 (1991): 233–54. For a response, see William Lane Craig, "Prof. Grünbaum on Creation," *Erkenntnis* 40 (1994): 325–41.

26. Brian Leftow puts this nicely when he writes, "If God existed in time once time existed and time had a first moment, then God would have a first moment of existence: there would be a moment before which He did not exist, because there was no 'before' that moment. . . . Yet even if He . . . had a first moment of existence, one could still call God's existence unlimited were it understood that He would have existed even if time did not. For as long as this is true, we cannot infer from God's having had a first moment of

is, as it were, the moment at which God enters time. His act of creation is thus simultaneous with the origination of the universe.

In response, Grünbaum has opposed this suggestion with the following argument:

1. The proponent of simultaneous, asymmetric causation must furnish a generally accepted criterion for distinguishing one of two causally connected simultaneous events as the cause of the other, if simultaneous, asymmetric causation is possible.
2. There is no generally accepted account of causal directionality.
3. Therefore, there can be no simultaneous, asymmetric cause of the big bang.[27]

This argument, if successful, would eliminate all purported instances of simultaneous, asymmetric causation, not just a cause of the big bang. Nevertheless, Grünbaum's argument is unsound, we think, because premise 1 is so obviously false. *First,* why must the proponent of simultaneous, asymmetric causation furnish a *generally accepted* criterion of causal directionality in order for such causation to be possible? Is this not an extravagant demand? Grünbaum fails to appreciate there is no generally accepted account of causation at all today. But should we therefore infer that causation is impossible or nonexistent?

Compare the situation in contemporary epistemology. There is today no generally accepted account of justification or rational warrant with respect to beliefs we hold to be true; but should we therefore infer that knowledge is impossible? Deconstructionists and other postmodernists may think so, but we doubt that Grünbaum would be ready to follow in their train. There is no reason to think that the possibility of simultaneous causation depends upon our being able to come up with an uncontroversial criterion of causal directionality.

Second, what reason is there, indeed, to think that the possibility of simultaneous, asymmetric causation depends upon our being able to produce any kind of criterion of causal directionality at all? Our enunciation of a criterion for distinguishing a cause from its effect

existence that God *came into* existence or would not have existed save if time did" (Brian Leftow, *Time and Eternity,* Cornell Studies in Philosophy of Religion [Ithaca, N.Y.: Cornell University Press, 1991], 269; cf. 201). Senor has dubbed such a model of divine eternity "accidental temporalism" (Thomas D. Senor, "Divine Temporality and Creation *ex nihilo,*" *Faith and Philosophy* 10 [1993]: 88). See further William Lane Craig, "Timelessness and Creation," *Australasian Journal of Philosophy* 74 (1996): 646–56.

27. Adolf Grünbaum, "Some Comments on William Craig's 'Creation and Big Bang Cosmology,'" *Philosophia Naturalis* 31 (1994): 225–36. For a response, see William Lane Craig, "A Response to Grünbaum on Creation and Big Bang Cosmology," *Philosophia Naturalis* 31 (1994): 237–49.

is an epistemic affair; the existence of simultaneous causation is a matter of ontology. A criterion helps us to *discern* simultaneous, asymmetric causes in the world; but to suggest that said criterion somehow *constitutes* such causal relations in reality is verificationism at its most implausible. Grünbaum has not suggested any incoherence or difficulty in simultaneous, asymmetric causation; if there are such causes in the world, they do not have to wait around for us to discover some criterion for distinguishing them.

Third, there is no reason to think that in order for specific cases of simultaneous, asymmetric causation to be possible or discernible, one must be able to furnish a general criterion broad enough to cover all such alleged cases. All one needs is a way of distinguishing cause from effect in the specific case. Now in the case of the hypothesis of theological creationism, we have a logically airtight means of distinguishing cause from effect. It is metaphysically impossible for God to be caused by the world, since if God exists, his nature is such that he exists necessarily. By contrast the world's existence is metaphysically contingent (as is evident from its beginning to exist). This entails that there is *no possible world* in which God is caused by the big bang.

Hence, it is easy for the theist to explain in what sense God is causally prior to the universe or the big bang: God and the universe are causally related, and if the universe were not to exist, God would nevertheless exist, whereas there is no possible world in which the universe exists without God. Thus, it seems to us that Grünbaum's objection to a supernatural cause for the origin of the universe is unsuccessful.

The non-theist might raise a metaphysical objection to the scenario we have sketched of the Creator's status sans the universe. It requires that we conceive of a timeless, personal agent, and some philosophers have argued that such a notion is self-contradictory.[28] For it is a necessary condition of personhood that an individual be capable of remembering, anticipating, reflecting, deliberating, deciding, and so forth. But these are inherently temporal activities. Therefore, there can be no atemporal persons.

The fallacy of this reasoning is that it conflates *common* properties of persons with *essential* properties of persons. The sorts of activities delineated above are certainly common properties of temporal persons. But that does not imply that such properties are essential to personhood. Arguably, what is necessary and sufficient for personhood

28. See discussion and references in William Lane Craig, "Divine Timelessness and Personhood," *International Journal for Philosophy of Religion* 43 (1998): 109–24.

is self-consciousness and free volition, and these are not inherently temporal. In his study of divine timelessness, John Yates writes:

> The classical theist may immediately grant that concepts such as reflection, memory, and anticipation could not apply to a timeless being (nor to any omniscient being), but this is not to admit that the key concepts of consciousness and knowledge are inapplicable to such a deity. . . . There does not seem to be any essential temporal element in words like . . . "understand," to "be aware," to "know," and so on. . . . An atemporal deity could possess maximal understanding, awareness, and knowledge in a single, all-embracing vision of himself and the sum of reality.[29]

Similarly, God could possess a free, changeless intention of the will to create a universe with a temporal beginning. Thus, neither self-consciousness nor free volition entail temporality. But since these are plausibly sufficient for personhood, there is no incoherence in the notion of a timeless, personal Creator of the universe.

More recently Smith has argued, "The thesis that the universe has an originating divine cause is logically inconsistent with all extant definitions of causality and with a logical requirement upon these and all possible valid definitions or theories of causality."[30] Smith shows that the typical analyses of the causal relation in terms of temporal priority, spatio-temporal contiguity, and nomological relatedness are inapplicable to the event of God's willing that the big bang occur and the event of the occurrence of the big bang. Therefore, these two events cannot, on the customary analyses, be regarded as cause and effect.

Counterfactual analyses of causation—such as David Lewis's, according to which c causes e if and only if (1) c and e are both events that occur, and (2) if c had not occurred, e would not have occurred—fare no better in Smith's view. For if c is God's willing and e is the big bang, it is true that if e had not occurred, then c would not have occurred. But this implies that the big bang is the cause of God's willing, which is false. Lewis avoids the problem of spurious reverse causal dependence by stipulating that if e had not occurred, then c would have occurred but failed to cause e. But since God is omnipotent and his willing necessarily effective, such a stipulation cannot be made in the present case. Thus, under no extant analysis of causality can God be said to cause the big bang.

Smith's argument may be formulated as follows:

29. John C. Yates, *The Timelessness of God* (Lanham, Md.: University Press of America, 1990), 173.

30. Quentin Smith, "Causation and the Logical Impossibility of a Divine Cause," *Philosophical Topics* 24 (1996): 169–70.

4. If the claim that God caused the big bang cannot be analyzed in terms of extant definitions of causality, then God cannot have caused the big bang.
5. The claim that God caused the big bang cannot be analyzed in terms of extant definitions of causality.
6. Therefore, God cannot have caused the big bang.

Is this argument sound and persuasive? We think not.

Consider premise 4. We see no reason to think that this premise is true. In general, arguments to the effect that some intuitively intelligible notion cannot be analyzed in terms of current philosophical theories ought to make us suspect the adequacy of those theories rather than reject the commonsense notion. The idea that God caused the universe is intuitively intelligible. A cause is, loosely speaking, something that produces something else and in terms of which the thing that is produced can be explained. That notion certainly applies to God's causing the universe. Indeed, God's causing certain effects is analogous to our acting as agents to bring about certain effects. We certainly conceive of ourselves as causes, and, intuitively, God should count as a cause as well. But Smith's argument, if successful, could be generalized to prove that God is not a cause of anything whatsoever.

If God's acting as a cause cannot be analyzed in terms of current philosophical definitions of causation, then so much the worse for those definitions! That only shows that the definitions are inadequate as unrestricted accounts. Indeed, the standard procedure in terms of which proposed definitions of causality are assessed is to postulate counterexamples of intuitively obvious cases of causation and then show how the definition fails to accommodate these examples. In the same way, if God's being a cause cannot be accommodated by some philosophical definition of causality, then that plausibly constitutes a counterexample to the definition that shows its inadequacy as a general metaphysical analysis of the causal relation, however adequate it might be for scientific purposes.[31]

31. In Quentin Smith, "The Concept of a Cause of the Universe," *Canadian Journal of Philosophy* 23 (1993): 1–24, Smith actually arrives at this conclusion himself. He states, "Extant definitions of causality are incorrect since they do not cohere in the proper way with the concept of a cause of the universe. . . . This entails that either there is some other (as yet undiscovered) definition of a cause that is correct or that a cause is indefinable. In the latter case, the concept of a cause would be primitive and the causal relation a simple relation known only by ostension (as is arguably the case with such relations as *being in contact with* or *being earlier than*). I know of no means of discovering or formulating a correct definition of a cause and know of no reason to think that there is such a definition. Accordingly, I think it is reasonable to conclude that the causal relation is indefinable.

Moreover, there is no reason to believe that we have arrived at the final and correct analysis of causation. In fact, there is good reason to believe the opposite. The definitions discussed by Smith are exclusively concerned with natural, even physical, causes. They were not intended to cover such recondite cases as divine causation of the origin of the universe. It is hardly surprising, therefore, that these analyses should fail to capture this notion. Smith simply ignores analyses of causation that are not currently fashionable but which were crafted in the context of a theistic metaphysic and are consonant with God's being the cause of the origin of the universe.

One such example is the account of efficient causation and creation given by Francisco Suarez in his monumental *Disputationes metaphysicae*.[32] In his lengthy introduction to his translation of questions 20 to 22 of Suarez's work, Freddoso argues that Suarez's account of causality not only enables one to construe God's creation of the universe as an instance of causation, but that it also contrasts favorably with empiricist accounts of causality offered by contemporary philosophers such as Mackie, Lewis, van Fraassen, and Tooley.

Finally, Smith just assumes that an analysis of the causal relation can be given. But it could be held that such a relation is conceptually primitive, in which case we should not expect a successful reductive analysis to exist that will cover all cases. The plethora of competing extant analyses and the recognized deficiencies of all of them lend credibility to this viewpoint.

What about premise 5? It seems to us that there are contemporary analyses of causation, however inadequate, that can accommodate God's causing the big bang. Consider Lewis's analysis of causation. According to Lewis, *c* causes *e* if and only if *c* and *e* are both events that occur and if *c* had not occurred, *e* would not have occurred. Now God's willing the big bang clearly satisfies this definition: God's willing and the big bang are both events that occur, and if God's willing had not occurred,

---

One way to avoid this conclusion would be to reject the assumption that the various examples of causes of the big bang . . . are genuine examples of causes. . . . I would say that claims that God's creation of the big bang singularity and other examples given . . . are not cases of possible causation are counterintuitive and are *ad hoc* attempts to retain a counterexampled theory. It is more plausible to think that a cause cannot be defined than to think that a mind's creation of a big bang singularity could not be a causal act" (ibid., 1, 24). Smith came to think God's relation to the big bang is not causal because no cause is logically sufficient for its effect. But Smith does not justify why the actions of an omnipotent being would not be exceptions to this rule.

32. Francisco Suarez, *On Creation, Conservation, and Concurrence: "Metaphysical Disputations 20, 21, and 22,"* trans. with introduction and notes by Alfred J. Freddoso (South Bend, Ind.: St. Augustine's Press, 2002).

the big bang would not have occurred. But Smith rejoins, "But if the big bang had not occurred, God's willing would not have occurred. So is the big bang the cause of God's willing?" Obviously not; but what this calls into question is the *adequacy* of Lewis's analysis, not whether divine causation satisfies it.

Lewis remedies the problem by stipulating that if *e* had not occurred, *c* would still have occurred but failed to cause *e*. But this remedy will not work for divine causation. Actually, Lewis's remedy will not work for many natural causes either, since in some cases the counterfactual statement, "If *e* had not occurred, *c* would not have occurred," is true. So what Lewis's definition gives is not an analysis of "*c* causes *e*" but rather an analysis of "*c* and *e* are causally related," and it fails to specify the *direction* of causation. But the theist faces no problem there: for, as we have said, it is metaphysically impossible for God's willing to have an external cause. There is no possible world in which the big bang causes God's volition. Therefore, given Lewis's analysis of "*c* and *e* are causally related" and the impossibility of the big bang's causing God's willing, it follows that God's willing causes the big bang. Thus, divine causation satisfies Lewis's definition of causality.

Again, there are analyses of agent causation that are even more relevant in the case of divine causation than the analyses surveyed by Smith. Smith considers exclusively event causation, but it may be disputed whether this is the correct conception to apply to God's case. Smith contends that considerations of agent causation are not germane to the discussion because we are not concerned with the relation between God (the agent) and his act of willing (the effect), but with the relation between his act of willing (an event) and the big bang (an event). Yet not all proponents of agent causation construe agent causation as a relation between an agent and his volitions. Some proponents of agent causation hold that an agent does not cause his volitions, but that by freely willing he brings about some intended event.[33] In the case at hand, God brings about the big bang by an exercise of his active power. "God's willing that the big bang occur" properly describes an *action*, not an *event*. The event in this case is the big bang, and the cause of that event is God, who, by willing, brought about the big bang. Thus, it is simply wrongheaded to think of the big bang as caused by the event of God's willing rather than by God himself.[34]

33. See E. J. Lowe, *A Survey of Metaphysics* (Oxford: Oxford University Press, 2002), 205–10.

34. See J. P. Moreland, "Libertarian Agency and the Craig/Grünbaum Debate about Theistic Explanation of the Initial Singularity," *American Catholic Philosophical Quarterly* 81 (1998): 539–54. I (Dr. Craig) am indebted to my colleague for several interesting discussions pertinent to agency and creation.

Hence, neither premise 4 nor 5 commends itself to us as more plausibly true than its contradictory. Smith recognizes these deficiencies of his argument, but he falls back to what he considers an impregnable position: "*c* is a cause of *e*" entails "*c* is not a logically sufficient condition of *e*."[35] This entailment precludes God's being the cause of the big bang because God's willing that the big bang occur is a logically sufficient condition of the big bang. This is because God is omnipotent, and thus his will is necessarily successful. There is no possible world in which God wills the big bang and yet the big bang fails to occur. Therefore, God cannot be the cause of the big bang.

This argument seems quite fanciful. If successful, it can be generalized to show that God cannot cause anything. Thus, precisely *because* he is omnipotent, God is utterly impotent—a strange inference! If being omnipotent entails inability to cause anything, then we are using "cause" in a highly technical sense that is not incompatible with God's bringing about the big bang, which is, after all, the issue. Whether or not God "causes" the big bang, it is still up to him whether it occurs or not, and it occurs only by virtue of his willing that it occur. If it seems that bringing about the big bang does involve a causal relation, then we shall simply reject Smith's entailment principle. Only someone who is already a naturalist would be tempted to think that that principle is true. Thus, Smith's argument is either question-begging or not incompatible with God's bringing about the big bang.

Smith considers such a response and insists that it is the theist who begs the question, since in every other case of causation, causes are not logically sufficient conditions of their effects. There is, he says, no justification for exempting God's alleged acts of causation from this principle. We need to have some independent reason for thinking that the relation between God and the big bang is a causal relation. Three things may be said about this response: *First,* since only God is omnipotent, it is hardly surprising that his case should be the sole exception to the principle that causes are not logically sufficient for their effects. God is so exceptional a being that he will in general not fit into our customary schemata. For example, it is a general principle that "*S* believes *p*" is not a logically sufficient condition of "*p.*" But since God is essentially omniscient, in God's case his believing *p* is a logically sufficient condition of *p*. Should we therefore conclude that God has no beliefs? In the same way, because God is omnipotent, are we to think that his will has no effects?

Second, there are other plausible counterexamples to Smith's principle. For example, change is plausibly a cause of the existence of time,

---

35. Smith, "Logical Impossibility of a Divine Cause," 176.

at least on a relational view of time. The occurrence of events actually brings time into existence. If there were an absolutely quiescent state, then time would not exist. But if a change occurs, time is immediately produced. Such a relation is plausibly causal; it is certainly not like the purely logical relation between, say, a two-dimensional figure's having three sides and its having three angles. Time is something altogether distinct from change, since time can go on, even most relationalists agree, even though change should cease.[36] Change, if it occurs, would seem to cause time to exist. Yet change necessarily causes time: There is no possible world in which change is going on without time. Change is thus logically sufficient for the existence of time, but is also plausibly a cause of time's existence.

Third, the reason that the relation between God and the big bang—or any other event he brings about—is causal is the close resemblance between God and ourselves as agents. Doubtless our deepest intuitions about causality are rooted in our own ability to bring about effects by an intentional exertion of our power. But God is a personal agent like ourselves. The difference between him and us is that his power is so great that he is infallible in bringing about his undertakings. Is his status as a cause now to be doubted because he is infallible? Hardly! In short, Smith's objection does not pose a serious obstacle to thinking that the big bang has a supernatural or divine cause.

Conclusion

All of the above objections have been considered as attempted justification of the naturalistic position that the universe, rather than being created by God, sprang into being uncaused out of nothing. But the premises of those objections strike us, at least, as far less perspicuous than the proposition that whatever begins to exist has a cause. It is far more plausible to deny one of those premises than to affirm what Hume called the "absurd Proposition" that something might arise without a cause,[37] that the universe, in this case, should have popped into existence uncaused, out of nothing. Therefore, it is far more plausible to believe in the classic doctrine of *creatio ex nihilo*.

36. Sydney Shoemaker, "Time without Change," *Journal of Philosophy* 66 (1969): 363–81.

37. David Hume to John Stewart, Feb. 1754, in *The Letters of David Hume*, 2 vols., ed. J. Y. T. Greig (Oxford: Clarendon, 1932), 1:187.

Subject Index

Scripture Index